Modern MANDARIN CHINESE Grammar

Modern Mandarin Chinese Grammar provides an innovative reference guide to Mandarin Chinese, combining traditional and function-based grammar in a single volume.

The *Grammar* is divided into two parts. Part A covers traditional grammatical categories such as phrase order, nouns, verbs, and specifiers. Part B is carefully organized around language functions and notions such as:

- Communication strategies
- Making comparisons
- Giving and seeking information
- Expressing apologies, regrets, and sympathies

The two parts of the *Grammar* are closely linked by extensive cross-references, providing a grammatical and functional perspective on many patterns. All grammar points and functions are richly illustrated with examples, with a strong focus on contemporary usage.

Main features of the *Grammar* include:

- Examples given in simplified characters, traditional characters and romanization (pinyin)
- Clear explanations and accessible descriptions
- Particular attention to areas of particular difficulty for learners of Mandarin Chinese

Implementing feedback from users of the first edition of the *Grammar*, this second edition has been revised throughout to offer expanded explanations, examples, cross-referencing, and indexing and brand new chapters on aspect, resultative verbs, directional verbs, and "ba" sentences.

This is the ideal reference grammar for learners of Mandarin Chinese at all levels, from elementary to advanced. No prior knowledge of grammatical terminology is assumed and a glossary of grammatical terms is provided. This *Grammar* is accompanied by the *Modern Mandarin Chinese Grammar Workbook* (978-0-415-83488-9) which features related exercises and activities.

Claudia Ross is Professor of Chinese Language and Linguistics in the Department of Modern Languages at the College of the Holy Cross in Worcester, Massachusetts, USA.

Jing-heng Sheng Ma is Emeritus Professor of Chinese Studies at Wellesley College, Massachusetts, USA.

Routledge Modern Grammars
Series concept and development – Sarah Butler

Other books in the series
Modern French Grammar, Second Edition
Modern French Grammar Workbook, Second Edition

Modern German Grammar, Second Edition
Modern German Grammar Workbook, Second Edition

Modern Italian Grammar, Third Edition
Modern Italian Grammar Workbook, Second Edition

Modern Brazilian Portuguese Grammar
Modern Brazilian Portuguese Grammar Workbook

Modern Russian Grammar
Modern Russian Grammar Workbook

Modern Spanish Grammar, Third Edition
Modern Spanish Grammar Workbook, Third Edition

Modern Japanese Grammar
Modern Japanese Grammar Workbook

Modern MANDARIN CHINESE Grammar

A Practical Guide

Second Edition

Claudia Ross
Jing-heng Sheng Ma

LONDON AND NEW YORK

First published 2006 by Routledge

This second edition published 2014
by Routledge
2 Park Square, Milton Park, Abingdon, Oxon OX14 4RN

and by Routledge
711 Third Avenue, New York, NY 10017

Routledge is an imprint of the Taylor & Francis Group, an informa business

© 2006, 2014 Claudia Ross and Jing-heng Sheng Ma

The right of Claudia Ross and Jing-heng Sheng Ma to be identified as the authors of this work has been asserted by them in accordance with sections 77 and 78 of the Copyright, Designs and Patents Act 1988.

All rights reserved. No part of this book may be reprinted or reproduced or utilised in any form or by any electronic, mechanical, or other means, now known or hereafter invented, including photocopying and recording, or in any information storage or retrieval system, without permission in writing from the publishers.

Trademark notice: Product or corporate names may be trademarks or registered trademarks, and are used only for identification and explanation without intent to infringe.

British Library Cataloguing in Publication Data
A catalogue record for this book is available from the British Library

Library of Congress Cataloging in Publication Data
Ross, Claudia.
　Modern Mandarin Chinese grammar : a practical guide / Claudia Ross, Jing-heng Sheng Ma. – Second Edition.
　　pages cm. – (Routledge Modern grammars)
　Includes bibliographical references and index.
　1. Chinese language–Grammar.　2. Mandarin dialects–Grammar.　3. Mandarin dialects–Self-instruction.　4. Chinese language–Textbooks for foreign speakers–English.　I. Ma, Jing-heng Sheng.　II. Title.
　PL1107.R65 2014
　495.1′82421–dc23
　　　　　　　　　　　　　　　　　　　　　　　　　　　　　　　　　　　2013034333

ISBN: 978-0-415-82715-7 (hbk)
ISBN: 978-0-415-82714-0 (pbk)
ISBN: 978-1-315-81475-9 (ebk)

Typeset in Times New Roman
by Graphicraft Limited, Hong Kong

Printed and bound by CPI Group (UK) Ltd, Croydon, CR0 4YY

Contents

Acknowledgments xv
Introduction xvi
How to use this book xvii
Glossary of grammatical terms xviii
A note on Chinese characters xxvi

Part A Structures 1

1 **Overview of pronunciation and Pinyin romanization** 3
   1.1 The Mandarin syllable *3*
   1.2 Pinyin romanization *4*

2 **Syllable, meaning, and word** 6
   2.1 The special status of the Mandarin syllable *6*
   2.2 Multi-syllable tendency in Mandarin words *7*
   2.3 Word-specific tone changes *8*
   2.4 Change to neutral tone *9*
   2.5 Incorporating foreign words and naming foreign objects *10*

3 **The Chinese writing system: an overview** 12
   3.1 Traditional and simplified characters *12*
   3.2 The structure of Chinese characters: the radical and the phonetic *12*
   3.3 The traditional classification of characters *14*
   3.4 Character stroke order: 笔顺/筆順 *bǐshùn* *16*

4 **Phrase order in the Mandarin sentence** 17
   4.1 Basic phrase order *17*
   4.2 The position of direct and indirect objects *17*
   4.3 The position of prepositional phrases *18*
   4.4 The position of location phrases *18*
   4.5 The position of 'time when' phrases *18*
   4.6 The relative order of the 'time when' phrase and the location phrase *19*
   4.7 The position of adverbs *19*
   4.8 The position of negation *19*
   4.9 The position of duration phrases *19*
   4.10 Order within the noun phrase *20*
   4.11 Phrase order in questions *20*
   4.12 The position of aspect particles *21*

v

CONTENTS

5 Nouns — 22
- 5.1 Common nouns *22*
- 5.2 Pronouns *23*
- 5.3 Proper nouns *26*

6 Numbers — 28
- 6.1 Mandarin numbers 0–99 *28*
- 6.2 Number 100 and higher *29*
- 6.3 Formal characters for numbers *31*
- 6.4 Ordinal numbers *31*
- 6.5 Estimates and approximations *32*
- 6.6 Fractions, percentages, decimals, half, and multiples *33*
- 6.7 Lucky and unlucky numbers *36*
- 6.8 Numbers used in phrases and expressions *36*
- 6.9 一 *yī* as a marker of sequence *37*
- 6.10 Numbers that are used as words *37*

7 Specifiers and demonstratives — 38
- 7.1 这/這 *zhè* 'this' and 那 *nà* 'that' as demonstratives *38*
- 7.2 这/這 *zhè, zhèi* 'this/these' and 那 *nà, nèi* 'that/those' as specifiers *39*
- 7.3 这儿/這兒 *zhèr* and 这里/這裏 *zhèlǐ* 'here,' 那儿/那兒 *nàr* and 那里/那裏 *nàlǐ* 'there' *39*
- 7.4 Question words that correspond to specifiers *40*

8 Classifiers — 41
- 8.1 The structure of phrases involving classifiers *41*
- 8.2 Choosing the classifier *41*
- 8.3 Omission of the head noun *44*
- 8.4 Classifiers that occur without a noun *44*
- 8.5 Money and prices *45*

9 Noun phrases — 47
- 9.1 Modifying a noun with a specifier and/or number *47*
- 9.2 Modifying a noun with all other modifiers: modification with 的 *de* *48*
- 9.3 Omission of the particle 的 *de* *51*
- 9.4 Noun modifiers in a series *51*
- 9.5 Omission of the head noun *52*
- 9.6 Modification with 之 *zhī* *52*

10 Adjectival verbs — 54
- 10.1 Negation of adjectival verbs *54*
- 10.2 Yes–no questions with adjectival verbs *55*
- 10.3 Modification by intensifiers *55*
- 10.4 Two-syllable preference *56*
- 10.5 Comparative meaning *56*
- 10.6 Superlative meaning *57*
- 10.7 Adjectival verbs and comparison structures *57*
- 10.8 Linking adjectival verbs *57*
- 10.9 Adjectival verbs and expressions that indicate change over time *58*
- 10.10 Adjectival verbs and sentence final 了 *le* *58*

CONTENTS

11 Stative verbs   59
- 11.1   Negation of stative verbs   *59*
- 11.2   Modification by intensifiers   *60*
- 11.3   Indicating completion, past time, and change of state   *60*
- 11.4   The equational verb 是 *shì* 'be'   *61*
- 11.5   The equational verb 姓 *xìng* 'be family named'   *63*
- 11.6   The verb of possession and existence: 有 *yǒu* 'have,' 'exist'   *64*
- 11.7   The location verb 在 *zài* 'be located at'   *65*

12 Modal verbs   66
- 12.1   Expressing possibility: 会/會 *huì*   *66*
- 12.2   Expressing ability   *66*
- 12.3   Expressing permission: 可以 *kěyǐ*   *67*
- 12.4   Expressing obligations   *68*
- 12.5   Expressing prohibitions   *69*
- 12.6   Grammatical properties of modal verbs   *70*

13 Action verbs   72
- 13.1   Indicating that an action is complete   *72*
- 13.2   Indicating that an action has been experienced in the past   *73*
- 13.3   Negating actions   *73*
- 13.4   Asking about actions   *74*
- 13.5   Open-ended action verbs   *75*
- 13.6   Change-of-state action verbs   *77*

14 Prepositions and prepositional phrases   79
- 14.1   The grammar of the prepositional phrase in the Mandarin sentence   *79*
- 14.2   Basic functions of prepositions   *80*
- 14.3   Prepositions that also function as verbs   *84*

15 Adverbs   85
- 15.1   General properties of adverbs   *85*
- 15.2   Adverbs with logical function: 也 *yě*, 都 *dōu*, 还/還 *hái*, 就 *jiù*, 只 *zhǐ*, and 才 *cái*   *86*

16 Conjunctions   92
- 16.1   Conjunctions that indicate an 'additive' or 'and' relationship   *92*
- 16.2   Conjunctions that indicate a disjunctive or 'or' relationship   *93*

17 Aspect   94
- 17.1   Perfective aspect   *94*
- 17.2   Durative aspect   *97*
- 17.3   Experiential aspect   *101*
- 17.4   A comparison of aspectual distinctions   *102*

18 Resultative verbs   103
- 18.1   Structure of resultative verbs   *103*
- 18.2   Action verb heads   *103*
- 18.3   Resultative suffixes   *104*
- 18.4   Resultative verbs in affirmative and negative sentences   *107*
- 18.5   Asking yes–no questions with resultative verbs   *108*
- 18.6   The potential form of resultative verbs   *109*
- 18.7   Resultative suffixes with figurative or idiomatic meaning   *112*

19 Directional verbs — 114
- 19.1 Structure of directional verbs *114*
- 19.2 Motion verbs *114*
- 19.3 Directional suffixes *115*
- 19.4 Sentences with directional verbs *116*
- 19.5 The potential form of directional verbs *119*
- 19.6 Asking yes–no questions with directional verbs *119*
- 19.7 Directional verbs and directional suffixes with figurative or idiomatic meaning *120*

20 把 *bǎ* sentences: The 'disposal' construction — 122
- 20.1 The structure of 把 *bǎ* sentences *122*
- 20.2 Properties of the subject and object in 把 *bǎ* sentences *122*
- 20.3 Properties of the verb in 把 *bǎ* sentences *124*
- 20.4 Negation in 把 *bǎ* sentences *126*
- 20.5 Adverbs and modal verbs in 把 *bǎ* sentences *126*

21 The passive — 128
- 21.1 The structure of the Mandarin passive *128*
- 21.2 The passive and negation *129*
- 21.3 Conditions for using the passive in Mandarin *130*
- 21.4 Differences between the passive markers 被 *bèi*, 叫 *jiào*, and 让/讓 *ràng* *130*
- 21.5 Additional functions of 让/讓 *ràng*, 叫 *jiào*, and 给/給 *gěi* *130*
- 21.6 Other Mandarin structures that highlight the affected object and de-emphasize the agent *131*

Part B Situations and functions — 133

22 Names, kinship terms, titles, and terms of address — 135
- 22.1 Names: 姓名 *xìngmíng* *135*
- 22.2 Kinship terms *136*
- 22.3 Titles *137*
- 22.4 Addressing others *139*
- 22.5 Addressing new acquaintances and negotiating terms of address *140*
- 22.6 Name cards and business cards *142*
- 22.7 Addressing letters and envelopes *143*

23 Introductions — 147
- 23.1 The general format of introductions *147*
- 23.2 Sample introductions *148*
- 23.3 Common occupations and fields of study *149*

24 Greetings and goodbyes — 151
- 24.1 Greetings in conversations *151*
- 24.2 Saying goodbye in conversations *153*
- 24.3 Greetings and goodbyes in letters *155*

CONTENTS

25 Basic strategies for communication   159
- 25.1 Attracting someone's attention   *159*
- 25.2 Responding to a call for attention   *160*
- 25.3 Checking whether people have understood you   *160*
- 25.4 Indicating understanding or lack of understanding   *160*
- 25.5 Requesting repetition or clarification of spoken language   *161*
- 25.6 Asking for assistance in identifying a Chinese character   *161*
- 25.7 Providing information about the identification of Chinese characters   *161*
- 25.8 Signaling that you are following the speaker   *162*
- 25.9 Interrupting a speaker   *162*
- 25.10 Using fillers   *162*
- 25.11 Formal development of a topic   *162*

26 Telecommunications and e-communications: telephones, the internet, and faxes   165
- 26.1 Making and receiving phone calls; sending and receiving faxes and email messages   *165*
- 26.2 Dialing a number and entering a number   *167*
- 26.3 Using the internet   *167*
- 26.4 Telephone etiquette   *167*
- 26.5 Writing and reciting phone numbers and fax numbers   *168*

27 Negating information   170
- 27.1 Negation of verbs and verb phrases   *170*
- 27.2 The relative order of negation and adverbs   *172*
- 27.3 Words that occur with negation   *172*
- 27.4 不 *bù* in resultative and directional verbs   *173*
- 27.5 Literary markers of negation: 無 *wú* and 非 *fēi*   *174*

28 Asking questions and replying to questions   176
- 28.1 Yes–no questions   *176*
- 28.2 Asking for agreement   *180*
- 28.3 Choosing between alternatives with 还是/還是 *háishi* 'either–or' questions   *181*
- 28.4 Rhetorical questions   *181*
- 28.5 Follow-up questions with 呢 *ne*   *182*
- 28.6 Content questions   *182*

29 Expressing identification, possession, and existence   187
- 29.1 Expressing identification   *187*
- 29.2 Expressing possession   *188*
- 29.3 Expressing existence   *190*

30 Describing people, places, and things   192
- 30.1 Equational sentences: identifying or describing the subject with a noun phrase in the predicate   *192*
- 30.2 Describing the subject with a predicate that is an adjectival verb   *192*
- 30.3 Identifying or describing a noun with a modifying phrase   *193*
- 30.4 Asking questions about the attributes of a person, place, or thing   *193*
- 30.5 Describing an item in terms of the material that it is made of   *194*
- 30.6 Describing nouns in terms of attributes that imply comparison   *195*
- 30.7 Describing people in terms of age   *195*
- 30.8 Describing the weather   *197*
- 30.9 Talking about illness and other medical conditions   *199*

CONTENTS

31 Describing how actions are performed — 201
- 31.1 Describing the general or past performance of an action with a manner adverbial phrase *201*
- 31.2 Asking about the performance of an action *203*
- 31.3 Describing the performance of an entire action with an adverbial modifier *204*

32 Indicating result, conclusion, potential, and extent — 206
- 32.1 Indicating the result or conclusion of an action with resultative verbs *206*
- 32.2 Indicating the ability to reach a conclusion or result: the potential infixes 得 *de* and 不 *bu* *210*
- 32.3 Summary of the functions of resultative verbs *211*
- 32.4 Indicating the ability to perform the verb: the potential suffixes 得了 *deliǎo* and 不了 *buliǎo* *212*
- 32.5 Resultative suffixes with special meanings or properties *213*
- 32.6 Indicating the extent or result of a situation *216*

33 Making comparisons — 217
- 33.1 Similarity *217*
- 33.2 Difference *222*
- 33.3 More than *223*
- 33.4 Less than *228*
- 33.5 Comparative degree *231*
- 33.6 Superlative degree *232*
- 33.7 Relative degree *232*

34 Talking about the present — 233
- 34.1 Time expressions that indicate present time *233*
- 34.2 Using 在 *zài* and 正在 *zhèngzài* to indicate ongoing actions in present time *234*
- 34.3 Using the final particle 呢 *ne* to indicate ongoing situations in present time *234*
- 34.4 Using 着/著 *zhe* to emphasize ongoing duration or an ongoing state in the present time *235*
- 34.5 Indicating present time by context *236*
- 34.6 Negation in present time situations *236*
- 34.7 Talking about actions that begin in the past and continue to the present *236*
- 34.8 Describing situations that are generally true *237*

35 Talking about habitual actions — 238
- 35.1 Expressing habitual time with the word 每 *měi* 'every/each' *238*
- 35.2 Expressing habitual time with 天天 *tiāntiān* and 年年 *niánnián* *238*
- 35.3 Adverbs that describe habitual action *239*

36 Talking about the future — 241
- 36.1 Time words that refer to future time *241*
- 36.2 Adverbs that refer to future time *241*
- 36.3 Indicating future time with the modal verb 会/會 *huì* *242*
- 36.4 Verbs that refer to the future *243*

CONTENTS

37 Indicating completion and talking about the past — 244
- 37.1 Marking an action as complete: perfective aspect 了 *le* 244
- 37.2 Talking about sequence with perfective 了 *le* 245
- 37.3 Indicating that an action did not occur in the past 245
- 37.4 Asking whether an action has occurred 246
- 37.5 Indicating that an action occurred again in the past: 又 *yòu* verb 了 *le* 247
- 37.6 Talking about past experience: verb suffix 过/過 *guo* 247
- 37.7 Comparing the aspect markers 过/過 *guo* and 了 *le* 249
- 37.8 Time words and adverbs that refer to past time 249
- 37.9 Focusing on a detail of a past event with 是 . . . 的 *shì . . . de* 251

38 Talking about change, new situations, and changing situations — 253
- 38.1 Indicating that a situation represents a change 253
- 38.2 Comparing sentences with and without sentence final 了 *le* 254
- 38.3 Indicating change over time 255
- 38.4 Nouns and verbs that express change 256

39 Talking about duration and frequency — 259
- 39.1 Specifying the length of an action with a duration phrase 259
- 39.2 Emphasizing ongoing duration 262
- 39.3 Indicating the ongoing duration of a background event 263
- 39.4 Indicating frequency 264

40 Expressing additional information — 266
- 40.1 也 *yě* 'also' 266
- 40.2 还/還 *hái* 'in addition, also' 266
- 40.3 还有/還有 *hái yǒu* 'in addition' 267
- 40.4 并且/並且 *bìngqiě* 'moreover' 267
- 40.5 再说/再說 *zài shuō* 'besides, moreover, to put it another way' 267
- 40.6 而 *ér* 'and, but' 267
- 40.7 和 *hé* and 跟 *gēn* 'and' 268
- 40.8 不但 . . . 而且 . . . *búdàn . . . érqiě . . .* 'not only . . . but also . . .' 268
- 40.9 又 . . . 又 . . . *yòu . . . yòu . . .* 'both . . . and . . .' 268
- 40.10 除了 . . . 以外 *chúle . . . yǐwài* 'besides . . .' 268
- 40.11 另外 *lìngwài* 'in addition,' '(an)other' 269

41 Expressing contrast — 270
- 41.1 Expressing contrast with paired connecting words 270
- 41.2 Adverbs that indicate contrast 271
- 41.3 Qualifying a statement with an adjectival verb or stative verb 273

42 Expressing sequence — 274
- 42.1 Expressing the relationship 'before' 274
- 42.2 Expressing the relationship 'after' in a single sentence 275
- 42.3 Indicating that one event happens first and another event happens afterwards 279
- 42.4 Indicating 'afterwards' in a separate sentence 280
- 42.5 Comparing 以前 *yǐqián* 'before' with 以后/以後 *yǐhòu* 'after' 280

CONTENTS

43 Expressing simultaneous situations — 282
- 43.1 Indicating that one situation is the background for another situation *282*
- 43.2 Indicating that two actions occur at the same time *283*
- 43.3 Indicating that two actions occur in the same time frame *283*
- 43.4 Describing a subject in terms of two qualities that exist at the same time *283*
- 43.5 Indicating that a situation is reached at a specific point in time *284*
- 43.6 Presenting simultaneous situations *284*

44 Expressing cause and effect or reason and result — 285
- 44.1 Expressing cause and effect or reason and result in a single sentence *285*
- 44.2 Introducing the cause or reason *286*
- 44.3 Introducing the effect or result *288*
- 44.4 Inquiring about cause or reason *288*

45 Expressing conditions — 290
- 45.1 'If . . . then' conditional sentences *290*
- 45.2 'even if' *292*
- 45.3 'as long as' *292*
- 45.4 'only if,' 'unless' *292*
- 45.5 'otherwise' *292*

46 Expressing 'both,' 'all,' 'every,' 'any,' 'none,' 'not any,' and 'no matter how' — 294
- 46.1 Expressing 'both' and 'all' *294*
- 46.2 Expressing 'none' *296*
- 46.3 Expressing 'every' *296*
- 46.4 Expressing 'every,' 'any,' 'not any,' and 'no matter how' with question words *297*

47 Expressing location and distance — 303
- 47.1 Location *303*
- 47.2 Indicating that an object exists or does not exist at a location *308*
- 47.3 Using location as a description *309*
- 47.4 Talking about distance *310*
- 47.5 Asking about distance *312*

48 Talking about movement, directions, and means of transportation — 314
- 48.1 Talking about 'going' and 'coming' *314*
- 48.2 Talking about turning *315*
- 48.3 Talking about crossing *316*
- 48.4 Talking about arriving *316*
- 48.5 Talking about means of transportation *316*
- 48.6 Asking about locations and asking for directions *318*
- 48.7 Asking for and giving directions: sample conversations *319*
- 48.8 Talking about directional movement *319*

49 Talking about clock time and calendar time — 321
- 49.1 Clock time *321*
- 49.2 Calendar time *325*

CONTENTS

50 Expressing obligations and prohibitions — 332
  50.1 Expressing obligations *332*
  50.2 Expressing prohibitions: must not, should not *334*

51 Expressing commands and permission — 337
  51.1 Commands *337*
  51.2 Permission *339*

52 Expressing ability and possibility — 341
  52.1 Expressing ability *341*
  52.2 Expressing possibility *342*

53 Expressing desires, needs, preferences, and willingness — 344
  53.1 Expressing desires *344*
  53.2 Expressing needs *345*
  53.3 Expressing preferences *345*
  53.4 Expressing willingness *346*

54 Expressing knowledge, advice, and opinions — 347
  54.1 Expressing knowledge *347*
  54.2 Advice and opinions *348*

55 Expressing fear, worry, and anxiety — 353
  55.1 Expressing fear of something *353*
  55.2 Expressing nervousness or anxiety *354*
  55.3 Indicating that something is scary *355*
  55.4 Indicating that something scares someone *355*

56 Expressing speaker attitudes and perspectives — 356
  56.1 Interjections *356*
  56.2 Sentence final particles *358*

57 Topic, focus, and emphasis — 359
  57.1 Introducing a topic *359*
  57.2 Focus *361*
  57.3 Emphasis *365*

58 Guest and host — 367
  58.1 Welcoming the guest *367*
  58.2 Offering food and drink *368*
  58.3 Inviting the guest to get comfortable *368*
  58.4 Saying goodbye and seeing the guest off *368*
  58.5 Additional expressions involving guest and host *369*

59 Giving and responding to compliments — 370
  59.1 Cultural conventions regarding praise *370*
  59.2 Expressions used in deflecting praise *370*
  59.3 Compliments and appropriate responses *371*

60 Expressing satisfaction and dissatisfaction — 372
  60.1 Expressing satisfaction *372*
  60.2 Expressing dissatisfaction *373*

CONTENTS

61 Expressing gratitude and responding to expressions of gratitude — 375
    61.1 Expressing gratitude *375*
    61.2 Replying to expressions of gratitude *376*

62 Invitations, requests, and refusals — 377
    62.1 Invitations *377*
    62.2 Requests *380*
    62.3 Refusals *381*
    62.4 Abandoning a request *383*

63 Expressing apologies, regrets, sympathy, and bad news — 384
    63.1 Apologies and regrets *384*
    63.2 Expressing sympathy *386*
    63.3 Conveying bad news *386*

64 Expressing congratulations and good wishes — 388
    64.1 General expressions of congratulations and good wishes *388*
    64.2 Fixed phrases of congratulations and good wishes for special events *389*
    64.3 Replying to expressions of congratulations and good wishes *390*

Index — 391

Acknowledgments

We are grateful to the many people who have assisted us in the preparation of this second edition of the Modern Mandarin Chinese Grammar. We particularly thank Baozhang He and Pei-Chia Chen for their careful reading of the entire manuscript and for their suggestions and corrections, and for the many readers who sent us feedback on the first edition. We thank the Routledge editors for their help and patience. We thank our family members for their encouragement and help, Lester Ross, Jocelyn Ross, Adam Ross, and Weiyi Ma.

References consulted

Chapter 1
The classification of finals in Chapter 1 is from John Defrancis, *Beginning Chinese*, 2nd revised edition, New Haven: Yale University Press, 1976.

Chapter 3
Yuen-ren Chao, *A Grammar of Spoken Chinese*, Berkeley: University of California Press, 1968.
John DeFrancis (ed.) *ABC Chinese–English Dictionary*, Honolulu: University of Hawaii Press, 1996.
John DeFrancis, *Beginning Chinese*, 2nd revised edition, New Haven: Yale University Press, 1976.
Jerry Norman, *Chinese*, Cambridge: Cambridge University Press, 1988.
L. Wieger, *Chinese Characters*, New York: Paragon Book Reprint Corp., 1965.

Chapter 12
The source of the legal example in Chapter 12 is the Child Welfare Law of the Republic of China, Section 1, article 3.

Chapter 22
The information on names is based on a survey published in the 香港星島日報 **xiānggǎng xīng dǎo rìbào** (*Hong Kong and Singapore Daily News*) in 2002 and reported in 大參考总 **dà cān kǎo zǒng** (*VIP Reference*) vol. 1640, July 28, 2002.

Chapter 50
The source of the legal examples in Chapter 50 is the Economic Contract Law of the PRC (as amended 1993) as cited in Claudia Ross and Lester Ross, 'Language and Law,' in Karen G. Turner, James V. Feinerman, and R. Kent Guy (eds) *The Limits of the Rule of Law in China*, Seattle: University of Washington Press, 2000, pp. 221–70.

Claudia Ross and Jing-heng Sheng Ma

Introduction

This book is divided into two sections: 'Structures' and 'Situations and functions.'

Part A 'Structures' is a concise grammar of Mandarin Chinese organized in the familiar and traditional way, providing an overview of the Chinese writing system and describing the major features of Mandarin grammar. This section should be used for reference when you want to know something about a form or structure. For example, if you want to review the structure of the noun phrase, or how to form numbers, or the structure of the passive form, you should consult this section.

Part B 'Situations and functions' is organized in terms of how to do things with language, and it is the longer of the two sections. For example, if you want to know how to address someone, how to say 'no,' how to make comparisons, or how to apologize, you should consult this section.

Often, the same ground is covered in both parts of this book, although the emphasis is different in each section. Related sections are linked by cross-referencing, indicated by arrows in the margin of the page directing you to another section. Related functions are also cross-referenced throughout the book. You should always follow the cross-reference links so that you have a complete picture of the expression that you are exploring and can use it correctly and accurately.

Topics covered in this book are listed in the table of contents and in the index, and you should use them to help you find words and topics quickly and easily. Notice that the index is an alphabetical listing that includes keywords in English and in Pinyin romanization. For example, if you want to know how to indicate that you have had an experience in the past you can look in the index for the English expression 'experiential aspect' or for the word **guò** (过/過).

In this book, we use traditional grammatical terms to explain the structures of Mandarin. The terms are presented in the glossary at the beginning of this book. Once you are familiar with the grammatical terms you will find them helpful in understanding the grammar and in expressing yourself accurately.

We hope that you will find this book useful and informative. We look forward to learning how you use the book, and to receiving your suggestions on how it can be improved.

Claudia Ross and Jing-heng Sheng Ma

How to use this book

This book brings together two different types of resources to help you to understand Mandarin Chinese. They are presented in two parts: Part A: 'Structures' and Part B: 'Situations and functions.'

When you want to review some aspect of Mandarin grammar such as how to describe a noun or where to put the prepositional phrase in a sentence, you should consult Part A. On the other hand, when you want to know how to apologize, or how to address someone, or how to emphasize something, you should consult Part B. Some topics are covered in more than one chapter of the book. For example, the verb suffix 过/過 **guò** is included in 'Structures' in Chapters 11, 13, and 17, and also in 'Situations and functions' in Chapter 37, 'Indicating completion and talking about the past.' Arrows in the left-hand margin of each page indicate additional sections of the book in which a topic is discussed. You should follow the cross-references and read everything about the topic that you are exploring in order to get a full picture of its structure and functions.

Some topics can be expressed differently depending upon the level of formality in a specific situation. Where appropriate, we have indicated the level of formality associated with expressions. See, for example, 'Prepositions and prepositional phrases' (Chapter 14, section 14.2.8) and 'Greetings and goodbyes' (Chapter 24, section 24.3).

This book provides the most common ways of expressing the major structures and functions in Mandarin. Native speakers of Mandarin differ in their use of some expressions, and we have tried to note standard variations. In your study of Mandarin, you will come across structures and expressions that are not included in this book. You should add them to your repertoire as you continue to strengthen your language skills.

To help you to consolidate your overall knowledge of Chinese, we begin this book with a brief overview of Mandarin pronunciation and an introduction to the Chinese writing system. For a more detailed coverage of pronunciation, consult a beginning level Mandarin textbook. For more information about the Chinese writing system, consult the references cited in the Acknowledgments.

Claudia Ross and Jing-heng Sheng Ma

Glossary of grammatical terms

Adverbs

Adverbs are words that precede and modify a verb or verb phrase.

他们都很忙。
他們都很忙。
Tāmen *dōu* hěn máng.
They are *all* very busy.

弟弟已经回家了。
弟弟已經回家了。
Dìdi *yǐjing* huí jiā le.
Younger brother *already* went home.

Sentence adverbs occur at the beginning of a sentence and indicate the relationship of information in a conversation or written text.

孩子小的时候，父母照顾他们。后来，父母老了，该是孩子照顾父母了。
孩子小的時候，父母照顧他們。後來，父母老了，該是孩子照顧父母了。
Háizi xiǎo de shíhou, fùmǔ zhàogù tāmen. Hòulái, fùmǔ lǎo le, gāi shì háizi zhàogù fùmǔ le.
When children are young, parents take care of them. Afterwards, when the parents are old, the children should take care of the parents.

▶ 15, 31, 34, 35, 36, 37, 38, 39, 40, 46, 47

Classifiers

Classifiers are words that occur after a number and/or specifier and before a noun. Some grammars refer to classifiers as 'measure words.' Classifiers often need not be translated into English.

一杯水	那本书 那本書	这两个人 這兩個人
yī *bēi* shuǐ	**nà *běn* shū**	**zhè liǎng *gè* rén**
one [*glass of*] water	that [*volume of*] book	these two [*classifier*] people

▶ 8

Clauses

Clauses are dependent sentences, that is, sentences that occur within a larger sentence.

Some verbs take clauses as their objects:

她说她今天很忙。
她說她今天很忙。
Tā shuō *tā jīntiān hěn máng*.
She said *she is very busy today*.

GLOSSARY OF GRAMMATICAL TERMS

> 我知道他没有钱。
> 我知道他沒有錢。
> Wǒ zhīdao *tā méi yǒu qián.*
> I know *he doesn't have any money.*

Clauses may also serve as subjects:

> 她昨天跟你说话并不表示她愿意当你的女朋友。
> 她昨天跟你說話並不表示她願意當你的女朋友。
> *Tā zuótiān gēn nǐ shuō huà* bìng bù biǎoshì tā yuànyi dāng nǐ de nǚ péngyou.
> (The fact that) *she spoke with you yesterday* does not mean that she is willing to be your girlfriend.

Complements

Some Mandarin grammars distinguish a class of *verb complements*, words or phrases that follow the verb and augment its meaning in some way. Included in the class of verb complements are result complements, potential complements, directional complements, manner complements, and degree complements. These various verb complements participate in different grammatical structures and perform different communication functions, and we therefore do not group them together in this book. Complements of result and direction participate in the same kinds of grammatical structures, and we discuss them in Chapters 18 and 19, along with their potential forms. We also discuss complements of result along with other structures that function to indicate result in Chapter 32. Complements of degree function as intensifiers for adjectival verbs, and we discuss them in Chapter 10. Complements of manner function to indicate the way that actions are performed, and we discuss them in Chapter 31. Here are the sections of this book in which each complement is included.

Result complements

▶ 18, 32.1

Directional complements

▶ 19, 48.8

Potential complements

▶ 18.6, 19.5, 32.2

Degree complements

▶ 10.3

Manner complements

▶ 31.3

Conjunctions

Conjunctions are words that connect two nouns or noun phrases to form a noun phrase.

> 妈妈和爸爸都会说中国话。
> 媽媽和爸爸都會說中國話。
> Māma *hé* bàba dōu huì shuō Zhōngguó huà.
> Mom *and* Dad can both speak Chinese.

▶ 16

Demonstratives see **Specifiers and demonstratives**

Direct objects see **Objects**

GLOSSARY OF GRAMMATICAL TERMS

Final particles

Final particles are syllables that occur at the end of the sentence and indicate a speech act or speaker perspective.

我们吃饭吧！
我們吃飯吧！
Wǒmen chī fàn *ba*!
Let's eat! (suggestion)

我得走了。再不走就晚咯。
Wǒ děi zǒu le. Zài bù *zǒu* jiù wǎn *lo*.
I'd better go now. If I don't go, I will be late. (obviousness)

▶ 28.1.1, 28.5, 34.3, 38.1, 56.2

Grammatical particles

Grammatical particles are syllables that convey grammatical meaning, for example 的 **de** (noun modification), 得 **de** (postverbal adverbial modification), 地 **de** (preverbal adverbial modification), 了 **le** (completed action), 着/著 **zhe** (duration).

▶ 9, 31, 37, 39

Indirect objects see Objects

Intensifiers

Intensifiers are words that precede and modify stative verbs, adjectival verbs, and modal verbs.

我<u>很</u>喜欢他。	那本书<u>太</u>贵了。	你<u>真</u>会跳舞。
我<u>很</u>喜歡他。	那本書<u>太</u>貴了。	你<u>真</u>會跳舞。
Wǒ *hěn* xǐhuan tā.	**Nà běn shū *tài* guì le.**	**Nǐ *zhēn* huì tiào wǔ.**
I like him *a lot*.	That book is *too* expensive.	You can *really* dance.

▶ 10.3, 11.2, 12.6.3

Nouns

Nouns are words that can be directly preceded by a specifier and/or number + classifier.

一本书　　那本书
一本書　　那本書
yī běn *shū* 　**nà běn *shū***
one *book* 　that *book*

Noun phrases

Noun phrases are nouns and their modifiers.

▶ 9

Numbers

Number words.

▶ 6

Objects

There are two different types of objects, *direct* and *indirect*.

The direct object is generally the noun phrase affected by or created by the action of the verb. The direct object generally follows the verb, though it may also be topicalized (see **Topics**).

我每天在图书馆看书。
我每天在圖書館看書。
Wǒ měitiān zài túshūguǎn kàn *shū*.
I read *books* in the library every day.

我已经吃晚饭了。
我已經吃晚飯了。
Wǒ yǐjing chī *wǎnfàn* le.
I have already eaten *dinner*.

The indirect object refers to the recipient of the object noun phrase. In Mandarin, only a small number of verbs take a direct and indirect object. These include 给/給 **gěi** 'give' and 送 **sòng** 'present as a gift.' In all cases, the indirect object precedes the direct object.

我不要给他钱。
我不要給他錢。
Wǒ bù yào gěi *tā* qián.
I don't want to give *him* money.

For most verbs, the recipient is expressed as the object of a preposition and not as an indirect object.

我给她写了一封信。
我給她寫了一封信。
Wǒ gěi *tā* xiě le yī fēng xìn.
I wrote *her* a letter. (I wrote a letter to *her*.)

Predicates

The predicate of a sentence includes a verb and any object(s) or complements of the verb. It may also include negation, adverbs, prepositional phrases, and phrases that indicate time when, duration, or frequency.

Prepositional phrases

Prepositional phrases consist of a preposition and its following noun phrase. In Mandarin, the prepositional phrase typically precedes the verb phrase.

我在家吃饭。
我在家吃飯。
Wǒ *zài jiā* chī fàn.
I eat *at home*.

我到图书馆去了。
我到圖書館去了。
Wǒ *dào túshūguǎn* qù le.
I went *to the library*.

Prepositional phrases that indicate where the object winds up as the result of the action generally follow the verb.

他跳到床上。
Tā tiào dào chuáng shàng.
He jumped onto the bed.

Prepositions

Prepositions are words that indicate the relationship of a noun phrase to a verb, for example 在 **zài** 'at,' 到 **dào** 'to,' 给/給 **gěi** 'to/for,' 替 **tì** 'for.'

▶ 14

GLOSSARY OF GRAMMATICAL TERMS

Pronouns

Pronouns are words that take the place of a noun or noun phrase.

<u>王明</u>是学生。
<u>王明</u>是學生。
<u>**Wáng Míng**</u> **shì xuésheng.**
<u>Wang Ming</u> is a student.

<u>他</u>是学生。
<u>他</u>是學生。
<u>**Tā**</u> **shì xuésheng.**
<u>He</u> is a student.

我不认识<u>那两个人</u>。
我不認識<u>那兩個人</u>。
Wǒ bù rènshi <u>**nà liǎng gè rén**</u>**.**
I don't know <u>those two people</u>.

我不认识<u>他们</u>。
我不認識<u>他們</u>。
Wǒ bù rènshi <u>**tāmen**</u>**.**
I don't know <u>them</u>.

▶ 5.2

Sentences

Normally, a full sentence includes a subject and a predicate. The sentence may begin with a topic.

topic + subject + predicate

那个孩子，脾气很坏。
那個孩子，脾氣很壞。
Nàge háizi, píqi hěn huài.
That child has a bad temper. (lit. 'That child, the temper is bad.')

Specifiers and demonstratives

Specifiers are words that translate as 'this/these' or 'that/those' and describe a noun.

<u>这</u>本书很有意思。
<u>這</u>本書很有意思。
<u>**Zhè**</u> **běn shū hěn yǒu yìsi.**
<u>This</u> book is very interesting.

These same words, when used to 'point' to an object, are 'demonstratives.'

<u>这</u>是中国毛笔。
<u>這</u>是中國毛筆。
<u>**Zhè**</u> **shì Zhōngguó máobǐ.**
<u>This</u> is a Chinese writing brush.

▶ 7

Subjects

The subject is the noun or noun phrase about which information is provided in the predicate. In Mandarin, the subject of a sentence occurs before the verb phrase. It can be omitted if it is understood from the overall context of the sentence. Typically, a subject is omitted if it is identical in reference to the subject of the preceding sentence.

我看了电影。( )九点钟就回家了。
我看了電影。( )九點鐘就回家了。
Wǒ kàn le diànyǐng. ( ) jiǔdiǎn zhōng jiù huí jiā le.
I saw a movie. At nine o'clock *I* returned home.

GLOSSARY OF GRAMMATICAL TERMS

Topics

Generally speaking, the topic is the noun or noun phrase that the sentence, paragraph, or narrative is about. The topic occurs at the beginning of a sentence, and is often distinct from the subject.

> 中国菜，我特别喜欢吃家常豆腐。
> 中國菜，我特別喜歡吃家常豆腐。
> **Zhōngguo cài, wǒ tèbié xǐhuan chī jiācháng dòufu.**
> (As for) *Chinese food*, I especially like to eat homestyle beancurd.

In Mandarin, the object of the verb may sometimes occur in 'topic' position, at the beginning of the sentence, before the subject.

> 羊肉，我不太喜欢吃。
> 羊肉，我不太喜歡吃。
> **Yángròu, wǒ bù tài xǐhuan chī.**
> *Mutton*, I don't particularly like to eat (it).

A sentence need not begin with a topic.

Verbs

Verbs are words that can be directly negated, or modified by an adverb, or that can serve as the 'yes' answer to yes–no questions. Verbs are the main word in the predicate, and a Mandarin sentence must include a verb. Verbs that take one or more objects are called transitive, and verbs that do not take an object are called intransitive. Mandarin has the following types of verbs.

Adjectival verbs

Adjectival verbs are verbs that can be translated as adjectives in English, for example 大 **dà** 'big,' 好 **hǎo** 'good,' 贵/貴 **guì** 'expensive.' Adjectival verbs are usually intransitive. Note that adjectival verbs do not occur with 是 **shì** 'be.'

Say this	Not this
他很高。	*他是很高。
Tā hěn gāo.	**Tā shì hěn gāo.**
He is very *tall*.	

▶ 10

Stative verbs

(a) Stative verbs are verbs that express states, for example 喜欢/喜歡 **xǐhuan** 'like,' 像 **xiàng** 'resemble.'

> 我喜欢他。
> 我喜歡他。
> **Wǒ xǐhuan tā.**
> I *like* him.

(b) Stative verbs are linking verbs, for example 是 **shì** 'be,' 姓 **xìng** 'be family named,' 有 **yǒu** 'have, exist.'

> 她有很多朋友。
> **Tā yǒu hěn duō péngyou.**
> She *has* many friends.

▶ 11

xxiii

GLOSSARY OF GRAMMATICAL TERMS

Modal verbs

Modal verbs are verbs that express ability, permission, or obligation, for example 会/會 **huì** 'can' (mentally able), 能 **néng** 'can' (physically able), 可以 **kěyǐ** 'may' (have permission), 得 **děi** 'must/have to.' Modal verbs can serve as the one word answer to yes–no questions, but in complete sentences they are always followed by a verb phrase complement.

▶ 12

Action verbs

Action verbs are verbs that refer to events. There are two kinds of action verbs:

- Open-ended action verbs express open-ended actions, such as 跑 **pǎo** 'run,' 写/寫 **xiě** 'write,' and 听/聽 **tīng** 'listen.' Most open-ended action verbs in Mandarin are transitive.
- Change-of-state action verbs express actions that refer to a change of state and have no duration, such as 坐 **zuò** 'sit (down),' 忘 **wàng** 'forget,' and 放 **fàng** 'put (down), place.'

▶ 13

Verb complements (*see* **Complements**)

Verb phrases

The verb phrase includes the modal verb, the verb, and any objects of the verb. (*See also* Predicates)

他每天看电视。
他每天看電視。
Tā měitiān *kàn diànshì*.
He *watches television* every day.

爸爸给我钱。
爸爸給我錢。
Bàba *gěi wǒ qián*.
Dad *gives me money*.

他会开车。
他會開車。
Tā *huì kāi chē*.
He *can drive (a car)*.

我请你吃晚饭。
我請你吃晚飯。
Wǒ *qǐng nǐ chī wǎnfàn*.
I *invite you to eat dinner*.

A note on grammatical categories and grammatical category shift

In Mandarin, a word may belong to more than one grammatical category. For example, some words may serve as both a verb and a preposition.

		Verb	*Preposition*
给/給	**gěi**	give	to/for
到	**dào**	arrive	to
在	**zài**	be located	at

GLOSSARY OF GRAMMATICAL TERMS

Out of context, it is not possible to say whether the word 给/給 **gěi** or 到 **dào** or 在 **zài** is a preposition or a verb. However, in the context of a sentence or phrase, the category of the word is clear:

Preposition

> 我想到中国去。
> 我想到中國去。
> **Wǒ xiǎng *dào* Zhōngguó qù.**
> I want *to* China go
> I want to go *to* China.

Verb

> 你什么时候到？
> 你甚麼時候到？
> **Nǐ shénme shíhòu *dào*?**
> When are you *arriving*?

Some textbooks and grammars provide special labels for words that can function as more than one category of word. For example, the label 'coverb' is used in many textbooks for words that can be both prepositions and verbs.

▶ 14.3

A note on Chinese characters

Certain traditional characters have more than one standard form. Here are some examples. This book uses the characters in the first column. An overview of the origin, structure, and systems of Chinese characters is presented in Chapter 3.

裏	裡	lǐ
著	着	zhè
叫	呌	jiào
為	爲	wèi

In addition, the word **zuò** when used as the verb 'do' can be written as 做 or 作. This book uses the form 做. In compounds such as 工作 **gōngzuò** 'work,' **zuò** is written as 作.

Part A

Structures

1

Overview of pronunciation and Pinyin romanization

1.1 The Mandarin syllable

The syllable in Mandarin Chinese can be made up of three parts: an initial consonant, a final, and a tone. For example, the syllable **má** 麻 is made up of the initial **m**, the final **a**, and the rising tone [´]. Syllables need not have an initial consonant. The syllable **è** 饿/餓 is made up of the final **e** and the falling tone [`]. In addition, a syllable may lack a tone. Syllables that do not have a tone are referred to as having *neutral tone*.

This section presents a brief overview of the initials, finals, and tones of Mandarin. Initials and finals are presented in Pinyin romanization. For a guide to their pronunciation, please consult a beginning level Mandarin textbook.

1.1.1 Initials

The Mandarin initials are presented here in the traditional recitation order:

Type of sound	*Initial*			
1 bilabial	b	p	m	f
2 alveolar	d	t	n	l
3 velar	g	k	h	
4 palatal	j	q	x	
5 retroflex	zh	ch	sh	r
6 alveolar affricate/fricative	z	c	s	

1.1.2 Finals

Finals are listed by initial vowel.

a finals	a an ang ai ao
o/e finals	o e en eng ei ou ong er
u finals	u ua uo uai ui uan un uang ueng
i finals	i ia iao ie iu ian in iang ing iong
ü finals	ü üe üan ün

1.1.3 Tones

Tone is the pitch contour of the syllable. Mandarin has four contour tones and a neutral tone. In most romanization systems of Mandarin, the tone is indicated by a diacritic over a vowel, or as a number following the syllable.

OVERVIEW OF PRONUNCIATION AND PINYIN ROMANIZATION

The following chart illustrates the contour of the four Mandarin tones when a syllable is spoken in *isolation*, that is, when it is neither preceded nor followed by another syllable.

1 level pitch ˉ
2 rising pitch ´
3 falling-rising pitch ˇ
4 falling pitch ˋ

The contour of a tone may change depending upon the following syllable. This is often called *tone sandhi*. Tone change is typically not indicated in the Pinyin spelling of words.

The third tone is the only tone that changes independent of the meaning of the syllable.

When a third tone occurs before another third tone, it is pronounced as a rising (second) tone.

$3 + 3 \rightarrow 2 + 3$

hěn hǎo → **hén hǎo** 很好 very good

When a third tone occurs before any other tone, it is pronounced as a low tone. This low tone is often called a *half third tone*.

mǎi shū → **ma̱i shū** 买书/買書 buy books

Tone is an inherent part of the Mandarin syllable, and Mandarin uses tones to distinguish meaning in the same way that the choice of a consonant or a vowel distinguishes meaning. Notice how tone determines the meaning of the following syllable.

Tone			
1	**mā** (ma1)	妈/媽	mother
2	**má** (ma2)	麻	numb
3	**mǎ** (ma3)	马/馬	horse
4	**mà** (ma4)	骂/罵	scold
neutral	**ma** (ma5)	吗/嗎	question particle

▶ 2.3

1.2 Pinyin romanization

Mandarin is written with Chinese characters, but characters do not provide consistent information about pronunciation. Therefore, Mandarin is typically studied via a transcription. Many transcription systems have been devised for Mandarin Chinese in China and in the West. Most of these are based on the Roman alphabet, and are therefore termed 'romanization' systems. In 1958, the People's Republic of China established *Hanyu Pinyin* (usually referred to as Pinyin) as its standard romanization system. Because of the widespread use of this system of Pinyin in Chinese language teaching around the world, it is used to transcribe the Chinese words in this book.

1.2.1 Placement of tone mark in Pinyin

If a final includes three vowels, or two vowels and a final consonant, the tone mark is written over the second vowel:

kuài   huán   biān   qióng

If a final includes two vowels and no final consonant, the tone mark is placed over the first vowel, unless the first vowel is **i** or **u**:

āi   áo   ěi   òu
      iā   ié   iǔ
uà   ué   uǐ   uò

1.2.2 Some additional Pinyin conventions

- 'u' after the initials **j**, **q**, and **x** is pronounced **ü** but is written as **u**.
- When 'i' and 'ü' begin a syllable, they are written as **yi** and **yu**.
- When 'u' begins a syllable, it is written as **wu**.
- In two-syllable words, when the boundary between syllables is not clear from the Pinyin spelling and more than one interpretation of the boundary is possible, an apostrophe is used to separate the syllables. For example, if the second syllable begins with a vowel, an apostrophe is used: **Xī'ān** 西安 vs. **xiān** 先.

2

Syllable, meaning, and word

2.1 The special status of the Mandarin syllable

2.1.1 The syllable and meaning

One of the features of Chinese is that each syllable is associated with a meaning. For example, the Mandarin word for bus station/train station or bus stop/train stop is 车站/車站 **chēzhàn**. The syllable 车/車 **chē** means vehicle and the syllable 站 **zhàn** means stand. Occurring together as a word, 车站/車站 **chēzhàn** is very nearly the sum of its parts: vehicle stand.

Some words in English have the kind of structure that Mandarin has, but for most English words, syllables need not have independent meaning. For example, the English word 'lettuce' consists of two syllables: 'let' and 'tuce.' These individual syllables do not have meaning on their own, and it makes no sense to ask about the meaning of 'let' or of 'tuce' in the word 'lettuce.' In contrast, with very few exceptions, the individual syllables of Mandarin words have identifiable meanings, and when learning new words, it makes good sense to note the meanings of the individual syllables.

NOTES

1 In Chinese, a small number of syllables are not associated with a meaning. The most common is the noun suffix 子 **zǐ**. See **2.2.1.1**.
2 A multi-syllable Mandarin word is not always simply the sum of its parts. For example, the word 故事 **gùshì** 'story' is composed of the syllables 故 **gù** 'former, previous' and 事 **shì** 'situation, incident.'

2.1.2 The syllable and Chinese characters

In Chinese, the syllable is associated with a Chinese character as well as a meaning. When a syllable is associated with more than one meaning, it is generally the case that each meaning is written with a different character. For example, Mandarin has a number of meanings associated with the pronunciation **zhàn**. Each meaning is written with a different character:

蘸	**zhàn**	dip in liquid (like a pen in ink)
占/佔	**zhàn**	occupy
战/戰	**zhàn**	fight
栈/棧	**zhàn**	storehouse
绽/綻	**zhàn**	split; burst open
站	**zhàn**	to stand; a stop, a stand

Because of these differences, the status of the syllable is much more important in Chinese than in English. Conversely, the status of the word is less important in Chinese than in English.

2.2 Multi-syllable tendency in Mandarin words

Although Mandarin syllables have meanings, they often combine to form words. Here is a short list of Mandarin syllables and words that they form.

Syllable				*Word*		
学/學	xué	study, study of		学生/學生	xuésheng	student
生	shēng	give birth to; grow		出生	chūshēng	be born, birth
出	chū	go out, produce		出口	chūkǒu	export; exit
口	kǒu	mouth, opening		出版	chūbǎn	publish
版	bǎn	printing block/printing		学校/學校	xuéxiào	school
校	xiào	school		校长/校長	xiàozhǎng	principal
长/長	zhǎng	head, one in charge		中学/中學	zhōngxué	middle school
中	zhōng	middle				
图/圖	tú	chart		图片/圖片	túpiàn	picture
片	piàn	a slice, a part		地图/地圖	dìtú	map
地	dì	earth				
书/書	shū	book				
馆/館	guǎn	place (for activities)		图书馆/圖書館	túshūguǎn	library
饭/飯	fàn	rice		饭馆/飯館	fànguǎn	restaurant

2.2.1 Strategies that create and maintain the two-syllable word

The most common length of Mandarin words is two syllables, and a number of common word formation strategies exist which help to create and maintain the two-syllable word.

2.2.1.1 The suffix 子 *zǐ*

One-syllable words may be turned into two-syllable words by the addition of the suffix 子 **zǐ**. This suffix adds little or no meaning to the word. It usually occurs in neutral tone (**zi**).

Some nouns occur in contemporary Mandarin only with the 子 **zi** suffix, for example 孩子 **háizi** 'child,' 房子 **fángzi** 'house,' 屋子 **wūzi** 'room,' 本子 **běnzi** 'notebook,' 袜子/襪子 **wàzi** 'socks.'

Some words can occur with or without the suffix. These include 车/車 **chē** → 车子/車子 **chēzi** 'car,' 鞋 **xié** → 鞋子 **xiézi** 'shoe,' 盘/盤 → 盘子/盤子 **pánzi** 'plate,' 票 **piào** → 票子 **piàozi** 'ticket.'

> NOTE
>
> In the Beijing dialect of Mandarin, the suffix 儿/兒 **(é)r** is routinely added to words in many categories, especially to nouns and classifiers. 儿/兒 **r** suffixation adds a retroflex (**r**) sound but no additional syllable to the word. If a word ends in a final consonant, the 儿/兒 **r** suffix replaces the final consonant: 份 **fèn** → 份儿/份兒 **fèr** 'a portion,' 玩 **wán** → 玩儿/玩兒 **wár** 'to play,' 电影/電影 **diànyǐng** → 电影儿/電影兒 **diànyǐr** 'movie,' etc. The suffix may also replace a vowel in the final: 孩 **hái** → 孩儿/孩兒 **hár** 'child.'
>
> In this book, we write **-r** suffixed words in terms of their changed pronunciation. That is, we write **wár** and not **wánr** or **wán'er**.

2.2.1.2 Location suffixes

Location words may be suffixed with 头/頭 **tóu**, 面 **miàn**, or 边/邊 **biān** to make them two-syllable words: 下头/下頭 **xiàtou** 'below,' 外面 **wàimian** 'outside,' 左边/左邊 **zuǒbiān** 'left side,' etc.

In Mandarin spoken in southern China and Taiwan, the specifiers 这/這 **zhè**, 那 **nà, nèi** and 哪 **nǎ, něi** are suffixed with 里/裏 when they are used as location words: 这里/這裏 **zhèlǐ** 'here,' 那里/那裏 **nàlǐ** 'there,' and 哪里?/哪裏? **nǎlǐ?** 'where?'

▶ 7.3, 47.1

SYLLABLE, MEANING, AND WORD

2.2.1.3 Abbreviation

Words and phrases that are longer than two syllables are often abbreviated to two syllables. The two syllables that form the new, abbreviated word are typically the first syllable of each of the words in the phrase or the first two syllables of the first word in the phrase, though other combinations occur.

超级市场/超級市場	**chāojí shìchǎng**	supermarket	→	超市 **chāoshì**
公共汽车/公共汽車	**gōnggòng qìchē**	public bus	→	公车/公車 **gōngchē**
飞机场/飛機場	**fēijīchǎng**	airport	→	机场/機場 **jīchǎng**

2.3 Word-specific tone changes

In addition to the tone changes mentioned in section 1.1.3 for all third-tone syllables, there are certain tone changes that occur in specific words.

2.3.1 Tone change in the word 不 *bù*

不 **bù** changes to **bú** when it occurs before another fourth-toned syllable in the same word, phrase, or breath group:

	4–4	→	*2–4*
不对/不對 not correct	bù duì	→	bú duì
不必 need not	bù bì	→	bú bì

2.3.2 Tone change in the numbers 一 *yī* '1,' 七 *qī* '7,' and 八 *bā* '8'

The tone of the numbers 一 **yī** '1,' and, less commonly, 七 **qī** '7,' and 八 **bā** '8' may change to second tone **yí**, **qí**, and **bá** before a fourth-toned syllable in the same word, phrase, or breath group:

	1–4	→	*2–4*
一共 altogether	yīgòng	→	yígòng
一定 certainly	yīdìng	→	yídìng
一辈子 a lifetime	yī bèizi	→	yí bèizi
七块钱/七塊錢 seven dollars	qī kuài qián	→	qí kuài qián
八倍 eightfold	bā bèi	→	bá bèi

Change to neutral tone | **2.4**

In addition, 一 **yī** changes to fourth tone before syllables with first, second, or third tone.

		1–1	→	*4–1*
一张/一張 one sheet (e.g. of paper)		**yī zhāng**	→	**yì zhāng**
		1–2	→	*4–2*
一条/一條 one thin strip (e.g. of news)		**yī tiáo**	→	**yì tiáo**
		1–3	→	*4–3*
一碗 one bowl		**yī wǎn**	→	**yì wǎn**

2.4 Change to neutral tone

In Beijing and northern China, certain syllables lose their original tone and are pronounced as neutral tone. This tone change does not occur in Taiwan, where all syllables retain their original tones.

▶ 1.1.3

The complete conditions for change to neutral tone are complex, but here are some general rules for the change of a second syllable to neutral tone.

- The second syllable is a repetition of the first syllable:

	tone-tone	→	*tone-neutral*
太太 Mrs	**tàitài**	→	**tàitai**
弟弟 younger brother	**dìdì**	→	**dìdi**
谢谢/謝謝 thank you	**xièxiè**	→	**xièxie**
看看 take a look	**kànkàn**	→	**kànkan**

- The second syllable is a suffix that does not contribute a meaning to the word. This includes the suffix 子 **zǐ** and the directional suffixes 头/頭 **tóu**, 面 **miàn**, and 边/邊 **biān**:

	tone-tone	→	*tone-neutral*
孩子 child	**háizǐ**	→	**háizi**
里头/裏頭 inside	**lǐtóu**	→	**lǐtou**

SYLLABLE, MEANING, AND WORD

2.5

- The meaning of the second syllable is the same as or overlaps with the meaning of the first syllable:

	tone-tone	→	tone-neutral
衣服 clothing	**yīfú**	→	**yīfu**

衣 **yī**
clothing

服 **fú**
clothing

| 事情 matter/situation | **shìqíng** | → | **shìqing** |

事 **shì**
situation

情 **qíng**
situation

The second syllable retains its tone when it adds to and expands the meaning of the first syllable. Examples include:

学期/學期	学/學	期
xuéqī	**xué**	**qī**
semester	study	interval

作法	作	法
zuòfǎ	**zuò**	**fǎ**
method of doing	do	method

看完	看	完
kànwán	**kàn**	**wán**
finish reading	read	finish

Sometimes, the use of full or neutral tone in the second syllable makes a difference in meaning. Here are two examples:

老子	**Lǎo Zǐ**	Laozi, the Taoist philosopher
老子	**lǎozi**	used to refer to one's father, or, humorously, to oneself
孙子	**Sūn zǐ**	5th C BC treatise on the art of war
孙子	**sūnzi**	grandson

2.5 Incorporating foreign words and naming foreign objects

Chinese has not borrowed freely from other languages. However, when it incorporates foreign words into the language, it typically uses the following strategies:

- Adapting the foreign pronunciation to conform to the syllable structure of Chinese.

    Names

    | 罗斯福/羅斯福 | **Luósīfú** | Roosevelt |
    | 加缪/加繆 | **Jiāmóu** | Camus |
    | 丘吉尔/邱吉爾 | **Qiūjí'ěr** | Churchill |
    | 拿破仑/拿破崙 | **Nápòlún** | Napoleon |
    | 莎士比亚/莎士比亞 | **Shāshìbǐyà** | Shakespeare |

10

Incorporating foreign words and naming foreign objects — 2.5

Objects

| 比萨/比薩 | **bǐsà** | pizza |
| 汉堡包/漢堡包 | **hànbǎobāo** | hamburger |

▶ 1.1

- Forming new words based on meaning or function.
- When new items enter China, they often lose their foreign pronunciation and get new Chinese names that reflect their meaning or function. Here are some examples:

电视/電視	**diànshì**	television (electric vision)
电脑/電腦	**diànnǎo**	computer (electric brain)
微波炉/微波爐	**wēibō lú**	microwave oven (micro-wave-stove)
手机/手機	**shǒujī**	cell phone/mobile phone (hand machine)
热狗/熱狗	**règǒu**	(lit.) hot dog
卫星/衛星	**wèixīng**	satellite (protection star)

- Forming new words based on meaning while preserving the foreign pronunciation.

万维网/萬維網	**wàn wéi wǎng**	the World Wide Web (a net of 10,000 connections)
可乐/可樂	**kělè**	cola (it can make you happy)
拖拉机/拖拉機	**tuōlājī**	tractor (drag pull machine)
摩托车/摩托車	**mótuō chē**	motorcycle (a vehicle you touch and support with your hands)
信用卡	**xìnyòng kǎ**	credit card (trust card)
吉普车/吉普車	**jípǔchē**	jeep (lucky widely used vehicle)

Foreign companies often follow this principle when translating the names of their companies and their products into Chinese.

可口可乐/可口可樂	**Kěkǒukělè**	Coca Cola [soft drink] (pleasant to drink and it can make you happy)
福特	**Fútè**	Ford [automobiles] (happiness – exceptional)
汰渍/汰漬	**Tàizì**	Tide [laundry detergent] (eliminate stains and sludge)

3

The Chinese writing system: an overview

Although transcription systems can be used to write Chinese, Chinese characters are the basis of written communication in China. This chapter presents an overview of Chinese characters.

3.1 Traditional and simplified characters

There are two standard systems of characters in current use: traditional characters and simplified characters. Simplified characters are the official characters used in mainland China and Singapore. Traditional characters are the official characters used in Taiwan and other parts of the Chinese-speaking world.

Most characters in the traditional and simplified systems are identical. However, in the simplified character system, many frequently used characters have been simplified from their traditional, more complex form. Here are some examples.

Traditional	*Simplified*	*Pronunciation*	*Meaning*
國	国	**guó**	country
東	东	**dōng**	east
車	车	**chē**	car
買	买	**mǎi**	buy
寫	写	**xiě**	write

A simplified way of writing characters has existed for hundreds of years. Simplified characters were used in informal documents and in some forms of calligraphy before they were adopted by mainland China as the official form. Therefore, although the two forms now have some political significance, you may encounter simplified characters in use in Taiwan and traditional characters in use in mainland China.

3.2 The structure of Chinese characters: the radical and the phonetic

3.2.1 The radical

All Chinese characters contain a *radical*, a sequence of strokes that broadly categorize the character in terms of meaning.

In the set of traditional characters, there are 214 radicals. In the set of simplified characters, there are 189 radicals. Some radicals may occur as independent characters. Others only occur as part of a character.

The structure of Chinese characters: the radical and the phonetic

3.2

Here is a list of some of the most common radicals, including their simplified form if there is one.

Traditional radical	Alternate form	Radicals with simplified forms	Meaning
人	亻		person
刀	刂		knife
力			energy
水	氵		water
門		门	door
土			earth
竹	⺮		bamboo
口			mouth
囗			enclosure
心	忄		heart
火	灬		fire
木			wood
日			sun
食		饣	eat, food
艸	艹	艹	grass
言		讠	language
金		钅	metal/gold

When a radical is simplified, the simplified form is used in all of the characters in which it occurs. Here are some examples.

Traditional	Simplified	Pronunciation	Meaning
話	话	**huà**	speech
錢	钱	**qián**	money
鋼	钢	**gāng**	steel
飯	饭	**fàn**	rice
餓	饿	**è**	hungry

3.2.2 The phonetic

Some characters are radicals by themselves. Examples include:

水	**shuǐ**	water
木	**mù**	wood
人	**rén**	person

However, most characters include a radical and additional sets of strokes. Often, these additional strokes provide a hint at the pronunciation of the character. When they do, they are called the *phonetic*.

13

THE CHINESE WRITING SYSTEM: AN OVERVIEW

Here are examples of characters with phonetics. As you can see, the pronunciation of the phonetic may be identical or similar to the pronunciation of the character.

Character	Phonetic: the character sounds like...
问/問 **wèn** to ask	门/門 **mén** door
间/間 **jiān** between	
简/簡 **jiǎn** simple	
们/們 **men** plural marker	
清 **qīng** clear	青 **qīng** blue or green
情 **qíng** situation, sentiment	
请/請 **qǐng** to request	
河 **hé** river	可 **kě** approve, can
哥 **gē** older brother	

Noting phonetic information is a helpful way to remember characters. However, the phonetic rarely provides complete information about the pronunciation of a character.

3.3 The traditional classification of characters

Chinese characters originated during the early Shang dynasty or the late Xia dynasty, in the seventeenth century BC. One of the earliest Chinese dictionaries, the *Shuowen Jiezi*, compiled in AD 121, established a classification of characters that is still used today. The classification identified the following six categories based on structure and representation of meaning.

3.3.1 Pictographs 象形 *xiàngxíng*

Pictographs originated as pictures of objects. They represent only a small portion of Chinese characters. The modern forms are stylized versions of the ancient forms. Here are comparisons of the Shang Dynasty forms with the modern forms of the same characters.

Shang form	Modern form	Meaning
〲	水 **shuǐ**	water
☉	日 **rì**	sun
⬭	目 **mù**	eye

The traditional classification of characters 3.3

3.3.2 Ideographs 指事 *zhǐ shì*

Ideographs represent abstract meanings, often having to do with spatial orientation. Only a small number of characters are ideographs. Examples are presented here.

Shang form	Modern form	Meaning
二	上 **shàng**	above
一	下 **xià**	below
𠅘	中 **zhōng**	middle (picture of a target hit by an arrow)

3.3.3 Associative compounds 会意/會意 *huì yì*

The meaning of these characters is reflected in the meaning of their component parts.

Character			Composed of					
好	**hǎo**	good	女	**nǚ**	woman	+ 子	**zǐ**	child
话/話	**huà**	speech	言	**yán**	language	+ 舌	**shé**	tongue

3.3.4 Phonetic compounds 形声/形聲 *xíngshēng*

Phonetic compounds are the most common type of Chinese character and are discussed in 3.2.2 above.

3.3.5 False borrowings 假借 *jiǎjiè*

False borrowings involve the use of a character to refer to another word with identical pronunciation but different meaning. For example, the word for 'wheat,' written as 来/來, a picture of the wheat plant, was 'borrowed' to write the abstract concept 'come,' which, at the time, had the same pronunciation as the word for wheat. The character for 'wheat' was later revised to distinguish it from the character for 'come.' In present-day writing, 'wheat' is written as 麦/麥 **mài** and 'come' is written as 来/來 **lái**. The similarity in the characters can be seen in the traditional form of the characters. Note that the pronunciation of the two words is no longer identical, though they still rhyme.

3.3.6 Semantic derivations 转注/轉注 *zhuǎnzhù*

Characters are considered 转注/轉注 **zhuǎnzhù** when they are used to represent a meaning that is derived from the original meaning of the character. For example, the character 网/網 **wǎng**, originally a picture of a fishing net, is used to refer to networks in general. It is the character used in one of the Chinese translations of the World Wide Web: 万维网/萬維網 **wàn wéi wǎng**. The simplified character for net, 网, is the older form of the character.

THE CHINESE WRITING SYSTEM: AN OVERVIEW

3.4 Character stroke order: 笔顺/筆順 *bǐshùn*

3.4.1 Basic rules of stroke order

Each Chinese character contains a precise number of strokes written in a fixed order. Below are the basic rules of stroke order for the writing of Chinese characters.

Rule	*Example*
1 Horizontal (横 **héng**) precedes vertical (竖/豎 **shù**).	十
2 Left falling stroke (撇 **piě**) precedes right falling stroke (捺 **nà**).	人
3 First top, then bottom.	三
4 First left, then right.	他
5 First outside, then inside.	月
6 First complete the inside of a box, then seal the box.	日
7 First center, then sides.	小
8 First horizontal (横 **héng**), then left falling stroke (撇 **piě**), then right falling stroke (捺 **nà**).	大

3.4.2 Special stroke order rules

Rule	*Example*
1 Write the dot (点/點 **diǎn**) last if it is positioned at the top right corner of a character.	我
2 Write the dot (点/點 **diǎn**) last if it is positioned inside a character.	太
3 If the character includes the curved left-falling stroke (横折撇/橫摺撇 **héng zhé piě**) and one other component, write the curved left-falling stroke last.	建
4 If the character consists of more than one horizontal stroke (横 **héng**) and vertical stroke (竖/豎 **shù**), write the vertical stroke first, and the horizontal stroke at the bottom last.	上
5 If a character has a horizontal stroke (横 **héng**) in the middle, write the horizontal stroke last.	女

4

Phrase order in the Mandarin sentence

4.1 Basic phrase order

The basic order of the Mandarin sentence is

topic + subject + predicate

A sentence need not have an overt topic. In addition, if the subject is understood from the context of the sentence, it is often omitted from the sentence.

The predicate consists of everything in the sentence except for the topic and subject, including the verb, its objects, negation, adverbial modifiers, prepositional phrases, and aspect particles. The following sections present the order of these constituents.

▶ 8.1, 15.1, 17, 20.1, 21.1, 39.1, 46.2, 46.3, 57

4.2 The position of direct and indirect objects

In the neutral sentence in which nothing is emphasized, the direct and indirect objects of the verb follow the verb. We refer to the verb and its objects as the *verb phrase*.

If there is an indirect object, it precedes the direct object.

subject + verb + indirect object + direct object

他给我一本书。
他給我一本書。
Tā gěi wǒ yī běn shū.
He gave (gives) me one book.

Most verbs take only a direct object.

subject + verb + direct object

我看了那些书。
我看了那些書。
Wǒ kàn le nà xiē shū.
I read those books.

The object may also occur before the subject for emphasis. In this position it is *topicalized*.

▶ 57

PHRASE ORDER IN THE MANDARIN SENTENCE **4.5**

4.3 The position of prepositional phrases

Prepositional phrases generally occur right before the verb and its objects.

subject + prepositional phrase + verb + direct object

他跟他的女朋友吃晚饭。
他跟他的女朋友吃晚飯。
Tā gēn tā de nǔ péngyou chī wǎnfàn.
He eats dinner with his girlfriend.

▶ 14

4.4 The position of location phrases

The location phrase, the phrase that indicates where an action occurs, is a type of prepositional phrase. It always occurs before the verb phrase.

subject + location phrase + verb phrase

我在家吃饭。
我在家吃飯。
Wǒ zài jiā chī fàn.
I eat at home.

Within the location phrase, the order of constituents is from the largest to the smallest. Letters are addressed following this principle.

中国北京潮阳区建国门外大街一号
中國北京潮陽區建國門外大街一號
Zhōngguó Běijīng Cháoyáng qū Jiànguó mén wài dà jiē yī hào
China Beijing Chaoyang District Jianguo Gate Outer Road Number 1 → Number 1, Jianguo Gate Outer Road, Chaoyang District, Beijing, China

▶ 22.7

4.5 The position of 'time when' phrases

A phrase that indicates the 'time when' a situation takes place occurs at the beginning of the predicate.

subject + time when + predicate

我	每天	喝咖啡。
Wǒ	**měitiān**	**hē kāfēi.**

I drink coffee every day.

他	每天	跟他的女朋友吃晚饭。
他	每天	跟他的女朋友吃晚飯。
Tā	**měitiān**	**gēn tā de nǔ péngyou chī wǎnfàn.**

He eats dinner with his girlfriend every day.

If 'time when' is emphasized or contrasted with another time, it may occur before the subject:

昨天我不太舒服。今天已经没问题了。
昨天我不太舒服。今天已經沒問題了。
Zuótiān wǒ bù tài shūfu. Jīntiān yǐjing méi wèntí le.
Yesterday I was a bit uncomfortable. Today it is no longer a problem.

The position of duration phrases 4.9

Within the 'time when' phrase, the order of constituents is from the largest block of time to the smallest block of time:

一九九八年二月十五日
yī jiǔ jiǔ bā nián èryuè shíwǔ rì
1998 year February 15 → February 15, 1998

昨天晚上八点钟
昨天晚上八點鐘
zuótiān wǎnshang bā diǎn zhōng
yesterday evening 8 o'clock → 8 o'clock last night

4.6 The relative order of the 'time when' phrase and the location phrase

When a sentence includes both a 'time when' phrase and a location phrase, 'time when' generally occurs before location.

subject + time when + location + verb phrase

我每天在家吃饭。
我每天在家吃飯。
Wǒ měitiān zài jiā chī fàn.
I eat at home every day.

4.7 The position of adverbs

Adverbs occur at the beginning of the predicate, before the verb and any prepositional phrase. Adverbs usually occur after the 'time when' phrase.

我上个月只看了一个电影。
我上個月只看了一個電影。
Wǒ shàng gè yuè *zhǐ* kàn le yī gè diànyǐng.
Last month I *only* saw one movie.

▶ 15

4.8 The position of negation

Negation occurs before the verb and any prepositional phrase. It usually occurs after an adverb, though certain adverbs may either precede or follow negation.

▶ 15, 27.2

4.9 The position of duration phrases

Duration phrases are time phrases that indicate the length of time that an action occurs. Duration phrases directly follow the verb. Unlike English, there is no preposition associated with the expression of duration in Mandarin.

我在中国住了三年。
我在中國住了三年。
Wǒ zài Zhōngguó zhù le *sān nián*.
I in China lived *three years*. → I lived in China *for three years*.

19

我昨天晚上睡了八个钟头。
我昨天晚上睡了八個鐘頭。
Wǒ zuótiān wǎnshang shuì le *bā gè zhōngtóu*.
I yesterday evening slept *eight hours*. → I slept *for eight hours* yesterday.

▶ 39

4.10 Order within the noun phrase

The main noun in the noun phrase, the *head noun*, occurs as the last word in the phrase. All phrases that describe or *modify* the head noun occur before the head noun.

那本很有意思的书
那本很有意思的書
nà běn hěn yǒu yìsi de *shū*
that very interesting *book*

▶ 9

4.11 Phrase order in questions

In Mandarin, the order of phrases in questions is identical to the order of phrases in statements. Unlike English and many European languages, Mandarin questions are not characterized by a special question word order.

Statement

我喜欢他。
我喜歡他。
Wǒ xǐhuan *tā*.
I like *him*.

Content question

你喜欢谁?
你喜歡誰?
Nǐ xǐhuan *shéi*?
Who do you like?

Yes–no question

你喜欢他吗?
你喜歡他嗎?
Nǐ xǐhuan *tā* ma?
Do you like *him*?

▶ 28

4.12 The position of aspect particles

Mandarin indicates the *aspect* of an event; that is, the way that the event is viewed by the speaker, with three different aspect particles, 了 **le** *perfective*, 着/著 **zhe** *durative*, and 过 **guo** *experiential*. These aspect particles directly follow the verb (or, for the perfective particle 了 **le**, either the verb or verb + object phrase) and always occur in neutral tone. Sentences that include the durative aspect particle 着/著 **zhe** often also include the words 在 **zài** or 正在 **zhèng zài** at the beginning of the verb phrase.

我已经吃饭了。
我已經吃飯了。
Wǒ yǐjing chī fàn le.
I've already eaten.

他们吃着饭呢。
他們吃著飯呢。
Tāmen chīzhe fàn ne.
They are eating.

你吃过中国饭吗?
你吃過中國飯嗎?
Nǐ chīguo Zhōngguó fàn ma?
Have you eaten Chinese food before?

▶ 17

5
Nouns

In Mandarin, the same form of the noun is used in subject and object position.

Subject	Object
猫吃鱼。	我养猫。
貓吃魚。	我養貓。
Māo chī yú.	**Wǒ yǎng *māo*.**
Cats eat fish. (or) *The cat* eats fish.	I raise *a cat/cats*.
他学中文。	我喜欢他。
他學中文。	我喜歡他。
Tā xué Zhōngwén.	**Wǒ xǐhuan *tā*.**
He studies Chinese.	I like *him*.

With the exception of the written form of the third person pronoun, **tā** (see 5.2 below), Mandarin nouns are not marked for gender, and there is not the distinction between masculine, feminine, and neuter found in many European languages. The properties of Mandarin nouns are described here.

5.1 Common nouns

Most nouns are common nouns. Their referents may be concrete (纸/紙 **zhǐ** 'paper,' 桌子 **zhuōzi** 'table,' 水 **shuǐ** 'water') or abstract (思想 **sīxiǎng** 'thought,' 原则/原則 **yuánzé** 'principle,' 自由 **zìyóu** 'freedom'). Mandarin makes no grammatical distinction between 'mass' and 'count' nouns.

Mandarin common nouns have a single, invariant form. They do not reflect number, and the same form of the noun is used whether the noun is singular or plural. When no number is used with a noun, the noun is understood to be neither singular nor plural, but simply unspecified for number. In addition, nouns that occur without any modifiers or descriptions have a general rather than a specific reference. For example, 书/書 **shū** refers to 'book' in general and not to any specific book.

When it is necessary to indicate the number of a noun, the noun is modified by a *number + classifier* phrase. The classifier is <u>required</u> after the number. *Number + noun* without an intervening classifier is ungrammatical. Compare the following:

Say this	Not this
一本书/一本書	*一书/一書
yì běn shū	**yì shū**
one book	

Say this	Not this
三个人/三個人	*三人
sān gè rén	**sān rén**
three people	

▶ 6, 8

Pronouns

5.2

When a specifier 这/這 **zhè, zhèi** 'this/these,' 那 **nà, nèi** 'that/those,' or the question specifier 哪 **nǎ, něi** 'which' modifies the noun, it also must be followed by a classifier or number + classifier. If the number is 'one,' the number may be omitted.

这(一)本书	那两本书	哪三本书?
這(一)本書	那兩本書	哪三本書?
zhè (yì) běn shū	**nà liǎng běn shū**	**nǎ sān běn shū?**
this book	those two books	which three books?

▶ 7

A small number of common nouns referring to people can be suffixed with -们/們 **men**, the suffix that also marks the plural form of pronouns (see section 5.2 below).

同志们/同志們	**tóngzhìmen**	comrades
孩子们/孩子們	**háizimen**	children
学生们/學生們	**xuéshengmen**	students

This use of -们/們 **men** with common nouns is relatively rare. It conveys a sense of inclusion and is sometimes used when addressing an audience.

同学们，今天我们听马老师作的报告。
同學們，今天我們聽馬老師作的報告。
Tóngxuémen, jīntiān wǒmen tīng Mǎ lǎoshī zuò de bàogào.
Fellow students, today we are going to listen to a report by teacher Ma.

When a noun is suffixed with -们/們 **men** it cannot be further modified with any kind of modifying phrase, including a number + classifier phrase.

Say this	*Not this*
我们的同学	*我们的同学们
我們的同學	我們的同學們
wǒmen de tóngxué	**wǒmen de tóngxuémen**
our fellow students	
三个孩子	*三个孩子们
三個孩子	三個孩子們
sān gè háizi	**sān gè háizimen**
three children	

▶ 9

5.2 Pronouns

Mandarin has first, second, and third person pronouns and a reflexive pronoun.

Mandarin pronouns have the following properties:

- Pronouns are not distinguished in terms of grammatical role. The same pronouns are used for subject, object, possession, etc.
- Pronouns have singular and plural forms. The suffix -们/們 **men** is added to the singular form to make it the plural form.
- Gender is not reflected in the spoken language. The written language has distinctions for the second and third person pronouns, though only the third person gender distinction is commonly used.

NOUNS 5.2

	Singular	Plural
First person	我 wǒ I/me	我们/我們 wǒmen we/us (exclusive or neutral) 咱们/咱們 zánmen we (inclusive)
Second person	你 nǐ (masculine or neutral) 妳 nǐ (feminine) you	你們 nǐmen you
Third person	他 tā (masculine or neutral) 她 tā (feminine) 它/牠 tā (non-human or inanimate) he/she/it	他们/他們 tāmen (masculine or non-specific for gender) 她们/她們 tāmen (feminine) they/them
Reflexive	自己 zìjǐ self	

5.2.1 The reflexive pronoun 自己 zìjǐ 'self'

Mandarin has only one reflexive pronoun, and it is not marked for person or gender. To indicate person, the reflexive may optionally be preceded by the relevant personal pronoun.

我自己　　　　　我们自己/我們自己
wǒ zìjǐ　　　　　**wǒmen zìjǐ**
myself　　　　　ourselves

你自己　　　　　你们自己/你們自己
nǐ zìjǐ　　　　　**nǐmen zìjǐ**
yourself　　　　yourselves

他自己/她自己　　他们自己/他們自己
tā zìjǐ　　　　　**tāmen zìjǐ**
himself, herself　themselves

自己 zìjǐ 'self' is also used without a personal pronoun. When it occurs in object position, it is understood to refer to the subject:

你在中国一定得把自己照顾好。
你在中國一定得把自己照顧好。
Nǐ zài Zhōngguó yīdìng děi bǎ zìjǐ zhàogù hǎo.
When *you* are in China you certainly should take good care of *yourself*.

没有人不喜欢自己的。
沒有人不喜歡自己的。
Méi yǒu rén bù xǐhuan zìjǐ de.
No *one* doesn't like *him/herself*.

自己 zìjǐ 'self' may be used to indicate contrast with another noun phrase or pronoun:

我希望他们结婚，可是我自己不想结婚。
我希望他們結婚，可是我自己不想結婚。
Wǒ xīwàng tāmen jiéhūn, kěshì wǒ zìjǐ bù xiǎng jiéhūn.
I hope they will get married, but I *myself* don't plan to get married.

这是我自己的事。你不用管。
這是我自己的事。你不用管。
Zhè shì wǒ zìjǐ de shì. Nǐ bù yòng guǎn.
This is my affair. You need not be concerned with it.

Pronouns

5.2.2 The inclusive pronoun 咱们/咱們 *zánmen* 'we'

The inclusive pronoun 咱们/咱們 **zánmen** 'we' is used in northern dialects of Mandarin. 咱们/咱們 **zánmen** 'we' refers to the speaker, other people associated with the speaker, and to the addressee. When a speaker uses 咱们/咱們 **zánmen** 'we' as the subject, he or she includes <u>you</u> in the remarks.

咱们都是自己人。
咱們都是自己人。
Zánmen dōu shì zìjǐ rén.
We are all family. (We, including you, are all one family.)

'Inclusive' 咱们/咱們 **zánmen** contrasts with an 'exclusive' use of 'we' that is associated with 我们/我們 **wǒmen**. In the exclusive sense, 我们/我們 **wǒmen** refers to the speaker and others associated with the speaker but not to the addressee.

我们欢迎你。
我們歡迎你。
Wǒmen huānyíng nǐ.
We welcome you.

咱们/咱們 **zánmen** only has the inclusive meaning. In addition, 咱们/咱們 **zánmen** is only used as subject, and never as object.

我们/我們 **wǒmen** can have either inclusive or exclusive meaning and it occurs as subject and object. It is much more commonly used than 咱们/咱們 **zánmen**.

5.2.3 Modification of pronouns

Pronouns represent an entire noun phrase. Therefore, in general, they are not further modified. However, Mandarin has a small number of literary expressions in which the pronoun is modified:

可怜的我
可憐的我
kělián de wǒ
poor me

美丽的她
美麗的她
měilì de tā
pretty her

善良的高老师
善良的高老師
shànliáng de Gāo lǎoshī
good-hearted professor Gao

5.2.4 Possession involving pronouns

Mandarin does not have possessive pronouns. The meaning of possessive pronouns is conveyed by *pronoun* + 的 *de*.

我的朋友
wǒ de péngyou
my friend

他的小狗
tā de xiǎogǒu
his puppy

NOUNS

5.3

Here is a table showing the Mandarin equivalent of English possessive pronouns. When *pronoun* + 的 *de* is followed by a noun, the English equivalent is *my*, *your*, *his/her*, *our*, and *their*. When *pronoun* + 的 *de* is <u>not</u> followed by a noun, the English equivalent is *mine*, *yours*, *his/hers*, *ours*, and *theirs*.

Singular		*Plural*	
my/mine	我的 **wǒ de**	our/ours	我们的/我們的 **wǒmen de**
			咱们的/咱們的 **zánmen de**
your/yours	你的 **nǐ de**	your/yours	你们的/你們的 **nǐmen de**
his (her)/his (hers)	他的 (她的) **tā de**	their/theirs	他们的/他們的 **tāmen de**
Reflexive one's	自己的 **zìjǐ de**		
Interrogative whose?	谁的？/誰的？ **shéi de?**		

这是我的书。
這是我的書。
Zhè shì wǒ de shū.
This is my book.

这是我的，那是你的。
這是我的，那是你的。
Zhè shì wǒ de, nà shì nǐ de.
This is *mine*, that is *yours*.

▶ 9.2.1.2, 29.2.2

5.3 Proper nouns

Proper nouns include personal names, place names, names of companies, names of schools, etc.

牛津大学
牛津大學
Niújīn Dàxué
Oxford University

伦敦/倫敦
Lúndūn
London

万里长城/萬里長城
Wànlǐ Chángchéng
The Great Wall

喜玛拉雅山脉/喜瑪拉雅山脈
Xǐmǎlāyǎ shān mài
Himalayan Mountains

Proper nouns 5.3

Proper nouns, like pronouns, typically occur without additional modification. As is the case with pronouns, Mandarin has a small number of literary expressions in which the proper noun may be modified. Here are some examples.

可爱的王美玲
可愛的王美玲
kě'ài de Wáng Měilíng
charming Wang Meiling

山清水秀的台湾
山清水秀的臺灣
shānqīng shuǐxiù de Táiwān
Taiwan of green hills and clear streams → beautiful Taiwan

地大物博的美国
地大物博的美國
dìdà wùbó de Měiguó
America vast in territory and rich in resources

▶ 5.2.3

6

Numbers

6.1 Mandarin numbers 0–99

6.1.1 Numbers 0–10

0	〇 or 零 **líng**			
1	一 **yī**	6	六 **liù**
2	二 **èr**, 两/兩 **liǎng**	7	七 **qī**
3	三 **sān**	8	八 **bā**
4	四 **sì**	9	九 **jiǔ**
5	五 **wǔ**	10	十 **shí**

The number 2 occurs in two forms.

- When counting without a classifier, the number 2 is always 二 **èr**.

   一　二　三　四　五
   yī – èr – sān – sì – wǔ
   　1　 2　 3　 4　 5

- When it occurs in a phrase with a classifier, the number 2 is 两/兩 **liǎng**.

   两本书
   兩本書
   liǎng běn shū
   two books

   两个人
   兩個人
   liǎng gè rén
   two people

▶ 9.1

Telephone numbers are recited as a series of single digits from 0 to 9. When reciting a telephone number, the number 2 is always 二 **èr**.

   我的电话号码是八六二二五六〇二。
   我的電話號碼是八六二二五六〇二。
   Wǒ de diànhuà hàomǎ shì bā liù èr èr wǔ liù líng èr.
   My phone number is 8 6 2 2 5 6 0 2.

▶ 26.5

6.1.2 Numbers 11–19

The numbers 11–19 consist of the number 10 [十 **shí**] followed by the numbers 1 [一 **yī**] through 9 [九 **jiǔ**] as follows. Note that the number 12 is 十二 **shí'èr** and not *十两/十兩 **shí liǎng**.

11	十一	**shíyī**	16	十六	**shíliù**
12	十二	**shí'èr**	17	十七	**shíqī**
13	十三	**shísān**	18	十八	**shíbā**
14	十四	**shísì**	19	十九	**shíjiǔ**
15	十五	**shíwǔ**			

6.1.3 Numbers 20–90

The numbers 20, 30, 40, etc. consist of the numbers 2 [二 **èr**] through 9 [九 **jiǔ**] followed by the number 10 [十 **shí**] as follows:

20	二十	**èrshí**	60	六十	**liùshí**
30	三十	**sānshí**	70	七十	**qīshí**
40	四十	**sìshí**	80	八十	**bāshí**
50	五十	**wǔshí**	90	九十	**jiǔshí**

The numbers 21, 22, etc. are formed as follows:

21	二十一	**èrshíyī**	57	五十七	**wǔshíqī**
22	二十二	**èrshí'èr**	68	六十八	**liùshíbā**
35	三十五	**sānshíwǔ**	74	七十四	**qīshísì**
46	四十六	**sìshíliù**	99	九十九	**jiǔshíjiǔ**

6.2 Number 100 and higher

6.2.1 100, 1,000, 10,000, and 100,000,000

Chinese has distinct words for multiples of 100, 1,000, 10,000, and 100,000,000 as follows:

Hundreds	百 **bǎi**	100	一百 **yī bǎi**
Thousands	千 **qiān**	1,000	一千 **yī qiān**
Ten thousands	万/萬 **wàn**	10,000	一万/一萬 **yī wàn**
Hundred millions	亿/億 **yì**	100,000,000	一亿/一億 **yī yì**

These number words function as classifiers. Therefore, the number 2 is usually 两/兩 **liǎng** when it occurs immediately before the word for 'hundred,' 'thousand,' or 'ten-thousand': 两百/兩百 **liǎng bǎi**, 两千/兩千 **liǎng qiān**, 两万/兩萬 **liǎng wàn**, etc. In many regional dialects of Mandarin, 二百 **èr bǎi**, 二千 **èr qiān**, 二万/二萬 **èr wàn**, etc. is also acceptable.

6.2.2 Forming numbers through 9,999

Numbers up to 9,999 follow the same pattern as in English:

352		三百 **sān bǎi**	五十 **wǔshí**	二 **èr**
1,670	一千 **yī qiān**	六百 **liù bǎi**	七十 **qīshí**	
3,482	三千 **sān qiān**	四百 **sì bǎi**	八十 **bāshí**	二 **èr**
9,222	九千 **jiǔ qiān**	二百 or 两百/兩百 **èr bǎi** or **liǎng bǎi**	二十 **èrshí**	二 **èr**

NUMBERS

6.2

6.2.3 'Zero' as a placeholder

The word 〇/零 **líng** may be used when the 'hundreds' place or the 'tens' place is empty, provided there is a number before and after 〇/零 **líng**. For example, it can be used to mark the 'hundreds' place when the thousands and tens are filled, as in the following number.

7,066	七千	零	六十	六
	qī qiān	**líng**	**liù shí**	**liù**

It can be used to mark the 'tens' place when the hundreds and single numbers are filled, as in the following number.

9,102	九千	一百	〇	二
	jiǔ qiān	**yī bǎi**	**líng**	**èr**

When two consecutive places are empty, 〇/零 **líng** occurs only once.

6,006	六千	零	六
	liù qiān	**líng**	**liù**

6.2.4 Forming numbers 10,000 to 100,000,000

Languages read numbers in terms of the categories that they distinguish. English distinguishes tens, hundreds, thousands, millions, and up. Numbers between one thousand and one million are read in terms of the numbers of thousands that they contain.

Chinese distinguishes the categories of tens, hundreds, thousands, ten-thousands, and hundred millions. Numbers between ten thousand and one-hundred million are read in terms of the number of *ten-thousands* that they contain. Compare the way that English and Chinese read the following numbers.

	English	*Chinese*
1,000	one thousand	一千 **yī qiān** one thousand
10,000	ten thousand	一万/一萬 **yī wàn** one ten-thousand
100,000	one hundred thousand	十万/十萬 **shí wàn** ten ten-thousands
1,000,000	one million	百万/百萬 **bǎi wàn** one hundred ten-thousands
10,000,000	ten million	千万/千萬 **qiān wàn** one thousand ten-thousands
100,000,000	one hundred million	亿/億 **yì**
1,000,000,000	one billion	十亿/十億 **shí yì** ten one hundred-millions

Observe how these numbers are read in Chinese.

	亿/億 *yì*	万/萬 *wàn*	千 *qiān*	百 *bǎi*	十 *shí*
25,250		两万 兩萬 **liǎng wàn**	五千 **wǔqiān**	二百 **èrbǎi**	五十 **wǔshí**
225,250		二十二万 二十二萬 **èrshí'èr wàn**	五千 **wǔqiān**	二百 **èrbǎi**	五十 **wǔshí**

Ordinal numbers | **6.4**

	亿/億 *yì*	万/萬 *wàn*	千 *qiān*	百 *bǎi*	十 *shí*
2,225,250		两百二十二万 兩百二十二萬 liǎngbǎi èrshí'èr wàn	五千 wǔqiān	二百 èrbǎi	五十 wǔshí
22,225,250		两千二百二十二万 兩千二百二十二萬 liǎngqiān èrbǎi èrshí'èr wàn	五千 wǔqiān	二百 èrbǎi	五十 wǔshí
522,225,250	五亿 五億 wǔ yì	两千二百二十二万 兩千二百二十二萬 liǎngqiān èrbǎi èrshí'èr wàn	五千 wǔqiān	二百 èrbǎi	五十 wǔshí

6.3 Formal characters for numbers

To discourage forgery, Chinese numbers are sometimes written using the following special set of characters. The numerals on Chinese currency are written with these special characters.

	Ordinary form	Special form	
1	一	壹	yī
2	二	贰	èr
3	三	叁	sān
4	四	肆	sì
5	五	伍	wǔ
6	六	陆	liù
7	七	柒	qī
8	八	捌	bā
9	九	玖	jiǔ
10	十	拾	shí
100	百	佰	bǎi
1000	千	仟	qiān

Chapter 8 presents the words and phrases associated with money.

▶ 8.5

6.4 Ordinal numbers

To make a number ordinal, add the prefix 第 **dì** before the number:

1st	第一	**dì yī**	20th	第二十	**dì èrshí**
2nd	第二	**dì èr**	50th	第五十	**dì wǔshí**
3rd	第三	**dì sān**	77th	第七十七	**dì qīshíqī**
4th	第四	**dì sì**	83rd	第八十三	**dì bāshí sān**
5th	第五	**dì wǔ**	95th	第九十五	**dì jiǔshíwǔ**
6th	第六	**dì liù**	100th	第一百	**dì yìbǎi**
10th	第十	**dì shí**	1,000th	第一千	**dì yìqiān**

NOTE In ordinal numbers, 'second' is always 第二 **dì èr** and never *第两/第兩 **dì liǎng**.

NUMBERS

6.5 Estimates and approximations

To indicate that a quantity is 'more or less' the stated number, use the phrase 左右 **zuǒyòu** 'more or less,' as follows:

number + classifier (+ noun) + 左右 zuǒyòu

五十个(人)左右
五十個(人)左右
wǔshí gè (rén) zuǒyòu
about 50 (people) (50 people more or less)

一百块钱左右
一百塊錢左右
yībǎi kuài qián zuǒyòu
around $100 ($100 more or less)

To indicate that a quantity is almost but not quite the stated amount, use 差不多 **chàbuduō** + number 'almost number.'

差不多 chàbuduō + number + classifier (+ noun)

差不多五十个(人)
差不多五十個(人)
chàbuduō wǔshí gè (rén)
almost 50 people

差不多一百块(钱)
差不多一百塊(錢)
chàbuduō yībǎi kuài (qián)
almost $100

To indicate that a quantity is greater than or equal to the stated number, use 以上 **yǐshàng** 'or more.' For a more formal expression with the same meaning, use 之上 **zhī shàng**.

number (+ classifier + noun) + 以上 yǐshàng/之上 zhī shàng

五十(个人)以上	五十(个人)之上
五十(個人)以上	五十(個人)之上
wǔshí (gè rén) yǐshàng	**wǔshí (gè rén) zhī shàng**
50 (people) or more	50 (people) or more

To indicate that the actual number is less than or equal to the stated number, use 以下 **yǐxià** 'or fewer.' For a more formal expression with the same meaning, use 之下 **zhī xià**.

number (+ classifier + noun) + 以下 yǐxià/之下 zhī xià

五十(个人)以下	五十(个人)之下
五十(個人)以下	五十(個人)之下
wǔshí (gè rén) yǐxià	**wǔshí (gè rén) zhī xià**
50 (people) or less	50 (people) or less
50 or fewer (people)	50 or fewer (people)

To indicate that the actual time lies within a specified period of time, use 以內 **yǐnèi**. For a more formal expression with the same meaning, use 之內 **zhī nèi**.

一年以内	一年之內
yì nián yǐnèi	**yì nián zhī nèi**
within one year	within one year

Fractions, percentages, decimals, half, and multiples

To indicate the actual number is more than the stated number, use 多 **duō** 'more than.'

> *number* + 多 **duō** + *classifier* (+ *noun*)

> 五十多个人
> 五十多個人
> **wǔshí duō gè rén**
> more than 50 people

To indicate an approximation within a small range, use two numbers in a sequence as follows:

> 我一两天就回来。
> 我一兩天就回來。
> **Wǒ yì liǎng tiān jiù huí lai.**
> I'll come back in a day or two.

> 这个东西卖三四块钱。
> 這個東西賣三四塊錢。
> **Zhège dōngxi mài sān sì kuài qián.**
> This thing sells for three or four dollars.

This expression can be used together with 左右 **zuǒyòu**:

> 这个东西卖三四块钱左右。
> 這個東西賣三四塊錢左右。
> **Zhège dōngxi mài sān sì kuài qián zuǒyòu.**
> This thing sells for around three or four dollars.

6.6 Fractions, percentages, decimals, half, and multiples

6.6.1 Fractions

To indicate fractions, use the pattern:

> X 分 之 Y
>   **fēn zhī**

> 三分之一
> **sān fēn zhī yī**
> one-third $\frac{1}{3}$

Note that the 'whole' is expressed first and the 'part of the whole' is expressed second.

$\frac{1}{4}$	四分之一	**sì fēn zhī yī**
$\frac{2}{5}$	五分之二	**wǔ fēn zhī èr**
$\frac{9}{10}$	十分之九	**shí fēn zhī jiǔ**
$\frac{7}{9}$	九分之七	**jiǔ fēn zhī qī**
$\frac{1}{15}$	十五分之一	**shíwǔ fēn zhī yī**

6.6.2 Percentages

Percentages are expressed as *parts of 100*. The expression used for percentages is the same as for fractions, but the 'whole' is always 百 **bǎi** '100':

> 百 分 之 + number
> **bǎi fēn zhī**   number

10%	百分之十	**bǎi fēn zhī shí**
25%	百分之二十五	**bǎi fēn zhī èrshíwǔ**
37%	百分之三十七	**bǎi fēn zhī sānshíqī**
66%	百分之六十六	**bǎi fēn zhī liùshíliù**
99%	百分之九十九	**bǎi fēn zhī jiǔshíjiǔ**

NUMBERS

6.6.3 Decimals

Decimals are recited as a series of single digits and zeros after a decimal point. The decimal point is read as 点/點 **diǎn**:

1.1	一点一/一點一	yī diǎn yī
2.5	(二 or) 两点五/(二 or) 兩點五	(èr or) liǎng diǎn wǔ
14.56	十四点五六/十四點五六	shísì diǎn wǔ liù
30.808	三十点八零八/三十點八零八	sānshí diǎn bā líng bā
8.06	八点〇六/八點〇六	bā diǎn líng liù

If there is no number before the decimal point, the fraction may optionally be recited as 〇点/點 (XXX) **líng diǎn** (XXX):

| .35 | 〇点三五/〇點三五 | líng diǎn sān wǔ |
| .27 | 〇点二七/〇點二七 | líng diǎn èr qī |

NOTE Chinese often omits the final zero after a decimal point. For example, $8.60 may also be written as $8.6.

6.6.4 Indicating 'half'

The word 半 **bàn** means 'half.'

To indicate *half of something*, place 半 **bàn** before the classifier associated with the thing.

半碗饭/半碗飯
bàn wǎn fàn
half a bowl of rice

半本书/半本書
bàn běn shū
half a book

半杯水
bàn bēi shuǐ
half a glass of water

▶ 8

To indicate *one or more things and a half*, place 半 **bàn** immediately after the classifier associated with the thing:

number + classifier + 半 ***bàn***

三碗半(饭)/三碗半(飯)
sān wǎn bàn (fàn)
three and a half bowls (of rice)

三本半(书)/三本半(書)
sān běn bàn (shū)
three and a half volumes (of books)

三杯半(水)
sān bēi bàn (shuǐ)
three and a half cups (of water)

To indicate 'half' in time expressions, see Chapter 49.

▶ 49.1.1, 49.1.3.2, 49.1.4

Fractions, percentages, decimals, half, and multiples   **6.6**

6.6.5 Indicating multiples of a quantity with 倍 *bèi*

倍 **bèi** is a classifier and is always preceded by a number: 一倍 **yī bèi**, 两倍/兩倍 **liǎng bèi**, 三倍 **sān bèi**, etc.

一倍 **yī bèi** means 'one fold,' or 'one time more than a given quantity.' 两倍/兩倍 **liǎng bèi** means 'twofold,' 三倍 **sān bèi** means 'threefold,' etc.

倍 **bèi** often occurs with expressions that imply an increase:

> 价格都增加了一倍了。
> 價格都增加了一倍了。
> **Jiàgé dōu zēngjiā le yī bèi le.**
> Prices have all doubled (increased by one-fold).

> 今年这本书比去年贵了一倍。
> 今年這本書比去年貴了一倍。
> **Jīnnián zhè běn shū bǐ qùnián guì le yī bèi.**
> This year this book is twice as expensive as it was last year.

倍 **bèi** also occurs in equational sentences such as the following:

> 我的书是你的书的两倍。
> 我的書是你的書的兩倍。
> **Wǒ de shū shì nǐ de shū de liǎng bèi.**
> I have twice as many books as you.
> (lit. 'My books are the equivalent of two times your books.')

If 半 **bàn** 'half' occurs, it follows 倍 **bèi**:

> 今年学中文的学生是去年的一倍半。
> 今年學中文的學生是去年的一倍半。
> **Jīnnián xué Zhōngwén de xuésheng shì qùnián de yī bèi bàn.**
> The number of students studying Chinese this year is $1\frac{1}{2}$ times greater than last year.

▶ 6.6.4

6.6.6 Discounts, sales, and percentage off the price

The expression for a discount or sale is the verb phrase 打折 **dǎ zhé**.

Discounts are expressed as a percentage of the original or full price.

九折 **jiǔ zhé** is 90% of the original price, or 10% off. 七点五折/七點五折 **qīdiǎn wǔ zhé** is 75% of the original price, or 25% off. Here are additional examples of discounts. Discounts are written with either Chinese or Arabic numerals.

8 折 **bā zhé**	80% of original price	20% off
5 折 **wǔ zhé**	50% of original price	50% off

or

or

半折 **bàn zhé**	half of original price	
二折 **èr zhé**	20% of original price	80% off
一折 **yī zhé**	10% of original price	90% off

To find out if an item is discounted or on sale, you can ask:

打折吗?	or	打不打折?	or	有折吗?
打折嗎?				有折嗎?
Dǎ zhé ma?		**Dǎ bù dǎ zhé?**		**Yǒu zhé ma?**
Do you discount?		Do you discount?		Is there a discount?

NUMBERS | **6.8**

To find out how much of a discount there is, you can ask:

打几折？/打幾折？
Dǎ jǐ zhé?
How much discount is there?

▶ 28

6.7 Lucky and unlucky numbers

Some numbers have special significance in Chinese based on their value in traditional Chinese numerology or because they are near-homophones with a word with positive or negative connotations. Here are some numbers with special significance.

Numbers with negative connotations – unlucky numbers

四 **sì** (near homophone with 死 **sǐ** 'to die')
五 **wǔ** (near homophone with 无/無 **wú** 'nothing')

Numbers with positive connotations – lucky numbers

六 **liù** (near homophone with 留 **liú** 'remain, leftover/excess')
八 **bā** (near homophone with 发/發 **fā** 'prosperity')

The special significance of odd and even numbers

- 单号/單號 **dānhào** 'odd numbers.' Odd-numbered items are appropriate for funerals and other sad occasions.
- 双号/雙號 **shuānghào** 'even numbers.' Even-numbered items (except for the number 4) are appropriate for weddings and other happy occasions.

6.8 Numbers used in phrases and expressions

Numbers, especially sequential numbers, are often used in Chinese phrases.

1's and 2's

一清二楚
yī qīng èr chǔ
perfectly clearly

他说得一清二楚。
他說得一清二楚。
Tā shuō de yī qīng èr chǔ.
He said it perfectly clearly.

3's and 4's

张三李四
張三李四
Zhāng Sān Lǐ Sì
John Doe and Mary Smith (ordinary people)

不三不四
bù sān bù sì
neither here nor there, questionable, no good

Numbers that are used as words

7's and 8's

乱七八糟
亂七八糟
luàn qī bā zāo
a mess/disorganized

七上八下
qī shàng bā xià
be in an unsettled state of mind

6.9 一 yī as a marker of sequence

In addition to functioning as a number, the word 一 yī is also used to indicate sequence in the following structure:

一 *yī* + *verb*
as soon as verb occurs . . .

他一看见他孩子就很高兴。
他一看見他孩子就很高興。
Tā yī kànjian tā háizi jiù hěn gāoxìng.
As soon as he sees (his) children he is happy.

▶ 42.3.3

6.10 Numbers that are used as words

Numbers that are homophonous or near homophones with words may be used as abbreviations for words. This kind of substitution is particularly common on the internet and in written advertisements and signs. Examples include:

    5 3 0   五三零
               wǔ sān líng
               （我想你）
               (wǒ xiǎng nǐ)
               I'm thinking of you – I miss you.

    5 2 0   五二〇
               wǔ èr líng
               （我爱你）
               (wǒ ài nǐ)
               I love you

    8 8   八八
               bā bā
               （拜拜）
               (bàibài)
               bye bye

7

Specifiers and demonstratives

这/這 **zhè** and 那 **nà** have two functions.

They can be used as *demonstratives*, or words that are used to point out an item:

> 那是我的手机。
> 那是我的手機。
> *Nà* **shì wǒ de shǒujī.**
> *That* is my cellphone.

They can be used as *specifiers*, or words that occur as part of a noun phrase and that identify specific items:

> 这三本书
> 這三本書
> *zhè* **sān běn shū**
> *these* three books

When used as specifiers, these words each have an alternative pronunciation. 这/這 may be pronounced **zhè** or **zhèi**. 那 may be pronounced **nà** or **nèi**. The choice of pronunciation varies by speaker and region of China.

7.1 这/這 *zhè* 'this' and 那 *nà* 'that' as demonstratives

As demonstratives, 这/這 **zhè** 'this' and 那 **nà** 'that' refer to an entire noun phrase, either a concrete object or an abstract concept. They always occur at the beginning of the sentence, and they serve as the subject of the sentence. They can occur in statements or in questions.

> 那是中文字典。
> **Nà shì Zhōngwén zìdiǎn.**
> That is a Chinese dictionary.

> 这是我的书。
> 這是我的書。
> **Zhè shì wǒ de shū.**
> This is my book.

> 那是什么?
> 那是甚麼?
> **Nà shì shénme?**
> What is that?
> (lit. 'That is what?')

> 这是什么意思?
> 這是甚麼意思?
> **Zhè shì shénme yìsi?**
> What is the meaning of this?
> (lit. 'This is what meaning?')

38

7.2 这/這 zhè, zhèi 'this/these' and 那 nà, nèi 'that/those' as specifiers

When they are used as specifiers, 这/這 **zhè**, **zhèi** 'this/these' and 那 **nà**, **nèi** 'that/those' are part of a noun phrase. They occur before the number if there is one, and before the classifier and the noun in this order:

specifier + (number) + classifier + noun

▶ 6, 8, 9

Here are examples of noun phrases that begin with specifiers. Following each noun phrase there is an example showing how the noun phrase is used in a sentence.

Noun phrase that begins with a specifier	*Sample sentence with the noun phrase*
这三本书 這三本書 **zhè sān běn shū** these three books	这三本书都很贵。 這三本書都很貴。 *Zhè sān běn shū* dōu hěn guì. *These three books* are all expensive.
这种音乐 這種音樂 **zhè zhǒng yīnyuè** this kind of music	我很喜欢这种音乐。 我很喜歡這種音樂。 Wǒ hěn xǐhuan *zhè zhǒng yīnyuè.* I like *this kind of music* very much.
那个人 那個人 **nàge rén** that person	那个人很聪明。 那個人很聰明。 *Nàge rén* hěn cōngming. *That person* is very intelligent.
那个电影 那個電影 **nàge diànyǐng** that movie	我要看那个电影。 我要看那個電影。 Wǒ yào kàn *nàge diànyǐng.* I want to see *that movie.*

Notice that 这/這 **zhè**, **zhèi** and 那 **nà**, **nèi** do not have separate singular and plural forms.

7.3 这儿/這兒 zhèr and 这里/這裏 zhèlǐ 'here,' 那儿/那兒 nàr and 那里/那裏 nàlǐ 'there'

这儿/這兒 **zhèr** (这里/這裏 **zhèlǐ**) 'here' and 那儿/那兒 **nàr** (那里/那裏 **nàlǐ**) 'there' indicate location. 这儿/這兒 **zhèr** 'here' and 那儿/那兒 **nàr** 'there' are used in the north of China, including Beijing. 这里/這裏 **zhèlǐ** and 那里/那裏 **nàlǐ** are used in the south of China, including Taiwan. The meaning and use of 这儿/這兒 **zhèr** and 这里/這裏 **zhèlǐ** is the same, as is the meaning and use of 那儿/那兒 **nàr** and 那里/那裏 **nàlǐ**. Each member of the pair is interchangeable in our examples here and throughout this book.

这儿/這兒 **zhèr** 'here' and 那儿/那兒 **nàr** 'there' may occur at the beginning of the sentence as the subject. As subjects, they may optionally be preceded by the location preposition 在 **zài** 'at.'

(在)这儿有很多商店。
(在)這兒有很多商店。
(Zài) zhèr yǒu hěn duō shāngdiàn.
Here (in this location) are a lot of shops.

(在)那儿没有停车场。
(在)那兒沒有停車場。
(Zài) nàr méi yǒu tíngchē cháng.
There (in that location) there aren't any parking lots.

SPECIFIERS AND DEMONSTRATIVES

When they are not the subject, 这儿/這兒 **zhèr** 'here' and 那儿/那兒 **nàr** 'there' must be preceded by the location preposition 在 **zài** 'at.'

> 我在这儿工作。
> 我在這兒工作。
> **Wǒ zài zhèr gōngzuò.**
> I work here.

> 我在那儿买东西。
> 我在那兒買東西。
> **Wǒ zài nàr mǎi dōngxi.**
> I shop there.

▶ 14

People cannot serve as location nouns. To make a person into a location, follow it with a location specifier.

> 请到我这儿来。
> 請到我這兒來。
> **Qǐng dào wǒ zhèr lái.**
> Please come to me. [to my location]

> 我们今天晚上去小王那儿吃饭。
> 我們今天晚上去小王那兒吃飯。
> **Wǒmen jīntiān wǎnshang qù Xiǎo Wáng nàr chī fàn.**
> Tonight we'll go to Xiao Wang's to eat.

7.4 Question words that correspond to specifiers

- 哪 **nǎ/něi** 'which?' is the question word that corresponds to the specifier 那 **nà**.

Question	Answer
你要哪本书？	（我要）那本（书）。
你要哪本書？	（我要）那本（書）。
Nǐ yào nǎ běn shū?	**(Wǒ yào) nà běn (shū).**
Which book do you want?	(I want) that (book).
(lit. 'You want which book?')	

- 哪儿/哪兒 **nǎr** 'where?' is the question word that corresponds to the location words 这儿/這兒 **zhèr** 'here' and 那儿/那兒 **nàr** 'there.'

Question	Answer
哪儿有书店？	那儿有书店。
哪兒有書店？	那兒有書店。
Nǎr yǒu shūdiàn?	**Nàr yǒu shūdiàn.**
Where is there a bookstore?	There is a bookstore *there*.
你在哪里工作？	我在这里工作。
你在哪裏工作？	我在這裏工作。
Nǐ zài *nǎlǐ* gōngzuò?	**Wǒ zài *zhèlǐ* gōngzuò.**
Where do you work?	I work *here*.

▶ 28.6

8

Classifiers

8.1 The structure of phrases involving classifiers

A classifier is a word that occurs between the specifier and/or number and the noun. In Chinese, a classifier always occurs between a specifier or number and a noun in this order:

specifier + number + classifier + noun

Specifier and/or number + classifier + noun forms a *noun phrase*.

NOTES
1 Classifiers are sometimes referred to as 'measure words.'
2 In English, mass nouns such as 'coffee,' 'rice,' and 'sand' occur with classifiers. In Chinese, all nouns occur with classifiers when they are preceded by a specifier and/or number.

▶ 6, 7, 9

Here are examples of noun phrases with specifiers, numbers, classifiers, and nouns. The classifier is emphasized in each example. The classifier is often omitted when a Mandarin noun phrase is translated into English.

Specifier + classifier + noun	*Number + classifier + noun*	*Specifier + number + classifier + noun*
这个人	三本书	这两碗饭
這個人	三本書	這兩碗飯
zhège rén	sān **běn** shū	zhè liǎng **wǎn** fàn
this person	three books	these two *bowls* of rice
那个学校	三杯咖啡	那三本书
那個學校		那三本書
nàge xuéxiào	sān **bēi** kāfēi	nà sān **běn** shū
that school	three *cups* of coffee	those three books

8.2 Choosing the classifier

8.2.1 Nouns and associated classifiers

Most nouns are associated with a particular classifier. Classifiers are often not predictable from the noun so they must be memorized. Some dictionaries indicate the classifier associated with a noun.

41

CLASSIFIERS

Noun	Classifier	Noun phrase
书/書 **shū** book	本 **běn** volume	三本书/三本書 **sān běn shū** three books
纸/紙 **zhǐ** paper	张/張 **zhāng** sheet	一张纸/一張紙 **yī zhāng zhǐ** one piece of paper
钢笔/鋼筆 **gāngbǐ** pen	枝 **zhī** branch	这枝钢笔/這枝鋼筆 **zhè zhī gāngbǐ** this pen
房子 **fángzi** house	所 **suǒ** building	一所房子 **yī suǒ fángzi** one house
猫/貓 **māo** cat	只/隻 **zhī** classifier for animals	两只猫/兩隻貓 **liǎng zhī māo** two cats
车/車 **chē** car	辆/輛 **liàng** classifier for cars	三辆车/三輛車 **sān liàng chē** three cars
椅子 **yǐzi** chair	把 **bǎ** classifier for things with handles	一把椅子 **yī bǎ yǐzi** one chair
桌子 **zhuōzi** table	张/張 **zhāng** sheet	那张桌子/那張桌子 **nà zhāng zhuōzi** that table
照片 **zhàopiàn** photograph	张/張 **zhāng** sheet	这张照片/這張照片 **zhè zhāng zhàopiàn** this photograph
电影/電影 **diànyǐng** movie	部 **bù** classifier for film	一部电影/一部電影 **yī bù diànyǐng** one movie
衣服 **yīfu** clothing	件 **jiàn** classifier for items	这件衣服/這件衣服 **zhè jiàn yīfú** this article of clothing
树/樹 **shù** tree	棵 **kē** classifier for trees	一棵树/一棵樹 **yī kē shù** a tree
人 **rén** person	个/個 **gè** classifier for people and many other nouns	一个人/一個人 **yī gè rén** one person

NOTE: 位 **wèi** is a polite classifier for people. When it is used, the noun typically does not occur:

| 一位 | **yī wèi** | one person |
| 两位/兩位 | **liǎng wèi** | two people |

Choosing the classifier 8.2

8.2.2 Classifiers that indicate a property of the noun

Some classifiers indicate a property of the noun. These classifiers are often translated into English:

Shape of noun	张/張 **zhāng** a flat sheet	一张纸/一張紙 **yī zhāng zhǐ** a sheet of paper	
The shape of the container of the noun	杯 **bēi** cup	一杯茶 **yī bēi chá** a cup of tea	
The weight of the noun	斤 **jīn** 0.5 kilograms	一斤苹果 **yī jīn píngguǒ** 0.5 kilograms of apples	
The value of the noun	毛 **máo** dime	一毛钱/一毛錢 **yī máo qián** a dime's worth of money	

Different classifiers may be used to describe a noun in different ways.

Noun	*Classifier*	*Noun phrase*
饭/飯 **fàn** rice	碗 **wǎn** bowl	一碗饭/一碗飯 **yī wǎn fàn** one bowl of rice
饭/飯 **fàn** rice	斤 **jīn** 0.5 kilograms	两斤饭/兩斤飯 **liǎng jīn fàn** one kilogram of rice
面包/麵包 **miànbāo** bread	条/條 **tiáo** loaf	一条面包/一條麵包 **yī tiáo miànbāo** a loaf of bread
面包/麵包 **miànbāo** bread	块/塊 **kuài** slice/piece	一块面包/一塊麵包 **yī kuài miànbāo** a slice of bread
水 **shuǐ** water	瓶 **píng** bottle	一瓶水 **yī píng shuǐ** a bottle of water
水 **shuǐ** water	杯 **bēi** glass	一杯水 **yī bēi shuǐ** a glass of water
水 **shuǐ** water	壶/壺 **hú** pot/vase	一壶水/一壺水 **yī hú shuǐ** a pot/vase of water
花 **huā** flower	瓶 **píng** bottle	一瓶花 **yī píng huā** a vase of flowers
花 **huā** flower	束 **shù** bouquet	一束花 **yī shù huā** a bouquet of flowers

43

CLASSIFIERS

8.2.3 个/個 gè, the general classifier

The most commonly used classifier is 个/個 gè. It is used with many different nouns including people and things. It does not contribute any meaning to the noun phrase in which it occurs. It is generally pronounced with neutral tone.

一个人/一個人
yī gè rén
a person

一个问题/一個問題
yī gè wèntí
a problem/a question

一个东西/一個東西
yī gè dōngxi
a thing (a physical object)

In mainland China, in informal speech, 个/個 gè can be used as the classifier for almost any noun, even those with an established classifier. This phenomenon is sometimes referred to as 个化/個化 **gè huà** 'ge-ization.'

一个车/一個車
yī gè chē
(compare with 一辆车/一輛車 **yī liàng chē**) a car

一个房子/一個房子
yī gè fángzi
(compare with 一所房子 **yī suǒ fángzi**) a house

8.3 Omission of the head noun

In modern Mandarin, if a noun phrase includes a specifier and/or a number, the classifier may not be omitted. However, the head noun may be omitted from the noun phrase.

Say this	*Not this*
三本书 [or] 三本 三本書 **sān běn shū** [or] **sān běn** three books [or] three	*三书 三書 **sān shū**
那个学校 [or] 那个 那個學校 [or] 那個 **nàge xuéxiào** [or] **nàge** that school [or] that one	*那学校 那學校 **nà xuéxiào**

▶ 7, 9

8.4 Classifiers that occur without a noun

The words for 'day' and 'year' are classifiers. They may be preceded by a number, and they are never followed by a noun.

天 **tiān** day   一天 **yī tiān** one day   两天/兩天 **liǎng tiān** two days
年 **nián** year   一年 **yī nián** one year   两年/兩年 **liǎng nián** two years

▶ 34.1, 36.1, 37.8, 49.2

8.5 Money and prices

In Chinese, money and prices are expressed as noun phrases. The units of money, dollars, dimes, and cents are expressed by classifiers. The word for money, 钱/錢 **qián**, is a noun, and may occur at the end of the noun phrase.

In informal and spoken contexts, the classifiers for money are as follows:

块/塊	**kuài**	dollar
毛	**máo**	dime
分	**fēn**	cent

分 **fēn** represents 1 cent to 9 cents. Multiples of 10 cents are represented by 毛 **máo**.

五块/五塊	三毛	八分	钱/錢	= $5.38
wǔ kuài	**sān máo**	**bā fēn**	**qián**	
四十八块/塊	九毛	六分	钱/錢	= $48.96
sìshíbā kuài	**jiǔ máo**	**liù fēn**	**qián**	

The number 2 in the phrases '2 dollars,' '2 dimes' (20 cents), or '2 cents' may be either 二 **èr** or 两/兩 **liǎng**.

三块/三塊	四毛	二分	钱/錢	= $3.42
sān kuài	**sì máo**	**èr fēn**	**qián**	
		or		
		两分/兩分		
		liǎng fēn		

The noun 钱/錢 **qián** 'money' need not occur in a money phrase. If it is absent, the classifier that immediately precedes it may also be absent.

四十八块/塊	九毛	六	= $48.96
sìshíbā kuài	**jiǔ máo**	**liù**	

If the classifier is absent, the number 2 can only be represented as 二 **èr** and not as 两/兩 **liǎng**.

三块/三塊	四毛	二	= $3.42
sān kuài	**sì máo**	**èr**	

Chinese also has the following formal written classifiers for dollars and dimes.

元/圓	**yuán**	dollar
角	**jiǎo**	dime

These are the classifiers used on currency and in formal financial transactions.

For the formal characters for numbers, see

▶ 6.3

When 元/圓 **yuán** and 角 **jiǎo** are used, the noun 钱/錢 **qián** does not occur in the money phrase. 元/圓 **yuán** and 角 **jiǎo** are often not used together in the same price. 角 **jiǎo** tends to occur only when the denomination is smaller than one 元/圓 **yuán**.

Formal/written

$3.00	三元/圓	**sān yuán**
$0.60	六角	**liù jiǎo**

To ask 'how much money?' say 多少钱？/多少錢？ **duōshao qián?**

这两本书多少钱？
這兩本書多少錢？
Zhè liǎng běn shū duōshao qián?
How much (money) are these two books?

CLASSIFIERS 8.5

To ask how many dollars, dimes, or cents, say:

几块钱？/幾塊錢？　**jǐ kuài qián?** how many dollars?
几毛钱？/幾毛錢？　**jǐ máo qián?** how many dimes?
几分钱？/幾分錢？　**jǐ fēn qián?** how many cents?

这本书几块钱？
這本書幾塊錢？
Zhè běn shū jǐ kuài qián?
How many dollars does this book cost? (How much is this book?)

一瓶水几毛钱？
一瓶水幾毛錢？
Yī píng shuǐ jǐ máo qián?
How many dimes does a bottle of water cost? (How much is a bottle of water?)

一块糖几分钱？
一塊糖幾分錢？
Yī kuài táng jǐ fēn qián?
How many cents does a piece of candy cost? (How much is a piece of candy?)

46

9

Noun phrases

A noun phrase consists of a noun and any words that describe or 'modify' the noun. Here is an example of a noun phrase with the noun emphasized.

三个大老虎
三個大老虎
sān gè dà *láohǔ*
three big *tigers*

Additional examples of noun phrases are presented below.

In this chapter, we refer to the noun that is being described or modified as the *head noun* and to the words or phrases that describe or modify the head noun as the *modifier*.

In Mandarin Chinese, the relative position of modifier and noun is constant:

> In Chinese, all noun modifiers occur before the head noun.

9.1 Modifying a noun with a specifier and/or number

Nouns can be modified by

    a specifier ('this,' 'that,' 'which?')
    or a number ('four,' 'twenty'),
    or a specifier and number together ('these four,' 'those twenty,' 'which two?')

In Mandarin, the classifier associated with the noun being modified must be included in the modifying phrase. The entire phrase precedes the head noun as follows:

specifier + classifier + noun

那	本	书
那	本	書
nà	**běn**	**shū**
that		book

number + classifier + noun

两	本	书
兩	本	書
liǎng	**běn**	**shū**
two		books

NOUN PHRASES

9.2

specifier + number + classifier + noun

那	三	个	人
那	三	個	人
nà	**sān**	**gè**	**rén**
those	three		people

哪	三	个	人
哪	三	個	人
nǎ	**sān**	**gè**	**rén**
which	three		people?

▶ 6, 7, 8

9.2 Modifying a noun with all other modifiers: modification with 的 *de*

Noun modifiers may also be nouns, pronouns, verbs, or phrases that include a verb. These kinds of modifiers are typically followed by the particle 的 **de**, and the noun phrase has the following form:

*modifier + 的 **de** + head noun*

▶ 5

NOTE

In English, when a modifier includes a verb, the modifier occurs after the head noun as a relative clause introduced by a relative pronoun ('who,' 'whom,' 'which') or a complementizer ('that'). In these examples, the modifier of the noun is presented in square brackets.

the book [that I bought]
the people [who spoke to you]

In Mandarin, <u>all</u> modifiers precede the head noun. In addition, Mandarin has no words that correspond to relative pronouns or complementizers. Do not attempt to translate them into Chinese.

9.2.1 Examples of noun phrases with different types of modifiers

9.2.1.1 Modifiers that are nouns

Modifier	Head noun	Noun phrase
孩子	衣服	孩子的衣服
háizi	**yīfu**	**háizi de yīfu**
child	clothing	children's clothing
车/車	速度	车的速度 / 車的速度
chē	**sùdù**	**chē de sùdù**
car	speed	the speed of a/the car
马老师 / 馬老師	学生 / 學生	马老师的学生 / 馬老師的學生
Mǎ lǎoshī	**xuésheng**	**Mǎ lǎoshī de xuésheng**
Professor Ma	student(s)	Professor Ma's student(s)
美国 / 美國	城市	美国的城市 / 美國的城市
Měiguó	**chéngshì**	**Měiguó de chéngshì**
America	city	America's city (cities)/a city (cities) in America.

48

Modifying a noun with all other modifiers: modification with 的 *de*   **9.2**

9.2.1.2 Modifiers that are pronouns

Modifier	Head noun	Noun phrase
我 **wǒ** I (my)	车/車 **chē** car	我的车 我的車 **wǒ de chē** my car
他 **tā** he (his)	家 **jiā** home	他的家 **tā de jiā** his home
你们 你們 **nǐmen** you (your)	书 書 **shū** book(s)	你们的书 你們的書 **nǐmen de shū** your book(s)

Notice that *pronoun* + 的 *de* serves the same function as a possessive pronoun in English and other languages. There are no possessive pronouns in Mandarin.

See Chapter 5 for a table showing the Mandarin equivalent of English possessive pronouns.

▶ 5.2.4, 29.2.2

9.2.1.3 Modifiers that are adjectival verbs

Modifier	Head noun	Noun phrase
很贵 很貴 **hěn guì** very expensive	车/車 **chē** car	很贵的车 很貴的車 **hěn guì de chē** a very expensive car

▶ 10

9.2.1.4 Modifiers that are stative verbs

Modifier	Head noun	Noun phrase
喜欢 喜歡 **xǐhuan** like	车/車 **chē** car	我喜欢的车 我喜歡的車 **wǒ xǐhuan de chē** a car that I like

▶ 11

9.2.1.5 Modifiers that are action verbs

Modifier	Head noun	Noun phrase
写 寫 **xiě** write	字 **zì** character	写的字 寫的字 **xiě de zì** a character that is written
来 來 **lái** come	人 **rén** people/person	来的人 來的人 **lái de rén** the people who have come/the person who has come

▶ 13

49

NOUN PHRASES

9.2.1.6 Modifiers that are *verb* + *object*

Modifier	Head noun	Noun phrase
唱歌儿 唱歌兒 **chàng gēr** sing song	女孩子 **nǚ háizi** girl	唱歌儿的女孩子 唱歌兒的女孩子 **chàng gēr de nǚ háizi** the girl who is singing
卖书 賣書 **mài shū** sell book	人 **rén** person	卖书的人 賣書的人 **mài shū de rén** the person who sells books

9.2.1.7 Modifiers that are *prepositional phrase* + *verb*

Modifier	Head noun	Noun phrase
在公园里玩 在公園裏玩 **zài gōngyuán lǐ wán** play in the park	人 **rén** people/person	在公园里玩的人 在公園裏玩的人 **zài gōngyuán lǐ wán de rén** people who are playing in the park
从日本来 從日本來 **cóng Rìběn lái** come from Japan	学生 學生 **xuésheng** student	从日本来的学生 從日本來的學生 **cóng Rìběn lái de xuésheng** a student who has come from Japan

▶ 14

9.2.1.8 Modifiers that are *subject* + *verb* sequences

Modifier	Head noun	Noun phrase
他喜欢 他喜歡 **tā xǐhuan** he likes	东西 東西 **dōngxi** things	他喜欢的东西 他喜歡的東西 **tā xǐhuan de dōngxi** the things that he likes
我们看 我們看 **wǒmen kàn** we see/we saw	电影 電影 **diànyǐng** movie	我们看的电影 我們看的電影 **wǒmen kàn de diànyǐng** the movie that we saw

9.2.1.9 Modifiers that are question words

Modifier	Head noun	Noun phrase
谁 誰 **shéi** who	书 書 **shū** book	谁的书? 誰的書? **shéi de shū?** whose book?
哪儿 哪兒 **nǎr** where	饭馆 飯館 **fànguǎn** restaurant	哪儿的饭馆? 哪兒的飯館? **nǎr de fànguǎn?** a restaurant located where?

▶ 28.6, 30.4.2

9.3 Omission of the particle 的 *de*

The particle 的 **de** is sometimes omitted from the modifier.

的 **de** may be omitted:

- when the modifier is an unmodified one-syllable adjectival verb.

    贵的车/貴的車 **guì de chē** → 贵车/貴車 **guì chē** expensive car

    but not

    很贵的车/很貴的車 **hěn guì de chē** → *很贵车/很貴車 **hěn guì chē**

- when the modifier is closely associated with the noun, describing, for example, nationality:

    美国的人/美國的人 **Měiguó de rén** → 美国人/美國人 **Měiguó rén** American person

- or a close personal relationship in which the modifier is a pronoun:

    我的爸爸 **wǒ de bàba** → 我爸爸 **wǒ bàba** my father

9.4 Noun modifiers in a series

In Mandarin Chinese, a noun may be modified by any number of modifiers.

- The modifiers occur in a series before the head noun.
- A modifier that is a specifier and/or a number ends with a classifier. All other modifiers may end in the particle 的 **de**.
- The head noun occurs only once, at the end of the series of modifiers.

Here are examples of noun phrases in which the head noun is modified by a series of modifiers. Each modifying phrase is included in [square brackets].

我们[昨天看的][刚出来的][中国的]电影
我們[昨天看的][剛出來的][中國的]電影
wǒmen [zuótiān kàn de] [gāng chūlái de] [Zhōngguó de] diànyǐng
we [yesterday see] [just come out] [China] *movie*
the Chinese *movie* that just came out that we saw yesterday

[你给我介绍的][那两个][很聪明的]留学生
[你給我介紹的][那兩個][很聰明的]留學生
[nǐ gěi wǒ jièshào de] [nà liǎng gè] [hěn cōngming de] liúxuéshēng
[you introduced to me] [those two] [very smart] *exchange students*
those two very smart *exchange students* who you introduced me to

Modifiers may occur in any order. However, modifiers involving inherent personal characteristics often occur closer to the head noun.

[穿毛衣的][很可爱的]小孩子
[穿毛衣的][很可愛的]小孩子
[chuān máoyī de] [hěn kě'ài de] xiǎo háizi
[wearing a sweater] [very cute] *child*
the very cute *child* who is wearing a sweater

NOUN PHRASES

Noun modifiers involving specifiers and numbers often occur first in a sequence of modifiers, though they may also occur closer to the head noun for emphasis or contrast.

[那个][戴眼镜的][很高的]人
[那個][戴眼鏡的][很高的]人
[nàge] [dài yǎnjìng de] [hěn gāo de] rén
[that]   [wear glasses]   [very tall]   *person*
that very tall *person* who wears glasses

[很高的][戴眼镜的][那个]人
[很高的][戴眼鏡的][那個]人
[hěn gāo de] [dài yǎnjìng de] [nàge] rén
that very tall *person* who wears glasses

9.5 Omission of the head noun

When the head noun is predictable from the context, it may be omitted. The presence of 的 **de** or a classifier at the end of a phrase identifies the phrase as a noun phrase modifier. When the head noun is omitted, 的 **de** cannot be omitted.

这是谁做的菜?　　　　　　　　这是马老师做的(__)。
這是誰做的菜?　　　　　　　　這是馬老師做的(__)。
Zhè shì shéi zuò de cài?　　**Zhè shì Mǎ lǎoshī zuò de (__).**
This is food cooked by whom?　This is (food) cooked by Professor Ma.

你喜欢什么样的菜?　　　　　　我特别喜欢红烧的(__)。
你喜歡甚麼樣的菜?　　　　　　我特別喜歡紅燒的(__)。
Nǐ xǐhuan shénme yàng de cài?　**Wǒ tèbié xǐhuan hóngshāo de (__).**
What kind of dishes do you like?　I especially like red cooked (ones).

你要买哪本书?　　　　　　　　我要那本(书)。
你要買哪本書?　　　　　　　　我要那本(書)。
Nǐ yào mǎi nǎ běn shū?　　**Wǒ yào nà běn (shū).**
Which book do you want to buy?　I want that (one).

多少钱?　　　　　　　　　　　三块(钱)。
多少錢?　　　　　　　　　　　三塊(錢)。
Duōshǎo qián?　　　　　　**Sān kuài (qián).**
How much money?　　　　　　Three dollars.

9.6 Modification with 之 *zhī*

之 **zhī** is the marker of noun modification in literary Chinese, and it is used for this purpose in certain literary expressions in modern Chinese, including the following. These instances of 之 **zhī** are not interchangeable with 的 **de**.

Percentages and fractions

三分之一
sān fēn zhī yī
one-third $\frac{1}{3}$

百分之十
bǎi fēn zhī shí
10%

▶ 6.6.1, 6.6.2

Modification with 之 zhī   9.6

Time phrases and sequence

之后/之後 zhīhòu 'after' (以后/以後 yǐhòu)

> 三年之后
> 三年之後
> **sān nián zhīhòu**
> three years afterward/after three years

之前 zhīqián 'before, previous' (以前 yǐqián)

> 第二次世界战争之前
> 第二次世界戰爭之前
> **dì èrcì shìjiè zhànzhēng zhīqián**
> before the Second World War

▶ 42.1, 42.2

之内 zhīnèi 'within, including' (cf. 以内 yǐnèi)

> 我三天之内一定做得完。
> **Wǒ sāntiān zhīnèi yīdìng zuòdewán.**
> I will definitely be able to finish within three days.

▶ 6.5

53

10

Adjectival verbs

Adjectival verbs translate into adjectives in English. They include 高 **gāo** 'be tall,' 贵/貴 **guì** 'be expensive,' 小 **xiǎo** 'be small,' 大 **dà** 'be big,' 好 **hǎo** 'be good,' etc.

Mandarin adjectival verbs, unlike English adjectives, are *not* preceded by a linking verb such as the verb 是 **shì** 'be.'

Say this	*Not this*
他高。	*他是高。
Tā gāo.	**Tā shì gāo.**
He is tall.	
那本书贵。	*那本书是贵。
那本書貴。	那本書是貴。
Nà běn shū guì.	**Nà běn shū shì guì.**
That book is expensive.	
那个学校大。	*那个学校是大。
那個學校大。	那個學校是大。
Nàge xuéxiào dà.	**Nàge xuéxiào shì dà.**
That school is big.	

The properties of adjectival verbs are discussed below.

NOTE 是 **shì** may occur before adjectival verbs, but only for emphasis.

▶ 57.3

10.1 Negation of adjectival verbs

Adjectival verbs are negated by 不 **bù**. They are never negated by 没/沒 **méi**.

他不高。	*他没/沒高。
Tā bù gāo.	**Tā méi gāo.**
He is not tall.	
那本书不贵。	*那本书没贵。
那本書不貴。	那本書沒貴。
Nà běn shū bù guì.	**Nà běn shū méi guì.**
That book is not expensive.	
那个人不好。	*那个人没好。
那個人不好。	那個人沒好。
Nàge rén bù hǎo.	**Nàge rén méi hǎo.**
That person is not good.	

10.2 Yes–no questions with adjectival verbs

Adjectival verbs can occur in yes–no questions formed by 吗/嗎 **ma** or the *verb-not-verb* structure.

那个学校大吗?
那個學校大嗎?
Nàge xuéxiào dà ma?
Is that school big?

那个学校大不大?
那個學校大不大?
Nàge xuéxiào dà bù dà?
Is that school big?

▶ 28.1

10.3 Modification by intensifiers

Adjectival verbs can be modified by intensifiers. Most intensifiers precede the adjectival verb.

Intensifier		*Intensifier + adjectival verb*	
很 **hěn**	very	很好 **hěn hǎo**	be very good
真 **zhēn**	really	真好 **zhēn hǎo**	be really good
比较/比較 **bǐjiào**	rather	比较好/比較好 **bǐjiào hǎo**	be rather good
相当/相當 **xiāngdāng**	quite	相当好/相當好 **xiāngdāng hǎo**	be quite good
特别 **tèbié**	especially	特别好 **tèbié hǎo**	be especially good
非常 **fēicháng**	extremely	非常好 **fēicháng hǎo**	be extremely good
尤其 **yóuqí**	especially	尤其好 **yóuqí hǎo**	be especially good
极其/極其 **jíqí**	extremely	极其好/極其好 **jíqí hǎo**	be extremely good
太 **tài**	too	太好 **tài hǎo**	be too good
更 **gèng**	more	更好 **gèng hǎo**	be even better
最 **zuì**	most	最好 **zuì hǎo**	be best

55

ADJECTIVAL VERBS

The intensifier suffixes 得很 **de hěn** 'very,' 极了/極了 **jíle** 'extremely,' and 得不得了 **debù déliǎo** 'extremely' follow the adjectival verb. They are sometimes referred to as degree complements or complements of degree.

> 好得很
> **hǎo de hěn**
> be very good
>
> 好极了
> 好極了
> **hǎojíle**
> be terrific
>
> 好得不得了
> **hǎo de bùdéliǎo**
> be terrific

Stative verbs and the modal verbs 会/會 **huì** and 能 **néng** can also be modified by intensifiers, but they do not take intensifier suffixes.

▶ 11.2, 12.6.3

10.4 Two-syllable preference

Adjectival verbs generally occur in two-syllable phrases. In affirmative form, when no special emphasis is intended, one-syllable adjectival verbs are usually preceded by 很 **hěn**. When negated, 不 **bù** provides the additional syllable.

> 他很高。　　　　　　　他不高。
> **Tā hěn gāo.**　　　　　**Tā bù gāo.**
> He is tall.　　　　　　He is not tall.
>
> 那本书很贵。　　　　　那本书不贵。
> 那本書很貴。　　　　　那本書不貴。
> **Nà běn shū hěn guì.**　**Nà běn shū bù guì.**
> That book is expensive.　That book is not expensive.

10.5 Comparative meaning

Adjectival verbs do not have a distinct comparative form. However, in certain contexts they have comparative meaning.

They have comparative meaning when the context implies a comparison:

> Q: 谁高？/誰高？　　　A: 他高。
> **Shéi gāo?**　　　　　　**Tā gāo.**
> Who is tall?　　　　　　He is tall.
> or　　　　　　　　　　 or
> Who is taller?　　　　　He is taller.

They have comparative meaning when they occur in comparison structures:

> 他比你高。
> **Tā bǐ nǐ gāo.**
> He is taller than you.

▶ 30.6, 33

Linking adjectival verbs　　　　　　　　　　　　　　　　　　　　**10.8**

They have comparative meaning when followed by 一点/一點 **yīdiǎn** *a little more*.

> 可以<u>便宜一点</u>吗?
> 可以<u>便宜一點</u>嗎?
> **Kěyǐ *piányi yīdiǎn* ma?**
> *Can it be a little cheaper?*

They also have comparative meaning when they occur in structures that indicate change.

▶ 10.9

To explicitly express comparative meaning, precede the adjectival verb with the intensifier 更 **gèng** or the expression 还(要)/還(要) **hái (yào)**.

> 他更高。　　　　他还(要)高。
> 　　　　　　　　他還(要)高。
> **Tā gèng gāo.**　**Tā hái (yào) gāo.**
> He is (even) taller.　He is (even) taller.

▶ 33.5

10.6 Superlative meaning

Adjectival verbs do not have a distinct superlative form. To express the superlative meaning, precede the adjectival verb with the intensifier 最 **zuì** 'most.'

> 他最高。　　　　那本书最贵。
> 　　　　　　　　那本書最貴。
> **Tā zuì gāo.**　**Nà běn shū zuì guì.**
> He is the tallest.　That book is the most expensive.

▶ 33.6

10.7 Adjectival verbs and comparison structures

Adjectival verbs are used in comparison structures.

Comparison structures involving 比 **bǐ** 'more than' and 没有/沒有 **méi yǒu** 'less than' typically end with an adjectival verb or a modified adjectival verb.

> 我比你高。
> **Wǒ bǐ nǐ gāo.**
> I am taller than you.

> 我没有你高。
> 我沒有你高。
> **Wǒ méi yǒu nǐ gāo.**
> I am not as tall as you.

▶ 33

10.8 Linking adjectival verbs

The adverb 又 **yòu** can be used to link adjectival verbs as follows. The structure is used to convey the meaning 'both . . . and . . .'

> 那个男的<u>又高又大</u>。
> 那個男的<u>又高又大</u>。
> **Nàge nán de *yòu gāo yòu dà*.**
> That guy is *both big and tall*.

ADJECTIVAL VERBS

那双鞋子很好。又便宜又舒服。
那雙鞋子很好。又便宜又舒服。
Nà shuāng xiézi hěn hǎo. Yòu piányi yòu shūfu.
That pair of shoes is really good. They are *both cheap and comfortable*.

▶ 40.9

10.9 Adjectival verbs and expressions that indicate change over time

10.9.1 越来越 *yuè lái yuè* adjectival verb 'more and more' adjectival verb

东西越来越贵。
東西越來越貴。
Dōngxi yuè lái yuè guì.
Things are more and more expensive.

10.9.2 越 *yuè* action verb 越 *yuè* adjectival verb 'the more' (action), 'the more' (adjectival verb)

他越说越快。
他越說越快。
Tā yuè shuō yuè kuài.
The more he speaks, the faster he speaks.

▶ 38.3

10.10 Adjectival verbs and sentence final 了 *le*

Sentence final 了 **le** may occur at the end of a sentence with an adjectival verb to indicate change.

你高了。
Nǐ gāo le.
You have gotten taller.

When the intensifier 太 **tài** 'too' modifies an adjectival verb, the adjectival verb is typically followed by sentence final 了 **le**.

东西太贵了。
東西太貴了。
Dōngxi tài guì le.
Things are too expensive.

你太聪明了。
你太聰明了。
Nǐ tài cōngming le.
You're too smart.

▶ 38.1

11

Stative verbs

Stative verbs describe situations that do not involve action. Examples of stative verbs include 喜欢/喜歡 **xǐhuan** 'like,' 爱/愛 **ài** 'love,' 像 **xiàng** 'resemble,' 想 **xiǎng** 'want,' 要 **yào** 'want,' 需要 **xūyào** 'need,' 怕 **pà** 'fear,' 尊敬 **zūnjìng** 'respect,' 感谢/感謝 **gǎnxiè** 'appreciate,' 懂 **dǒng** 'understand,' 信 **xìn** 'believe,' and 想念 **xiǎngniàn** 'miss.' Certain stative verbs have special meanings and properties and will be discussed separately below. They include the equational verbs 是 **shì** 'be' and 姓 **xìng** 'be family named,' the verb 有 **yǒu** 'have,' 'exist,' and the location verb 在 **zài** 'be located at.'

Stative verbs are similar to adjectival verbs in their form of negation, their occurrence with intensifiers, and their use in comparison structures.

▶ 10.1, 10.3, 33

11.1 Negation of stative verbs

Most stative verbs may only be negated by 不 **bù**. The stative verb 有 **yǒu** 'have' may only be negated by 没/沒 **méi**.

不 *bù negates most stative verbs*	没/沒 *méi only negates* 有 *yǒu*
他不像他爸爸。 **Tā bù xiàng tā bàba.** He doesn't resemble his dad.	
他不怕狗。 **Tā bù pà gǒu.** He is not afraid of dogs.	
我不要钱。 我不要錢。 **Wǒ bù yào qián.** I don't want money.	
	他没有车。 他沒有車。 **Tā méi yǒu chē.** He doesn't have a car.

▶ 27

59

STATIVE VERBS

11.2 Modification by intensifiers

Stative verbs, like adjectival verbs, can be preceded and modified by intensifiers. The intensifiers are emphasized in each of the following sentences.

我们<u>很</u>尊敬他。
我們<u>很</u>尊敬他。
Wǒmen *hěn* zūnjìng tā.
We all respect him *a lot*.

我<u>很</u>想念你。
Wǒ *hěn* xiǎngniàn nǐ.
I miss you *a lot*.

我<u>真</u>怕这种人。
我<u>真</u>怕這種人。
Wǒ *zhēn* pà zhè zhǒng rén.
I'm *really* afraid of this kind of person.

他<u>特别</u>需要你的支持。
Tā *tèbié* xūyào nǐ de zhīchí.
He *especially* needs your support.

For a complete list of intensifiers, see section 10.3.

▶ 10.3, 12.6.3

11.3 Indicating completion, past time, and change of state

The verb suffixes 了 **le** and 过/過 **guo** cannot be used to indicate the *completion* or *past time* of a stative verb. To indicate that a state existed in the past, use a time expression or adverb that refers to the past.

我<u>小的时候</u>怕狗。
我<u>小的時候</u>怕狗。
Wǒ *xiǎo de shíhou* pà gǒu.
When I was small I was afraid of dogs.

我<u>以前</u>很喜欢吃口香糖。
我<u>以前</u>很喜歡吃口香糖。
Wǒ *yǐqián* hěn xǐhuan chī kǒuxiāngtáng.
I *used to* like to chew gum. (lit. '*Before*, I liked to chew gum.')

When a stative verb is followed by 了 **le**, it indicates *change of state*.

我懂了!
Wǒ dǒng le!
I understand (now)!

▶ 37.1, 38

The equational verb 是 *shì* 'be'   11.4

NOTE

Some verbs can function as a stative verb and as an action verb.

    有 *yǒu* as a stative verb   有 *yǒu* as an action verb

    她很有钱。   她有了一笔钱。
    她很有錢。   她有了一筆錢。
    Tā hěn yǒu qián.   **Tā yǒu le yī bǐ qián.**
    She has a lot of money.   She has acquired a sum of money.
    She is rich.

▶ Glossary of grammatical terms

11.4 The equational verb 是 *shì* 'be'

是 **shì** 'be' joins two noun phrases and indicates an equational relationship between them.

    她是大学生。
    她是大學生。
    Tā shì dàxuésheng.
    She is a college student.

    王老师是英国人。
    王老師是英國人。
    Wáng lǎoshī shì Yīngguó rén.
    Professor Wang is British.

The negation of 是 **shì** is 不是 **bù shì**.

    她不是大学生。
    她不是大學生。
    Tā bù shì dàxuésheng.
    She is not a college student.

    王老师不是英国人。
    王老師不是英國人。
    Wáng lǎoshī bù shì Yīngguó rén.
    Professor Wang is not British.

是 **shì** is used less often than the English verb 'be.' In particular, in Mandarin, 是 **shì** is ordinarily not used with adjectival verbs or stative verbs. In most circumstances,

    Say this   *Not this*

    我的弟弟很高。   *我的弟弟是很高。
    Wǒ de dìdi hěn gāo.   **Wǒ de dìdi shì hěn gāo.**
    My younger brother is very tall.

    他很聪明。   *他是很聪明。
    他很聰明。   他是很聰明。
    Tā hěn cōngming.   **Tā shì hěn cōngming.**
    He is very intelligent.

是 **shì** is only used with adjectival verbs or stative verbs for special emphasis, especially contrastive emphasis.

    你是很高！
    Nǐ *shì* hěn gāo!
    You really are tall!

61

STATIVE VERBS | 11.4

那本书是很贵。
那本書是很貴。
Nà běn shū *shì* hěn guì.
That book *is* expensive (despite what you claim).

他是很聪明。
他是很聰明。
Tā *shì* hěn cōngming.
He really is intelligent (despite what you may think).

是 **shì** can be used for contrastive emphasis with action verbs.

我是明天走，不是今天走。
Wǒ shì míngtiān zǒu, bù shi jīntiān zǒu.
I am leaving tomorrow. I am not leaving today.

▶ 37.9, 57.2.4, 57.3

是 **shì** is not used to indicate location or existence.

▶ 11.6.3, 11.7

When the object of 是 **shì** includes a number (for example, when it refers to money, age, time, etc.) 是 **shì** can be omitted in affirmative form.

那本书(是)五块钱。
那本書(是)五塊錢。
Nà běn shū (shì) wǔ kuài qián.
That book is $5.00.

我妹妹(是)十八岁。
我妹妹(是)十八歲。
Wǒ mèimei (shì) shíbā suì.
My younger sister is 18 years old.

现在(是)八点钟。
現在(是)八點鐘。
Xiànzài (shì) bādiǎn zhōng.
It is now 8 o'clock.

However, when the object is negated, 是 **shì** cannot be omitted.

Say this	*Not this*
那本书不是五块钱。 那本書不是五塊錢。 **Nà běn shū bù shì wǔ kuài qián.** That book is not $5.00.	*那本书不五块钱。 那本書不五塊錢。 **Nà běn shū bù wǔ kuài qián.**
我妹妹不是十八岁。 我妹妹不是十八歲。 **Wǒ mèimei bù shì shíbā suì.** My younger sister is not 18 years old.	*我妹妹不十八岁。 我妹妹不十八歲。 **Wǒ mèimei bù shíbā suì.**
现在不是八点钟。 現在不是八點鐘。 **Xiànzài bù shì bādiǎn zhōng.** It is not 8 o'clock now.	*现在不八点钟。 現在不八點鐘。 **Xiànzài bù bādiǎn zhōng.**

11.5 The equational verb 姓 *xìng* 'be family named'

是 **shì** is used to focus on some detail of a situation; for example, the time, place, or participants in a situation, or the material that something is made from.

> 他是昨天来的。
> 他是昨天來的。
> **Tā shì zuótiān lái de.**
> It was yesterday that he came. (He came *yesterday*.)

> 我是在大学学中文。
> 我是在大學學中文。
> **Wǒ shì zài dàxué xué Zhōngwén.**
> It is at the university where I study Chinese. (I study Chinese *at university*.)

> 我的耳环是(用)金子作的。
> 我的耳環是(用)金子作的。
> **Wǒ de ěrhuán shì (yòng) jīnzi zuò de.**
> My earrings are made of gold.

▶ 30.7.1, 37.9, 57.2.4

11.5 The equational verb 姓 *xìng* 'be family named'

To tell someone your family name or to indicate the family name of another person, use 姓 **xìng**.

> 我姓罗。
> 我姓羅。
> **Wǒ xìng Luó.**
> My family name is Luo.

> 她姓马。
> 她姓馬。
> **Tā xìng Mǎ.**
> Her family name is Ma.

The negation of 姓 **xìng** is 不姓 **bù xìng**.

> 我不姓李。我姓罗。
> 我不姓李。我姓羅。
> **Wǒ bù xìng Lǐ. Wǒ xìng Luó.**
> My family name isn't Li. My family name is Luo.

To ask someone's family name, say:

> 你姓什么?
> 你姓甚麼?
> **Nǐ xìng shénme?**
> What is your family name?

The very polite way to ask someone's family name is:

> 你贵姓?
> 你貴姓?
> **Nǐ guì xìng?**
> (What is) your honorable family name?

▶ 22

STATIVE VERBS

11.6 The verb of possession and existence: 有 *yǒu* 'have,' 'exist'

有 *yǒu* has two meanings: 'have' and 'exist.'

11.6.1 有 *yǒu* used to express possession

有 *yǒu* means 'have' when the subject is something that can have possessions. This includes people, animals, or any other noun that can be described as 'having' things:

我有一个弟弟。
我有一個弟弟。
Wǒ yǒu yī gè dìdi.
I have a younger brother.

那个书店有很多旧书。
那個書店有很多舊書。
Nàge shūdiàn yǒu hěn duō jiù shū.
That bookstore has many old books.

中国有很多名胜古迹。
中國有很多名勝古跡。
Zhōngguó yǒu hěn duō míng shèng gǔ jì.
China has many scenic spots and historical sites.

▶ 29.2.1

11.6.2 有 *yǒu* used to express existence

有 *yǒu* indicates existence when the subject is a location. The most common English translation of this meaning is 'there is' or 'there are.'

房子后头有一个小湖。
房子後頭有一個小湖。
Fángzi hòutou yǒu yī gè xiǎo hú.
Behind the house there is a small lake.

那儿有很多人排队。
那兒有很多人排隊。
Nàr yǒu hěn duō rén pái duì.
There are a lot of people there waiting in line.

▶ 47.1

11.6.3 Possession vs. existence

The meanings of possession and existence are closely related, and often a Chinese sentence with 有 *yǒu* can be interpreted as conveying either possession or existence. The difference in interpretation typically depends upon whether the subject is understood to be a possessor or a location.

美国大学有很多留学生。
美國大學有很多留學生。
Měiguó dàxué yǒu hěn duō liúxuéshēng.
American universities have many exchange students.
There are many exchange students in American universities.

这个图书馆有很多中文书。
這個圖書館有很多中文書。
Zhège túshūguǎn yǒu hěn duō Zhōngwén shū.
This library has a lot of Chinese books.
There are a lot of Chinese books in this library.

1.6.4 Negation of 有 *yǒu*

The negation of 有 **yǒu** is always 没有/沒有 **méi yǒu**.

> 我没有弟弟。
> 我沒有弟弟。
> **Wǒ méi yǒu dìdi.**
> I do not have a younger brother.

> 房子后头没有湖。
> 房子後頭沒有湖。
> **Fángzi hòutou méi yǒu hú.**
> There is no lake behind the house.

> 这个图书馆没有很多中文书。
> 這個圖書館沒有很多中文書。
> **Zhège túshūguǎn méi yǒu hěn duō Zhōngwén shū.**
> This library does not have a lot of Chinese books.
> There aren't a lot of Chinese books in this library.

▶ 27.1.2

11.7 The location verb 在 *zài* 'be located at'

To indicate location, use 在 **zài**.

> 他在家。
> **Tā zài jiā.**
> He is at home.

> 图书馆在公园的北边。
> 圖書館在公園的北邊。
> **Túshūguǎn zài gōngyuán de běibiān.**
> The library is north of the park.

Notice that English uses the verb 'be' and the preposition 'at' to express this meaning.

The negation for 在 **zài** is 不在 **bù zài**.

> 他不在家。
> **Tā bù zài jiā.**
> He is not at home.

> 图书馆不在公园的北边。
> 圖書館不在公園的北邊。
> **Túshūguǎn bù zài gōngyuán de běibiān.**
> The library is not to the north of the park.

在 **zài** also functions as a preposition. As a preposition, it indicates the location where an action occurs. Depending upon the sentence, it may be translated into English as 'at,' 'in,' or 'on.'

> 他在家吃饭。
> 他在家吃飯。
> **Tā zài jiā chī fàn.**
> He eats at home.

> 孩子在公园里玩。
> 孩子在公園裏玩。
> **Háizi zài gōngyuán lǐ wán.**
> The children play in the park.

▶ 14, 47.1

12

Modal verbs

Modal verbs occur before a verb and express the meanings of possibility, ability, permission, obligation, and prohibition.

12.1 Expressing possibility: 会/會 *huì*

明天会下雨。
明天會下雨。
Míngtiān huì xià yǔ.
It may rain tomorrow.

我希望我们将来会有机会再见。
我希望我們將來會有機會再見。
Wǒ xīwàng wǒmen jiānglái huì yǒu jīhuì zài jiàn.
I hope that in the future we will have the chance to meet again.

Notice that this meaning of 会/會 *huì* also implies future time.

▶ 36.3

12.2 Expressing ability

12.2.1 会/會 *huì*

会/會 *huì* expresses innate ability or ability based on learning and knowledge. The negative is 不会/不會 *bù huì*.

她会说中文。
她會說中文。
Tā huì shuō Zhōngwén.
She can speak Chinese.

我不会写那个字。
我不會寫那個字。
Wǒ bù huì xiě nàge zì.
I can't write that character.

▶ 52.1, 54.1.2

Expressing permission: 可以 *kěyǐ*　　　　**12.3**

12.2.2 能 *néng*

能 **néng** expresses physical ability or the unobstructed ability to perform some action. 不能 **bù néng** is used when performance is obstructed.

> 你能不能把桌子搬到那边去？
> 你能不能把桌子搬到那邊去？
> **Nǐ néng bù néng bǎ zhuōzi bān dào nàbiān qù?**
> Can you move this table over there?
> (lit. 'Can you take this table and move it over there?')

> 他的嗓子疼，不能说话。
> 他的嗓子疼，不能說話。
> **Tā de sǎngzi téng, bù néng shuō huà.**
> His throat is sore. He can't speak.

> 现在在修路。不能过。
> 現在在修路。不能過。
> **Xiànzài zài xiū lù. Bù néng guò.**
> The road is being repaired now. You can't cross it.

▶ 52.1.3

12.2.3 可以 *kěyǐ*

可以 **kěyǐ** is sometimes used to express knowledge-based or physical ability. The negative is 不可以 **bù kěyǐ**.

> 你可以不可以写你的名字？
> 你可以不可以寫你的名字？
> **Nǐ kěyǐ bù kěyǐ xiě nǐ de míngzi?**
> Can you write your name?

> 她已经八十岁了，可是还可以骑自行车。
> 她已經八十歲了，可是還可以騎自行車。
> **Tā yǐjing bāshí suì le, kěshì hái kěyǐ qí zìxíngchē.**
> She is already eighty years old but can still ride a bicycle.

12.3 Expressing permission: 可以 *kěyǐ*

The primary use of 可以 **kěyǐ** is to express permission to perform an action. The negative is 不可以 **bù kěyǐ**.

> 妈妈说我可以跟你去看电影。
> 媽媽說我可以跟你去看電影。
> **Māma shuō wǒ kěyǐ gēn nǐ qù kàn diànyǐng.**
> Mom said I can go with you to see a movie.

> 你才十六岁。不可以喝酒。
> 你才十六歲。不可以喝酒。
> **Nǐ cái shíliù suì. Bù kěyǐ hē jiǔ.**
> You are only 16 years old. You cannot drink alcohol.

▶ 51.2

MODAL VERBS

12.4 Expressing obligations

Obligations may be strong (*must*) or weak (*should*). In Mandarin, as in English, negation often changes the force of the words used to express obligation. This section presents a brief overview of the use of modal verbs to express obligations. For more on expressing obligations, see Chapter 50.

12.4.1 Strong obligation: must, have to

The Mandarin words used to indicate strong obligation (*must*) are 必须/必須 bìxū, 必得 bìděi, and 得 děi. 必得 bìděi and 必须/必須 bìxū are more formal than 得 děi. 必须/必須 bìxū is used in legal pronouncements and in other formal spoken and written contexts.

必须/必須 *bìxū*

> 婚前必须做健康检查。
> 婚前必須做健康檢查。
> **Hūn qián bìxū zuò jiànkāng jiǎnchá.**
> Before you get married you must have a physical exam.

必得 *bìděi*

> 医生说我每天必得吃药。
> 醫生說我每天必得吃藥。
> **Yīshēng shuō wǒ měitiān bìděi chī yào.**
> The doctor says I must take medicine every day.

得 *děi*

> 住院以前得先付钱。
> 住院以前得先付錢。
> **Zhù yuàn yǐqián děi xiān fù qián.**
> Before being admitted to the hospital you must first pay a fee.

▶ 50.1.1

12.4.2 Weak obligation – social and moral obligation: should, ought to

The modal verbs used to express weak obligations (*should*) associated with social or moral responsibilities include 应该/應該 yīnggāi, 该/該 gāi, 应当/應當 yīngdāng, and 当/當 dāng. 应当/應當 yīngdāng is more formal than 应该/應該 yīnggāi and can be used in formal texts including legal documents. 该/該 gāi is used in informal speech. 应/應 yīng is used in formal texts including legal documents. For illustrations of legal uses, see

▶ 50.1.2

应该/應該 *yīnggāi*

> 学生应该认真地学习。
> 學生應該認真地學習。
> **Xuésheng yīnggāi rènzhēn de xuéxí.**
> Students should study conscientiously.

该/該 *gāi*

> 你该早一点睡觉。
> 你該早一點睡覺。
> **Nǐ gāi zǎo yīdiǎn shuì jiào.**
> You should go to sleep a little earlier.

Expressing prohibitions   **12.5**

应当/應當 *yīngdāng*

> 孩子应当尊敬父母。
> 孩子應當尊敬父母。
> **Háizi yīngdāng zūnjìng fùmǔ.**
> Children should respect their parents.

▶ 50.1.2

12.4.3 Using modal verbs to express negative obligations: need not, do not have to

不必 **bù bì** expresses negative obligation, using the syllable 必 **bì** that occurs in the strong obligation modal verbs 必得 **bìděi** and 必须/必須 **bìxū**. For additional ways to express negative obligations, see 50.1.3.

> 你去看朋友的时候不必送礼物。
> 你去看朋友的時候不必送禮物。
> **Nǐ qù kàn péngyou de shíhou bù bì sòng lǐwù.**
> When you visit friends, it is not necessary to bring a gift.

12.5 Expressing prohibitions

The following phrases involving modal verbs are used to express prohibitions. For additional phrases used in expressing prohibitions, see

▶ 50.2

不可以 **bù kěyǐ** 'not allowed to'

> 考试的时候不可以说话。
> 考試的時候不可以說話。
> **Kǎoshì de shíhou bù kěyǐ shuō huà.**
> During the test you cannot speak.

不能 **bù néng** 'cannot'

> 这些书都是内部刊物。你不能借。
> 這些書都是內部刊物。你不能借。
> **Zhè xiē shū dōu shì nèi bù kānwù. Nǐ bù néng jiè.**
> Those books are all restricted publications. You can't borrow them.

> 这件事情，我不能告诉你。
> 這件事情，我不能告訴你。
> **Zhè jiàn shìqing, wǒ bù néng gàosu nǐ.**
> (As for) this matter, I can't tell you about it.

不许/不許 **bù xǔ** 'must not, not allowed'

不许/不許 **bù xǔ** is used in formal speech and writing.

> 图书馆里不许抽烟、吃东西。
> 圖書館裏不許抽煙、吃東西。
> **Túshūguǎn lǐ bù xǔ chōu yān, chī dōngxi.**
> You are not allowed to smoke or eat (things) in the library.

▶ 50.2.1

MODAL VERBS

12.6 Grammatical properties of modal verbs

12.6.1 Negation of modal verbs

Modal verbs are always negated with 不 **bù** and never with 没/沒 **méi**.

Say this

他不会说中文。
他不會說中文。
Tā bù huì shuō Zhōngwén.
He can't speak Chinese.

你不应该抽烟。
你不應該抽煙。
Nǐ bù yīnggāi chōu yān.
You shouldn't smoke.

Not this

*他没会说中文。
他沒會說中文。
Tā méi huì shuō Zhōngwén.

*你没应该抽烟。
你沒應該抽煙。
Nǐ méi yīnggāi chōu yān.

Modal verbs indicating weak obligation, 会/會 **huì**, 可以 **kěyǐ**, 能 **néng**, 应该/應該 **yīnggāi**, and 应当/應當 **yīngdāng**, have the properties of stative verbs.

▶ 11

12.6.2 Questions with modal verbs

Modal verbs can serve as the verb in *verb-not-verb* questions, and they can be used as the short, one word answers to yes–no questions.

Question

你会不会说中文?
你會不會說中文?
Nǐ huì bù huì shuō Zhōngwén?
Can you speak Chinese?

我可以不可以借你的车?
我可以不可以借你的車?
Wǒ kěyǐ bù kěyǐ jiè nǐ de chē?
Can I borrow your car?

你能不能帮助我?
你能不能幫助我?
Nǐ néng bù néng bāngzhù wǒ?
Can you help me?

我们该不该交作业?
我們該不該交作業?
Wǒmen gāi bù gāi jiāo zuòyè?
Should we hand in our homework?

Response

会。
會。
Huì.
(I) can.

可以。
可以。
Kěyǐ.
(You) can.

能。
能。
Néng.
(I) can.

该。
該。
Gāi.
(We) should.

▶ 28

12.6.3 Modification by intensifiers

会/會 **huì** and 能 **néng** can be modified by intensifiers.

那个人很会跳舞。
那個人很會跳舞。
Nàge rén hěn huì tiào wǔ.
That person can really dance.

Grammatical properties of modal verbs 12.6

中国人很能吃苦。
中國人很能吃苦。
Zhōngguórén hěn néng chī kǔ.
Chinese people can endure a lot of hardship.

For a complete list of intensifiers, see 10.3.

▶ 10.3, 11.2

12.6.4 Modal verbs and expressions that indicate change over time

会/會 **huì**, 能 **néng**, and 可以 **kěyǐ** can be used in the structures 越来越 **yuè lái yuè** and 越 verb 越 verb **yuè** verb **yuè** verb to indicate change over time.

他越来越会说话。
他越來越會說話。
Tā yuè lái yuè huì shuō huà.
He is becoming more and more elegant (diplomatic) in his speech.

他越来越能适应英国的生活了。
他越來越能適應英國的生活了。
Tā yuè lái yuè néng shìyìng Yīngguó de shēnghuó le.
Little by little he is getting used to British life.

我越来越可以适应这种天气了。
我越來越可以適應這種天氣了。
Wǒ yuè lái yuè kěyǐ shìyìng zhè zhǒng tiānqì le.
Little by little, I've become able to cope with this kind of weather.

▶ 38.3

12.6.5 Modal verbs and adverbs

The modal verbs that indicate strong obligation, 必须/必須 **bìxū**, 必得 **bìděi**, and 得 **děi**, are similar to adverbs.

They cannot serve as the verb in *verb-not-verb* questions.

Say this	*Not this*
你必须马上回家吗？	*你必须不必须马上回家？
你必須馬上回家嗎？	你必須不必須馬上回家？
Nǐ bìxū mǎshàng huí jiā ma?	**Nǐ bìxū bù bìxū mǎshàng huí jiā?**
Do you have to go right home?	
我们得在这儿注册吗？	*我们得不得在这儿注册？
我們得在這兒註冊嗎？	我們得不得在這兒註冊？
Wǒmen děi zài zhèr zhù cè ma?	**Wǒmen děi bù děi zài zhèr zhù cè?**
Do we have to register here?	

The modal 得 **děi** cannot be used as the one-word answer to yes–no questions:

Question	*Respond with this*	*Not this*
今天得注册吗？	今天得注册。	*得。
今天得註冊嗎？	今天得註冊。	
Jīntiān děi zhù cè ma?	**Jīntiān děi zhù cè.**	**Děi**
Do we have to register today?	We have to register today.	
	or	
	对。/對。	
	Duì.	
	Correct.	

71

13

Action verbs

Action verbs are verbs that describe doing things. They include 买/買 **mǎi** 'shop,' 学/學 **xué** 'study,' 看 **kàn** 'look at,' 'watch,' 'read,' 吃 **chī** 'eat,' 睡 **shuì** 'sleep,' 去 **qù** 'go,' 唱 **chàng** 'sing,' 洗 **xǐ** 'wash,' etc.

This chapter shows you how to talk about completed, past, and ongoing actions, and introduces the overall properties of action verbs. There are two kinds of action verbs, those that describe open-ended actions, and those that describe actions that cause a change. The last two sections of this chapter present the characteristics of these two types of verbs.

13.1 Indicating that an action is complete

To indicate that an action is complete – that is, that it is viewed as a bounded event – follow the action verb or the verb + object with the perfective particle 了 **le**.

The location of 了 **le**, either after the action or after the verb + object phrase, depends upon properties of the object.

If the object consists of a noun phrase without any modification, that is, without a preceding specific, number, classifier, or description phrase, 了 **le** typically follows the object.

> 她买东西了。
> 她買東西了。
> **Tā mǎi dōngxi le.**
> She bought things.

> 她到图书馆去了。
> 她到圖書館去了。
> **Tā dào túshūguǎn qù le.**
> She went to the library.

If the object includes a description, including a specifier, a number + classifier, a question word involving quantity, or any other description, 了 **le** occurs directly after the verb.

> 我看了那个电影。
> 我看了那個電影。
> **Wǒ kàn le nàge diànyǐng.**
> I saw that movie.

> 他吃了两碗饭。
> 他吃了兩碗飯。
> **Tā chī le liǎng wǎn fàn.**
> He ate two bowls of rice.

Negating actions 13.3

你点了几个菜？
你點了幾個菜？
Nǐ diǎn le jǐge cài?
How many dishes did you order?

我借了我同屋的车。
我借了我同屋的車。
Wǒ jiè le wǒ tóngwū de chē.
I borrowed my roommate's car.

▶ 17, 37.1

13.2 Indicating that an action has been experienced in the past

To indicate that the subject had the experience of performing some action in the past, follow the action verb with the verb suffix 过/過 **guo**. The verb suffix 过/過 **guo** is used when talking about actions that the subject does not perform on a regular basis or for actions that happened in the remote past. It is not used when talking about actions that have occurred recently.

我看过那个电影。
我看過那個電影。
Wǒ kànguo nàge diànyǐng.
I've seen that movie before.

我来过这里。
我來過這裏。
Wǒ láiguo zhèlǐ.
I've been here before.

▶ 17, 37.6

13.3 Negating actions

13.3.1 Indicating that an action does not occur or will not occur

To indicate that an action does not occur or will not occur, negate the action verb with 不 **bù**.

我不吃肉。
Wǒ bù chī ròu.
I don't eat meat.

台北从来不下雪。
臺北從來不下雪。
Táiběi cónglái bù xià xuě.
It does not snow in Taipei.

明天是星期六。我们不上课。
明天是星期六。我們不上課。
Míngtiān shì xīngqīliù. Wǒmen bù shàng kè.
Tomorrow is Saturday. We don't attend class.

73

ACTION VERBS

13.3.2 Indicating that an action did not occur in the past

To indicate that an action did not occur in the past, negate the action verb with 没/沒 (有) **méi (yǒu)**.

我今天没(有)吃早饭。
我今天沒(有)吃早飯。
Wǒ jīntiān méi (yǒu) chī zǎofàn.
I didn't eat breakfast today.

我没买电脑。
我沒買電腦。
Wǒ méi mǎi diànnǎo.
I didn't buy a computer.

▶ 27.1.2, 37.3

When a verb is negated with 没/沒 (有) **méi (yǒu)**, it cannot be suffixed with 了 **le**. It can, however, be suffixed with 过/過 **guo**.

▶ 37.6

Say this	Not this
我没吃过日本菜。	*我没吃了日本菜。
我沒吃過日本菜。	我沒吃了日本菜。
Wǒ méi chīguo Rìběn cài.	**Wǒ méi chī le Rìběn cài.**
I have never eaten Japanese food before.	

▶ 37.6

13.4 Asking about actions

To ask if an action generally occurs, will occur, or is complete, ask a yes–no question.

13.4.1 Yes-no questions with 吗/嗎 *ma*

你学中文吗?
你學中文嗎?
Nǐ xué Zhōngwén ma?
Do you study Chinese?

你今天晚上去图书馆吗?
你今天晚上去圖書館嗎?
Nǐ jīntiān wǎnshang qù túshūguǎn ma?
Are you going to the library tonight?

你吃饭了吗?
你吃飯了嗎?
Nǐ chī fàn le ma?
Have you eaten?

Open-ended action verbs   **13.5**

13.4.2 Verb-not-verb yes–no questions

To ask a yes–no question about whether an action generally occurs or will occur, use 不 **bù** and ask:

> *(subject) verb* 不 *bù verb (object)*
>
> 你学不学中文？
> 你學不學中文？
> **Nǐ xué bù xué Zhōngwén?**
> Do you study Chinese?
>
> 你今天晚上去不去图书馆？
> 你今天晚上去不去圖書館？
> **Nǐ jīntiān wǎnshang qù bù qù túshūguǎn?**
> Are you going to the library tonight?

To ask a yes–no question about whether an action is complete, use 没有/沒有 **méi yǒu**:

> *(subject) verb (object)* 了 *le* 没有/沒有 *méi yǒu*
>
> 你吃饭了没有？
> 你吃飯了沒有？
> **Nǐ chī fàn le méi yǒu?**
> Have you eaten?

13.5 Open-ended action verbs

Open-ended action verbs refer to actions that can have duration and can be performed for a period of time. Examples of open-ended action verbs include 念 **niàn** 'study/read aloud,' 买/買 **mǎi** 'shop,' 写/寫 **xiě** 'write,' 学/學 **xué** 'study,' 跑 **pǎo** 'run,' 吃 **chī** 'eat,' 玩 **wán** 'play,' and 唱 **chàng** 'sing.'

13.5.1 Duration of open-ended actions

To indicate the duration of an open-ended action verb, follow the verb with a duration expression. In the following examples, the verb is emphasized.

> 他在中国住了一年。
> 他在中國住了一年。
> **Tā zài Zhōngguó *zhù* le yīnián.**
> He *lived* in China for a year.
>
> 他每天看一个钟头的报。
> 他每天看一個鍾頭的報。
> **Tā měitiān *kàn* yī gè zhōngtou de bào.**
> He *reads* a newspaper for one hour every day.

▶ 39.1

To emphasize the ongoing action of an open-ended action verb without specifying the length of the duration, follow the verb with the durative aspect particle 着/著 **zhe**. 在 **zài** and 呢 **ne** often occur with 着/著 **zhe**. 在 **zài** occurs before the verb and 呢 **ne** occurs at the end of the sentence.

> 他在说着话呢。
> 他在說著話呢。
> **Tā zài shuōzhe huà ne.**
> He is speaking.

▶ 17, 39.2

ACTION VERBS

13.5

13.5.2 Open-ended action verbs and obligatory objects

Open-ended action verbs are typically followed by an *obligatory object*, a noun phrase that serves as the direct object of the verb. Many open-ended action verbs have a *default object*, an object that automatically occurs with the verb.

Default objects contribute little or no meaning to the *verb + object* phrase and are typically not translated into English.

Open-ended action verb	Default object	Verb + object	Example sentence
说 說 **shuō** speak	话 話 **huà** speech	说话 說話 **shuō huà** speak	他们在说话呢。 他們在說話呢。 **Tāmen zài shuō huà ne.** They are speaking.
看 **kàn** read	书 書 **shū** book	看书 看書 **kàn shū** read	我喜欢看书。 我喜歡看書。 **Wǒ xǐhuan kàn shū.** I like to read.
吃 **chī** eat	饭 飯 **fàn** rice	吃饭 吃飯 **chī fàn** eat	我们吃饭吧! 我們吃飯吧! **Wǒmen chī fàn ba!** Let's eat!
写 寫 **xiě** write	字 **zì** character	写字 寫字 **xiě zì** write	他不会写字。 他不會寫字。 **Tā bù huì xiě zì.** He can't write.
画 畫 **huà** paint	画儿 畫兒 **huàr** picture	画画儿 畫畫兒 **huà huàr** paint	他会画画儿。 他會畫畫兒。 **Tā huì huà huàr.** He can paint.
唱 **chàng** sing	歌儿 歌兒 **gēr** song	唱歌儿 唱歌兒 **chàng gēr** sing	他周末跟朋友唱歌儿。 他週末跟朋友唱歌兒。 **Tā zhōumò gēn péngyou chàng gēr.** He sings with friends at the weekend.
洗 **xǐ** wash	澡 **zǎo** bathe	洗澡 **xǐ zǎo** wash; bathe	孩子不喜欢洗澡。 孩子不喜歡洗澡。 **Háizi bù xǐhuan xǐ zǎo.** Children do not like to bathe.
睡 **shuì** sleep	觉 覺 **jiào** a sleep	睡觉 睡覺 **shuì jiào** sleep	你几点钟睡觉? 你幾點鐘睡覺? **Nǐ jǐdiǎn zhōng shuì jiào?** What time do you go to sleep?

When an object with fuller meaning is used, it replaces the default object.

For example:

- 'to eat' is 吃饭/吃飯 **chī fàn**
  'to eat *dumplings*' is 吃饺子/吃餃子 **chī jiǎozi** and not
  *吃饭饺子/吃飯餃子 **chī fàn jiǎozi**.
- 'to write' is 写字/寫字 **xiě zì**
  'to write *English*' is 写英文/寫英文 **xiě Yīngwén** and not
  *写字英文/寫字英文 **xiě zì Yīngwén**

Change-of-state action verbs   **13.6**

- 'to read' is 看书/看書 **kàn shū**
'to read *a newspaper*' is 看报/看報 **kàn *bào*** and not
*看书报/看書報 **kànshū bào**.

The direct object may be absent when it can be inferred from the context of the sentence.

> Q: 你吃了晚饭吗?   A: 吃了。
> 你吃了晚飯嗎?
> **Nǐ chī le wǎnfàn ma?**   **Chī le.**
> Did you eat dinner?   I ate (dinner).

When it receives special emphasis, the direct object may occur at the beginning of the sentence as the topic, instead of after the verb.

> 那个电影我还没看过。
> 那個電影我還沒看過。
> **Nàge diànyǐng wǒ hái méi kànguo.**
> That movie, I still haven't seen (it).

▶ 57.1.2.1

13.6 Change-of-state action verbs

Change-of-state verbs describe events in which the action of the verb results in a change. Here are some examples of change-of-state verbs.

坐	**zuò**	to sit (a change from standing to sitting)
站	**zhàn**	to stand (a change from sitting to standing)
放	**fàng**	to put/place (a change of location)
挂/掛	**guà**	to hang (a change of location)
离开/離開	**líkāi**	to depart (a change of location)
穿	**chuān**	to put on (clothing – on the torso and legs)
戴	**dài**	to put on (clothing – on the head, neck, and hands)
病	**bìng**	to become sick (a change of health)
到	**dào**	to arrive (a change of location from 'not here' to 'here')
去	**qù**	to go (a change of location from 'here' to 'not here')

13.6.1 Change-of-state verbs and duration

Change-of-state verbs have no duration. However, some change-of-state actions bring about a resulting state. Verbs that indicate this state may be suffixed with 着/著 **zhe** to focus on the ongoing nature of the state. Here are some examples. A list of additional change-of-state verbs with related ongoing states is presented in 13.6.2.

> 孩子都在屋子里坐着。
> 孩子都在屋子裡坐著。
> **Háizi dōu zài wūzi li zuòzhe.**
> *The children are all sitting in the room.*

> 墙上挂着一张画儿。
> 牆上掛著一張畫兒。
> **Qiángshàng guàzhe yī zhāng huàr.**
> *There is a painting hanging on the wall.*

ACTION VERBS

13.6.2 Change-of-state verbs and stative verbs

Many change-of-state verbs also function as stative verbs.

		Change-of-state verb	*Stative verb*
坐	zuò	to sit down	to be seated
站	zhàn	to stand up	to be standing
戴	dài	to put on (clothing, on head, neck, arms)	to wear
穿	chuān	to put on (clothing, on torso and legs)	to wear
病	bìng	to become sick	to be sick
挂/掛	guà	to hang (something up)	to be hanging
贴/貼	tiē	to attach	to be attached

▶ Glossary of grammatical terms, 17.2.2

14

Prepositions and prepositional phrases

Prepositions occur before a noun phrase and indicate some relationship between the noun phrase and the main verb of the sentence. The preposition plus its noun phrase forms a prepositional phrase.

14.1 The grammar of the prepositional phrase in the Mandarin sentence

Here are the two rules to follow when using prepositional phrases.

Rule 1. **In Mandarin, the prepositional phrase occurs immediately before the verb phrase.**

Compare this with English, in which the prepositional phrase occurs immediately *after* the verb phrase.

    他们　　　[给弟弟]　　　[买了冰淇淋]。
    他們　　　[給弟弟]　　　[買了冰淇淋]。
    Tāmen　　[gěi dìdi]　　　[mǎi le bīngqilín].
    They [for younger brother] [buy ice cream]
    They bought ice cream for younger brother.

    她　　　　[跟同学]　　　　[聊天]。
    她　　　　[跟同學]　　　　[聊天]。
    Tā　　　　[gēn tóngxué]　　[liáo tiān].
    She [with classmates] [chat]
    She chats with classmates.

There is one exception to this rule. If the prepositional phrase indicates where the subject is located as a result of the action, the prepositional phrase follows the verb.

    他跳到床上。   **Tā tiào dào chuáng shàng.**   He jumped onto the bed.

Rule 2. **Nothing occurs between the preposition and its noun phrase object.**

- The suffixes 了 **le**, 着/著 **zhe**, and 过/過 **guo** follow verbs, but not prepositions:

    Say this   *Not this*
    他在中国住过一年。   *他在过中国住一年。
    他在中國住過一年。   他在過中國住一年。
    Tā zài Zhōngguó zhùguo yīnián. **Tā zàiguo Zhōngguó zhù yīnián.**
    He lived in China for a year.

    我昨天跟他说话了。   *我昨天跟了他说话。
    我昨天跟他說話了。   我昨天跟了他說話。
    Wǒ zuótiān gēn tā shuō huà le. **Wǒ zuótiān gēn le tā shuō huà.**
    I spoke with him yesterday.

PREPOSITIONS AND PREPOSITIONAL PHRASES   14.2

- Adverbs occur before the prepositional phrase. They do not occur between the prepositional phrase and the main verb.

Say this	Not this
请你马上到我家来。 請你馬上到我家來。 **Qǐng nǐ *mǎshàng* dào wǒ jiā lái.** Please come to my home *immediately*.	*请你到我家马上来。 請你到我家馬上來。 **Qǐng nǐ dào wǒ jiā *mǎshàng* lái.**
我一定跟你去看电影。 我一定跟你去看電影。 **Wǒ *yīdìng* gēn nǐ qù kàn diànyǐng.** I will *definitely* go with you to see a movie.	*我跟你一定去看电影。 我跟你一定去看電影。 **Wǒ gēn nǐ *yīdìng* qù kàn diànyǐng.**

▶ 15.1

14.2 Basic functions of prepositions

Here are the most common Mandarin prepositions, arranged according to function. The prepositional phrase is emphasized in each example. The last category includes prepositions that are only used in formal speech and writing.

14.2.1 Prepositions that indicate location in time or space – no movement involved

在 *zài* 'at, in, on'

他每天晚上在家吃饭。
他每天晚上在家吃飯。
Tā měitiān wǎnshang *zài jiā* chī fàn.
He eats *at home* every evening.

每天在公园里玩。
他們每天在公園裏玩。
Tāmen měitiān *zài gōngyuán lǐ* wán.
They play *in the park* every day.

在 *zài* is optional in time expressions:

我(在)两点钟来找你，行吗？
我(在)兩點鐘來找你，行嗎？
Wǒ *(zài) liǎng diǎn zhōng* lái zhǎo nǐ, xíng ma?
I'll come looking for you *at 2 o'clock*, okay?

14.2.2 Prepositions that indicate an action performed toward a reference point – no movement involved

对/對 *duì* 'to, toward'

他对你说了什么话？
他對你說了甚麼話？
Tā *duì nǐ* shuō le shénme huà?
What did he say *to you*?

向 *xiàng* 'toward'

他一直向外面看。
Tā yīzhí *xiàng wàimian* kàn.
He keeps looking *(to the) outside*.

Basic functions of prepositions

14.2.3 Prepositions that indicate joint performance of an action

跟 *gēn* 'with'

> 她每天跟他朋友吃午饭。
> 她每天跟他朋友吃午飯。
> **Tā měitiān *gēn tā péngyou* chī wǔfàn.**
> She eats lunch *with her friends* every day.

This use of 跟 *gēn* 'with' overlaps with that of the conjunction 跟 *gēn* 'and.'

▶ 16.1

14.2.4 Prepositions that indicate movement of the subject

从/從 *cóng* 'from': movement from a location

> 他慢慢地从宿舍走出来了。
> 他慢慢地從宿舍走出來了。
> **Tā mànmān de *cóng sùshè* zǒuchūlái le.**
> He slowly walked *out of the dormitory*.

到 *dào* 'to': movement to a location that is the destination

> 他想到餐厅去找朋友。
> 他想到餐廳去找朋友。
> **Tā xiǎng *dào cāntīng* qù zhǎo péngyou.**
> He's thinking about going *to the cafeteria* to look for his friends.

往 *wǎng*, 'toward' a location

> 往西边走。
> 往西邊走。
> **Wǎng xībian zǒu.**
> Go *(toward the) west*.

进/進 *jìn* 'into' a location

> 他进城去了。
> 他進城去了。
> **Tā *jìn chéng* qù le.**
> He went *into the city*.

从/從 *cóng* and 到 *dào* may occur in sequence in the same sentence:

> 从宿舍 到邮局 怎么走?
> 從宿舍 到郵局 怎麼走?
> **Cóng sùshè dào yóujú zěnme zǒu?**
> How do you go *from the dormitory to the post office*?

14.2.5 Prepositions that indicate transfer of something from one noun phrase to another

给/給 *gěi* 'to, for'

> 她给我买书了。
> 她給我買書了。
> **Tā *gěi wǒ* mǎi shū le.**
> She bought a book *for me*.

PREPOSITIONS AND PREPOSITIONAL PHRASES | **14.2**

跟 gēn 'from'

> 他跟我借书了。
> 他跟我借書了。
> **Tā gēn wǒ jiè shū le.**
> He borrowed a book *from me*.

向 xiàng 'from'

> 他向我借书了。
> 他向我借書了。
> **Tā xiàng wǒ jiè shū le.**
> He borrowed a book *from me*.

14.2.6 Prepositions that indicate the beneficiary of an action performed by another

给/給 gěi 'for, on behalf of'

> 她给我写信了。
> 她給我寫信了。
> **Tā gěi wǒ xiě xìn le.**
> She wrote a letter *for me* (on my behalf).
> (This can also mean: She wrote a letter *to me*.)

替 tì 'for, on behalf of'

> 明天请你替我教书。
> 明天請你替我教書。
> **Míngtiān qǐng nǐ tì wǒ jiāo shū.**
> Please teach *for me* tomorrow.

14.2.7 Prepositions that mark the agent in passive sentences

被 bèi 'by'

> 我的皮包被人家偷走了。
> **Wǒ de píbāo bèi rénjiā tōuzǒu le.**
> My wallet was stolen *by* someone.

叫 jiào 'by'

> 我的课本叫朋友弄丢了。
> 我的課本叫朋友弄丟了。
> **Wǒ de kèběn jiào péngyou nòngdiū le.**
> My textbook was lost *by* my friend.

让/讓 ràng 'by'

> 他们的房子让火烧了。
> 他們的房子讓火燒了。
> **Tāmen de fángzi ràng huǒ shāo le.**
> Their house was burned down *by* the fire.

▶ 21

Basic functions of prepositions 14.2

NOTE

The preposition is part of the following fixed expressions:

跟 (someone) 开玩笑
跟 (someone) 開玩笑
gēn (someone) **kāi wánxiào**
to play a joke on (someone)

> 他哥哥喜欢跟他开玩笑。
> 他哥哥喜歡跟他開玩笑。
> **Tā gēge xǐhuan gēn tā kāi wánxiào.**
> His older brother likes to play jokes on him.

对 (something) 有兴趣
對 (something) 有興趣
duì (something) **yǒu xìngqù**
to be interested in (something)

> 我对科学有兴趣。
> 我對科學有興趣。
> **Wǒ duì kēxué yǒu xìngqù.**
> I am interested in science.

14.2.8 Prepositions used in formal speech and formal written language

To indicate beneficiary or recipient

为/為 *wèi* 'for/on behalf of'

> 我们应该为人民服务。
> 我們應該為人民服務。
> **Wǒmen yīnggāi *wèi* rénmín fúwù.**
> We should serve the people.
> (serve *for the people*)

To indicate the source (no movement)

由 *yóu* 'from'

> 由此可见，人民都喜欢自由。
> 由此可見，人民都喜歡自由。
> ***Yóu* cǐ kě jiàn, rénmín dōu xǐhuan zìyóu.**
> You can see *from* this that everyone likes freedom.

To indicate location in time or space

于/於 *yú* 'at, in, on'

> 谨定于三月十五日在人民大会堂开会。
> 謹定於三月十五日在人民大會堂開會。
> **Jǐndìng *yú* sānyuè shíwǔ rì zài rénmín dàhuìtáng kāi huì.**
> The meeting is respectfully set at March 15 in the Great Hall of the People.

To indicate a point in time (no movement)

自从/自從 *zìcóng* 'from, (ever) since'

> 自从中国开放以后，人民的生活水平提高了。
> 自從中國開放以後，人民的生活水平提高了。
> ***Zìcóng* Zhōngguó kāifàng yǐhòu, rénmín de shēnghuó shuǐpíng tígāo le.**
> *Ever since China began to open up*, the standard of living of its people has improved.

83

PREPOSITIONS AND PREPOSITIONAL PHRASES

14.3 Prepositions that also function as verbs

Many prepositions also function as verbs.

	As a preposition	*As a verb*
在 zài	*at* 他在家吃饭。 他在家吃飯。 **Tā zài jiā chī fàn.** He eats *at* home.	*exist; be located at* 他在家。 **Tā zài jiā.** He *is at* home.
给/給 gěi	*to/for* 他给我买了毛衣。 他給我買了毛衣。 **Tā gěi wǒ mǎi le máoyī.** He bought a sweater *for* me.	*give* 她给我这件毛衣了。 她給我這件毛衣了。 **Tā gěi wǒ zhè jiàn máoyī le.** She *gave* me this sweater.
到 dào	*to* 你什么时候到图书馆去？ 你甚麽時候到圖書館去？ **Nǐ shénme shíhòu dào túshūguǎn qù?** When are you going *to* the library?	*arrive* 他什么时候到？ 他甚麽時候到？ **Tā shénme shíhòu dào?** What time does he *arrive*?
对/對 duì	*to, toward* 你应该对客人很客气。 你應該對客人很客氣。 **Nǐ yīnggāi duì kèren hěn kèqi.** You should be polite *to* guests.	*correct* Q: 你是英国人，对吗？ 　　你是英國人，對嗎？ 　　**Nǐ shì Yīngguórén, duì ma?** 　　You are British, *right*? A: 对。 　　對。 　　**Duì.** 　　*Correct*.
跟 gēn	*with* 他每天跟朋友聊天。 **Tā měitiān gēn péngyou liáo tiān.** He chats *with* friends every day.	*follow* 不要老跟着我。 不要老跟著我。 **Bù yào lǎo gēnzhe wǒ.** Don't *follow* me all the time.

You can identify a word as either a preposition or a verb by observing the other words with which it occurs.

- Prepositions are always followed by an object noun phrase and a verb phrase. If a word is not followed by both an object noun phrase and a verb phrase, it is not a preposition.

Verb: followed by a noun phrase but no verb phrase	*Preposition: followed by a noun phrase and a verb phrase*
她给我这件毛衣了。 她給我這件毛衣了。 **Tā gěi wǒ zhè jiàn máoyī le.** She *gave* me this sweater.	她给我买了这件毛衣了。 她給我買了這件毛衣了。 **Tā gěi wǒ mǎi le zhè jiàn máoyī le.** She bought this sweater *for* me.
他在家。 **Tā zài jiā.** He *is at* home.	他在家吃饭。 他在家吃飯。 **Tā zài jiā chī fàn.** He is eating *at* home.

▶ Glossary of grammatical terms

15

Adverbs

Adverbs are words that modify the verb or verb phrase.

15.1 General properties of adverbs

In Mandarin, adverbs occur at the beginning of the verb phrase, before the verb and any prepositional phrase.

Most adverbs must precede negation, but some adverbs may occur before or after negation.

她一定不去。 **Tā yīdìng bù qù.** She's definitely not going.	*and also*	她不一定去。 **Tā bù yīdìng qù.** She may not go. (She is not definitely going.)
她也许不去。 她也許不去。 **Tā yéxǔ bù qù.** Perhaps she won't go.	*but not*	*她不也许去 她不也許去 **Tā bù yéxǔ qù.**
她并不喜欢我。 她並不喜歡我。 **Tā bìng bù xǐhuan wǒ.** She doesn't like me at all.	*but not*	*她不并喜欢我。 她不並喜歡我。 **Tā bù bìng xǐhuan wǒ.**

▶ 27.2

Unlike verbs, adverbs typically cannot be the one word answer to a yes–no question.

Question	*Respond with this*	*Not this*
他们经常在那个饭馆吃饭吗？ 他們經常在那個飯館吃飯嗎？ **Tāmen jīngcháng zài fànguǎn chī fàn ma?** Do they often eat at that restaurant?	对。 對。 **Duì.** Correct. *or* 他们经常在那儿吃饭。 他們經常在那兒吃飯。 **Tāmen jīngcháng zài nàr chī fàn.** They often eat there.	*经常。 經常。 **Jīngcháng.**

85

ADVERBS

Question	Respond with this	Not this
你已经吃了吗？	对。	*已经。
你已經吃了嗎？	對。	已經。
Nǐ yǐjing chī le ma?	**Duì.**	**Yǐjing.**
Have you already eaten?	Correct.	
	or	
	我已经吃了。	
	我已經吃了。	
	Wǒ yǐjing chī le.	
	I have already eaten.	

Mandarin has a number of structures that are *adverbial* in function in that they describe the way an action is performed. See

▶ 31

Adjectival verbs, stative verbs, and modal verbs may be modified by intensifiers such as 很 **hěn** 'very,' 太 **tài** 'too,' and 真 **zhēn** 'really.'

▶ 10.3, 11.2, 12.6.3

Adverbs add many different kinds of meaning to a sentence. This chapter presents adverbs that have *logical* functions. Other adverbs are presented throughout this book in chapters that focus on the meanings associated with the specific adverbs.

▶ 27.1, 34, 35, 36.2, 37, 38, 40, 41.2

15.2 Adverbs with logical function: 也 *yě*, 都 *dōu*, 还/還 *hái*, 就 *jiù*, 只 *zhǐ*, and 才 *cái*

15.2.1 也 *yě* 'also, in addition'

也 **yě** is used to introduce a second verb phrase. It never follows negation.

也 **yě** can be used to introduce a second verb phrase that adds additional information about the subject.

小王学中文。他也学日文。
小王學中文。他也學日文。
Xiǎo Wáng xué Zhōngwén. Tā yě xué Rìwén.
Little Wang studies Chinese. He also studies Japanese.

When the subjects are identical in reference, the second subject may be omitted:

小王学中文，也学日文。
小王學中文，也學日文。
Xiǎo Wáng xué Zhōngwén, yě xué Rìwén.
Little Wang studies Chinese and also studies Japanese.

也 **yě** can be used to indicate that two different subjects share similar properties or perform the same action.

小王很高。小李也很高。
Xiǎo Wáng hěn gāo. Xiǎo Lǐ yě hěn gāo.
Little Wang is very tall. Little Li also is very tall.

小王上大学。小李也上大学。
小王上大學。小李也上大學。
Xiǎo Wáng shàng dàxué. Xiǎo Lǐ yě shàng dàxué.
Little Wang attends college. Little Li also attends college.

▶ 40.1

Adverbs with logical function: 也 *yě*, 都 *dōu*, 还/還 *hái*, 就 *jiù*, 只 *zhǐ*, and 才 *cái* **15.2**

Since 也 *yě* introduces additional information it can sometimes be translated by 'and' in English. However, it is very different from English 'and.' 'And' can connect almost any kind of phrase; 也 *yě* can only occur before verbs or verb phrases.

Compare this Mandarin example and its English translation.

> 我学中文，也学中国历史。
> 我學中文，也學中國歷史。
> **Wǒ xué Zhōngwén, yě xué Zhōngguó lìshǐ.**
> I study Chinese and I also study Chinese history.

Chinese conjunctions that join noun phrases and convey the meaning of the English 'and' include 和 *hé* and 跟 *gēn*.

> 我学中文和中国历史。
> 我學中文和中國歷史。
> **Wǒ xué Zhōngwén hé Zhōngguó lìshǐ.**
> I study Chinese and Chinese history.

▶ 40.7

15.2.2 都 *dōu* 'all, both'

都 *dōu* can indicate that a verb phrase is true for the entire subject.

> 我们都学中文。
> 我們都學中文。
> **Wǒmen dōu xué Zhōngwén.**
> We all study Chinese.

> 小王和小李都学中文。
> 小王和小李都學中文。
> **Xiǎo Wáng hé Xiǎo Lǐ dōu xué Zhōngwén.**
> Little Wang and Little Li both study Chinese.

都 *dōu* can indicate that a verb is true for multiple objects. Typically, when 都 *dōu* refers to objects, the objects occur before the verb as the topic of the sentence.

> 中文，日文，他都学。
> 中文，日文，他都學。
> **Zhōngwén, Rìwén, tā dōu xué.**
> Chinese, Japanese, he studies them both.

▶ 57.1

都 *dōu* before a verb without an object can be used to express the meaning 'completely.'

> 我都懂。
> **Wǒ dōu dǒng.**
> I understand everything.

都 *dōu* can occur with a question word to indicate that something is universally true.

> 她什么都会。
> 她甚麼都會。
> **Tā shénme dōu huì.**
> She can do everything.

> 她什么时候都很忙。
> 她甚麼時候都很忙。
> **Tā shénme shíhòu dōu hěn máng.**
> She is always busy.

▶ 46.4

ADVERBS

都 **dōu** can occur before or after negation. The relative position of negation and 都 **dōu** reflects a difference in meaning.

The sequence 都 **dōu** + *negation* conveys the meaning 'all not.'

都 **dōu** before negation may indicate that the negated verb phrase is true for the entire subject.

> 他们都没学中文。
> 他們都沒學中文。
> **Tāmen dōu méi xué Zhōngwén.**
> They have not all studied Chinese.

都 **dōu** before negation can also indicate that the negated verb is true for the entire object. Often, when 都 **dōu** refers to the object, the object is topicalized.

> 猪肉，牛肉我都不吃。
> 豬肉，牛肉我都不吃。
> **Zhūròu, niúròu wǒ dōu bù chī.**
> Pork, beef, I don't eat either.

都 **dōu** after negation indicates that negation is not true for the entire subject or that it is not true for the entire object. The sequence *negation* + 都 **dōu** can often be translated into English as 'not all.'

> 我们不都是中国人。她是美国人，他是英国人。只有我是中国人。
> 我們不都是中國人。她是美國人，他是英國人。只有我是中國人。
> **Wǒmen bù dōu shì Zhōngguó rén. Tā shì Měiguó rén, tā shì Yīngguó rén. Zhǐ yǒu wǒ shì Zhōngguó rén.**
> We are not all Chinese. She is American, he is English. Only I am Chinese.

> 美国人不都有钱。有的有钱，有的没有钱。
> 美國人不都有錢。有的有錢，有的沒有錢。
> **Měiguó rén bù dōu yǒu qián. Yǒu de yǒu qián, yǒu de méi yǒu qián.**
> Not all Americans have money. Some have money, some don't have money.

15.2.3 还/還 *hái* 'in addition, still, also, else'

还/還 **hái** marks the continuation of a situation or introduces additional actions performed by the subject. It can never follow negation.

> 他们还在这儿。
> 他們還在這兒。
> **Tāmen hái zài zhèr.**
> They are still here.

> 你还学中文吗？
> 你還學中文嗎？
> **Nǐ hái xué Zhōngwén ma?**
> Are you still studying Chinese?

> 我要买书，还要买纸。
> 我要買書，還要買紙。
> **Wǒ yào mǎi shū, hái yào mǎi zhǐ.**
> I want to buy books. (I) also want to buy paper.

> 你还要买什么？
> 你還要買甚麼？
> **Nǐ hái yào mǎi shénme?**
> What else do you want to buy?

Adverbs with logical function: 也 *yě*, 都 *dōu*, 还/還 *hái*, 就 *jiù*, 只 *zhǐ*, and 才 *cái* | **15.2**

还/還 **hái** may introduce additional information about a noun phrase. In this function it is similar to 也 **yě** 'also.'

> 他会说中文，还会说日文。
> 他會說中文，還會說日文。
> **Tā huì shuō Zhōngwén, hái huì shuō Rìwén.**
> He can speak Chinese (and) can also speak Japanese.

还没(有)/還沒(有) **hái méi (yǒu)** translates into English as 'not yet' or 'still.'

> 他还没回来呢。
> 他還沒回來呢。
> **Tā hái méi huí lái ne.**
> He hasn't returned yet. (He still hasn't returned.)

▶ 40.2

还有/還有 **hái yǒu** is a phrase that occurs at the beginning of a sentence or clause and introduces additional information. It can be translated into English as 'in addition.'

NOTE

> 她的男朋友很和气。还有，他很帅！
> 她的男朋友很和氣。還有，他很帥！
> **Tā de nán péngyou hěn héqi. Hái yǒu, tā hěn shuài!**
> Her boyfriend is very friendly. In addition, he is really cute!

▶ 40.3

15.2.4 就 *jiù* 'only, uniqueness'

When 就 **jiù** precedes a verb phrase that is not linked to another verb phrase, it conveys the meaning of uniqueness.

In some sentences, this meaning is best translated by the English word 'only':

> 我就有一块钱。
> 我就有一塊錢。
> **Wǒ jiù yǒu yī kuài qián.**
> I only have one dollar.

In some contexts, 就 **jiù** conveys precise identification of a noun phrase. If the noun phrase is a person or place, there may be no English equivalent for 就 **jiù**.

王：	你找谁? 你找誰?	林：	我找王美玲。	王：	我就是。
Wáng:	**Nǐ zhǎo shéi?**	Lín:	**Wǒ zhǎo Wáng Měilíng.**	Wáng:	**Wǒ *jiù shì*.**
Wang:	Who are you looking for?	Lin:	I am looking for Wang Meiling.	Wang:	That's me.

If the noun phrase is part of a location phrase, 就 **jiù** may be translated as 'right' or 'precisely.'

Q:	赵经理的办公室在哪儿? 趙經理的辦公室在哪兒? **Zhào jīnglǐ de bàngōngshì zài nǎr?** Where is Manager Zhao's office?	A:	她的办公室<u>就在这儿</u>。 她的辦公室<u>就在這兒</u>。 **Tā de bàngōngshì *jiù zài zhèr*.** Her office *is right here*.
Q:	图书馆在哪儿? 圖書館在哪兒? **Túshūguǎn zài nǎr?** Where is the library?	A:	<u>就在火车站的对面</u>。 <u>就在火車站的對面</u>。 ***Jiù zài huǒchēzhàn de duìmiàn.*** *Right across from the train station.*

ADVERBS

就 **jiù** is also used to link two verb phrases and to signal a relationship of sequence between them.

> 我看了报以后就睡觉。
> 我看了報以後就睡覺。
> **Wǒ kàn le bào yǐhòu jiù shuì jiào.**
> After I read the newspaper I will go to sleep.

> 她很聪明。一学就会。
> 她很聰明。一學就會。
> **Tā hěn cōngming. Yī xué jiù huì.**
> She is really smart. As soon as she studies it, she gets it.

▶ 42.2.2.1

就 **jiù** usually precedes negation, but it may also follow negation.

> 这件事情不就是我一个人知道。
> 這件事情不就是我一個人知道。
> **Zhè jiàn shìqing bù jiù shì wǒ yī gè rén zhīdao.**
> (As for) this matter, it is not just I who knows.

15.2.5 只 *zhǐ* 'only'

只 **zhǐ** can be used interchangeably with 就 **jiù** to express the meaning 'only.' It does not have any of the other meanings or functions associated with 就 **jiù**.

> 我只有一块钱。
> 我只有一塊錢。
> **Wǒ zhǐ yǒu yī kuài qián.**
> I only have one dollar.

Like 就 **jiù**, 只 **zhǐ** typically precedes negation, but may also follow it.

> 这件事情不只是我一个人知道。
> 這件事情不只是我一個人知道。
> **Zhè jiàn shìqing bù zhǐ shì wǒ yī gè rén zhīdao.**
> (As for) this matter, it is not just I who knows.

15.2.6 才 *cái* 'only, only then'

才 **cái** indicates that something is less than expected. In sentences in which there is only a single verb, 才 **cái** may be translated into English as 'only.'

> 他才认识五个字。
> 他才認識五個字。
> **Tā cái rènshi wǔ gè zì.**
> He only knows (recognizes) five characters [and that is fewer than one would expect].

> 那个孩子才一岁。当然还不会说话。
> 那個孩子才一歲。當然還不會說話。
> **Nàge háizi cái yīsuì. Dāngrán hái bù huì shuō huà.**
> That child is only one year old. Of course (s/he) can't speak yet.

> 我今天才挣了三百元。
> **Wǒ jīntiān cái zhèng le sānbǎi yuán.**
> Today I only earned 300 yuan (300 dollars).

Adverbs with logical function: 也 *yě*, 都 *dōu*, 还/還 *hái*, 就 *jiù*, 只 *zhǐ*, and 才 *cái* — **15.2**

When 才 **cái** is used to link two verb phrases as in the following sentences, it may be translated as 'only then.'

> 她做完了功课才睡觉。
> 她做完了功課才睡覺。
> **Tā zuòwán le gōngkè cái shuì jiào.**
> She finishes doing her homework and only then goes to sleep.

> 那本书我看了两次才懂。
> 那本書我看了兩次才懂。
> **Nà běn shū wǒ kàn le liǎng cì cái dǒng.**
> That book, I read it twice and only then understood (it).

▶ 42.2.2.2

才 **cái** never follows negation.

In sentences with 才 **cái**, perfective 了 **le** does not occur in the main clause.

15.2.7 而已 *éryǐ* 'and that is all'

In Taiwan, the sentence final expression 而已 **éryǐ** 'and that is all' is commonly used to reinforce the sense of *only* contributed by 就 **jiù**, 只 **zhǐ**, and 才 **cái**.

> 我只有五块钱而已。
> 我只有五塊錢而已。
> **Wǒ zhǐ yǒu wǔ kuài qián éryǐ.**
> I only have five dollars (and that is all).

> 他就写了一个字而已。
> 他就寫了一個字而已。
> **Tā jiù xiě le yī gè zì éryǐ.**
> He only wrote one character (and that is all).

The meaning 'only if' is expressed with the sentence initial phrase 除非 **chúfēi**.

▶ 45.4

91

16

Conjunctions

Conjunctions are words that join phrases belonging to the same grammatical category and indicate a relationship between them. Mandarin conjunctions include the following.

16.1 Conjunctions that indicate an 'additive' or 'and' relationship

16.1.1 和 *hé*

王明和李安是大学生。
王明和李安是大學生。
Wáng Míng hé Lǐ Ān shì dàxuéshēng.
Wang Ming and Li An are college students.

16.1.2 跟 *gēn*

北京跟上海都是很值得去看的地方。
Běijīng gēn Shànghǎi dōu shì hěn zhíde qù kàn de dìfang.
Beijing and Shanghai are both places worth seeing.

跟 **gēn** also functions as a preposition.

▶ 14

16.1.3 同 *tóng*

我同他的关系很不错。
我同他的關係很不錯。
Wǒ tóng tā de guānxi hěn bù cuò.
The relationship between him and me is not bad (really good).

16.1.4 与/與 *yǔ*

我们对中国的文化与历史都很有兴趣。
我們對中國的文化與歷史都很有興趣。
Wǒmen duì Zhōngguó de wénhuà yǔ lìshǐ dōu hěn yǒu xīngqù.
We are really interested in Chinese culture and history.

NOTE 同 **tóng** is used in southern China and is not common in the north. 与/與 **yǔ** is used in literary phrases.

16.2 Conjunctions that indicate a disjunctive or 'or' relationship

16.2.1 还是/還是 *háishi* 'or'

还是/還是 *háishi* is used in questions that ask the addressee to choose between two alternatives, only one of which can be true or possible. It conveys the sense of 'either . . . or.' 还是/還是 *háishi* questions often end with 呢 **ne**.

Q: 你是来旅游的还是来学习的？
你是來旅遊的還是來學習的？
Nǐ shì lái lǚyóu de háishi lái xuéxí de?
Did you come for vacation or to study?

A: 我是来学习的。
我是來學習的。
Wǒ shì lái xuéxí de.
I came to study.

Q: 你要喝红茶还是喝花茶呢？
你要喝紅茶還是喝花茶呢？
Nǐ yào hē hóng chá háishi hē huā chá ne?
Do you want to drink black tea or jasmine tea?
(In Chinese: red tea or jasmine tea?)

A: 我要喝红茶。
我要喝紅茶。
Wǒ yào hē hóng chá.
I want to drink black tea.

还是/還是 *háishi* precedes verb phrases. However, if the second verb phrase begins with 是 **shì**, 是 **shì** is usually omitted.

Q: 你是美国人还是英国人呢？
你是美國人還是英國人呢？
Nǐ shì Měiguórén háishi Yīngguórén ne?
Are you American or British?

A: 我是美国人。
我是美國人。
Wǒ shì Měiguórén.
I'm American.

还是/還是 *háishi* is sometimes included in an answer to a 还是/還是 *háishi* question to mark the preferred alternative. In this usage, 还是/還是 *háishi* functions as an adverb and not as a conjunction.

Q: 你想这个问题，是现在讨论好还是以后再讨论好？
你想這個問題，是現在討論好還是以後再討論好？
Nǐ xiǎng zhège wèntí, shì xiànzài tǎolùn hǎo háishi yǐhòu zài tǎolùn hǎo?
(As for) this question, do you think we should talk about it now or later?

A: 我想还是以后再讨论好。
我想還是以後再討論好。
Wǒ xiǎng háishi yǐhòu zài tǎolùn hǎo.
I think we should talk about it later.

▶ 15, 28.3

16.2.2 或者 *huòzhě* 'or'

或者 *huòzhě* 'or' is used in statements to present two alternatives, both of which are possible.

Q: 你要今天去长城还是明天去长城？
你要今天去長城還是明天去長城？
Nǐ yào jīntiān qù Chángchéng háishi míngtiān qù Chángchéng?
Do you want to go to the Great Wall today or tomorrow?

A: 今天去或者明天去都行。
Jīntiān qù huòzhě míngtiān qù dōu xíng.
Today and tomorrow are both okay.

Mandarin conjunctions are much more restricted than English conjunctions in the grammatical categories that they join. In Mandarin, the 'and' conjunctions only join noun phrases. The 'or' conjunctions only join verb phrases.

Most Mandarin connecting words are adverbs. They are presented in the relevant chapters on sentence connection.

▶ 41.2, 42.2.2, 43, 44, 45

17

Aspect

Aspect refers to the way that an action is viewed, either from the outside, as a bounded event, or from the inside, as an ongoing situation. Languages differ as to whether aspectual distinctions are signaled in the grammar. In Mandarin, they are. Mandarin grammar marks three different aspectual distinctions—perfective, durative, and experiential—each signaled by a verb suffix: 了 **le** *perfective*, 着/著 **zhe** *durative*, and 过/過 **guo** *experiential*. These suffixes, often referred to as *aspect particles*, directly follow the verb (or, for perfective 了 **le**, either the verb or verb + object phrase). Mandarin also signals *progressive aspect* with pre-verbal 在 **zài** or the phrase 正在 **zhèngzài**. Progressive aspect is discussed section 17.2.1.

17.1 Perfective aspect

The perfective aspect marker 了 **le** signals that an action is viewed as bounded and complete.

17.1.1 Perfective 了 *le* in simple sentences

17.1.1.1 The location of perfective 了 le in simple sentences

了 **le** follows the object of the verb if the object is an unmodified noun, such as the object in the verb phrases 吃饭/吃飯 **chī fàn** 'eat,' 说话/說話 **shuō huà** 'speak,' 写字/寫字 **xiě zì** 'write,' 看书/看書 **kàn shū** 'read,' 洗澡 **xǐ zǎo** 'bathe,' and 看电视/看電視 **kàn diànshì** 'watch television.'

> 我已经吃饭了。
> 我已經吃飯了。
> **Wǒ yǐjing chī fàn le.**
> I have already eaten.

> 他们昨天在宿舍看电视了。
> 他們昨天在宿舍看電視了。
> **Tāmen zuótiān zài sùshè kàn diànshì le.**
> They watched television in the dorm yesterday.

了 **le** directly follows the verb if the object of the verb is a modified noun. Modified nouns are nouns with any kind of modifier, including:

> *specifier + classifier + noun*
> 我看了那个电影。
> 我看了那個電影。
> **Wǒ kàn le nàge diànyǐng.**
> I saw that movie.

Perfective aspect　　　　　　　　　　　　　　　　　　　　**17.1**

    (specifier) + number + classifier + noun

    我看了(这)两本书。
    我看了(這)兩本書。
    Wǒ kàn le (zhè) liǎng běn shū.
    I read (these) two books.

    (number + classifier +) description phrase + noun

    我吃了(一碗)牛肉面。
    我吃了(一碗)牛肉麵。
    Wǒ chī le (yī wǎn) niúròu miàn.
    I ate (a bowl of) beef noodles.

    我借了他的车。
    我借了他的車。
    Wǒ jiè le tā de chē.
    I borrowed his car.

▶ 7, 8, 9

7.1.1.2 Stating that an action does not or has not happened

Perfective 了 **le** only occurs in affirmative sentences, never in negative sentences. This is because it signals that an action is viewed as a complete, bounded event. Actions that do not happen can never be seen as complete or bounded.

To indicate that an action *does not happen*, negate the action verb with 不 **bù**.

    他不吃早饭。
    他不吃早飯。
    Tā bù chī zǎofàn.
    He does not eat breakfast.

To indicate that an action *has not happened*, negate the ENTIRE action verb phrase with 没/沒 **méi**, or 没有/沒有 **méi yǒu**. If the action includes a prepositional phrase, 没/沒 **méi** precedes the prepositional phrase.

    他没吃早饭。
    他沒吃早飯。
    Tā méi chī zǎofàn.
    He did not eat breakfast.

    我没给他打电话。
    我沒給他打電話。
    Wǒ méi gěi tā dǎ diànhuà.
    I did not phone him.

▶ 13.3.2, 27.1.2, 37.3

7.1.1.3 Asking whether actions are complete

To ask whether an action is complete, use a 吗/嗎 question or a verb-not-verb yes–no question as follows.

    你吃饭了吗?
    你吃飯了嗎?
    Nǐ chī fàn le ma?
    Have you eaten?

    你吃饭了没有?
    你吃飯了沒有?
    Nǐ chī fàn le méi yǒu?
    Have you eaten?

ASPECT 17.1

你看完了那本书吗？
你看完了那本書嗎？
Nǐ kànwán le nǎ běn shū ma?
Have you finished reading that book?

你看完了那本书没有？
你看完了那本書沒有？
Nǐ kànwán le nǎ běn shū méi yǒu?
Have you finished reading that book?

▶ 37.4

17.1.2 Perfective 了 *le* in sequence sentences

Perfective aspect 了 **le** may be used in narrative sequence sentences that can be translated as 'after VP$_1$, VP$_2$.' 了 **le** can co-occur with other markers of sequence in these sentences: the adverb 就 **jiù** and the noun 以后/以後 **yǐhòu** 'after.'

我吃了饭以后就给你打电话。
我吃了飯以後就給你打電話。
Wǒ chī le fàn yǐhòu jiù gěi nǐ dǎ diànhuà.
After I eat I will phone you.

Sometimes, perfective 了 **le** is the only explicit marker of sequence in a sequence sentence.

你到了宿舍请给我打电话。
你到了宿舍請給我打電話。
Nǐ dào le sùshè qǐng gěi wǒ dǎ diànhuà.
(After) you arrive at the dorm, phone me.

Sequence can also be inferred without perfective 了 **le**.

我回家以后就给你打电话。
我回家以後就給你打電話。
Wǒ huí jiā yǐhòu jiù gěi nǐ dǎ diànhuà.
After I return home, I will phone you.

To indicate that the entire sequence is a complete bounded event, include perfective 了 **le** in the second clause, following the guidelines for the placement of perfective 了 **le** in section 17.1.1.1.

他吃了饭就走了。
他吃了飯就走了。
Tā chī le fàn jiù zǒu le.
After he ate, he left.

学生做完了功课就交给老师了。
學生做完了功課就交給老師了。
Xuésheng zuòwán le gōngkè jiù jiāo gěi lǎoshī le.
After the students finished their work, they handed it to the teacher.

These sentences have two instances of 了 **le**. The one that follows the first verb indicates sequence. The one that occurs in the second clause indicates that the sequence is a complete event.

▶ 42.2.3, 42.2.4

17.1.3 Perfective aspect vs. past tense

Aspect is different from tense. While aspect focuses on the internal or external properties of events, tense anchors events to time, marking them as past, present, or future. There is some

Durative aspect **17.2**

overlap between perfective aspect in Mandarin and past tense in English, especially in simple affirmative sentences. But there are many times when perfective aspect and past tense do not overlap. Here are the major differences between tense in English and perfective aspect in Mandarin.

- Perfective aspect is only a feature of action verbs. Stative verbs, adjectival verbs, and modal verbs cannot be followed by perfective 了 le. In English, tense is a feature of all verbs.
- Perfective aspect is only a feature of verbs in affirmative form. In English, tense is a feature of verbs in affirmative and negative sentences.
- In narrative sequence sentences, perfective aspect can occur in the first clause to signal sequence. In English, the verbs in sequence sentences are marked for relative tense, not sequence.

17.2 Durative aspect

Durative aspect focuses on the internal structure of a situation and signals that it is ongoing. Mandarin marks durative aspect in two ways, with the verb suffix 着/著 zhe, and with pre-verbal 在 zài or 正在 zhèngzài. Sentences with durative aspect often end with the final particle 呢 ne.

着/著 zhe and 在 zài/正在 zhèngzài focus on different types of duration. 着/著 zhe indicates that a verb describes a *continuous* situation. We will refer to it here as the *durative suffix*. 在 zài and 正在 zhèngzài focus on the progression of a situation over time. 正在 zhèngzài focuses on the progression of a situation that is happening *now*, and can often be translated as 'right now.' 在 zài and 正在 zhèngzài are sometimes referred to as *progressive markers*, and we will use that term here. Durative and progressive aspect markers can sometimes occur together to describe a situation, but there are times when only one or the other is appropriate.

▶ 17.2.3

17.2.1 Progressive markers

The progressive markers 在 zài and 正在 zhèngzài usually occur with open-ended action verbs, since actions can progress over time. 在 zài can also occur with certain adjectival verbs. See 17.2.3. 在 zài and 正在 zhèngzài immediately precede the verb phrase, including any prepositional phrase associated with the verb, and they can only occur in the main clause of a sentence.

subject 在 **zài** *verb phrase* (呢 **ne**)

他们在学习中文。
他們在學習中文。
Tāmen zài xuéxí Zhōngwén.
They are (in the middle of) studying Chinese.

他还在穿衣服呢。
他還在穿衣服呢。
Tā hái zài chuān yīfú ne.
He is still getting dressed. (He is still putting on clothes.)

我同屋在睡觉呢。
我同屋在睡覺呢。
Wǒ tóngwū zài shuì jiào ne.
My roommate is sleeping.

他们正在做作业呢。
他們正在做作業呢。
Tāmen zhèngzài zuò zuòyè ne.
They are doing homework right now.

ASPECT

她正在给妈妈打电话。
她正在給媽媽打電話。
Tā zhèngzài gěi māma dǎ diànhuà.
She's phoning her mom right now.

她在跟朋友唱歌。
她在跟朋友唱歌。
Tā zài gēn péngyou chàng gē.
She's singing with friends.

To negate sentences with progressive aspect, Beijing Mandarin speakers use 没/沒(有) **méi(yǒu)**:

他们没在学中文。
他們沒在學中文。
Tāmen méi zài xué Zhōngwén.
They are not studying Chinese.

Speakers from other Mandarin-speaking regions may also negate these sentences with 不 **bù**.

17.2.2 The durative aspect suffix 着/著 *zhe*

The durative aspect suffix 着/著 *zhe* emphasizes the durative nature of the action as an unchanging, ongoing situation.

着/著 **zhe** may occur as a suffix for open-ended action such as 吃 **chī** 'eat,' 说/說 **shuō** 'speak,' 睡 **shuì** 'sleep,' 洗 **xǐ** 'bath,' 看 **kàn** 'look at, read,' and 写/寫 **xiě** 'write.' When used with open-ended action verbs, it focuses on the ongoing nature of the action.

他们说着话呢。
他們說著話呢。
Tāmen shuō zhe huà ne.
They are (in the middle of the action of) speaking.

他们睡着觉呢。
他們睡著覺呢。
Tāmen shuì zhe jiào ne.
They are (in the middle of the action of) sleeping.

她哭着呢。
她哭著呢。
Tā kūzhe ne.
She's (in the middle of the action of) crying.

着/著 **zhe** can also be used as a suffix for change-of-state placement verbs such as 站 **zhàn** 'stand,' 坐 **zuò** 'sit,' 停 **tíng** 'stop,' 掛 **guà** 'hang,' 穿 **chuān** 'put on.' When used with change-of-state action verbs, the verb refers to the resulting state, and not to the action itself:

她穿着高跟鞋。
她穿著高跟鞋。
Tā chuānzhe gāogēnxié.
She is wearing (she is in) high-heeled shoes.

孩子都在屋子里坐着。
孩子都在屋子裡坐著。
Háizi dōu zài wūzi li zuòzhe.
The children are all sitting in the room.

墙上挂着一张画儿。
牆上掛著一張畫兒。
Qiángshàng guàzhe yī zhāng huàr.
There is a painting hanging on the wall.

17.2 Durative aspect

17.2.3 Duration vs. progression

Sometimes, either 着/著 **zhe** or 在 **zài** can occur with a verb. The choice of 着/著 **zhe** or 在 **zài** changes the sense of the verb in ways that illustrate the difference between the two types of durative aspect markers. Here are some examples.

穿着/穿著 *chuānzhe*

> 她穿着高跟鞋。
> 她穿著高跟鞋。
> **Tā chuānzhe gāogēnxié.**
> She is wearing (she is in) high-heels.

在穿 *zài chuān*

> 她在穿高跟鞋。
> **Tā zài chuān gāogēnxié.**
> She's putting on high heels.

The verb 穿 **chuān** means both 'put on (clothing on the torso or legs)' or 'wear (clothing on the torso or legs).' When suffixed with 着/著 **zhe**, which focuses on unchanging, durative situations, the verb must be interpreted as 'wear.' When preceded by the aspect marker 在 **zài**, which focuses on the progression of a situation, the verb must be interpreted as 'put on.'

Here are additional examples:

挂着/掛著 *guàzhe*

> 墙上挂着一张画儿。
> 牆上掛著一張畫兒。
> **Qiángshàng guàzhe yī zhāng huàr.**
> There is a painting hanging on the wall.

在挂 *zài guà*

> 爸爸在挂画儿呢。
> 爸爸在掛畫兒呢。
> **Bàba zài guà huàr ne.**
> Dad is hanging pictures.

挂 **guà** means 'hang (an object on a wall)' or 'be hanging (on a wall).' When someone is performing the action of hanging more than one picture, the action itself involves a progression that takes place over time. Preceding 挂 **guà** with the progressive aspect marker 在 **zài** emphasizes that ongoing progression. In contrast, once an item is hung on a wall, it remains hanging there, an unchanging state. Suffixing 挂 **guà** with 着/著 **zhe** emphasizes the ongoing, unchanging nature of the situation. The same contrast is illustrated in the following pair of sentences with 写/寫 **xiě** 'write.' When 写/寫 **xiě** is preceded by 在, the sentence emphasizes the ongoing progression of writing. When 写/寫 **xiě** is suffixed with 着/著 **zhe**, the sentence emphasizes the unchanging, ongoing nature of something that is written.

写着/寫著 *xiězhe*

> 门上写着你的名字。
> 門上寫著你的名字。
> **Ménshang xiězhe nǐ de míngzi.**
> Your name is written on the door.

在写/在寫 *zài xiě*

> 弟弟在写汉字。
> 弟弟在寫漢字。
> **Dìdi zài xiě Hàn zì.**
> Younger brother is writing Chinese characters.

ASPECT

Here are two examples, one with an action verb, one with an adjectival verb, that include both the durative suffix 着/著 **zhe** and the progressive marker 在 **zài**. In this first example with the open-ended action verb 开/開 **kāi** 'drive,' the suffix 着/著 **zhe** is acceptable with or without the second clause 不能打电话/不能打電話 **bù néng dǎ diànhuà** '(one) can't make a phone call.' But the use of 在 **zài** is only acceptable when the second clause occurs.

> 我在开着车呢，不能打电话。
> 我在開著車呢，不能打電話。
> **Wǒ zài kāizhe chē ne, bù néng dǎ diànhuà.**
> I am driving right now and can't make a phone call.

With or without the second clause, 开/開 **kāi** 'drive,' has duration. But only with the inclusion of the second clause does the situation involve a progression, in this case from driving to driving while making a phone call.

The following sentence, with the adjectival verb 热/熱 **rè** 'be hot,' is acceptable with or without 在 **zài**. Without 在 **zài** it means that the soup is in the state of being hot. With the inclusion of 在 **zài** the sentence means that the soup is 'becoming hot' or is 'being heated.' In other words, 在 **zài** adds a sense of progression to the action.

> 汤在热着呢。
> 湯在熱著呢。
> **Tāng zài rèzhe ne.**
> The soup is being heated.

17.2.4 Duration of a background event

The durative aspect marker 着/著 **zhe** is commonly used in complex sentences to indicate that an action is ongoing in the background while some other action occurs. This kind of sentence takes the following form.

> *subject verb₁-着/著 zhe (object₁), verb₂ (object₂)*

> 她听着音乐做作业。
> 她聽著音樂做作業。
> **Tā tīngzhe yīnyuè zuò zuòyè.**
> She is doing homework while listening to music. (background action: listening to music)

> 他们走着路谈话。
> 他們走著路談話。
> **Tāmen zǒuzhe lù tán huà.**
> They're chatting while walking. (background action: walking)

> 她坐着睡觉。
> 她坐著睡覺。
> **Tā zuòzhe shuì jiào.**
> She's sleeping sitting down. (background action: sitting)

> 别吃着东西开车。
> 別吃著東西開車。
> **Bié chīzhe dōngxi kāi chē.**
> Don't eat while you are driving. (background action: eating)

Progressive aspect cannot be used in sentences like these.

▶ 10, 13, 38, 43.2, 43.3

17.3 Experiential aspect

Experiential aspect focuses on an action that has occurred in the past and signals that it is relevant to the current discourse. Mandarin marks experiential aspect with the verb suffix 过/過 **guo**. 过/過 **guo** immediately follows the verb and typically occurs in neutral tone. It can only be used with action verbs, and conveys the meaning that the subject has done the action before.

> 我看过那个电影。
> 我看過那個電影。
> **Wǒ kànguo nàge diànyǐng.**
> I have seen that movie before.

> 我来过这里。
> 我來過這裏。
> **Wǒ láiguo zhèli.**
> I have been here before.

The experiential suffix 过/過 **guo** is appropriate in the following circumstances:

- when talking about actions that the subject does not perform on a regular basis:

    > 我去过中国。
    > 我去過中國。
    > **Wǒ qùguo Zhōngguó.**
    > I've been to China before. (I have had the experience of going to China.)

- when talking about actions that happened in the remote past:

    > 我小的时候听过那个故事。
    > 我小的時候聽過那個故事。
    > **Wǒ xiǎo de shíhou tīngguo nàge gùshi.**
    > When I was small (young), I heard that story.

- when talking about actions that are repeatable:

    > 我登过万里长城。
    > 我登過萬里長城。
    > **Wǒ dēngguo Wànlǐ Chángchéng.**
    > I climbed the Great Wall.

Actions that are not repeatable cannot be suffixed with 过/過 **guo**.

Say this	*Do not say this*
她高中毕业了。	*她高中毕业过。
她高中畢業了。	她高中畢業過。
Tā gāozhōng bìyè le.	**Tā gāozhōng bìyè guo.**
She graduated high school.	

A verb can be suffixed with both experiential 过/過 **guo** and perfective 了 **le**. When it is, 过/過 **guo** precedes 了 **le**. The meaning conveyed is that the subject has experienced the action of the verb and that the entire event is viewed in its entirety as closed and bounded.

> 那部电影我已经看过了，不要再看了。
> 那部電影我已經看過了，不要再看了。
> **Nà bù diànyǐng wǒ yǐjing kànguo le, bù yào zài kàn le.**
> I've already seen that movie before. I don't want to see it again.

ASPECT

The negation of verb-过/過 **guo** is 没/沒(有) **méi(yǒu)** + verb- 过/過 **guo**.

我没看过那部电影。
我沒看過那部電影。
Wǒ méi kànguo nà bù diànyǐng.
I have not seen that movie before.

我没来过这里。
我沒來過這裏。
Wǒ méi láiguo zhèli.
I have not been here before.

我没登过万里长城。
我沒登過萬里長城。
Wǒ méi dēngguo Wànlǐ Chángchéng.
I have not climbed the Great Wall before.

To ask whether the subject has performed an action before, ask a 吗/嗎 question or a verb-not-verb question as follows:

*subject verb-*过/過 *guo object* 吗/嗎 *ma?*

or

*subject verb-*过/過 *guo object* 没有/沒有 *méi yǒu?*

你看过那个电影吗？ 你看過那個電影嗎？ **Nǐ kànguo nàge diànyǐng ma?** Have you seen that movie?	你看过那个电影没有？ 你看過那個電影沒有？ **Nǐ kànguo nàge diànyǐng méi yǒu?** Have you seen that movie?
你登过万里长城吗？ 你登過萬里長城嗎？ **Nǐ dēngguo Wànlǐ Chángchéng ma?** Have you climbed the Great Wall?	你登过万里长城没有？ 你登過萬里長城沒有？ **Nǐ dēngguo Wànlǐ Chángchéng méi yǒu?** Have you climbed the Great Wall?

17.4 A comparison of aspectual distinctions

Aspectual distinctions are part of a system, so they exist in opposition to each other. Perfective aspect looks at the boundaries of events that occur in a time relevant to the present. Durative aspect looks at an action from the inside, focusing on the ongoing nature of the action. Experiential aspect, like perfective aspect, signals bounded events, but only events whose completion took place at a time remote from, or separated from, the present.

18

Resultative verbs

18.1 Structure of resultative verbs

Resultative verbs consist of an action verb 'head' and a resultative suffix:

action verb + resultative suffix

For example, the action verb 听/聽 **tīng** 'listen' + the resultative suffix 见/見 **jiàn** 'perceive' form the resultative verb 听见/聽見 **tīngjiàn** 'hear.' 'Listen' and 'hear' are related in meaning. 'Listen' is an open-ended action. 'Hear' is the perception of sounds that results from listening. English typically uses two different verbs to express actions and their results or conclusions. Mandarin uses the same verb for both, adding a resultative suffix to the action to indicate result or conclusion.

Aspect markers occur after the resultative suffix and never between the action verb head and the suffix. For example, to indicate that an action occurred and reached a particular conclusion or result, add perfective 了 **le** to the end of the resultative verb, and not between the action verb and the resultative suffix.

Say this	*Not this*
他写完了功课。 他寫完了功課。 **Tā xiěwánle gōngkè.** He finished doing (writing) his homework.	*他写了完功课。 他寫了完功課。 **Tā xiělewán gōngkè.**

▶ 13, 17

Similarly, when indicating that an action did not reach a particular result or conclusion, the resultative verb as a whole is negated with 没/沒 **méi** 'not.' 没/沒 **méi** can only occur at the beginning of a resultative verb, and may never occur between the action verb and resultative suffix.

Say this	*Not this*
我从来没写错过那个字。 我從來沒寫錯過那個字。 **Wǒ cónglái méi xiěcuòguo nàge zì.** I have never written that character incorrectly.	*我从来写没错过那个字。 我從來寫沒錯過那個字。 **Wǒ cónglái xiě méi cuòguo nàge zì.**

18.2 Action verb heads

The action verb head may be either an open-ended action verb or a change-of-state action verb.

Open-ended action verbs refer to actions that have duration and can be performed for a period of time. They include 说/說 **shuō** 'speak,' 写/寫 **xiě** 'write,' 吃 **chī** 'eat,' 听/聽 **tīng** 'listen,' 唱 **chàng** 'sing,' 睡 **shuì** 'sleep,' and many other verbs. Their meanings do not entail the completion or result of the action. For example, the open-ended action verb 找 **zhǎo** means

RESULTATIVE VERBS

'look for' something, not 'find' something, the open-ended action verb 买/買 **mǎi** means 'shop for' things, not 'buy' things, and the open-ended action verb 听/聽 **tīng** means 'listen to' something, not 'hear' something.

Change-of-state verbs refer to events in which the action of the verb results in a change. They include 站 **zhàn** 'stand up,' 坐 **zuò** 'sit down,' 放 **fàng** 'put or place' (something somewhere), 挂/掛 **guà** 'hang' (something up), and many other verbs.

▶ 13.5, 13.6

18.3 Resultative suffixes

Resultative suffixes contribute one of the following meanings to the resultative verb.

- They indicate the result of the action. These suffixes are often called 'complements of result' or 'result complements.'
  For example: 写/寫 **xiě** 'write' 写错/寫錯 **xiěcuò** 'write incorrectly'
- They indicate the conclusion of the action.
  For example: 写/寫 **xiě** 'write' 写完/寫完 **xiěwán** 'finish writing'

Here are common resultative endings, followed by examples of resultative verbs in which the endings occur. The list of resultative verbs is not exhaustive. Action verbs can freely combine with resultative suffixes as long as the action can be concluded in the way that the suffix indicates.

Resultative verbs with idiomatic meanings will be discussed at the end of this chapter.

NOTE
A third type of suffix, directional suffixes (sometimes called directional complements), also serve as suffixes on action verbs. Action verb + directional suffixes form directional verbs. The properties of directional verbs are very similar to those of resultative verbs.

▶ 19

18.3.1 Suffixes that indicate result: result complements

-到 **dào** 'reach, succeed, attain'

This suffix follows open-ended action verbs. It indicates that the subject has obtained or reached the object as a result of the action. (Similar in meaning to, but more commonly used than, the resultative suffix -着/著 **zháo**.)

买到/買到 **mǎidào** 'buy'
找到 **zhǎodào** 'find'
想到 **xiǎngdào** 'think of'
看到 **kàndào** 'see, locate something with one's eyes'
梦到/夢到 **mèngdào** 'dream of'

-着/著 **zháo** 'reach, succeed, attain'

This suffix follows open-ended action verbs. It indicates that the subject has obtained or reached the object as a result of the action. (*See also* the resultative suffix -到 **dào**.)

猜着/猜著 **cāizháo** 'guess correctly'
买着/買著 **mǎizháo** 'succeed in buying'
找着/找著 **zhǎozháo** 'find, succeed in locating'

-见/見 **jiàn** 'perceive'

This suffix follows open-ended action verbs that refer to perception. It indicates that the subject has successfully perceived some object by hearing, sight, or smell.

Resultative suffixes 18.3

  听见/聽見 **tīngjiàn** 'hear'
  看见/看見 **kànjiàn** 'see'
  闻见/聞見 **wénjiàn** 'smell, perceive by smelling'
  遇见/遇見 **yùjiàn** 'encounter'
  碰见/碰見 **pèngjiàn** 'run into, encounter, come across'

-懂 *dǒng* 'understand'

This suffix follows open-ended action verbs that refer to actions that provide information. It indicates that the subject understands the object as a result of performing the action.

  看懂 **kàndǒng** 'read and understand'
  听懂/聽懂 **tīngdǒng** 'listen and understand'

-会/會 *huì* 'master a skill'

This suffix follows open-ended action verbs, most commonly the verb 学/學 **xué** 'study.' It indicates that the subject has mastered the object as a result of performing the action.

  学会/學會 **xuéhuì** 'study to the point of mastery of some skill or subject matter'

-饱/飽 *bǎo* 'full'

This suffix follows open-ended action verbs, most commonly the verb 吃 **chī** 'eat.' It indicates that the subject has eaten until full.

  吃饱/吃飽 **chībǎo** 'eat to the point of being full'

-对/對 *duì* 'correct'

This suffix follows open-ended action verbs. It indicates that the subject has performed the action correctly.

  說对/說對 **shuōduì** 'speak correctly'
  写对/寫對 **xiěduì** 'write correctly'
  猜对/猜對 **cāiduì** 'guess correctly'
  做对/做對 **zuòduì** 'do correctly'

-错/錯 *cuò* 'incorrect, wrong'

This suffix follows open-ended action verbs. It indicates that the subject has performed the action incorrectly.

  说错/說錯 **shuōcuò** 'say incorrectly'
  写错/寫錯 **xiěcuò** 'write incorrectly'
  猜错/猜錯 **cāicuò** 'guess incorrectly'
  做错/做錯 **zuocuò** 'do incorrectly'

-清楚 *qīngchu* 'clearly'

This suffix follows open-ended action verbs that refer to thinking or communicating. It indicates that the action was performed clearly.

  看清楚 **kànqīngchu** 'see clearly'
  听清楚/聽清楚 **tīngqīngchu** 'listen clearly' (listen and be clear about the meaning)
  说清楚/說清楚 **shuōqīngchu** 'speak clearly'
  想清楚 **xiǎngqīngchu** 'think clearly'
  写清楚/寫清楚 **xiěqīngchu** 'write clearly'

-干净/乾淨 *gānjing* 'clean'

This suffix follows open-ended action verbs to do with cleaning. It indicates that the action is performed until the object is clean.

  洗干淨/洗乾淨 **xǐgānjing** 'wash (something) clean'
  擦干净/擦乾淨 **cāgānjing** 'wipe (something) clean'

RESULTATIVE VERBS

-开/開 **kāi** *'open, separate, (move) away'*

This suffix follows a limited number of action verbs whose meanings convey opening up or separation. The most common of these are presented here.

> 打开/打開 **dǎkāi** 'open'
> 开开/開開 **kāikāi** 'open'
> 拿开/拿開 **nákāi** 'take away'
> 推开/推開 **tuīkāi** 'push open/away'
> 离开/離開 **líkāi** 'separate'

18.3.2 Suffixes that indicate conclusion

-完 **wán** *'finish, complete, end'*

This suffix follows open-ended action verbs. It indicates that the subject has concluded performing the action.

> 吃完 **chīwán** 'finish eating'
> 唱完 **chàngwán** 'finish singing'
> 看完 **kànwán** 'finish reading'
> 写完/寫完 **xiěwán** 'finish writing'
> 用完 **yòngwán** 'use up'
> 做完 **zuòwán** 'finish doing'

-好 **hǎo** *'satisfaction, completion'*

This suffix follows open-ended action verbs. It indicates that the subject has performed the action and reached a successful conclusion.

> 做好 **zuòhǎo** 'do something and reach the desired conclusion'
> 预备好/預備好 **yùbèihǎo** 'finish satisfactory preparations'
> 修理好 **xiūlǐhǎo** 'fix successfully'
> 商量好 **shāngliánghǎo** 'reach an agreement'

-住 **zhù** *'hold on, constrain'*

This suffix follows change-of-state action verbs that have resulting states.

> 站住 **zhànzhù** 'stand still'
> 停住 **tíngzhù** 'stop'
> 抓住 **zhuāzhù** 'grab onto, catch'
> 管住 **guǎnzhù** 'control'
> 记住/記住 **jìzhù** 'remember'
> 拿住 **názhù** 'hold on'

-掉 **diào** *'drop, fall, lose'*

This suffix follows action verbs and change-of-state verbs that have no resulting state, that is, verbs for which, once the action is over, there is nothing left. It reinforces the completion and finality of the action.

> 忘掉 **wàngdiào** 'forget'
> 死掉 **sǐdiào** 'die'
> 甩掉 **shuǎidiào** 'throw off, get rid of'
> 坏掉/壞掉 **huàidiào** 'ruin'
> 卖掉/賣掉 **màidiào** 'sell out'
> 扔掉 **rēngdiào** 'throw away'

18.4 Resultative verbs in affirmative and negative sentences

In affirmative sentences, resultative verbs indicate that an action concludes in a particular way. When talking about actions that have already concluded, affirmative sentences with resultative verbs include the perfective aspect suffix 了 **le**.

> 我找到了我的手机。
> 我找到了我的手機。
> **Wǒ zhǎodàole wǒ de shǒujī.**
> I found my cellphone.

> 我已经用完了父母给我的钱。
> 我已經用完了父母給我的錢。
> **Wǒ yǐjing yòngwánle fùmǔ gěi wǒ de qián.**
> I have already spent the money that my parents gave to me.

> 你猜对了；我有三块钱。
> 你猜對了；我有三塊錢。
> **Nǐ cāiduìle; wǒ yǒu sān kuài qián.**
> You guessed it right; I have three dollars.

> 我们商量好了，今天晚上出去吃饭。
> 我們商量好了，今天晚上出去吃飯。
> **Wǒmen shāngliānghǎole, jīntiān wǎnshang chūqu chī fàn.**
> We've agreed, we're going out to eat tonight.

The object of the resultative verb may be topicalized.

> 这个字，你又写错了。
> 這個字，你又寫錯了。
> **Zhèige zì, nǐ yòu xiěcuòle.**
> You wrote this character wrong again.

Resultative verbs can also be used to talk about concluding an action in the future. In situations like these, the perfective aspect marker does not occur.

> 我明天能把这本书看完。
> 我明天能把這本書看完。
> **Wǒ míngtiān néng bǎ zhè běn shū kànwán.**
> I can finish reading this book tomorrow.

When a resultative verb is used in a negated sentence, the sentence conveys the information that some action was not or has not been completed. Negation is always 没/沒 **méi**, and it occurs right before the resultative verb.

> 今天的功课，我还没做完。
> 今天的功課，我還沒做完。
> **Jīntiān de gōngkè, wǒ hái méi zuòwán.**
> Today's homework, I haven't yet finished doing it.

> 还没预备好呢。
> 還沒預備好呢。
> **Hái méi yùbèihǎo ne.**
> I haven't finished preparing.

Perfective 了 **le** never occurs in negated sentences, but when talking about some action that has never occurred before, the experiential aspect marker 过/過 **guò** may occur right after the resultative verb.

> 她从来没做错过事。
> 她從來沒做錯過事。
> **Tā cónglái méi zuòcuòguo shì.**
> She's never done anything wrong before.

RESULTATIVE VERBS

18.5 Asking yes–no questions with resultative verbs

To ask a yes–no question with 吗/嗎 **ma**, simply end your question with 吗/嗎 **ma**.

我刚才说的话你听见了吗?
我剛才說的話你聽見了嗎?
Wǒ gāngcái shuō de huà nǐ tīngjiànle ma?
Did you hear what I just said?

You can also ask yes–no questions using one of the following *verb-not-verb* structures. Native speakers differ in their preferences for these forms. When using the verb + 了 **le** + 没有/沒有 **méi yǒu** form, the object is often omitted. 了 **le** is not used in the 有没有/有沒有 **yǒu méi yǒu** form.

(object) (subject) resultative verb 了 *le* 没有/沒有 *méi yǒu*

今天的功课你做完了没有?
今天的功課你做完了沒有?
Jīntiān de gōngkè nǐ zuòwánle méi yǒu?
Did you finish today's homework?

你吃饱了没有?
你吃飽了沒有?
Nǐ chībǎole méi yǒu?
Are you full? (Have you eaten until you are full?)

你的手机找到了没有?
你的手機找到了沒有?
Nǐ de shǒujī zhǎodàole méi yǒu?
Have you found your cellphone?

(subject) resultative verb 了 *le object* 没有/沒有 *méi yǒu*

你做完了今天的功课没有?
你做完了今天的功課沒有?
Nǐ zuòwánle jīntiān de gōngkè méi yǒu?
Have you finished today's homework?

(object) (subject) 有没有/有沒有 *yǒu méi yǒu resultative verb*

今天的功课你有没有做完?
今天的功課你有沒有做完?
Jīntiān de gōngkè nǐ yǒu méi yǒu zuòwán?
Have you finished today's homework?

你的手机有没有找到?
你的手機有沒有找到?
Nǐ de shǒujī yǒu méi yǒu zhǎodào?
Have you found your cellphone?

(subject) 有没有/有沒有 *yǒu méi yǒu resultative verb (object)*

你有没有做完今天的功课?
你有沒有做完今天的功課?
Nǐ yǒu méi yǒu zuòwán jīntiān de gōngkè?
Have you finished today's homework?

你有没有找到你的手机?
你有沒有找到你的手機?
Nǐ yǒu méiyǒu zhǎodào nǐ de shǒujī?
Have you found your cellphone?

▶ 32.1

The potential form of resultative verbs

18.6 The potential form of resultative verbs

The potential form of resultative verbs indicates that the subject is able to, or unable to, reach the desired result or conclusion. The potential is created by adding the potential infixes 得 **de** or 不 **bu** between the action verb head and the resultative suffix, as follows.

Affirmative potential form

> action verb + 得 *de* + resultative suffix
> do the action and be able to reach the conclusion or result

> 找得到 **zhǎodedào** 'able to find'
> 做得完 **zuòdewán** 'able to finish doing'
> 看得懂 **kàndedǒng** 'read and be able to understand'

Negative potential form

> action verb + 不 *bu* + resultative suffix
> do the action but be unable to reach the conclusion or result

> 找不到 **zhǎobudào** 'unable to find'
> 做不完 **zuòbuwán** 'unable to finish doing'
> 看不懂 **kànbudǒng** 'read but be unable to understand'

Aside from the potential infixes 得 **de** and 不 **bu**, nothing occurs between the action verb head and the resultative suffix.

Here are sentences with resultative verbs in the affirmative and negative potential form. Notice that the aspectual suffixes 了 **le** and 过/過 **guo** never occur when the potential form of a resultative verb is used.

> 你听得见他说的话吗?
> 你聽得見他說的話嗎?
> **Nǐ tīngdejian tā shuō de huà ma?**
> Can you hear what he is saying?

> 我想到了一个你想不到的办法。
> 我想到了一個你想不到的辦法。
> **Wǒ xiǎngdàole yí gè nǐ xiǎngbúdào de bànfa.**
> I thought of a method that you could not possibly imagine.

> 我的报告今天写不完。
> 我的報告今天寫不完。
> **Wǒ de bàogào jīntiān xiěbuwán.**
> I can't finish my paper today.

> 这个工作三天做不好。
> 這個工作三天做不好。
> **Zhèige gōngzuò sān tiān zuòbuhǎo.**
> I cannot finish this job (and do a good job on it) within three days.

▶ 32.2

18.6.1 Asking and answering yes–no questions in the potential form

To ask a yes–no question with 吗/嗎 **ma** involving a resultative verb in potential form, simply follow the statement with 吗/嗎 **ma**:

> 你听得懂中国话吗?
> 你聽得懂中國話嗎?
> **Nǐ tīngdedǒng Zhōngguóhuà ma?**
> Can you understand Chinese?

RESULTATIVE VERBS

18.6

那个山上有一个人，你看得见吗？
那個山上有一個人，你看得見嗎？
Nèige shānshàng yǒu yī gè rén, nǐ kàndejiàn ma?
There is a person on that mountain. Can you see him?

那个孩子很小，离得开母亲吗？
那個孩子很小，離得開母親嗎？
Nèige háizi hěn xiǎo, lídekāi mǔqin ma?
That child is very young. Can he be separated from his mother?

To ask a verb-not-verb yes–no question involving a resultative verb in potential form, state the affirmative potential form of the resultative verb followed by the negative potential form:

你听得见听不见他说的话？
你聽得見聽不見他說的話？
Nǐ tīngdejian tīngbujiàn tā shuō de huà?
Are you able or not able to hear what he said?

老师说的话，你记得住记不住？
老師說的話，你記得住記不住？
Lǎoshi shuō de huà, nǐ jìdezhù jìbuzhù?
Can you remember what the teacher said?

▶ 32.4.3

18.6.2 Resultative suffixes that only occur in the potential form

The following resultative suffixes only occur in the potential form.

-得了 **deliǎo** 'able to, able to finish the action'/-不了 **buliǎo** 'unable to, unable to finish the action.' These are often called the *potential suffixes*. They can be used with any activity verb. Here are examples.

你做了这么多菜，我怎么吃得了？
你做了這麼多菜，我怎麼吃得了？
Nǐ zuòle zhème duō cài, wǒ zěnme chīdeliǎo?
You made so much food. How am I going to finish it?

我牙疼，现在吃不了东西。
我牙疼，現在吃不了東西。
Wǒ yá téng, xiànzài chībuliǎo dōngxi.
My tooth aches. I can't eat anything right now.

他的坏习惯永远也改不了了。
他的壞習慣永遠也改不了了。
Tā de huài xíguàn yǒngyuǎn yě gǎibuliǎo le.
He will never be able to change his bad habits.

-得起 **deqǐ** 'afford to'/-不起 **buqǐ** 'unable to afford to.' These suffixes can be used with any activity verb that involves paying for something. Here are examples.

Q: 你买得起买不起那个汽车？
   你買得起買不起那個汽車？
   Nǐ mǎideqǐ mǎibuqǐ nèige qìchē?
   Can you afford to buy that car?

A: 我买不起，可是我爸爸买得起。
   我買不起，可是我爸爸買得起。
   Wǒ mǎibuqǐ, kěshi wǒ bàba mǎideqǐ.
   I cannot afford it, but my father can.

The potential form of resultative verbs | 18.6

北京的房子太贵了。一般人住不起了。
北京的房子太貴了。一般人住不起了。
Běijīng de fángzi tài guì le. Yībānrén zhùbuqǐ le.
Beijing houses have become too expensive. Ordinary people can't afford to live there anymore.

我们吃不起龙虾。
我們吃不起龍蝦。
Wǒmen chībuqǐ lóngxiā.
We can't afford to eat lobster.

-得下 **dexià** 'have room to accommodate (the object of the verb)'/-不下 **buxià** 'not have room to accommodate (the object of the verb)'

你吃得下这么多的菜吗?
你吃得下這麼多的菜嗎?
Nǐ chīdexià zhème duō de cài ma?
Can you eat so much food?

这间屋子住得下多少人?
這間屋子住得下多少人?
Zhè jiān wūzi zhùdexià duōshǎo rén?
How many people can this room accommodate?

这辆车坐得下九个人。
這輛車坐得下九個人。
Zhè liàng chē zuòdexià jiǔ gè rén.
This car can seat nine people.

这个箱子太小,放不下这件大衣。
這個箱子太小,放不下這件大衣。
Zhège xiāngzi tài xiǎo, fàngbùxià zhè jiàn dàyī.
This suitcase is too small; it cannot hold this overcoat.

-得过/過 **deguò** 'able to surpass (in doing the action of the verb)'/-不过/過 **buguò** 'unable to surpass (in doing the action of the verb).' This suffix can be used with any activity where it can be said that someone can outdo someone else. Here are examples.

你比得过他吗?
你比得過他嗎?
Nǐ bǐdeguò tā ma?
Can you out-do him?

喝酒,我比不过他。他很能喝酒。
喝酒,我比不過他。他很能喝酒。
Hē jiǔ, wǒ bǐbuguò tā. Tā hěn néng hē jiǔ.
I cannot out-do him when it comes to drinking. He can drink a lot.

-得及 **dejí** 'in time to do'/-不及 **bují** 'too late to do.' This suffix most commonly occurs with the verb 来/來 **lái** 'come.'

A: 飞机就要起飞了,再不走就来不及了。
飛機就要起飛了,再不走就來不及了。
Fēijī jiù yào qǐfēi le, zài bù zǒu jiù láibùjí le.
The airplane is going to take off. It will be too late if we don't leave now.

B: 别着急,还有十分钟,来得及。
別著急,還有十分鐘,來得及。
Bié zháojí, hái yǒu shí fēnzhōng, láidejí.
Don't worry, we still have ten minutes. We can make it.

RESULTATIVE VERBS

-不定 **budìng**. This suffix only occurs in the negative potential form. It is most commonly used as a suffix for the verb 说/說 **shuō** 'say.' 说不定 **shuōbudìng** means 'unable to say for sure, perhaps, possibly.'

> 太晚了，说不定他今天不会来了。
> 太晚了，說不定他今天不會來了。
> **Tài wǎnle, shuōbudìng tā jīntiān bù huì lái le.**
> It's too late, perhaps he won't come today.

-得动/動 **dedòng** 'able to move'/-不动/動 **budòng** 'unable to move'

> 他的行李太重了，一个人拿不动。
> 他的行李太重了，一個人拿不動。
> **Tā de xíngli tài zhòng le, yīge rén nábudòng.**
> His suitcase is too heavy. One person can't lift it all by himself.

> 这个汽车这么重，他推得动推不动？
> 這個汽車這麼重，他推得動推不動？
> **Zhège qìchē zhème zhòng, tā tuīdedòng tuībudòng?**
> This car is so heavy. Can he move it (by pushing)?

> 这块牛肉太老了，我咬不动。
> 這塊牛肉太老了，我咬不動。
> **Zhèi kuài niúròu tài lǎo le, wǒ yǎobudòng.**
> This piece of beef is too tough. I cannot chew it.

18.7 Resultative suffixes with figurative or idiomatic meaning

Some resultative suffixes have figurative or idiomatic meanings. Here are some examples. Notice that sentences with these resultative suffixes typically end with 了 **le**.

-死 **sǐ** 'extremely, terribly, to death'

> 忙死 **mángsǐ** 'busy to death'
> 貴死 **guìsǐ** 'so expensive it would put one in the grave'
> 累死 **lèisǐ** 'dead tired'
> 饿死/餓死 **èsǐ** 'starving to death'
> 笑死 **xiàosǐ** 'die laughing'
> 穷死/窮死 **qióngsǐ** 'dead broke'
> 急死 **jísǐ** 'worry to death'
> 吓死/嚇死 **xiàsǐ** 'frightened to death, scared to death'

> 这几天把我忙死了。
> 這幾天把我忙死了。
> **Zhèi jǐ tiān bǎ wǒ mángsǐ le.**
> I've been worked to death these past few days.

> 那个电影真可笑，把我笑死了。
> 那個電影真可笑，把我笑死了。
> **Nàge diànyǐng zhēn kěxiào, bǎ wǒ xiàosǐ le.**
> That movie was very funny. I could have died laughing.

-坏/壞 **huài** 'bad, badly, terribly.' When 坏/壞 **huài** is used as a resultative suffix, the sentence typically ends with 了 **le**.

> 吓坏/嚇壞 **xiàhuài** 'terrified'
> 累坏/壞 **lèihuài** 'dog-tired'
> 饿坏/餓壞 **èhuài** 'starving'
> 乐坏/樂壞 **lèhuài** 'wild with joy'
> 气坏/氣壞 **qìhuài** 'very angry'

18.7 Resultative suffixes with figurative or idiomatic meaning

今天我做了这么多事，真把我累坏了。
今天我做了這麼多事，真把我累壞了。
Jīntiān wǒ zuò le zhème duō shì, zhēn bǎ wǒ lèihuài le.
I did so much work today that it has made me terribly tired.

他今天考试得了100分，把他乐坏了。
他今天考試得了100分，把他樂壞了。
Tā jīntiān kǎoshì dé le 100 fēn, bǎ tā lèhuài le.
He got 100 percent on his test today; it made him so happy.

-扁 **biǎn** 'flat'

压扁/壓扁 **yābiǎn** 'flattened'
挤扁/擠扁 **jǐbiǎn** 'squeezed flat'

公共汽车上那么多人快要把我挤扁了。
公共汽車上那麼多人快要把我擠扁了。
Gōnggòng qìchē shàng nàme duō rén kuài yào bǎ wǒ jǐbiǎn le.
There were so many people on the bus that I was almost squished flat.

-疯/瘋 **fēng** 'crazy, mad'

气疯/氣瘋 **qìfēng** 'crazed with rage'
穷疯/窮瘋 **qióngfēng** 'crazed with poverty'
想疯/想瘋 **xiǎngfēng** 'at wit's end'

这个人真穷疯了，什么东西都要。
這個人真窮瘋了，甚麼東西都要。
Zhège rén zhēn qióngfēng le, shénme dōngxi dōu yào.
This person is crazed with poverty and will take anything.

In addition, the suffixes -得起 **deqǐ** and -不起 **buqǐ** are used idiomatically in the following verbs.

看得起 **kàndeqǐ** 'have a good opinion of; think highly of'
看不起 **kànbuqǐ** 'look down upon, despise'
对得起/對得起 **duìdeqǐ** 'treat someone fairly, do not let someone down'
对不起/對不起 **duìbuqǐ** 'disappoint someone, cause someone to be embarrassed or lose face.' (Also used as a fixed expression to express apologies for disappointing someone or causing them to lose face.)

别人都看不起他。
Biéren dōu kànbuqǐ tā.
Everyone looks down on him.

你不用功念书，对得起你父母吗？
你不用功念書，對得起你父母嗎？
Nǐ bù yònggōng niàn shū, duìdeqǐ nǐ fùmǔ ma?
How can you face your parents if you don't work hard at your studies?

你帮他很多忙，你对得起他了。
你幫他很多忙，你對得起他了。
Nǐ bāng tā hěn duō máng, Nǐ duìdeqǐ tā le.
You've helped him a lot. You've really treated him fairly.

不要对不起你的父母。
不要對不起你的父母。
Bù yào duìbuqǐ nǐ de fùmǔ.
Don't embarrass your parents.

不要做对不起朋友的事。
不要做對不起朋友的事。
Bù yào zuò duìbuqǐ péngyou de shì.
Don't do things that would make you not want to face your friends.

19

Directional verbs

19.1 Structure of directional verbs

Directional verbs consist of an action verb that involves motion (a motion verb) and a directional suffix.

motion verb + directional suffix

For example, the motion verb 坐 **zuò** 'sit' + the directional suffix 下 **xià** 'down' form the resultative verb 坐下 **zuòxià** 'sit down.'

Directional suffixes are also sometimes referred to as *directional complements*.

▶ 48.8

19.2 Motion verbs

Motion verbs referring to actions in which the subject moves include:

走 **zǒu** 'walk'	躺 **tǎng** 'lie (down)'
跑 **pǎo** 'run'	趴 **pā** 'lie on one's stomach'
跳 **tiào** 'jump'	跪 **guì** 'kneel'
飞/飛 **fēi** 'fly'	进/進 **jìn** 'enter'
爬 **pá** 'climb, crawl'	出 **chū** 'go out'
滚 **gǔn** 'roll'	起 **qǐ** 'rise'
站 **zhàn** 'stand'	回 **huí** 'return'
坐 **zuò** 'sit'	过/過 **guò** 'go across'

Motion verbs referring to actions in which the object moves include:

拿 **ná** 'take'	带/帶 **dài** 'carry'
送 **sòng** 'send (as a gift)'	搬 **bān** 'move'
放 **fàng** 'put'	挂/掛 **guà** 'hang'
寄 **jì** 'send (by mail)'	发/發 **fā** 'send (an email)'
开/開 **kāi** 'drive, open'	关/關 **guān** 'close'
穿 **chuān** 'put on (clothing, on the torso)'	戴 **dài** 'put on (clothing or accessories such as earrings, glasses, hearing aids, etc., on head, neck, arms, or hands)'

Directional suffixes

19.3 Directional suffixes

Directional suffixes are either simple or complex.

19.3.1 Simple directional suffixes

Simple directional suffixes consist of a single syllable that indicates the direction of motion. Here is a list of simple directional suffixes followed by directional verbs in which they occur. Note that the suffix is typically pronounced in neutral tone.

-下 *xià* 'down'

    坐下 **zuòxià** 'sit down'
    躺下 **tǎngxià** 'lie down'
    趴下 **pāxià** 'lie down on one's stomach'
    跪下 **guìxià** 'kneel; go down on one's knees'
    放下 **fàngxià** 'put down'

-上 *shàng* 'up, upward, better'

    关上/關上 **guānshàng** 'close (doors, windows, lights)'
    挂上/掛上 **guàshàng** 'hang up (pictures, flowers)'
    穿上 **chuānshàng** 'put on (clothes, shoes)'
    戴上 **dàishàng** 'put on (hats, gloves, eyeglasses)'

-来/來 *lái* 'movement toward the speaker'

    跑来/跑來 **pǎolái** 'run toward the speaker'
    走來 **zǒulái** 'walk toward the speaker'
    爬來 **pálái** 'crawl toward the speaker'
    飞来/飛來 **fēilái** 'fly toward the speaker'
    进来/進來 **jìnlái** 'come in'
    出来/出來 **chūlái** 'go out (toward the speaker)'
    起来/起來 **qǐlái** 'bring up, pick up'
    回来/回來 **huílái** 'return to a location (toward the speaker)'
    过来/過來 **guòlái** 'pass, travel across (toward the speaker)'

-去 *qù* 'movement away from the speaker toward a specific destination'

    跑去 **pǎoqù** 'run away from the speaker toward a specific destination'
    走去 **zǒuqù** 'walk away from the speaker toward a specific destination'
    爬去 **páqù** 'crawl away from the speaker toward a specific destination'
    飞去/飛去 **fēiqù** 'fly away from the speaker toward a specific location'
    进去/進去 **jìnqù** 'go in (away from the speaker)'
    出去 **chūqù** 'go out (away from the speaker)'
    回去 **huíqù** 'return to a location (away from the speaker)'
    过去/過去 **guòqù** 'pass, travel across (away from the speaker)'

-走 *zǒu* 'movement away from the speaker not directed toward a specific location'

    跑走 **pǎo zǒu** 'run away'
    飞走/飛走 **fēizǒu** 'fly away'
    拿走 **názǒu** 'take away'
    带走/帶走 **dàizǒu** 'carry away'

DIRECTIONAL VERBS

19.3.2 Complex directional suffixes

Complex directional suffixes have two parts. The first part indicates the absolute direction of movement: *up, down, into, out of, across,* or *returning to a location.* The second part indicates the direction of movement toward or away from the speaker.

Direction of motion   *Direction toward/away from speaker*

上 **shàng** 'up'   来/來 **lái** 'toward the speaker'
起 **qǐ** 'up'*   去 **qù** 'away from the speaker'
下 **xià** 'down'
进/進 **jìn** 'into'
出 **chū** 'out of'
过/過 **guò** 'pass a location'
回 **huí** 'return to a location'

*There is no corresponding suffix 起去 **qǐqù**.

Here are examples of action verbs with compound directional endings.

走下来/走下來 **zǒuxiàlái** 'walk down (toward the speaker)'
走下去 **zǒuxiàqù** 'walk down (away from the speaker)'
跑下来/跑下來 **pǎoxiàlái** 'run down (toward the speaker)'
跑下去 **pǎoxiàqù** 'run down (away from the speaker)'
拿出来/拿出來 **náchūlái** 'take out (toward the speaker)'
拿出去 **náchūqù** 'take out (away from the speaker)'
跳过来/跳過來 **tiàoguòlái** 'jump over (toward the speaker)'
爬上来/爬上來 **páshànglái** 'climb or crawl up (toward the speaker)'
走上来/走上來 **zǒushànglái** 'walk up (toward the speaker)'
走回来/走回來 **zǒuhuílái** 'walk back to a location (toward the speaker)'
走进来/走進來 **zǒujìnlái** 'walk in (toward the speaker)'
站起来/站起來 **zhànqǐlái** 'stand up'
滚出去 **gǔnchūqù** 'roll out (away from the speaker), get out of here (disrespectful colloquial expression)'
放下来/放下來 **fàngxiàlái** 'put down'
开回去/開回去 **kāihuíqù** 'drive back (to the original location)'
开过来/開過來 **kāiguòlái** 'drive across (toward the speaker)'
开过去/開過去 **kāiguòqù** 'drive across (away from the speaker)'

19.4 Sentences with directional verbs

Sentences with directional verbs may use basic Mandarin phrase order:

subject + verb + direct object

请你们坐下。
請你們坐下。
Qǐng nǐmen zuòxià.
Please sit down!

两个人走进来了。
兩個人走進來了。
Liǎng gè rén zǒujìnlái le.
Two people walked in.

一只小鸟飞来了，一只小鸟飞走了。
一隻小鳥飛來了，一隻小鳥飛走了。
Yī zhī xiǎo niǎo fēiláile, yī zhī xiǎoniǎo fēizǒu le.
One little bird flew over here, and the other one flew away.

Sentences with directional verbs

要是你看不懂，就别再看下去了。
Yàoshi nǐ kànbudǒng, jiù bié zài kànxiàqùle.
If you do not understand it, then don't continue reading it.

别说了！我听不下去了。
別說了！我聽不下去了。
Bié shuō le! We tīngbuxiàqù le.
Don't talk anymore! I cannot continue to listen anymore.

穿上你的大衣，戴上手套！
Chuānshàng nǐ de dàyī, dàishàng shǒutào!
Put on your overcoat and wear your gloves!

外边太冷了。请你关上窗户。
外邊太冷了。請你關上窗戶。
Wàibian tài lěng le. Qǐng nǐ guānshàng chuānghu.
It's too cold outside. Please shut the window.

19.4.1 Topicalization of the direct object

In sentences with directional verbs, the direct object is often topicalized, presented at the beginning of the sentence, or, when the conditions for 把 **bǎ** are met, included in the sentence as the object of 把 **bǎ**.

你的东西我都带来了。
你的東西我都帶來了。
Nǐ de dōngxi wǒ dōu dàilái le.
(As for) your things, I've brought them all here.

太冷了，快把窗户关上！
太冷了，快把窗戶關上！
Tài lěng le, kuài bǎ chuānghu guānshàng!
It's too cold. Hurry up and close the window!

把那个东西放下！
把那個東西放下！
Bǎ nàge dōngxi fàngxià!
Put that thing down!

▶ 20, 57.2.1

19.4.2 The position of the location phrase in sentences with directional verbs

Sentences with directional verbs with simple directional suffixes cannot include a location phrase. Sentences with directional verbs with complex directional suffixes can include a location phrase. The location phrase occurs between the first part of the suffix (the part that indicates absolute direction) and 来/來 **lái** or 去 **qù**.

verb of motion + direction + location + 来/來 lái or 去 qù

他爬上[山]去了。
Tā páshàng [shān] qù le.
He climbed up the mountain.

把我的车开回[家]去！
把我的車開回[家]去！
Bǎ wǒ de chē kāi huí [jiā] qù!
Drive my car home!

DIRECTIONAL VERBS   **19.4**

你不可以把汽车开进[公园]去。
你不可以把汽車開進[公園]去。
Nǐ bù kěyǐ bǎ qìchē kāijìn [gōngyuán] qù.
You are not allowed to drive your car into the park.

他走进[图书馆]去了。
他走進[圖書館]去了。
Tā zǒujìn [túshūguǎn] qù le.
He walked into the library.

我的同屋跑出[宿舍]来了。
我的同屋跑出[宿舍]來了。
Wǒ de tóngwū pǎochū [sùshè] lái le.
My roommate ran out of the dorm.

你能不能把自行车骑上[山]去?
你能不能把自行車騎上[山]去?
Nǐ néng bù néng bǎ zìxíngchē qí shàng [shān] qù?
Can you ride your bike up the mountain?

19.4.3 Negation with directional verbs

Negation occurs before the directional verb and can be 不 **bù** or 没 **méi** depending upon whether the sentence refers to a non-past or habitual action, or an action that has not been completed.

你不可以把车开进公园去。
你不可以把車開進公園去。
Nǐ bù kěyǐ bǎ chē kāijìn gōngyuán qù.
You can't drive your car into the park.

我还没把东西放下。
我還沒把東西放下。
Wǒ hái méi bǎ dōngxi fàngxià.
I haven't put my things down yet.

19.4.4 Aspectual suffixes with directional verbs

The perfective aspect suffix 了 **le** can occur with directional verbs. It occurs at the very end of the directional suffix.

他爬上山去了。
Tā páshàng shān qù le.
He climbed up the mountain.

她把书都拿回图书馆去了。
她把書都拿回圖書館去了。
Tā bǎ shū dōu náhuí túshūguǎn qù le.
She took all of the books back to the library.

Asking yes–no questions with directional verbs

19.5 The potential form of directional verbs

Like resultative verbs, most directional verbs also have a potential form. The potential is formed by the inclusion of the potential infixes 得 **de** or 不 **bu** between the motion verb and the directional suffix.

Affirmative potential form

> motion verb + 得 **de** + directional suffix
> 'able to perform the motion in the specified direction'

> 拿得来/拿得來 **nádelái** 'able to bring over'

> 那个东西你拿得来吗?
> 那個東西你拿得來嗎?
> **Nàge dōngxi nǐ nádelái ma?**
> Can you bring that thing over here?

> 坐得下 **zuòdexià** 'able to seat'

> 我的车坐得下六个人。
> 我的車坐得下六個人。
> **Wǒ de chē zuòdexià liù gè rén.**
> My car can seat six people.

Negative potential form

> motion verb + 不 **bu** + directional suffix
> 'unable to perform the motion in the specified direction'

> 穿不上 **chuānbushàng** 'unable to wear/put on'

> 那条裤子太小了。我穿不上。
> 那條褲子太小了。我穿不上。
> **Nà tiáo kùzi tài xiǎo le. Wǐ chuānbushàng.**
> Those slacks are too small. I can't put them on.

> 别说了！我听不下去了。
> 別說了！我聽不下去了。
> **Bié shuō le! Wǒ tīng bù xiàqù le.**
> Don't talk! I can't listen anymore.

> 你的车太大了，肯定开不进去。
> 你的車太大了，肯定開不進去。
> **Nǐ de chē tài dà le, kěndìng kāi bù jìnqu.**
> Your car is too big. You certainly can't drive it in.

▶ 18.6, 32.2

19.6 Asking yes–no questions with directional verbs

To ask a yes–no question with 吗/嗎 **ma** about an action involving a directional verb, simply place 吗/嗎 **ma** at the end of the sentence.

> 她把书都拿回图书馆去了吗?
> 她把書都拿回圖書館去了嗎?
> **Tā bǎ shū dōu náhuí túshūguǎn qù le ma?**
> Did she take all of the books back to the library?

DIRECTIONAL VERBS

When using a directional verb, verb-not-verb yes–no questions may take one of the following forms. Mandarin speakers differ in their preferences for these forms. When using the affirmative statement + 没有/沒有 **méi yǒu** form, the destination location (presented here in square brackets) is often omitted. 了 **le** does not occur in the 有没有/有沒有 **yǒu méi yǒu** form.

affirmative statement + 没有/沒有 *méi yǒu*

她把书都拿回[图书馆]去了没有？
她把書都拿回[圖書館]去了沒有？
Tā bǎ shū dōu náhuí [túshūguǎn] qù le méi yǒu?
Did she take all of the books back (to the library)?

subject + 有没有/有沒有 *yǒu méi yǒu* + *predicate*

她有没有把书都拿回图书馆去？
她有沒有把書都拿回圖書館去？
Tā yǒu méi yǒu bǎ shū dōu náhuí túshūguǎn qù?
Did she take all of the books back to the library?

To ask a verb-not-verb yes–no question about a directional expression in potential form, use the following structure

topic (object in sentence initial position) + subject + affirmative potential + negative potential

这么高的山，你上得去上不去？
這麼高的山，你上得去上不去？
Zhème gāo de shān, nǐ shàngdequ shàngbuqù?
A mountain this high, can you climb (up) it?

19.7 Directional verbs and directional suffixes with figurative or idiomatic meaning

考上 **kǎoshàng** *(directional verb)* 'pass an entrance exam and move up to the next level'

她考上大学了。
她考上大學了。
Tā kǎoshàng dàxué le.
She passed the college entrance exam.

考上 **kǎoshàng** is often used in the potential form.

Q: 你想他今年考得上考不上大学？
你想他今年考得上考不上大學？
Nǐ xiǎng tā jīnnián kǎodeshàng kǎobushàng dàxué?
Do you think he can pass the entrance examination and be admitted to college this year?

A: 他是一个好学生，我想他考得上。
他是一個好學生，我想他考得上。
Tā shì yī gè hǎo xuésheng, wǒ xiǎng tā kǎodeshàng.
He is a good student; I think he can pass the college examinations.

下去 **xiàqù** *(directional suffix)*. In addition to its literal meaning 'go down,' 下去 **xiàqù** is also used to contribute the meaning 'continue to (do the verb).'

说下去/說下去 **shuōxiàqù** 'keep talking'
看下去 **kànxiàqù** 'keep reading'
做下去 **zuòxiàqù** 'keep doing'
活下去 **huóxiàqù** 'go on living'
听下去/聽下去 **tīngxiàqù** 'keep listening'

Directional verbs and directional suffixes with figurative or idiomatic meaning 19.7

起來 **qǐlái** *(directional suffix)*. In addition to its literal meaning 'rise up,' 起來 **qǐlái** conveys the meaning 'begin to do the action of the verb.'

> 唱起来 **chàngqǐlai** 'begin to sing'
> 哭起来 **kūqǐlái** 'begin to cry'
> 打起来 **dǎqǐlái** 'begin to fight'

V-起來 **qǐlái** can also serve on pairs of verbs to indicate contrast.

> 中国菜，吃起来很容易，做起来很难。
> 中國菜，吃起來很容易，做起來很難。
> **Zhōngguó cài, chīqǐlái hěn róngyì, zuòqǐlái hěn nán.**
> Chinese food is easy to eat but hard to cook.

▶ 41

20
把 *bǎ* sentences: The 'disposal' construction

把 **bǎ** sentences focus on what happens to the object of a verb as the result of some action. They answer the question: *What does/did the subject do to the object?* 把 **bǎ** sentences can always be paraphrased as: *the subject takes/took the object and does/did (an action) with it.* The structure of 把 **bǎ** sentences is sometimes called the 'disposal construction.'

20.1 The structure of 把 *bǎ* sentences

把 **bǎ** sentences take the following form:

subject + 把 *bǎ object* + *action verb*

他把我的车偷走了。
他把我的車偷走了。
Tā bǎ wǒ de chē tōuzǒu le.
He stole my car away.

The 把 **bǎ** construction is widely used in Mandarin, but it may only be used when the object and the verb have certain properties.

20.2 Properties of the subject and object in 把 *bǎ* sentences

20.2.1 Properties of the subject

The subject in a 把 **bǎ** sentence must be capable of causing something to happen. This includes subjects that are animate such as people, animals, insects, etc., and also inanimate forces of nature such as rain, wind, earthquakes, floods, etc.

把 *bǎ sentences with animate subject*

我把英文翻成中文了。
Wǒ bǎ Yīngwén fānchéng Zhōngwén le.
I translated the English into Chinese.

谁把烤鸭吃光了。
誰把烤鴨吃光了。
Shéi bǎ kǎoyā chīguāng le.
Who ate (finished eating) the roast duck?

鸡把虫都吃了。
雞把蟲都吃了。
Jī bǎ chóng dōu chī le.
The chicken(s) ate all of the worms.

Properties of the subject and object in 把 bǎ sentences 20.2

把 *bǎ sentences with inanimate subjects*

> 昨天晚上大火把他们家烧了。
> 昨天晚上大火把他們家燒了。
> **Zuótiān wǎnshang dàhuǒ bǎ tāmen jiā shāo le.**
> Last night a big fire burned their home.

> 这几天真把妈妈忙坏了。
> 這幾天真把媽媽忙壞了。
> **Zhèjǐtiān zhēn bǎ māma mánghuài le.**
> These last few days have really worn Mom out.

Causation does not have to be deliberate or intentional.

> 他不知不觉地把所有的饺子都吃完了。
> 他不知不覺地把所有的餃子都吃完了。
> **Tā bùzhī-bùjué de bǎ suǒyǒu de jiǎozi dōu chīwán le.**
> Without realizing it, he ate up all the dumplings.

If you want to say that the subject deliberately caused something to happen, you can add an expression such as 故意/故意 **gùyì** 'deliberately' before 把 **bǎ**.

> 他故意把我的衣服弄坏了。
> 他故意把我的衣服弄壞了。
> **Tā gùyì bǎ wǒ de yīfu nònghuài le.**
> He deliberately ruined my clothes.

20.2.2 Properties of the object

- The object must refer to something definite or generic.
  Objects are definite if they have already been mentioned in the discourse, or if they are preceded by the specifier 这 **zhè** 'this, these' or 那 **nà** 'that, those,' or are modified by a description phrase.

> 我已经把那本书看完了。
> 我已經把那本書看完了。
> **Wǒ yǐjing bǎ nà běn shū kànwán le.**
> I already finished reading that book.

> 他把孩子的衣服都洗干净了。
> 他把孩子的衣服都洗乾淨了。
> **Tā bǎ háizi de yīfu dōu xǐ gānjìng le.**
> He washed the children's clothing clean.

Objects are generic if they refer to a group or class of objects in general rather than to a specific or definite object. When you say 'I like mustard on hot dogs,' both 'mustard' and 'hot dogs' have generic rather than definite or specific reference.

> 他经常把花儿送给女朋友。
> 他經常把花兒送給女朋友。
> **Tā jīngcháng bǎ huār sòng gěi nǚ péngyou.**
> He regularly sends his girlfriend flowers.

- The object must exist independently of the action of the verb.
  In 把 **bǎ** sentences, the verb can do something to the object, but it cannot create the object. Therefore, for example, you can use 把 **bǎ** to say that you revised an essay, but not that you wrote it.

> 她把文章改了改。
> **Tā bǎ wénzhāng gǎile gǎi.**
> She revised the essay.

把 *BĂ* SENTENCES: THE 'DISPOSAL' CONSTRUCTION

20.3

*她把文章写了写。
她把文章寫了寫。
Tā bǎ wénzhāng xiěle xiě.
(intended: She wrote the essay.)

Similarly, you can use 把 **bǎ** to say that you finished a painting, but not that you created it by painting it.

她把画儿画完了。
她把畫兒畫完了。
Tā bǎ huàr huàwán le.
She finished the painting.

*她把画儿画了。
她把畫兒畫了。
Tā bǎ huàr huà le.
(intended: She painted the painting.)

20.3 Properties of the verb in 把 *bǎ* sentences

The verb in 把 **bǎ** sentences must refer to a bounded, complete action that has an endpoint. There are a number of ways to add an endpoint to an action verb.

20.3.1 Adding an endpoint to a change-of-state verb

To add an endpoint to a change-of-state action verb such as 忘 **wàng** 'forget,' 丢 **diū** 'lose,' and 卖/賣 **mài** 'sell,' do one of the following.

- Follow the verb with the perfective aspect particle 了 **le**.

    我把他们的名字都忘了。
    我把他們的名字都忘了。
    Wǒ bǎ tāmen de míngzi dōu wàng le.
    I forgot their names.

▶ 17.1

- Follow the verb with a resultative ending such as 掉 **diào** + 了 **le**, which indicates that the action is complete.

    我把袜子给丢掉了。
    我把襪子給丟掉了。
    Wǒ bǎ wàzi gěi diūdiào le.
    I lost my socks.

▶ 18.3.2

- For change-of-state verbs that refer to placing an object in a location, such as 放 **fàng** 'put, place,' and 挂/掛 **guà** 'hang,' follow the verb with the location phrase that indicates where the object will be located as a result of the action.

    把你的鞋子放在门外。
    把你的鞋子放在門外。
    Bǎ nǐ de xiézi fàng zài mén wài.
    Put your shoes outside the door.

    她把画儿挂在墙上了。
    她把畫兒掛在牆上了。
    Tā bǎ huàr guà zài qiáng shàng le.
    She hung the picture on the wall.

▶ 14.1

Properties of the verb in 把 *bǎ* sentences   **20.3**

20.3.2 Adding an endpoint to an open-ended action verb

To add an endpoint to an open-ended action verb, do one of the following:

- Follow the verb with a directional suffix.

  你能不能把车开进去？
  你能不能把車開進去？
  Nǐ néng bù néng bǎ chē kāijìnqu?
  Can you drive the car in?

▶ 19

- Follow the verb with a resultative suffix that indicates the result or conclusion of the action.

  你睡觉以前得把功课准备好。
  你睡覺以前得把功課準備好。
  Nǐ shuì jiào yǐqián děi bǎ gōngkè zhǔnbèihǎo.
  Before you go to sleep you should finish preparing your course work.

▶ 18.3

NOTE: Resultative endings that indicate sensory perception, such as 见/見 **jiàn** 'to perceive' and 懂 **dǒng** 'to understand,' cannot be used as resultative complements in 把 **bǎ** sentences.

- Repeat the verb with the phrase V 一 **yī** V or V 了 **le** V.

  请把你的故事说一说。
  請把你的故事說一說。
  Qǐng bǎ nǐ de gùshi shuō yī shuō.
  Please tell your story.

  他把文章改了改。
  Tā bǎ wénzhāng gǎi le gǎi.
  He revised the essay.

- Follow the verb with a frequency phrase.

  我把那部电影看了两次。
  我把那部電影看了兩次。
  Wǒ bǎ nà bù diànyǐng kàn le liǎng cì.
  I saw that movie twice.

▶ 39.4

- Follow the verb with a manner adverbial.

  把你的东西再放得整齐一点。
  把你的東西再放得整齊一點。
  Bǎ nǐ de dōngxī zài fàng de zhěngqí yīdiǎn.
  Arrange your things a little bit neater.

  请把这条裤子改得短一点。
  請把這條褲子改得短一點。
  Qǐng bǎ zhè tiáo kùzi gǎi de duǎn yīdiǎn.
  Please make these slacks a little shorter.

  她把头发剪得短短的。
  她把頭髮剪得短短的。
  Tā bǎ toufà jiǎn de duǎnduǎn de.
  She cut her hair short.

▶ 31

把 *BǍ* SENTENCES: THE 'DISPOSAL' CONSTRUCTION

- Follow the verb with the durative aspect suffix 着/著 **zhe**.

    把这点儿钱带着。
    把這點兒錢帶著。
    Bǎ zhè diǎr qián dàizhe.
    Take this money.

▶ 17.2

- Follow the object with a phrase that refers to part of the object.

    他把功课只做了一半。
    他把功課只做了一半。
    Tā bǎ gōngkè zhǐ zuò le yībàn.
    He only did half the homework.

    她把蛋糕吃了两口。
    她把蛋糕吃了兩口。
    Tā bǎ dàngāo chī le liǎng kǒu.
    She ate two bites of the cake.

20.4 Negation in 把 *bǎ* sentences

In 把 **bǎ** sentences, negation occurs before 把 **bǎ** and not before the action verb.

If a 把 **bǎ** sentence refers to a future event, or to general or habitual action, negation is indicated with 不 **bù**. Prohibitions can be expressed with 别 **bié** or 不要 **bù yào** 'don't.'

不要把你的东西留在外边。
不要把你的東西留在外邊。
Bù yào bǎ nǐ de dōngxi liú zài wàibian.
Don't leave your things outside.

别把你的名字写错了。
別把你的名字寫錯了。
Bié bǎ nǐ de míngzi xiě cuò le.
Don't write your name incorrectly.

你不可以把这些东西带回家。
你不可以把這些東西帶回家。
Nǐ bù kěyǐ bǎ zhè xiē dōngxi dài huí jiā.
You can't take these things home.

If a 把 **bǎ** sentence refers to an event that did not occur, negation is 没/沒(有) **méi (yǒu)**.

他没把故事说清楚。
他沒把故事說清楚。
Tā méi bǎ gùshi shuō qīngchu.
He didn't tell the story clearly.

20.5 Adverbs and modal verbs in 把 *bǎ* sentences

Adverbs and modal verbs that refer to the entire action occur before 把 **bǎ**.

我已经把功课交给老师了。
我已經把功課交給老師了。
Wǒ yǐjing bǎ gōngkè jiāo gěi lǎoshī le.
I already gave my homework to the teacher.

Adverbs and modal verbs in 把 bǎ sentences — 20.5

你得把你的房间收拾收拾。
你得把你的房間收拾收拾。
Nǐ děi bǎ nǐ de fángjiān shōushi shōushi.
You should clean up your room.

When it refers to the entire action, the adverb 都 **dōu** occurs <u>after</u> 把 **bǎ** and its object, before the verb phrase.

他把房间都整理好了。
他把房間都整理好了。
Tā bǎ fángjiān dōu zhěnglǐ hǎo le.
He straightened up the room completely.

他把饺子都吃完了。
他把餃子都吃完了。
Tā bǎ jiǎozi dōu chīwán le.
He finished eating all the dumplings.

都 **dōu** can also occur before 把 **bǎ**. When it does, it refers to the subject of the sentence.

他们都把房间整理好了。
他們都把房間整理好了。
Tāmen dōu bǎ fángjiān zhěnglǐ hǎo le.
They all straightened up the room. (All of them did the action)

▶ 57.2.1

21

The passive

21.1 The structure of the Mandarin passive

In active sentences, the subject is typically the *agent*, the noun phrase that initiates the action, and the object of the verb is the noun phrase *affected by* the action of the verb.

subject	+ *verb*	+ *object*
agent		*affected object*
他	偷走了	我的车。
他	偷走了	我的車。
Tā	**tōuzǒu le**	**wǒ de chē.**

He stole my car.

In Mandarin passive sentences, the affected noun phrase occurs as the subject of the verb, and the agent occurs as the object of a passive marking preposition. As is typical with prepositional phrases, the prepositional phrase occurs before the verb:

subject + prepositional phrase + verb

▶ 14

NOTE The exception is when the prepositional phrase indicates the location of the object as a result of the action of the verb. In that case, the prepositional phrase follows the verb.

▶ 14.1

Mandarin has three passive marking prepositions (*passive markers*): 被 **bèi**, 叫 **jiào**, and 让/讓 **ràng**, all of which may be translated with English 'by.'

subject	+ *passive NP*		+ *verb*
affected NP	*agent*		
我的车	[被/叫/让]	他	偷走了。
我的車	[被/叫/讓]	他	偷走了。
Wǒ de chē	**[bèi/jiào/ràng]**	**tā**	**tōuzǒu le.**

My car was stolen by him.

In passive structures, the word 给/給 **gěi** is sometimes placed before the verb.

那本字典	[被/叫/让]	小李	给借走了。
那本字典	[被/叫/讓]	小李	給借走了。
Nà běn zìdiǎn	**[bèi/jiào/ràng]**	**Xiǎo Lǐ**	**gěi jièzǒu le.**

That dictionary was borrowed by Little Li.

The passive and negation

The presence of 给/給 **gěi** before the verb indicates that the sentence is passive, even when the passive markers 被 **bèi**, 叫 **jiào**, and 让/讓 **ràng** do not occur.

> 那个坏人给抓住了。
> 那個壞人給抓住了。
> **Nàge huàirén gěi zhuāzhù le.**
> That bad person was arrested.

The agent of a passive sentence need not be an animate entity. An inanimate entity, a force, or a situation may also function as the agent. For example:

> 他们的房子[被/叫/让]火烧了。
> 他們的房子[被/叫/讓]火燒了。
> **Tāmen de fángzi [bèi/jiào/ràng] huǒ shāo le.**
> Their house was burned by fire.

> 他被学校撤职了。
> 他被學校撤職了。
> **Tā bèi xuéxiào chèzhí le.**
> He was fired by the school.

An agent is obligatory when using the passive markers 叫 **jiào** and 让/讓 **ràng**. An agent is optional for the marker 被 **bèi**.

> 他被撤职了。
> 他被撤職了。
> **Tā bèi chèzhí le.**
> He was fired.

When the passive marker is followed by an object, all of the passive markers are interchangeable. Therefore, all remaining examples in this chapter will be illustrated with only one passive marker.

21.2 The passive and negation

The function of negated passive sentences is to indicate that some action has not occurred in the past. Therefore, negation in passive sentences is typically 没/沒(有) **méi (yǒu)**. 没/沒(有) **méi (yǒu)** must occur before the passive marking preposition, and never before the verb.

Say this	Not this
你的车没有被警察拖走。 你的車沒有被警察拖走。 **Nǐ de chē méi yǒu bèi jǐngchá tuōzǒu.** Your car wasn't towed away by the police.	*你的车被警察没有拖走。 你的車被警察沒有拖走。 **Nǐ de chē bèi jǐngchá méi yǒu tuōzǒu.**

The passive form can also be used when expressing prohibitions and warnings.

> 别被你的朋友给骗了。
> 別被你的朋友給騙了。
> **Bié bèi nǐ de péngyou gěi piàn le.**
> Don't let yourself be cheated by your friend.

> 我们作的事不要被别人知道。
> 我們作的事不要被別人知道。
> **Wǒmen zuò de shì bù yào bèi biéren zhīdao.**
> We shouldn't let other people know what we did. (lit. 'What we've done shouldn't be known by others.')

▶ 51.1.2

THE PASSIVE

21.3 Conditions for using the passive in Mandarin

The Mandarin passive is used under the following circumstances:

- To express adversity
  To indicate that the event has negative consequences or is in some way 'bad news' for the narrator, addressee, or affected noun:

  > 我的钱被小偷偷走了。
  > 我的錢被小偷偷走了。
  > **Wǒ de qián bèi xiǎotōu tōuzǒu le.**
  > My money was stolen by a thief.

  This association of the passive with bad news, once a signature feature of the passive in Mandarin, is becoming less common.

- To express surprise or astonishment

  > 我们的秘密被政府发现了。
  > 我們的祕密被政府發現了。
  > **Wǒmen de mìmì bèi zhèngfǔ fāxiàn le.**
  > Our secret was discovered by the government.

- To emphasize the affected noun phrase rather than the agent

  > 这儿的树都被人砍了。
  > 這兒的樹都被人砍了。
  > **Zhèr de shù dōu bèi rén kǎn le.**
  > The trees here were all cut down by people.

- To describe an action when the agent is unknown

  > 昨天银行被抢了。
  > 昨天銀行被搶了。
  > **Zuótiān yínháng bèi qiǎng le.**
  > The bank was robbed yesterday.

- To avoid mentioning the agent of an action

  > 我女儿被骗了。
  > 我女兒被騙了。
  > **Wǒ nǚ'ér bèi piàn le.**
  > My daughter was cheated.

21.4 Differences between the passive markers 被 *bèi*, 叫 *jiào*, and 让/讓 *ràng*

- Frequency: 被 **bèi** occurs more frequently in written or formal contexts than the other passive markers. In colloquial speech, 叫 **jiào** and 让/讓 **ràng** are more commonly used. Dialects differ in the preferred passive marker.
- Adversity: 被 **bèi** connotes stronger adversity than the other passive markers.

21.5 Additional functions of 让/讓 *ràng*, 叫 *jiào*, and 给/給 *gěi*

In addition to their role in passive sentences, 让/讓 **ràng**, 叫 **jiào**, and 给/給 **gěi** have other functions.

- 叫 **jiào** is also used as a verb meaning 'call,' or 'order.'
- 让/讓 **ràng** is also used as a verb meaning 'let' or 'allow.'

Other Mandarin structures that highlight the affected object & de-emphasize the agent   **21.6**

- 给/給 **gěi** is also used as a verb meaning 'give,' and as a preposition meaning 'to' or 'for/on behalf of.'

▶ 14

When the verb is not followed by an object noun phrase, 叫 **jiào** and 让/讓 **ràng** may sometimes be interpreted as either a passive marker or as a verb, and the sentence may be ambiguous.

> 教授让学生批评了。
> 教授讓學生批評了。
> **Jiàoshòu ràng xuésheng pīpíng le.**
> The professor was criticized by the students.
> (让/讓 **ràng** = passive marker: by the students)
> or
> The professor now allows the students to criticize.
> (让/讓 **ràng** = allow: allows the students)

In most cases, however, the context will make clear the function of 叫 **jiào**, or 让/讓 **ràng**, or 给/給 **gěi**, and only one interpretation will make sense. For example, the following sentence only makes sense if 让/讓 **ràng** is interpreted as 'allow' or 'let' and not as the passive marker 'by.'

> 妈妈让孩子吃饼干。
> 媽媽讓孩子吃餅乾。
> **Māma ràng háizi chī bǐnggān.**
> Mom let the children eat cookies. (*by the children . . .)

21.6 Other Mandarin structures that highlight the affected object and de-emphasize the agent

Mandarin has several different patterns that function to emphasize an affected object or to de-emphasize or avoid mentioning the agent. These include the following:

- Topicalization

> 支票，银行已经收到了。
> 支票，銀行已經收到了。
> **Zhīpiào, yínháng yǐjing shōudào le.**
> (As for) the check, the bank has already received it.

▶ 57.1.2.1

- The 把 **bǎ** construction

> 朋友把水果送来了。
> 朋友把水果送來了。
> **Péngyou bǎ shuǐguǒ sònglai le.**
> A friend sent the fruit as a gift.
> (A friend took the fruit and sent it as a gift.)

▶ 20, 57.2.1

- The 是 **shì** . . . 的 **de** construction

> 这本书是我教授写的。
> 這本書是我教授寫的。
> **Zhè běn shū shì wǒ jiàoshòu xiě de.**
> This book was written by my professor.
> (This book, it was my professor who wrote it.)

▶ 57.2.4

Part B

Situations and functions

22

Names, kinship terms, titles, and terms of address

22.1 Names: 姓名 *xìngmíng*

The order of a Chinese name is:

family name + given name

姓	名字
xìng	**míngzi**
王	莉花
Wáng	**Lìhuā**
张/張	伟明/偉明
Zhāng	**Wěimíng**

In this book we translate Chinese names using Chinese word order. That is, 王莉花 **Wáng Lìhuā** is translated as 'Wang Lihua' and not 'Lihua Wang.'

22.1.1 Family names

There are over 3500 Chinese family names. However, of these, only about 100 occur widely. This is probably the basis of the expression 老百姓 **lǎobǎixìng** 'the old 100 family names,' which is used to refer to 'the people' or 'the common man.'

The three most common Chinese family names are 李 **Lǐ**, 王 **Wáng**, and 张/張 **Zhāng**. The next most common family names, representing the overwhelming majority of Chinese people, are 刘/劉 **Liú**, 陈/陳 **Chén**, 杨/楊 **Yáng**, 赵/趙 **Zhào**, 黄 **Huáng**, 周 **Zhōu**, 吴/吳 **Wú**, 徐 **Xú**, 孙/孫 **Sūn**, 胡 **Hú**, 朱 **Zhū**, 高 **Gāo**, 林 **Lín**, 何 **Hé**, 郭 **Guō**, and 马/馬 **Mǎ**.

Most family names are a single character/single syllable in length. However, there are a small number of two-character/two-syllable Chinese family names. The most common are 司马/司馬 **Sīmǎ**, 司徒 **Sītú**, 欧阳/歐陽 **Ōuyáng**, and 皇甫 **Huángfǔ**.

22.1.2 Given names

A given name consists of one or two characters/syllables. There is no fixed inventory of given names in Chinese as there is in English such as Ruth, Michael, Lisa, and Mark. Instead, names express meaning, and families select as names, words or phrases with positive connotations that they wish to associate with their child. While this method of naming is also used in the West, it is the exception rather than the rule.

In the traditional naming process, the first character of a given name is a generational name: all children in the family who are of the same gender and in the same generation share the same first character in their given name. The second character reflects some other positive

NAMES, KINSHIP TERMS, TITLES, AND TERMS OF ADDRESS — 22.2

characteristic. Thus, brothers might be named 亦豪 **Yì Háo** (talent) and 亦强/亦強 **Yì Qiáng** (strength). Sisters might be named 颖怡/穎怡 **Yǐng Yí** (joyful) and 颖美/穎美 **Yǐng Měi** (beautiful).

Modern naming practice often does not include a generational name. This is especially common in mainland China. Instead, given names reflect positive attributes, and may be one or two syllables in length.

Given names are personal and somewhat private. In general, they are only used as terms of address by good friends and close acquaintances, and in closed settings such as a family, classroom, or office, where people are members of a well-defined group. Often, people use kinship terms and titles rather than names when addressing and referring to others.

22.2 Kinship terms

Here are the most commonly used kinship terms and the distinctions that they reflect.

22.2.1 Kinship terms for immediate family

Male			Female		
父亲/父親	**fùqin**	father	母亲/母親	**mǔqīn**	mother
爸爸	**bàba**	dad	妈妈/媽媽	**māma**	mom
哥哥	**gēge**	brother older than self	姐姐	**jiějie**	sister older than self
弟弟	**dìdi**	brother younger than self	妹妹	**mèimei**	sister younger than self

The reference point for siblings is oneself. For example, an older brother is a brother older than oneself. If you are male and have an older brother and a younger brother, then your younger brother has two older brothers.

Your family from your perspective

> 我有一个哥哥、一个弟弟。
> 我有一個哥哥、一個弟弟。
> **Wǒ yǒu yī gè gēge, yī gè dìdi.**
> I have one older brother and one younger brother.

Your family from your younger brother's perspective

> 我有两个哥哥，没有弟弟。
> 我有兩個哥哥，沒有弟弟。
> **Wǒ yǒu liǎng gè gēge, méi yǒu dìdi.**
> I have two older brothers and no younger brother.

Titles

22.2.2 Kinship terms for extended family

Paternal

祖父	zǔfù (fml)	grandfather
爷爷/爺爺	yéye (inf)	(father's father)
祖母	zǔmǔ (fml)	grandmother
奶奶	nǎinai (inf)	(father's mother)
叔叔	shūshu	uncle (on father's side)
姑姑	gūgu	aunt (on father's side)
堂哥	tánggē	male cousin older than self
堂弟	tángdì	male cousin younger than self
堂姐	tángjiě	female cousin older than self
堂妹	tángmèi	female cousin younger than self
公公	gōnggong	father-in-law (husband's father)
婆婆	pópo	mother-in-law (husband's mother)

Maternal

外公	wàigōng (fml)	grandfather
公公	gōnggōng (inf)	(mother's father)
外婆	wàipó (fml)	grandmother
姥姥	lǎolǎo (inf)	(mother's mother)
舅舅	jiùjiu	uncle (on mother's side)
阿姨	āyí	aunt (on mother's side)
表哥	biǎogē	male cousin older than self
表弟	biǎodì	male cousin younger than self
表姐	biǎojiě	female cousin older than self
表妹	biǎomèi	female cousin younger than self
岳父	yuèfù	father-in-law (wife's father)
岳母	yuèmǔ	mother-in-law (wife's mother)

fml = formal term, inf = informal term

22.3 Titles

Titles refer to gender and marital status, education, or occupation. When a name includes a title, the order of information is as follows:

family name	(+ given name)	+	title
王	莉花		博士
Wáng	**Lìhuā**		**bóshì**
			Ph.D. (Dr.)

Dr. Wang Lihua

Chinese people often use titles when addressing others or when talking about others. Titles may be used alone or with the family name and given name.

NOTE In Taiwan, the title generally follows the family name: *family name + title + given name*.

22.3.1 Titles that indicate gender and marital status

The most common titles used to reflect gender and marital status are:

先生	王先生
xiānsheng	**Wáng xiānsheng**
Mr.	Mr. Wang

太太	王太太
tàitai	**Wáng tàitai**
夫人	王夫人
fūren	**Wáng fūren**
Mrs.	Mrs. Wang

NAMES, KINSHIP TERMS, TITLES, AND TERMS OF ADDRESS 22.3

小姐	王小姐
xiǎojie	**Wáng xiǎojie**
女士	王女士
nǚshì	**Wáng nǚshì**
Miss	Miss Wang

NOTE

The titles 先生 **xiānsheng** 'Mr.,' 太太 **tàitai** 'Mrs.,' and 小姐 **xiǎojie** 'Miss' are standard expressions in Taiwan but are not commonly used in mainland China. There is no standardly used expression in mainland China for either Mr. or Mrs. The expression 姑娘 **gūniang** is gaining popularity as a way of addressing or referring to young women in mainland China, but it is only appropriate when used by those at least one generation older than the young woman. It is not used together with a name.

22.3.2 Professional titles

Commonly used professional titles include:

医生/醫生
yīshēng
doctor

大夫
dàifu
doctor

护士/護士
hùshì
nurse

师傅/師傅
shīfu
master (skilled person)

老师/老師
lǎoshī
teacher

教授
jiàoshòu
professor

律师/律師
lǜshī
lawyer

法官
fǎguān
judge, justice

主席
zhǔxí
chairperson of a political party, etc.

校长/校長
xiàozhǎng
principal

警察
jǐngchá
police officer

公关/公關
gōngguān
receptionist

秘书/祕書
mìshū
secretary

秘书长/祕書長
mìshūzhǎng
secretary general

主任
zhǔrèn
director of a department, chairperson of a department

司机/司機
sījī
driver; chauffeur

大使
dàshǐ
ambassador

总统/總統
zǒngtǒng
president, chief of state

经理/經理
jīnglǐ
manager

总经理/總經理
zǒngjīnglǐ
general manager
(abbreviated to 总/總 **zǒng** 王总/王總
 Wáng zǒng General Manager Wang)

博士 **bóshì**
doctor of philosophy (Ph.D.)

138

22.4 Addressing others

22.4.1 Addressing friends

Close friends may address each other using family name and given name together, or, if they are very close, by given name alone.

> 王莉花，早。
> **Wáng Lìhuā, zǎo.**
> Wang Lihua, good morning.
>
> 莉花，最近怎么样？
> 莉花，最近怎麼樣？
> **Lìhuā, zuì jìn zěnmeyàng?**
> Lihua, how have you been recently?

Friends or close acquaintances may also address each other using the prefix 老 **lǎo** 'old' or 小 **xiǎo** 'small' before the family name as follows:

| 老高 | **Lǎo Gāo** | Old Gao | 小高 | **Xiǎo Gāo** | Little Gao |
| 老王 | **Lǎo Wáng** | Old Wang | 小王 | **Xiǎo Wáng** | Little Wang |

老 **lǎo** and 小 **xiǎo** do not literally mean 'old' and 'little' here. 老 **lǎo** is used for those older than oneself, and 小 **xiǎo** is used for those younger than oneself.

22.4.2 Addressing family and others with kinship terms

In China, people use kinship terms rather than names to address relatives. Kinship terms are also used in informal contexts to address people who are not relatives. The term that is used depends upon the age and gender of the person whom you are addressing. Here are the kinship terms most commonly used when talking with people who are not your relatives.

大哥 **dà gē**
older brother (title for man near your age but older than you)

大姐 **dà jiě**
older sister (title for woman near your age but older than you)

叔叔 **shūshu**
uncle (title for man who is about your father's age)

阿姨 **āyí**
aunt (title for woman who is about your mother's age or older)

爷爷/爺爺 **yéye**
grandfather (title for man who is about your grandfather's age)

奶奶 **nǎinai**
grandmother (title for woman who is about your grandmother's age)

22.4.3 Colloquial terms of address used with strangers

The following terms are used in informal contexts to address strangers

小伙子	**xiǎo huǒzi**	young fellow (used to address young boys – very colloquial)
小朋友	**xiǎo péngyǒu**	little friend (commonly used to address children)
朋友	**péngyou**	friend (often used by shopkeepers to address customers)
帅哥/帥哥	**shuài gē**	handsome guy (used when addressing a young man one does not know, especially in the context of a restaurant or store)
美女	**měi nǚ**	beautiful girl (used when addressing a young women one does not know, especially in the context of a restaurant or store)

NAMES, KINSHIP TERMS, TITLES, AND TERMS OF ADDRESS

22.4.4 Using titles as terms of address

Titles are commonly used as terms of address. The titles 先生 **xiānsheng** 'Mr.,' 太太 **tàitai** 'Mrs.,' 小姐 **xiǎojie** 'Miss,' and 师傅/師傅 **shīfu** 'master' are used alone without any additional name to address strangers in a polite way. 师傅/師傅 **shīfu** 'master' is often used in mainland China as a polite way to address a man in relatively informal contexts. 小姐 **xiǎojie**, 姑娘 **gūniang**, and 美女 **měi nǚ** are used to address young women in service positions such as in restaurants and shops. 帅哥/帥哥 **shuài gē** is used to address young men in service positions. 夫人 **fūren** 'Mrs.' and 女士 **nǚshì** 'Miss' are very formal and their use is restricted to formal contexts such as speeches and formal events. The titles presented in 22.3.2 can all be used as terms of address. For occupations that are not used as titles or terms of address, see

▶ 23.3

22.5 Addressing new acquaintances and negotiating terms of address

When you meet someone for the first time, you need to determine how to address them. Since given names are not freely used, and family names are generally not used alone, an initial conversation usually includes some negotiation about terms of address. The most common expressions are as follows.

The neutral and most common way to inquire about someone's family name is:

> 你姓什么?
> 你姓甚麽?
> **Nǐ xìng shénme?**
> What is your family name? (neutral question)

A more formal and polite way to inquire about someone's family name is:

> 你貴姓? / 你贵姓
> **Nǐ guì xìng?**
> What is your family name? (polite, formal)

The most common way to reply to either of these questions is:

> 我姓(王)。
> **Wǒ xìng (Wáng).**
> My family name is (Wang).

A very polite and humble response to the formal question is:

> 敝姓(王)。
> **Bì xìng (Wáng).**
> My humble family name is (Wang).

While the polite form of the question is fairly common, the polite humble form of the response is rarely used.

The neutral and most common way to inquire about someone's family name and given name is:

> 你姓什么, 叫什么名字?
> 你姓甚麽, 叫甚麽名字?
> **Nǐ xìng shénme, jiào shénme míngzi?**
> What is your family name and what is your given name?

22.5 Addressing new acquaintances and negotiating terms of address

The neutral and most common way to respond to this question is:

> 我姓(王)，叫(莉花)。
> **Wǒ xìng (Wáng), jiào (Lìhuā).**
> My family name is (Wang), my given name is (Lihua).

The very polite way to inquire about someone's family name and given name is:

> 请问，尊姓大名？
> 請問，尊姓大名？
> **Qǐng wèn, zūnxìng dàmíng?**
> Excuse me, what is your (honorable) name?

The polite, humble response to this question is:

> 敝姓(王)，小名(建国)。
> 敝姓(王)，小名(建國)。
> **Bì xìng (Wáng), xiǎo míng (Jiànguó).**
> My humble family name is (Wang), and my small name is (Jianguo).

People often do not inquire about given names when they first meet. When you have established a friendship, you may inquire about a given name by asking:

> 你叫什么名字？
> 你叫甚麼名字？
> **Nǐ jiào shénme míngzi?**
> What is your name?

The reply to this question is either the family name plus the given name, or the given name alone:

> 我叫(王玫玲)。
> **Wǒ jiào (Wáng Méilíng).**
> I am called (Wang Meiling). (My name is Wang Meiling.)

To make a general inquiry about someone's identity, ask:

> 你是谁？
> 你是誰？
> **Nǐ shì shéi?**
> Who are you?

> 你是 . . . ?
> **Nǐ shì . . . ?**
> Are you . . . ?

> 你是哪位？
> **Nǐ shì něi wèi?**
> Who are you? (polite)

To learn how someone prefers to be addressed by you, ask:

> 我应该怎么称呼你？
> 我應該怎麼稱呼你？
> **Wǒ yīnggāi zěnme chēnghu nǐ?**
> How should I address you?

141

22.6 Name cards and business cards

Name cards and business cards are widely used in China, and people often exchange name cards when they meet for the first time. The information on a person's name card will help you to determine how to address him or her.

When handing your card to someone, use both hands, and give it to the person so that the writing is facing him or her. Receive a card with both hands, read the card, and thank the person who gave you the card or comment on the information on the card so that it is clear that you have read it. If business cards are exchanged during a meeting or a meal, it is customary to place the cards you receive on the table, arranged according to hierarchy, so that you can refer to them as you talk.

The organization of the Chinese name card or business card is typically as follows:

```
Business Organization

Title


                    NAME  education degree

                              (Contact information)

                              Address

                              Telephone number

                              Mobile phone number

                              Fax number
```

```
XX中文系

主任教授



              张惟康

                         电话：8666–8686

地址：中山南路10号        电传：8666–8687

                         手机：13058886666
```

Addressing letters and envelopes 22.7

In mainland China, cards written in Chinese are usually printed horizontally. In Taiwan, cards may also be printed vertically.

22.7 Addressing letters and envelopes

22.7.1 Special terms for the recipient (addressee) and the sender

The name of the recipient is typically followed by the recipient's title, or the title plus the expression 收 **shōu**, 启/啟 **qǐ**, or 大启/大啟 **dà qǐ**. 启/啟 **qǐ** and 大启/大啟 **dà qǐ** are more formal than 收 **shōu**. All three expressions mean 'recipient.'

The name of the sender may be followed by the expression 寄 **jì** or 缄/緘 **jiān**. 缄/緘 **jiān** is more formal than 寄 **jì**. Both expressions mean 'sender.'

NAMES, KINSHIP TERMS, TITLES, AND TERMS OF ADDRESS

22.7.2 The format of a horizontal envelope (commonly used in mainland China)

☐☐☐☐☐☐   stamp

Address of the recipient

Name of Recipient 启/啓（收）

Address of the sender, name of sender 缄/緘 **jiān**

☐☐☐☐☐☐   stamp

北京市新街口南大街十号

王建国先生大 启

南京中山路五号孙古缄

Addressing letters and envelopes 22.7

22.7.3 The format of a vertical envelope (commonly used in Taiwan)

[Envelope diagram showing layout with "stamp" box in upper left, "Recipient Name" in large characters down the center, "Recipient Address" to the right, "Sender Address & name" to the left, with 缄/緘 at bottom of sender column and 启/啟 at bottom of recipient name column. Postal code boxes appear at top right and bottom left.]

[Second envelope example showing: 北京市新街口南大街十号 (right column), 王建国先生大启 (center, large), 南京中山路五号孙古缄 (left column)]

In vertical format, addresses are written from top to bottom.

22.7.4 Terms used in addresses and their order of presentation

Addresses in China are presented from the largest unit to the smallest. If the postal code is included in the address, it occurs before the name of the city.

The major regional distinctions used in addresses in order of size are as follows:

省	县/縣	市	乡/鄉	镇/鎮	村
shěng	**xiàn**	**shì**	**xiāng**	**zhèn**	**cūn**
province	county	city	town	township	village

22.7 NAMES, KINSHIP TERMS, TITLES, AND TERMS OF ADDRESS

The terms used to refer to the units in street addresses differ somewhat in Taiwan and in mainland China. Here is a summary of the most common terms. The term 胡同 **hútong** 'alley' is used in Beijing, though as streets are restructured, alleys are being eliminated.

Terms used in Taiwan

段	**duàn**	section
区/區	**qū**	district
巷	**xiàng**	alley
弄	**lòng**	alley, lane
里	**lǐ**	neighborhood
路	**lù**	road, street
号/號	**hào**	number

Terms used in mainland China

区/區	**qū**	district
(大)街	**(dà)jiē**	street
路	**lù**	road, street
胡同	**hútong**	alley
号/號	**hào**	number

Two sample addresses in Beijing:

北京市西城区红星胡同18号
北京市西城區紅星胡同18號
Běijīng shì xīchéng qū hóngxīng hútong 18 hào
18 Red Star Alley, West District, Beijing

北京市新街口南大街十号
北京市新街口南大街十號
Běijīng shì xīn jiē kǒu nán dà jiē shí hào
10 South Xinjiekou Street, Beijing

In Beijing, street names often make reference to their location inside or outside of a traditional city gate. Here is an example:

建国门外大街
建國門外大街
Jiànguó mén wài dà jiē
the big street outside of the Jianguo Gate

Three sample addresses in Taiwan:

台北市和平东路一段162号
臺北市和平東路一段162號
Táiběi shì Hépíng dōng lù yī duàn 162 hào
162 Section 1 Hoping East Road, Taipei

40744台中市西屯区台中港路三段181号
40744臺中市西屯區臺中港路三段181號
40744 Táizhōng shì xī tún qū Táizhōng gǎng lù sān duàn 181 hào
181 Section 3 Taichung Harbor Road, Xitun District, Taichung, 40744

高雄县清水镇永康乡，镇南里冈山南路42号
高雄縣清水鎮永康鄉，鎮南裏岡山南路42號
Gāoxióng xiàn qīngshuǐ zhèn yǒngkāng xiāng, zhèn nán lǐ gāng shān nán lù 42 hào
42 South Gangshan Road, Zhennan Neighborhood, Yongkang Village, Qingshui Township, Gaoxiong (County)

For greetings and goodbyes in letters, see

▶ 24.3

23

Introductions

23.1 The general format of introductions

Formal introductions use the polite classifier for people, 位 **wèi**.

> 这位是刘晓东。这位是王玫玲。
> 這位是劉曉東。這位是王玫玲。
> **Zhè wèi shì Liú Xiǎodōng. Zhè wèi shì Wáng Méilíng.**
> This (person) is Liu Xiaodong. This (person) is Wang Meiling.

Neutral introductions have the following format.

> 这是刘晓东。这是王玫玲。
> 這是劉曉東。這是王玫玲。
> **Zhè shì Liú Xiǎodōng. Zhè shì Wáng Méilíng.**
> This is Liu Xiaodong. This is Wang Meiling.

The most common and neutral response to an introduction is:

> 你好。
> **Nǐ hǎo.**
> Hello. (lit. 'How are you?')

More formal responses to an introduction include:

> 很高兴认识你。
> 很高興認識你。
> **Hěn gāoxìng rènshi nǐ.**
> I'm very happy to meet you.

> 久仰。
> **Jiǔ yǎng.**
> I have wanted to make your acquaintance for a long time.

久仰 **jiǔ yǎng** is often said twice.

> 久闻大名。
> 久聞大名。
> **Jiǔ wén dàmíng.**
> I have heard so much about you. (lit. 'I have long heard of your great fame.')

or

> 久仰大名。
> **Jiǔ yǎng dàmíng.**
> I have heard so much about you. (lit. 'I have long admired your famous name.')

INTRODUCTIONS

23.2 Sample introductions

The following conversations illustrate informal and formal introductions. It is appropriate to include information about a person's work or field of study in an introduction. Following the conversations are the Mandarin terms for many common occupations and fields of study.

Conversation 1 (neutral level of formality)

    A: 这是李小姐，我的同学。她学地质学。
        這是李小姐，我的同學。她學地質學。
        Zhè shì Lǐ xiǎojie, wǒ de tóngxué. Tā xué dìzhìxué.

        这是我哥哥，张大年。他学语言学。
        這是我哥哥，張大年。他學語言學。
        Zhè shì wǒ gēge, Zhāng Dànián. Tā xué yǔyánxué.
        This is Miss Li, my classmate. She studies geology.
        This is my older brother, Zhang Danian. He studies linguistics.

    B: 你好。
        Nǐ hǎo.
        Hello.

    C: 你好。
        Nǐ hǎo.
        Hello.

Conversation 2 (more formal)

    A: 我给你们介绍介绍，这位是唐教授。这位是从美国来的司密斯先生。
        我給你們介紹介紹，這位是唐教授。這位是從美國來的司密斯先生。
        Wǒ gěi nǐmen jièshào jièshào, zhè wèi shì Táng jiàoshòu. Zhè wèi shì cóng Měiguó lái de Sī Mìsī xiānsheng.
        Allow me to introduce the two of you. This is Professor Tang. This is Mr. Smith from America.

    B: 久仰，久仰。
        Jiǔ yǎng, jiǔ yǎng.
        I have wanted to make your acquaintance for a long time now.

Conversation 3 (formal)

    A: 这位是有名的音乐家，马友友，这位是名导演，张艺谋。
        這位是有名的音樂家，馬友友，這位是名導演，張藝謀。
        Zhè wèi shì yǒumíng de yīnyuè jiā, Mǎ Yǒu-yǒu, zhè wèi shì míng dáoyǎn, Zhāng Yìmóu.
        This is the famous musician Ma You-you. This is the famous film director Zhang Yimou.

    B: 久仰大名。
        Jiǔ yǎng dàmíng.
        I have heard your name and have wanted to meet you for a long time.

    C: 彼此，彼此。
        Bícǐ, bícǐ.
        The feeling is mutual. (in reply to someone well known)

23.3 Common occupations and fields of study

Common professions

科学家/科學家
kēxuéjiā
scientist

作者
zuòzhě
writer

画家/畫家
huàjiā
artist

音乐家/音樂家
yīnyuè jiā
musician

记者/記者
jìzhě
reporter

会计/會計
kuàijì
accountant

农民/農民
nóngmín
farmer

工人
gōngrén
worker

牙医/牙醫
yá yī
dentist

救火员/救火員
jiùhuǒyuán
fireman

木匠
mùjiang
carpenter

水工
shuǐgōng
plumber

化工
huàgōng
chemical engineer

电工/電工
diàngōng
electrical engineer; electrician

业主/業主
yèzhǔ
owner of a business

小贩/小販
xiǎofàn
street vendor

NOTE These are not used as titles or as terms of address. For professions that are also used as titles and terms of address, see

▶ 22.3.2

Fields of study

会计学/會計學
kuàijì xué
accounting

人类学/人類學
rénlèixué
anthropology

人文科学/人文科學
rénwén kēxué
art (includes all performing arts)

亚洲学系/亞洲學系
yàzhōu xuéxì
Asian Studies

生物学/生物學
shēngwù xué
biology

化学/化學
huàxué
chemistry

资讯/資訊
zīxùn
information technology

地理学/地理學
dìlǐ xué
geography

地质学/地質學
dìzhì xué
geology

经济学/經濟學
jīngjì xué
economics

149

INTRODUCTIONS

历史/歷史
lìshǐ
history

医学/醫學
yīxué
medicine

哲学/哲學
zhé xué
philosophy

政治学/政治學
zhèngzhì xué
political science

宗教学/宗教學
zōngjiào xué
religious studies

戏剧学/戲劇學
xìjù xué
theater

数学/數學
shùxué
math

音乐学/音樂學
yīnyuè xué
music

物理学/物理學
wùlǐ xué
physics

心理学/心理學
xīnlǐ xué
psychology

社会学/社會學
shèhuì xué
sociology

语言学/語言學
yǔyán xué
linguistics

24

Greetings and goodbyes

This chapter contains the most common expressions used by Mandarin Chinese speakers when greeting others and saying goodbye in different contexts. The expressions here are those used by the majority of Mandarin speakers, but differences between mainland China and Taiwan are noted where relevant. In Chinese, greetings and goodbyes are typically not accompanied by body contact such as a handshake, hug, or kiss, though handshakes are becoming more common in cities.

Greetings are used to acknowledge the presence of another person. Chinese uses different kinds of greetings depending upon the relationship of speaker and addressee, the time of day in which the greeting is made, and whether or not contact is face-to-face. Greetings that take the form of questions typically need no response.

24.1 Greetings in conversations

24.1.1 Basic greeting

To greet casual acquaintances or to greet others in a shopping or business environment, or when meeting someone for the first time, or when answering the telephone, say:

> 你好。
> **Nǐ hǎo.**
> Hi. (How are you?)

The response to this greeting is:

> 你好。
> **Nǐ hǎo.**
> Hi. (How are you?)

Or, also possible, but less common:

> 好。谢谢。你呢?
> 好。謝謝。你呢?
> **Hǎo. Xièxie. Nǐ ne?**
> Fine. Thanks. And you?

NOTE: Until recently, the expression 你好 **nǐ hǎo** was primarily used when greeting foreigners, but in Chinese cities it is now widely used between native speakers of Chinese.

A more formal variation of this greeting uses the polite pronoun 您 **nín** 'you':

毛:	王经理，您好?	王:	好。
毛:	王經理，您好?	**Wáng:**	**Hǎo.**
Máo:	**Wáng jīnglǐ, nín hǎo?**	Wang:	Fine.
Mao:	Manager Wang, how are you?		

GREETINGS AND GOODBYES

24.1.2 Greetings with reference to time of day

The most common morning greeting is:

> 早。
> **Zǎo.**
> Good morning.

The response is:

> 早
> **Zǎo.**
> Good morning.

An alternative form of this greeting is:

> 早安。
> **Zǎo'ān.**
> Good morning.

or

> 早上好。
> **Zǎoshang hǎo.**
> Good morning.

There is no greeting associated with any other time of day.

24.1.3 Greeting people by calling them (叫 *jiào*)

In China, it is very common to greet others by making eye contact and calling them by name, title, or appropriate kinship term. To greet others in this way is to 叫 **jiào** 'call' them. This greeting can include 好 **hǎo** or 你好 **nǐ hǎo**.

罗老师！/羅老師！ **Luó lǎoshī!** Professor Ross!	张萌！/張萌！ **Zhāng Méng!** Zhang Meng!
王经理！/王經理！ **Wáng jīnglǐ!** Manager Wang!	阿姨好！ **Āyí hǎo!** How are you, Auntie!
小王！ **Xiǎo Wáng!** Little Wang!	老张你好！/老張你好！ **Lǎo Zhāng nǐ hǎo!** How are you, Old Zhang!

▶ 22.4

24.1.4 Greeting others by referring to their present activity

Relatives, friends, or close acquaintances may greet each other by referring to their present activity. Here are some examples.

吃饭去。 吃飯去。 **Chī fàn qù.** (I see that you are) Going off to eat.	上课吧！ 上課吧！ **Shàng kè ba!** Going to class, I assume.
回家呢？ **Huí jiā ne?** Are you going home?	上班呢。 **Shàng bān ne.** Going to work, right?

Saying goodbye in conversations

A variation of this kind of greeting is to ask about present activity.

你上哪儿去？
你上哪兒去？
Nǐ shàng nǎr qù?
Where are you going?

你到哪儿去？
你到哪兒去？
Nǐ dào nǎr qù?
Where are you going?

你去哪儿？
你去哪兒？
Nǐ qù nǎr?
Where are you going?

你今天去哪儿玩了？
你今天去哪兒玩了？
Nǐ jīntiān qù nǎr wán le?
Where are you heading off to play today?

干吗（呢）？ (informal/casual)
幹嗎（呢）？
Gànmá (ne)?
What are you up to?

忙什么呢？
忙甚麼呢？
Máng shénme ne?
What are you busy doing?

24.1.5 Greeting by asking about eating a meal

When greeting others around normal meal times, you can ask if they have eaten.

（你）吃（饭）了吗？ （你）吃（饭）了没有？
（你）吃（飯）了嗎？ （你）吃（飯）了沒有？
Nǐ chī (fàn) le ma? Nǐ chī (fàn) le méi yǒu
Have you eaten yet? Have you eaten yet?

24.1.6 Telephone greetings

The most common phone greetings are:

喂？
Wèi/Wéi. (It may be spoken in a rising or falling tone.)
Hello.

喂，你好。
Wéi, nǐ hǎo.
Hello, how are you?

24.2 Saying goodbye in conversations

24.2.1 Basic goodbyes

The most general way to say goodbye and to end a conversation is:

再见。/再見。
Zài jiàn.
Goodbye. (lit. 'again see' → 'see you again')

In Taiwan, and increasingly in mainland China, people also say:

拜拜。
Báibái. (also pronounced **bàibài**)
Bye bye. (borrowed from English 'bye bye')

If the participants in a conversation expect to see each other in the near future, they may use variations of 再见/再見 **zàijiàn** to say goodbye. These include:

一会儿见。
一會兒見。
Yīhuìr jiàn.
See you in a moment.

GREETINGS AND GOODBYES

回头见。
回頭見。
Huí tóu jiàn.
See you in a moment. (lit. 'See you in the turn of a head.')

明天见。
明天見。
Míngtiān jiàn.
See you tomorrow.

后天见。
後天見。
Hòutiān jiàn.
See you the day after tomorrow.

Other expressions indicating future time can be used before 见/見 **jiàn**.

24.2.2 Saying goodbye to a guest

To say goodbye to a guest, use one of these expressions:

慢走。
Màn zǒu.
Don't hurry off.

再来玩。
再來玩。
Zài lái wán.
Come again. (informal)

有空再来。
有空再來。
Yǒu kòng zài lái.
Come again when you have time.

走好。
Zǒu hǎo.
Take care.

To respond to a host when taking leave, use one of these expressions:

别送。
Bié sòng.
Don't see me off.

请留步。
請留步。
Qǐng liú bù.
Please do not bother to see me off. (more formal)

▶ 58.4.2

24.2.3 Saying goodbye to someone who is leaving on a trip

To say goodbye to someone who is leaving on a trip, say:

一路顺风。　　　　　　　　　　　　or　　一路平安。
一路顺風。
Yī lù shùn fēng.　　　　　　　　　　　　　**Yī lù píng'ān.**
Have a good trip.　　　　　　　　　　　　　Have a good trip.
(lit. 'Have a smooth wind for the entire road.')　(lit. 'Have peace for the entire road.')

Greetings and goodbyes in letters

24.3

24.2.4 Saying goodbye with reference to time of day

晚安。
Wǎn'ān.
Goodnight.

NOTE 晚安 **wǎn'ān** can only be used as a goodbye, and not as a greeting.

24.3 Greetings and goodbyes in letters

24.3.1 Greetings and salutations in letters

Letters begin with the name of the addressee.

In informal letters to someone with whom you have a close relationship, you may use the recipient's given name, or family name and given name. Sometimes these are followed by these kinship terms:

兄	xiōng	elder brother, a form of address used by males of the same generation
弟	dì	younger brother, a form of address used to a younger male
姊 or 姐	zǐ jiě	elder sister, a form of address used by females of the same generation
妹	mèi	younger sister, a form of address used to a younger female

建国兄：
建國兄：
Jiànguó xiōng:
Elder brother Jianguo:

美英姊：
Měiyīng zǐ:
Elder sister Meiying:

A more formal letter may begin with the addressee's family name, or family name and given name, followed by his or her title.

王建国先生：
王建國先生：
Wáng Jiànguó xiānsheng:
Mr. Wang Jianguo:

More formal letters may also begin with the name and title of the addressee following by a standard salutation. Note that the use of the family name makes the greeting more formal than the use of the given name alone.

The following phrases may also be used after the name and title of the addressee.

Polite and formal

钧鉴/鈞鑒 *jūnjiàn* 'for your perusal'

王先生钧鉴：
王先生鈞鑒：
Wáng xiānsheng jūnjiàn:
Mr. Wang, for your perusal:

王校长钧鉴：
王校長鈞鑒：
Wáng xiàozhǎng jūnjiàn:
Principal Wang, for your perusal:

155

GREETINGS AND GOODBYES

24.3

Polite but less formal

如晤 **rúwù** 'as if talking to you face-to-face'

> 建国兄如晤：
> 建國兄如晤：
> **Jiànguó xiōng rúwù:**
> Elder brother Jianguo, it is as if I were talking to you face-to-face:

惠鉴/惠鑒 **huìjiàn** 'please be kind enough to read the following letter'

> 美英姊惠鉴：
> 美英姊惠鑒：
> **Měiyīng zǐ huìjiàn:**
> Elder sister Meiying, please be kind enough to read the following letter:

The use of a formal title makes this salutation more formal:

> 美英女士惠鉴：
> 美英女士惠鑒：
> **Měiyīng nǚshì huìjiàn:**
> Ms. Meiying, please be kind enough to read the following letter:

This salutation is used in letters from a government department or organization to an individual.

台端 **táiduān** 'for your gracious perusal'

> 王先生台端：
> 王先生臺端：
> **Wáng xiānsheng táiduān:**
> Mr. Wang, for your gracious perusal:

24.3.2 Goodbyes in letters

The following expressions are used to close a letter. They occur after the body of the letter, before the name of the sender.

Expressions used to extend good wishes to the addressee

These expressions occur immediately after the body of the letter, before any additional greetings.

顺颂/順頌	**shùn sòng**	I take this opportunity to send regards and wish your well-being
祝	**zhù**	expressing good wishes
敬祝	**jìng zhù**	respectfully extending (good) wishes to you
敬颂/敬頌	**jìng sòng**	(I) extend good wishes
敬请/敬請	**jìng qǐng**	(I) respectfully extend (good) wishes
此颂/此頌	**cǐ sòng**	(I) extend good wishes

Wishes for good health and well-being

The following phrases are standard expressions of good wishes. They occur after one of the previous phrases, before the name of the sender. Note that many are linked to a specific season or to the new year.

春安	**chūn'ān**	a peaceful spring
夏安	**xià'ān**	your health, your well-being in the summer season
秋安	**qiū'ān**	your welfare in this autumn season
冬安	**dōng'ān**	your well-being in this winter season
教祺	**jiào qí**	(instructing you to have) good fortune [for teachers or educators]

Greetings and goodbyes in letters

岁祺/歲祺	suìqí	good fortune at the New Year
新禧	xīnxǐ	Happy New Year
道安	dào'ān	asking about your well-being
钧安	jūn'ān	your well-being
文安	wén'ān	your health

Expressions included with the signature

The following expressions are included after the name of the sender.

For letters written to someone of the same generation as oneself:

Less formal

| 上 | shàng | written by |

More formal

敬上	jìng shàng	respectfully presented
拜上	bài shàng	respectfully yours
拜启/拜啟	bài qǐ	respectfully report
再拜	zài bài	bow twice (a polite closing to a letter)

For very formal letters written to a superior

| 谨启/謹啟 | jǐn qǐ | cautiously and prudently respectfully present |
| 谨禀/謹稟 | jǐn bǐng | respectfully submitted |

In addition, if the addressee is referred to as 兄 **xiōng**, 弟 **dì**, 姊 **zǐ**, or 妹 **mèi** in the salutation, the writer typically prefixes the reciprocal generation term to his or her name in the closing. In other words, a male writer who greets his addressee with 兄 **xiōng** typically closes the letter by prefixing his name with 弟 **dì**. A female writer who greets her addressee with 姊 **zǐ** typically closes the letter by prefixing her name with 妹 **mèi**.

In the body of a letter, the name of the sender and the date of the letter are placed at the end of the letter.

Sample letters illustrating the format and the use of these expressions are presented here.

24.3.3 Sample letter outlines

24.3.3.1 Informal letter to a friend

丽历姊如晤：
麗歷姊如晤：
Lìlì zǐ rúwù:
Older sister Lili, as I talk to you face-to-face:
　　[body of the letter]
　　　　　　　顺颂
　　　　　　　順頌
　　　　　　　Shùn sòng
I take this opportunity to send regards and wish for your well-being

夏安
Xià'ān
peace in this summer season
　　　　　妹　王嘉玲　上
　　　　　　　　　一月十二日
　　　　　mèi　Wáng Jiālíng　shàng
　　　　　　　　　yī yuè shí'èr rì
Younger sister Wang Jialing
January 12

GREETINGS AND GOODBYES

24.3.3.2 Formal letter

张老师钧鉴：
張老師鈞鑒：
Zhāng lǎoshī jūn jiàn:
Professor Zhang, for your perusal:
    [body of the letter]

                敬颂
                敬頌
                Jìng sòng
                (I) extend good wishes

教祺
Jiào qí
good fortune

         学生　王美丽　拜上
                        五月十七日
         學生　王美麗　拜上
                        五月十七日
         xuésheng　Wáng Měilì　bài shàng
                        wǔ yuè shíqī rì
(Your) student, Wang Meili, I bow to you
                         May 17

24.3.3.3 Very formal letter

刘建安校长台端：
劉建安校長臺端：
Liú Jiàn'ān xiàozhǎng táiduān:
Principal Liu Jian'an, for your perusal:
    [body of the letter]

                此颂
                此頌
                Cǐ sòng
                (I) extend good wishes

道安
Dào'ān
Your health

         郭友情　谨禀
                        九月二十八日
         郭友情　謹稟
                        九月二十八日
         Guō Yǒuqíng　jǐn bǐng
                      jiǔ yuè èrshí bā rì
         Guo Youqing　respectfully submitted
                      September 28, 2004

For the format used in addressing envelopes, see

▶ 22.7

25

Basic strategies for communication

Languages have specific expressions that speakers use to start conversations and to keep them going. These expressions often reflect the degree of formality of the situation, the relationship of the participants in the conversation, and the attitudes of the speakers. This section presents the most commonly used expressions in Mandarin.

25.1 Attracting someone's attention

25.1.1 Attracting attention by using a name or title

In Mandarin, the most common way to attract someone's attention is to address them with their name, a title, or a kinship term.

▶ 22.4

马教授/馬教授	王玫玲
Mǎ jiàoshòu	**Wáng Méilíng**
Professor Ma	Wang Meiling
先生	小姐
Xiānsheng	**Xiǎojie**
Mr./sir	Miss

In mainland China, to politely get the attention of a male whom you do not know, you can say:

师傅/師傅　　**shīfu**　　master (as in, 'master craftsman')

Taxi drivers are typically addressed as:

司机/司機　　**sījī**　　driver

An informal way to attract someone's attention is by using the interjection:

欸　　　　**ēi**　　hey

25.1.2 Attracting attention by apologizing for the intrusion

麻烦你	对不起	劳驾
麻煩你	對不起	勞駕
máfan nǐ	**duìbuqǐ**	**láojià**
excuse me (I am bothering you)	excuse me (sorry for being rude)	excuse me (for creating extra work for you)

BASIC STRATEGIES FOR COMMUNICATION

25.1.3 Attracting attention by indicating that you want to ask a question

请问　　　　　　　　　　　(我想)打听一下
請問　　　　　　　　　　　(我想)打聽一下
qǐng wèn　　　　　　　　**(wǒ xiǎng) dǎting yí xià**
may I ask　　　　　　　　　I'd like to inquire for a moment

25.1.4 Attracting attention by asking for help

请帮(个)忙。　　　　　　　劳驾
請幫(個)忙。　　　　　　　勞駕
Qǐng bāng (gè) máng.　　**láojià**
Please help me.　　　　　　excuse me (for creating extra work for you)

Asking for help is an appropriate strategy when dealing with friends or acquaintances. It is not a good strategy when speaking with strangers, who may be reluctant to get involved in a troublesome situation. When speaking with strangers, apologizing for or acknowledging an intrusion (麻烦你/麻煩你 **máfan nǐ**) or beginning your request with a question (请问/請問 **qǐng wèn**) is more effective.

25.2 Responding to a call for attention

The most common way to respond to a call for attention is to use the phrase

什么事？
甚麼事？
Shénme shì?
What is the matter?/What do you want?

Other responses include

有事吗？　　　　　　　　　怎么了？
有事嗎？　　　　　　　　　怎麼了？
Yǒu shì ma?　　　　　　　**Zěnme le?**
Is something the matter?　　　What's the matter?

25.3 Checking whether people have understood you

清楚吗？　　　　　懂不懂？　　　　　懂吗？
清楚嗎？　　　　　懂不懂？　　　　　懂嗎？
Qīngchu ma?　　**Dǒng bù dǒng?**　　**Dǒng ma?**
Is it clear?　　　　Do you understand?　Do you understand?

25.4 Indicating understanding or lack of understanding

好。　　　　　　　　行。　　　　　　　　(我)懂(了)。
Hǎo.　　　　　　**Xíng.**　　　　　　　**(Wǒ) dǒng (le).**
Okay.　　　　　　　Okay.　　　　　　　　(I) understand (now).

我不懂。
Wǒ bù dǒng.
I don't understand.

25.5 Requesting repetition or clarification of spoken language

请你再说。
請你再說。
Qǐng nǐ zài shuō.
Please repeat./Please say it again.

(那是)什么意思?
(那是)甚麼意思?
(Nà shì) shénme yìsi?
What does that mean?

请你说慢一点。
請你說慢一點。
Qǐng nǐ shuō màn yīdiǎn.
Please speak a little slower.

25.6 Asking for assistance in identifying a Chinese character

怎么念?
怎麼唸?
Zěnme niàn?
How is it pronounced?

这个字怎么念?
這個字怎麼唸?
Zhège zì zěnme niàn?
How is this character pronounced?

怎么写?
怎麼寫?
Zěnme xiě?
How do you write it?

那个字怎么写?
那個字怎麼寫?
Nàge zì zěnme xiě?
How do you write that character?

'qīngchu' 怎么写?
'qīngchu' 怎麼寫?
'qīngchu' zěnme xiě?
How do you write the word 'qingchu'?

那个字是什么意思?
那個字是甚麼意思?
Nàge zì shì shénme yìsi?
What does that character mean?

25.7 Providing information about the identification of Chinese characters

The following strategies are commonly used to help a listener identify a character.

- Present a common word in which the character in question occurs

   「清楚」的「清」
   'qīngchu' de 'qīng'
   the 'qing' in 'qingchu'

   「朋友」的「友」
   'péngyou' de 'yǒu'
   the 'you' of 'pengyou'

- List the components of the character in question

「三点水」的「清」
「三點水」的「清」
'sāndiǎn shuǐ' de 'qīng'
the character 'qing' with the 'three dot water' radical

「木子」「李」
'mù' 'zǐ' 'Lǐ'
the character '李 **Lǐ**' that consists of the character '木 **mù**' and the character '子 **zǐ**'

25.8 Signaling that you are following the speaker

To indicate that you are following a speaker, say:

是，是	shì, shì	yes, yes
嗯，嗯	en, en	yeh, yeh
对，对/對，對	duì, duì	right, right

25.9 Interrupting a speaker

To interrupt a speaker say:

对不起/對不起　　**duìbuqǐ**　　excuse me

25.10 Using fillers

A filler is an expression that fills a pause in a conversation and keeps the conversation going. English uses expressions such as 'well,' 'mmm,' 'uh.' Mandarin uses these expressions:

那么/那麼	**nàme**	well
嗯，嗯	**en, en**	yeh
这个，这个…/這個，這個…	**zhège, zhège**	this, this…

25.11 Formal development of a topic

25.11.1 Opening remarks

To formally introduce a topic in a talk or written report, use the following expressions:

今天要谈到的问题是…
今天要談到的問題是…
Jīntiān yào tándào de wèntí shì…
The issue/problem we are going to discuss today is…

今天要讲的题目是…（今天要讨论的题目是…）
今天要講的題目是…（今天要討論的題目是…）
Jīntiān yào jiǎng de tímù shì…(jīntiān yào tǎolùn de tímù shì…)
The topic I am going to talk about today is…(The topic I am going to discuss today is…)

请各位多多指教。
請各位多多指教。
Qǐng gèwèi duōduō zhǐjiào.
I invite your comments and corrections. (used in formal speeches and written presentations)

▶ 57.1

Formal development of a topic | **25.11**

25.11.2 Introducing further points

To introduce additional points in a discussion or in writing, say:

首先	**shǒuxiān**	in the first place
第一	**dì yī**	first
除了 (noun phrase) 以外	**chúle** (noun phrase) **yǐwài**	besides (noun phrase)
还有/還有	**hái yǒu**	also, in addition
请看/請看	**qǐng kàn** (+ noun phrase)	please look at (noun phrase)

▶ 15.2.3, 40.3

25.11.3 Establishing a sequence

第一	**dìyī**	first
第二	**dì èr**	second
第三	**dì sān**	third
然后/然後	**ránhòu**	afterwards
后来/後來	**hòulái**	afterwards (only used to describe sequence in the past)

▶ 6.4, 42

25.11.4 Establishing references

To refer to information that is relevant to the conversation, use these expressions:

关于/關於 **guānyú** 'regarding (noun phrase)'

> 关于买飞机票的事，请你负责。
> 關於買飛機票的事，請你負責。
> **Guānyú mǎi fēijī piào de shì, qǐng nǐ fùzé.**
> As for buying the airplane tickets, please take charge.

至于/至於 **zhìyú** 'in reference to (noun phrase)'

> 至于定旅馆的事，你不必费心。
> 至於定旅館的事，你不必費心。
> **Zhìyú dìng lǚguǎn de shì, nǐ bù bì fèixīn.**
> As for making the hotel reservations, you don't have to bother (doing that).

甚至于/甚至於 **shènzhìyú** 'even, go so far as to (noun phrase or verb phrase)'

> 一切手续都办好了，甚至于你住的地方。
> 一切手續都辦好了，甚至於你住的地方。
> **Yīqiè shǒuxù dōu bànhǎo le, shènzhìyú nǐ zhù de dìfang.**
> All of the arrangements have been taken care of, even down to the place where you will live.

> 为什么有时候打开网页的速度很慢甚至于无法连接？
> 為什麼有時候打開網頁的速度很慢甚至於無法連接？
> **Wèishénme yǒu shíhòu dǎkāi wǎngyè de sùdù hěn màn shènzhìyú wúfǎ liánjie?**
> Why is it that sometimes it takes a very long time for a web page to open, sometimes not even connecting at all?

▶ 57.1.1

BASIC STRATEGIES FOR COMMUNICATION 25.11

25.11.5 Giving examples

To give examples, use these expressions to introduce your remarks:

比方说/比方說 **bǐfang shuō** *'for example' (+ sentence)*

> 中文跟英文不同。比方说，中文有声调，英文没有。
> 中文跟英文不同。比方說，中文有聲調，英文沒有。
> **Zhōngwén gén Yīngwén bù tóng. Bǐfang shuō, Zhōngwén yǒu shēngdiào, Yīngwén méi yǒu.**
> Chinese and English are different. For example, Chinese has tones, English doesn't have tones.

例如 **lìrú** *'for example' (+ sentence)*

> 请你说一下你是怎么学中文的，例如每天花多少时间，听多少时间录音，等等。
> 請你說一下你是怎麼學中文的，例如每天花多少時間，听多少時間錄音，等等。
> **Qǐng nǐ shuō yīxià nǐ shì zěnme xué Zhōngwén de, lìrú měitiān huā duōshao shíjiān, tīng duōshao shíjiān lùyīn, děng děng.**
> Please tell (me) how you study Chinese, for example, how many hours you spend every day, how long you listen to recordings, etc.

譬如 **pìrú** *'for example' (used the same way as* 例如 **lìrú***, but in more formal contexts)*

举例来说/舉例來說 **jǔlì láishuō** *'to give an example' (+ sentence)*

> 中国话有很多词可以重叠，举例来说，走走，哥哥，天天，等。
> 中國話有很多詞可以重疊，舉例來說，走走，哥哥，天天，等。
> **Zhōngguó huà yǒu hěn duō cí kěyǐ chóngdié, jǔ lì lái shuō, zǒu zǒu, gēge, tiāntiān, děng.**
> The Chinese language has a lot of words that can be reduplicated, for example, '**zou zou**,' '**gege**,' '**tiantian**,' etc.

25.11.6 Summarizing and concluding

To summarize and conclude, use these expressions to introduce your remarks:

总而言之/總而言之 **zǒng'éryánzhī** *'in other words, to put it another way'*

> 这件事我们已经谈了很多次了。总而言之，希望我们能互相信任。
> 這件事我們已經談了很多次了。總而言之，希望我們能互相信任。
> **Zhè jiàn shì wǒmen yǐjing tán le hěn duō cì le. Zǒng'éryánzhī, xīwàng wǒmen néng hùxiāng xìnrèn.**
> We've talked about this matter many times before. To put it another way, I hope we can trust each other.

总括来说/總括來說 **zǒngkuò láishuō** *'to sum up'*

> 总括来说，中国文字太复杂，需要改革。
> 總括來說，中國文字太複雜，需要改革。
> **Zǒngkuò láishuō, Zhōngguó wénzì tài fùzá, xūyào gǎigé.**
> To sum things up, the Chinese language is too complicated and needs to be revised.

最后/最後 **zuìhòu** *'finally'*

> 以下是我的看法，最后希望各位能多提意见。
> 以下是我的看法，最後希望各位能多提意見。
> **Yǐxià shì wǒde kànfǎ, zuìhòu xīwàng gè wèi néng duō tí yìjian.**
> What follows is my opinion. Finally, I hope that everyone will provide feedback.

26

Telecommunications and e-communications: telephones, the internet, and faxes

Telecommunications and e-communications play a major role in communication in China. This chapter presents expressions associated with the use of these technologies.

26.1 Making and receiving phone calls; sending and receiving faxes and email messages

26.1.1 Telephone and mobile phone/cell phone

给 (someone) 打电话/給 (someone) 打電話
gěi (someone) *dǎ* **diànhuà**
make a phone call to someone

> (请)给我打电话。
> (請)給我打電話。
> **(Qǐng) gěi wǒ *dǎ* diànhuà.**
> (Please) call me.

> 请打我的手机。
> 請打我的手機。
> **Qǐng *dǎ* wǒ de shǒujī.**
> Please call my mobile.

接电话/接電話
jiē **diànhuà**
receive a phone call

> 没人接电话。
> 沒人接電話。
> **Méi rén *jiē* diànhuà.**
> No one is *answering* the phone.

发短信   or   发短消息
發短信   發短消息
fā **duǎnxìn**   *fā* **duǎn xiāoxi**
send a text message

> 我给你发了短信。
> 我給你發了短信。
> **Wǒ gěi nǐ fā le duǎnxìn.**
> I sent you a text message.

165

TELECOMMUNICATIONS AND E-COMMUNICATIONS

收短信 or 收短消息
shōu **duǎnxìn** *shōu* **duǎn xiāoxi**
receive a text message

我收到了你的短信。
Wǒ shōudào le nǐ de duǎnxìn.
I received your text message.

26.1.2 Fax

发传真/發傳真
fā **chuánzhēn**
send a fax

收传真/收傳真
shōu **chuánzhēn**
receive a fax

我没收到你的传真。请你重发一次。
我沒收到你的傳真。請你重發一次。
Wǒ méi *shōudào* **nǐ de chuánzhēn. Qǐng nǐ chóng** *fā* **yīcì.**
I didn't *receive* your fax. Please *transmit* it again.

26.1.3 Email

电子信/電子信 or （电子）邮件/（電子）郵件
diànzǐ xìn **(diànzǐ) yóujiàn**
email email

发电子信 or 送电子邮件
發電子信 送電子郵件
fā **diànzǐ xìn** **sòng diànzǐ yóujiàn**
send an email send an email

接电子邮件/接電子郵件
jiē **diànzǐ yóujiàn**
receive an email

添加附件
tiānjiā **fùjiàn**
add an attachment

打开附件/打開附件
dǎkāi **fùjiàn**
open an attachment

请看附件。
請看附件。
Qǐng kàn fùjiàn.
Please see the attachment.

166

Telephone etiquette

26.2 Dialing a number and entering a number

拨电话号码/撥電話號碼
bō diànhuà hàomǎ
dial a phone number

> 在你刚拨的电话号码前请加 '○'。
> 在你剛撥的電話號碼前請加 '○'。
> **Zài nǐ gāng bō de diànhuà hàomǎ qián qǐng jiā 'líng.'**
> Please add 'zero' in front of the telephone number that you just dialed.

输入号码/輸入號碼
shūrù hàomǎ
enter a number

> 请输入你的客户号码。
> 請輸入你的客戶號碼。
> **Qǐng shūrù nǐ de kèhù hàomǎ.**
> Please enter your customer (account) number.

26.3 Using the internet

Basic vocabulary

万维网/萬維網
wàn wéi wǎng
internet

(世界)网路/(世界)網路
(shìjiè) wǎng lù
internet

因特网/因特網
yīn tè wǎng
internet

互联网/互聯網
hùlián wǎng
internet

网站/網站
wǎng zhàn
website

网页/網頁
wǎng yè
webpage

网路专家/網路專家
wǎnglù zhuānjiā
webmaster

网吧/網吧
wǎng bā
internet cafe

上网(路)/上網(路)
shàng wǎng (lù)
surf the web

26.4 Telephone etiquette

Telephone calls are answered with the phrase:

> 喂? **Wèi?** or **Wéi?**

喂? **Wèi?** (in either tone) is the equivalent of 'Hello' in English.

NOTE 喂 **wèi** can be used more broadly as an interjection to attract somebody's attention. When used in answering a phone call, it is said in second or fourth tone. Second tone is more polite and more commonly used. Fourth tone conveys a sense of impatience.

167

TELECOMMUNICATIONS AND E-COMMUNICATIONS

Increasingly, in the cities of China, the phrase used to answer a phone call is:

> 喂？你好。
> 喂？你好。
> **Wéi? Nǐ hǎo.**
> Hello. How are you?

To ask to speak to someone say:

> (张老师)在吗？
> (張老師)在嗎？
> **(Zhāng lǎoshī) zài ma?**
> Is (Professor Zhang) in?

or

> 我找(张老师)。她在吗？
> 我找(張老師)。她在嗎？
> **Wǒ zhǎo (Zhāng lǎoshī). Tā zài ma?**
> I'm looking for (Professor Zhang). Is she in?

If the party in question is not in, say:

> (她)不在。
> **(Tā) bù zài.**
> (She) is not in.

If you wish to leave a message say:

> 我要留言。
> **Wǒ yào liú yán.**
> I'd like to leave a message.

To arrange to get together with someone by phone say:

> 我们通电话。
> 我們通電話。
> **Wǒmen tōng diànhuà.**
> Let's be in touch by phone.

To describe problems reaching someone by phone say:

> (我)打不通。
> **(Wǒ) dǎbutōng.**
> (I am) unable to get through.

> 现在占线。
> 現在占線。
> **Xiànzài** *zhàn xiàn.*
> The line is busy.

26.5 Writing and reciting phone numbers and fax numbers

Phone and fax numbers are recited as a list of single digits. In mainland China, when reciting numbers, the number 1 (一) is pronounced **yāo**. In Taiwan it is pronounced **yī**. Phone and fax numbers are typically written with Arabic numerals and not with Chinese characters.

26.5 Writing and reciting phone numbers and fax numbers

Sample numbers

Phone, fax

6	5	2	7 – 3	3	7	8
liù	wǔ	èr	qī sān	sān	qī	bā

Cell phone

1	3	5	5	7	6	7	6	6	6	6
yī	sān	wǔ	wǔ	qī	liù	qī	liù	liù	liù	liù
or										
yāo	sān	wǔ	wǔ	qī	liù	qī	liù	liù	liù	liù

▶ 6.1.1

NOTE — Phone numbers that include the numerals 6 or 8 are considered particularly good and lucky. Those with the numeral 4 are less desirable. In mainland China, cell phone customers select and purchase their numbers from a list. Those with 6s and 8s are more expensive. Those with 4s are less expensive.

27

Negating information

27.1 Negation of verbs and verb phrases

The words that are used to negate verbs and verb phrases in Mandarin are 不 **bù** and 没/沒 **méi**. 不 **bù** and 没/沒 **méi** immediately precede the verb or anything that precedes and modifies the verb, including an adverb, a location phrase, or any other prepositional phrase.

> 他不喝酒。[negation + verb]
> **Tā bù *hē* jiǔ.**
> He doesn't *drink* (alcohol).

> 他不一定考得好。[negation + adverb]
> **Tā bù *yīdìng* kǎodehǎo.**
> It is not *certain* that he will do well on the exam. (He may not do well on the exam.)

> 他不在家吃饭。[negation + location prepositional phrase]
> 他不在家吃飯。
> **Tā bù *zài jiā* chī fàn.**
> He doesn't eat *at home*.

> 她没跟弟弟说话。[negation + prepositional phrase]
> 她沒跟弟弟說話。
> **Tā méi *gēn dìdi* shuō huà.**
> She didn't speak *with younger brother*.

In addition to the primary role of 不 **bù** and 没/沒 **méi** as markers of negation, they often serve to identify the aspect and time frame of events.

▶ 10.1, 11.1, 12, 13.3, 17, 37.3

27.1.1 不 *bù*

不 **bù** is the marker of negation for:

- adjectival verbs, stative verbs, and modal verbs

> 妹妹不高。(*adjectival verb*)
> **Mèimei bù *gāo*.**
> Younger sister is not *tall*.

> 我不喜欢他。(*stative verb*)
> 我不喜歡他。
> **Wǒ bù *xǐhuan* tā.**
> I don't *like* him.

> 十六岁的孩子不可以喝酒。(*modal verb*)
> 十六歲的孩子不可以喝酒。
> **Shíliù suì de háizi bù *kéyǐ* hē jiǔ.**
> 16-year-old children are not *allowed* to drink.

Negation of verbs and verb phrases | **27.1**

- negated manner adverbial phrases

    他考得不好。
    Tā kǎo de bù hǎo.
    He didn't do well on the test.

▶ 10.1, 11.1, 12.6.1, 31.1.2.2

- action verbs describing present, future, or habitual events

    他不吃肉。
    Tā bù _chī_ ròu.
    He does not _eat_ meat.

    我不学法语。
    我不學法語。
    Wǒ bù _xué_ Fáyǔ.
    I don't _study_ French.

▶ 13.3

27.1.2 没/沒 _méi_ and 没有/沒有 _méi yǒu_

没/沒 **méi** is the negation word that negates the verb 有 **yǒu**.

    他没有钱。
    他沒有錢。
    Tā méi yǒu qián.
    He doesn't have any money.

    公园里没有人。
    公園裏沒有人。
    Gōngyuán lǐ méi yǒu rén.
    There are no people in the park.

In addition, 没/沒 **méi** (or 没有/沒有 **méi yǒu**) negates action verbs under the following conditions:

The action is not complete

    我还没看完那本书。
    我還沒看完那本書。
    Wǒ hái méi kànwán nà běn shū.
    I still haven't finished reading that book.

The action did not happen in the past

    我昨天没吃晚饭。
    我昨天沒吃晚飯。
    Wǒ zuótiān méi chī wǎnfàn.
    Yesterday, I didn't eat dinner.

    我这个月都没看电影。
    我這個月都沒看電影。
    Wǒ zhège yuè dōu méi kàn diànyǐng.
    This month I haven't seen a movie.

When negation occurs at the end of the sentence in _verb-not-verb_ questions, 没/沒 **méi** must be followed by 有 **yǒu**.

    你看完了那本书没有?
    你看完了那本書沒有?
    Nǐ kànwán le nà běn shū méi yǒu?
    Have you finished reading that book?

▶ 13.3, 37.4

171

NEGATING INFORMATION

27.2 The relative order of negation and adverbs

Here are some general rules for the relative order of negation and adverbs. The adverbs are emphasized in each example.

- Most adverbs occur before negation.

    那本书，我还没看完。
    那本書，我還沒看完。
    Nà běn shū, wǒ *hái* méi kànwán.
    That book, I have not *yet* finished reading it.

    我喜欢吃中国饭，就不喜欢吃海参。
    我喜歡吃中國飯，就不喜歡吃海參。
    Wǒ xǐhuan chī Zhōngguó fàn, *jiù* bù xǐhuan chī hǎishēn.
    I like to eat Chinese food; I *just* don't like to eat sea slugs.

    他也许不认识你妹妹。
    他也許不認識你妹妹。
    Tā *yěxǔ* bù rènshi nǐ mèimei.
    Perhaps he doesn't know your younger sister.

- A small number of adverbs may occur either before or after negation. The order of negation and adverb influences the meaning of the sentence.

    我们都不会开车。
    我們都不會開車。
    Wǒmen *dōu* bù huì kāi chē.
    We *all* cannot drive (a car).

    我们不都会开车。有的会，有的不会。
    我們不都會開車。有的會，有的不會。
    Wǒmen bù *dōu* huì kāi chē. Yǒu de huì, yǒu de bù huì.
    Not *all* of us can drive a car. Some can, some can't.

    我一定不去。
    Wǒ *yīdìng* bù qù.
    I am *definitely* not going.

    我不一定去。
    Wǒ bù *yīdìng* qù.
    I am not *definitely* going. (I may not go.)

▶ 15.1

27.3 Words that occur with negation

27.3.1 Adverbs that occur with negation

Certain adverbs always occur with negation or in negative contexts. These include:

从来/從來 *cónglái* (+ negation) 'never'

    我从来没抽过烟。
    我從來沒抽過煙。
    Wǒ cónglái méi chōuguo yān.
    I've never smoked cigarettes.

不 bù in resultative and directional verbs **27.4**

根本 **gēnběn** (+ negation) 'absolutely not'

> 那样的话根本没有道理。
> 那樣的話根本沒有道理。
> **Nà yàng de huà gēnběn méi yǒu dàoli.**
> That kind of talk makes no sense.

并/並 **bìng** (+ negation) 'absolutely (not)'

> 我并不愿意跟他一起住。
> 我並不願意跟他一起住。
> **Wǒ bìng bù yuànyi gēn tā yīqǐ zhù.**
> I am absolutely not willing to live with him.
> (I am not at all willing to live with him.)

▶ 35.3

27.3.2 The noun modifier 任何 rènhé and negation

任何 **rènhé** 'any'

> 我没告诉任何人。
> 我沒告訴任何人。
> **Wǒ méi gàosu rènhé rén.**
> I didn't tell anyone.

27.4 不 bù in resultative and directional verbs

不 **bù** occurs between the verb and the resultative or directional suffix to indicate inability to achieve the result. Here are some examples.

吃完 **chīwán** 'finish eating'

> 我吃不完。
> **Wǒ chībuwán.**
> I am unable to finish eating (the food).

看见 **kànjian** 'see, perceive'

> 这个电影的字幕太小。我根本看不见。
> 這個電影的字幕太小。我根本看不見。
> **Zhège diànyǐng de zìmù tài xiǎo. Wǒ gēnběn kànbujiàn.**
> The subtitles in this movie are too small. I can't see them at all.

听懂/聽懂 **tīngdǒng** 'understand by listening'

> 他说得太快。我听不懂。
> 他說得太快。我聽不懂。
> **Tā shuōde tài kuài. Wǒ tīngbudǒng.**
> He speaks too quickly. I can't understand (by listening).

爬上去 **páshàngqu** 'climb up'

> 山太高。我爬不上去。
> **Shān tài gāo. Wǒ pábushàngqù.**
> The mountain is too tall. I can't climb up. (I can't climb it.)

▶ 18.6, 19.5, 32.2

173

NEGATING INFORMATION

27.5 Literary markers of negation: 無 *wú* and 非 *fēi*

The literary markers of negation 無 **wú** and 非 **fēi** occur in modern Mandarin as components of words. The following are commonly used words that include 無 **wú** and 非 **fēi**.

Expressions with 無 *wú*

无论/無論	**wúlùn**	no matter what
无论如何/無論如何	**wúlùn rú hé**	in any case, no matter what
无比/無比	**wúbǐ**	incomparable
无故/無故	**wúgù**	without reason; for no reason
无理/無理	**wúlǐ**	unreasonable; for no reason
毫无/毫無	**háowú**	not in the least, not at all

无论你去不去上课，我也不去。
無論你去不去上課，我也不去。
Wúlùn nǐ qù bù qù shàng kè, wǒ yě bù qù.
Whether or not you go to class, I am not going.

你无论如何得帮我这个忙。
你無論如何得幫我這個忙。
Nǐ wúlùn rúhé děi bāng wǒ zhège máng.
No matter what, you have to help me with this matter.

夏威夷的风景美丽无比。
夏威夷的風景美麗無比。
Xiàwēiyí de fēngjǐng měilì wúbǐ.
The scenery of Hawaii is so beautiful that no place can match it.

你为什么无缘无故打人？
你為甚麼無緣無故打人？
Nǐ wèi shénme wúyuán wúgù dǎ rén?
Why do you hit people for no reason at all?

你这真是无理取闹。
你這真是無理取鬧。
Nǐ zhè zhēn shì wúlǐ qǔnào.
You are really picking a fight for no reason.

毫无疑问，她是一个很好的学生。
毫無疑問，她是一個很好的學生。
Háowú yí wèn, tā shì yī gè hěn hǎo de xuésheng.
No doubt at all; she is a very good student.

Q: 你明天能来吗？　　　　　　　　A: 毫无问题。
　　你明天能來嗎？　　　　　　　　　　毫無問題。
　　Nǐ míngtiān néng lái ma?　　　　**Háowú wèntí.**
　　Are you able to come tomorrow?　　No problem.

Expressions with 非 *fēi*

非 (verb phrase) 不可	**fēi** (verb phrase) **bù kě**	must (verb phrase)
非得	**fēiděi**	must
非凡	**fēifán**	outstanding
非法	**fēifǎ**	illegal
非常	**fēicháng**	extraordinary, extremely

我非把中文学好不可。
我非把中文學好不可。
Wǒ fēi bǎ Zhōngwén xué hǎo bù kě.

Literary markers of negation: 無 *wú* and 非 *fēi*   **27.5**

I must master Chinese.

你今天下午非得把功课做完。
你今天下午非得把功課做完。
Nǐ jīntiān xiàwǔ fēi děi bǎ gōngkè zuòwán.
You must finish your homework this afternoon.

这次的庆祝会隆重非凡。
這次的慶祝會隆重非凡。
Zhè cì de qìngzhù huì lóngzhòng fēifán.
This celebration was extraordinarily ceremonious.

非法的生意我不会作的。
非法的生意我不會作的。
Fēifǎ de shēngyì wǒ bù huì zuò de.
I will never do any illegal business.

他的英文非常好。
Tā de Yīngwén fēicháng hǎo.
His English is extremely good.

28

Asking questions and replying to questions

Questions are used to ask for information. Here are the most common question types in Mandarin.

28.1 Yes–no questions

Yes–no questions are questions that can be answered with 'yes' or 'no.' In Mandarin, there are several ways to ask yes–no questions. Notice that unlike English, the overall phrase order of statements and yes–no questions is the same. In addition, no helping word equivalent to 'do' is involved in yes–no questions in Chinese.

28.1.1 Yes-no questions with 吗/嗎 *ma*

When 吗/嗎 **ma** is added to the end of a statement, it turns the statement into a yes–no question.

Statement	*Yes–no question*
她是中国人。	她是中国人吗?
她是中國人。	她是中國人嗎?
Tā shì Zhōngguo rén.	**Tā shì Zhōngguo rén ma?**
She is a Chinese person.	Is she a Chinese person?
他们卖橘子。	他们卖橘子吗?
他們賣橘子。	他們賣橘子嗎?
Tāmen mài júzi.	**Tāmen mài júzi ma?**
They sell tangerines.	Do they sell tangerines?
他会说中文。	他会说中文吗?
他會說中文。	他會說中文嗎?
Tā huì shuō Zhōngwén.	**Tā huì shuō Zhōngwén ma?**
He can speak Chinese.	Can he speak Chinese?

28.1.2 Yes-no questions with verb-not-verb structure

Yes–no questions may also be formed by repeating the first verb of the verb phrase in affirmative and negative form. Here are examples with different types of verbs.

Modal verbs

他<u>会</u>不<u>会</u>说中文?
他<u>會</u>不<u>會</u>說中文?
Tā *huì* bù *huì* shuō Zhōngwén?
Can he speak Chinese?

▶ 12.6.2

Yes–no questions 28.1

The equational verb 是 *shì 'to be'*

> 她是不是中国人？
> 她是不是中國人？
> **Tā *shì* bù *shì* Zhōngguo rén?**
> *Is* she a Chinese person?

▶ 11.5

Action verbs

> 他们卖不卖橘子？
> 他們賣不賣橘子？
> **Tāmen *mài* bù *mài* júzi?**
> Do they *sell* tangerines?

▶ 13.4.1

Stative verbs

> 你喜欢不喜欢他？
> 你喜歡不喜歡他？
> **Nǐ *xǐhuan* bù *xǐhuan* tā?**
> Do you *like* him?

or

> 你喜不喜欢他？
> 你喜不喜歡他？
> **Nǐ *xǐ* bù *xǐhuan* tā?**
> Do you like him?

▶ 11

Adjectival verbs

> 飞机票贵不贵？
> 飛機票貴不貴？
> **Fēijī piào *guì* bù *guì*?**
> Are airplane tickets *expensive*?

▶ 10.2

When the main verb of a sentence is 有 **yǒu**, the *verb-not-verb* question is 有没有/有沒有 **yǒu méi yǒu**.

> 你有没有钱？
> 你有沒有錢？
> **Nǐ yǒu méi yǒu qián?**
> Do you have money?

▶ 11.6.4, 13.4.2, 27.1.2

When the verb is followed by a direct object and no other phrase, *verb-not-verb* may be split. In this case, *not-verb* can occur immediately after the object.

> 他会说中文不会？
> 他會說中文不會？
> **Tā *huì* shuō Zhōngwén bù *huì*?**
> Can he speak Chinese?

> 她是中国人不是？
> 她是中國人不是？
> **Tā *shì* Zhōngguo rén bù *shì*?**
> Is she a Chinese person?

177

ASKING QUESTIONS AND REPLYING TO QUESTIONS

28.1

他们卖橘子不卖？
他們賣橘子不賣？
Tāmen mài júzi bù mài?
Do they sell tangerines?

你有钱没有？
你有錢沒有？
Nǐ yǒu qián méi yǒu?
Do you have money?

The *verb-not-verb* structure can be used to question whether an action is complete. In this case, 'not' must be 没有/沒有 **méi yǒu**. 没有/沒有 **méi yǒu** occurs after the direct object, at the end of the sentence.

你吃饭了没有？
你吃飯了沒有？
Nǐ chī fàn le méi yǒu?
Have you eaten?

NOTE Native speakers differ in where they put 了 **le** in sentences like these. Some speakers prefer to put 了 **le** after the object of the verb as in the example above. Some speakers prefer to put 了 **le** after the verb itself, as in the following example

你吃了饭没有？
你吃了飯沒有？
Nǐ chǐ le fàn méi yǒu?
Have you eaten?

▶ 13.4, 37.1

28.1.3 Yes-no questions with 是否 *shìfǒu*

是否 **shìfǒu** before the verb turns a statement into a yes–no question. 是否 **shìfǒu** questions are more common in written Chinese than in the spoken language.

Statement	是否 *shìfǒu* question
你喜欢他。 你喜歡他。 **Nǐ xǐhuan tā.** You like him.	你是否喜欢他？ 你是否喜歡他？ **Nǐ shìfǒu xǐhuan tā?** Do you like him (or not)?
他去过中国。 他去過中國。 **Tā qùguò Zhōngguó.** He has been to China.	他是否去过中国？ 他是否去過中國？ **Tā shìfǒu qùguò Zhōngguó?** Has he been to China (or not)?
他会说汉语。 他會說漢語。 **Tā huì shuō Hànyǔ.** He can speak Chinese.	他是否会说汉语？ 他是否會說漢語？ **Tā shìfǒu huì shuō Hànyǔ?** Can he speak Chinese (or not)?

28.1.4 Replying to yes-no questions

28.1.4.1 Replying 'yes'

There is no word 'yes' in Mandarin. To reply 'yes' to a yes–no question in 吗/嗎 **ma** form, in 是否 **shìfǒu** form, or in *verb-not-verb* form, repeat the verb.

178

Yes–no questions

28.1

吗/嗎 *ma* question	是否 *shìfǒu* question	Verb-not-verb question	Yes
她是中国人吗？ 她是中國人嗎？ **Tā *shì* Zhōngguo rén ma?** *Is* she a Chinese person?	她是否是中国人？ 她是否是中國人？ **Tā *shìfǒu shì* Zhōngguo rén?** *Is* she a Chinese person?	她是不是中国人？ 她是不是中國人？ **Tā *shì bù shì* Zhōngguo rén?** *Is* she a Chinese person?	是。 Shì. Yes.
他去过中国吗？ 他去過中國嗎？ **Tā *qùguò* Zhōngguó ma?** Has he *been* to China?	他是否去过中国？ 他是否去過中國？ **Tā *shìfǒu qùguò* Zhōngguó?** Has he *been* to China?	他去过中国没有？ 他去過中國沒有？ **Tā *qùguò* Zhōngguó *méi yǒu*?** Has he *been* to China?	去过。 去過。 Qùguò. Yes.
他会说中文吗？ 他會說中文嗎？ **Tā *huì* shuō Zhōngwén ma?** *Can* he speak Chinese?	他是否会说中文？ 他是否會說中文？ **Tā *shìfǒu huì* shuō Zhōngwén?** *Can* he speak Chinese?	他会不会说中文？ 他會不會說中文？ **Tā *huì bù huì* shuō Zhōngwén?** *Can* he speak Chinese?	会/會。 Huì. Yes.
你有钱吗？ 你有錢嗎？ **Nǐ *yǒu* qián ma?** Do you *have* money?	你是否有钱？ 你是否有錢？ **Nǐ *shìfǒu yǒu* qián?** Do you *have* money?	你有没有钱？ 你有沒有錢？ **Nǐ *yǒu méi yǒu* qián?** Do you *have* money?	有。 Yǒu. Yes.

8.1.4.2 Replying 'no'

If the question asks about present, future, or general time and the main verb of the sentence is any verb except for 有 **yǒu**, the 'no' answer is 不 **bù** + the verb.

If the question asks about a past or complete event or if the main verb of the question is 有 **yǒu**, the 'no' answer is 没有 **méi yǒu**.

Yes–no question	是否 *shìfǒu* question	Verb-not-verb question	No
她是中国人吗？ 她是中國人嗎？ **Tā *shì* Zhōngguo rén ma?** *Is* she a Chinese person?	她是否是中国人？ 她是否是中國人？ **Tā *shìfǒu shì* Zhōngguo rén?** *Is* she a Chinese person?	她是不是中国人？ 她是不是中國人？ **Tā *shì bù shì* Zhōngguo rén?** *Is* she a Chinese person?	不是。 Bù shì. No.
他去过中国吗？ 他去過中國嗎？ **Tā *qùguo* Zhōngguó ma?** Has he *been* to China?	他是否去过中国？ 他是否去過中國？ **Tā *shìfǒu qùguo* Zhōngguó?** Has he *been* to China?	他去过中国没有？ 他去過中國沒有？ **Tā *qùguo* Zhōngguó *méi yǒu*?** Has he *been* to China?	没有。 沒有 Méi yǒu. No.
他会说中文吗？ 他會說中文嗎？ **Tā *huì* shuō Zhōngwén ma?** *Can* he speak Chinese?	他是否会说中文？ 他是否會說中文？ **Tā *shìfǒu huì* shuō Zhōngwén?** *Can* he speak Chinese?	他会不会说中文？ 他會不會說中文？ **Tā *huì bù huì* shuō Zhōngwén?** *Can* he speak Chinese?	不会。 不會。 Bù huì. No.
你有钱吗？ 你有錢嗎？ **Nǐ *yǒu* qián ma?** Do you *have* money?	你是否有钱？ 你是否有錢？ **Nǐ *shìfǒu yǒu* qián?** Do you *have* money?	你有没有钱？ 你有沒有錢？ **Nǐ *yǒu méi yǒu* qián?** Do you *have* money?	没有。 沒有 Méi yǒu. No.

ASKING QUESTIONS AND REPLYING TO QUESTIONS

28.2 Asking for agreement

To ask someone for confirmation that information is correct:

Follow the statement with the tag question 对不对？/ 對不對？ *duì bù duì?* 'correct?' 'right?'

> 她是中国人，对不对？
> 她是中國人，對不對？
> **Tā shì Zhōngguo rén, duì bù duì?**
> She is a Chinese person, right?

Or, add 是不是 **shì bù shì** before the predicate:

> (subject) 是不是 **shì bù shì** predicate

> 她是不是会说中文？
> 她是不是會說中文？
> **Tā shì bù shì huì shuō Zhōngwén?**
> Can she speak Chinese?

To ask someone whether a situation is acceptable to him or her, follow the statement with one of the following tag questions:

好不好？ *hǎo bù hǎo?* or 好吗？/ 好嗎？ *hǎo ma?* 'okay?'

> 我们说中文，好不好？
> 我們說中文，好不好？
> **Wǒmen shuō Zhōngwén, hǎo bù hǎo?**
> Let's speak Chinese, okay?

行不行？ *xíng bù xíng?* or 行吗？/ 行嗎？ *xíng ma?* 'okay?'

> 我请小白跟我们一起吃饭，行不行？
> 我請小白跟我們一起吃飯，行不行？
> **Wǒ qǐng Xiǎo Bái gēn wǒmen yīqǐ chī fàn, xíng bù xíng?**
> I am inviting Little Bai to eat with us, okay?

可以吗？/ 可以嗎？ *kěyǐ ma?* 'okay?'

> 我跟你去看王老师，可以吗？
> 我跟你去看王老師，可以嗎？
> **Wǒ gēn nǐ qù kàn Wáng lǎoshī, kěyǐ ma?**
> I will go with you to see Professor Wang, okay?

To answer 'yes,' for tag questions, repeat the verb in the tag question. For 是不是 **shì bù shì** questions, say 是 **shì**.

To answer 'no,' for tag questions, say 不 **bù** + the verb in the tag question. For 是不是 **shì bù shì** questions, say 不 **bù**, optionally followed by the complete negated sentence without 是 **shì**.

Question	Yes	No
她是中国人，对不对？ 她是中國人，對不對？ **Tā shì Zhōngguo rén, duì bù duì?** She is a Chinese person, right?	对。 對。 Duì. Right.	不对。 不對。 Bù duì. Wrong.
我们说中文，好不好？ 我們說中文，好不好？ **Wǒmen shuō Zhōngwén, hǎo bù hǎo?** Let's speak Chinese, okay?	好。 Hǎo. Okay.	不好。 Bù hǎo. No.
她是不是会说中文？ 她是不是會說中文？ **Tā shì bù shì huì shuō Zhōngwén?** Can she speak Chinese?	是。 是。 Shì. Yes.	不。(她不会说中文。) 不。(她不會說中文。) Bù. (Tā bù huì shuō Zhōngwén.) No. (She can't speak Chinese.)

Rhetorical questions

28.3 Choosing between alternatives with 还是/還是 *háishi* 'either–or' questions

To ask someone to choose between alternatives, use 还是/還是 **háishi**. 还是/還是 **háishi** sentences often end with 呢 **ne**.

Usually, 还是/還是 **háishi** occurs before the verb phrase of each alternative.

(subject) VP₁ 还是/還是 **háishi** VP₂ 呢 **ne**

你喝茶还是喝啤酒呢？
你喝茶還是喝啤酒呢？
Nǐ hē chá háishi hē píjiǔ ne?
Will you drink tea or beer?

If the main verb of the sentence is 是 **shì**, 还是/還是 **háishi** can occur before the object noun or noun phrase.

她是学生还是老师呢？
她是學生還是老師呢？
Tā shì xuésheng háishi lǎoshī ne?
Is she a student or a teacher?

When both alternatives are sentences, 还是/還是 **háishi** occurs before the second sentence.

你觉得中文难还是日文难？
你覺得中文難還是日文難？
Nǐ juéde Zhōngwén nán háishi Rìwén nán?
Which do you think is more difficult: Chinese or Japanese?
(lit. '(Do) you think Chinese is difficult or Japanese is difficult?')

The first alternative may be preceded by 是 **shì**.

(是)中国大还是俄国大？
(是)中國大還是俄國大？
(Shì) Zhōngguó dà háishi Éguó dà?
Which is bigger, China or Russia? (lit. 'Is China big or is Russia big?')

To answer a 还是/還是 **háishi** question, select the alternative that you prefer. To indicate that a choice was made after careful consideration, it may be preceded by 是 **shì** or 还是/還是 **háishi**.

中国大。	or	是中国大。
中國大。		是中國大。
Zhōngguó dà.		**Shì Zhōngguó dà.**
China is bigger.		[I think] China is bigger.

我喝茶。	or	我还是喝茶。
我喝茶。		我還是喝茶。
Wǒ hē chá.		**Wǒ háishi hē chá.**
I'll drink tea.		I'd prefer to drink tea.

▶ 16.2.1

28.4 Rhetorical questions

To ask a question for which you think you know the answer, use 不是 **bù shì** + 吗/嗎 **ma**. 不是 **bù shì** occurs immediately before the predicate.

他<u>不是</u>已经毕业了吗？
他<u>不是</u>已經畢業了嗎？
Tā *bù shì* yǐjing bì yè le *ma*?

181

ASKING QUESTIONS AND REPLYING TO QUESTIONS   28.6

Hasn't he already graduated? (Isn't it the case that he's already graduated?)

你<u>不是</u>已经看过那部电影了吗?
你<u>不是</u>已經看過那部電影了嗎?
Nǐ bù shì yǐjing kànguo nà bù diànyǐng le ma?
Haven't you already seen that movie?

28.5 Follow-up questions with 呢 ne

呢 **ne** is used to follow up a question with another question. It is used to ask the same question as the first one, but about another subject or object. 呢 **ne** follows the new subject or object.

呢 *ne questions to ask about a new subject*

小白:	你(的)<u>弟弟</u>上大学了吗?
小白:	你(的)<u>弟弟</u>上大學了嗎?
Xiǎo Bái:	**Nǐ (de) dìdi shàng dàxué le ma?**
Little Bai:	Does *your younger brother* attend college?

小高:	上了。
Xiǎo Gāo:	**Shàng le.**
Little Gao:	Yes. [(He) attends.]

小白:	你(的)<u>妹妹</u>呢?
Xiǎo Bái:	**Nǐ (de) mèimei ne?**
Little Bai:	(What about) *Your younger sister*?

小高:	她也上了。
Xiǎo Gāo:	**Tā yě shàng le.**
Little Gao:	She also attends (college).

呢 *ne questions to ask about a new object*

小白:	你会说<u>中文</u>吗?
	你會說<u>中文</u>嗎?
	Nǐ huì shuō Zhōngwén ma?
Little Bai:	Can you speak *Chinese*?

小高:	会/會。
	Huì.
Little Gao:	Yes.

小白:	<u>日文</u>呢?
	Rìwén ne?
Little Bai:	*Japanese*?

小高:	不会/不會。
	Bù huì.
Little Gao:	No.

28.6 Content questions

Content questions are used to ask about the identity of a person, an object, a time, a location, or a quantity, or to seek an explanation or process. Mandarin content question words include the following:

Content questions 28.6

Content question word	Meaning	What it questions	Example phrase
谁 誰 **shéi**	who?	person	他是谁？ 他是誰？ **Tā shì shéi?** Who is he?
什么 甚麼 **shénme**	what?	concrete or abstract object	那是什么？ 那是甚麼？ **Nà shì shénme?** What is that?
什么时候 甚麼時候 **shénme shíhòu**	when?	time (including clock time)	你什么时候开始学中文？ 你甚麼時候開始學中文？ **Nǐ shénme shíhòu kāishǐ xué Zhōngwén?** When will you begin to study Chinese?
几点钟 幾點鐘 **jǐdiǎn zhōng**	when?	clock time	你几点钟回家？ 你幾點鐘回家？ **Nǐ jǐdiǎn zhōng huí jiā?** When are you going home?
什么地方 甚麼地方 **shénme dìfang**	what place/ where?	location	你在什么地方工作？ 你在甚麼地方工作？ **Nǐ zài shénme dìfang gōngzuò?** Where do you work?
哪儿 哪兒 **nǎr**	where?	location	你在哪儿工作？ 你在哪兒工作？ **Nǐ zài nǎr gōngzuò?**
哪里 哪裏 **nǎlǐ**			你在哪里工作？ 你在哪裏工作？ **Nǐ zài nǎlǐ gōngzuò?** Where do you work?
为什么 為甚麼 **wèi shénme**	why?	reason	你为什么学中文？ 你為甚麼學中文？ **Nǐ wèi shénme xué Zhōngwén?** Why do you study Chinese?
凭什么 憑甚麼 **píng shénme**	on what basis/ by what right?	reason	你凭什么逮捕我？ 你憑甚麼逮捕我？ **Nǐ píng shénme dàibǔ wǒ?** On what grounds are you arresting me?
怎么 怎麼 **zěnme**	how?	process	怎么走？ 怎麼走？ **Zěnme zǒu?** How do you go?
哪 **nǎ**	which?	specifier	你要买哪本书？ 你要買哪本書？ **Nǐ yào mǎi nǎ běn shū?** Which book do you want to buy?
几 幾 **jǐ**	how many? (usually 10 or less; used with countable nouns)	quantity	你想吃几个饺子？ 你想吃幾個餃子？ **Nǐ xiǎng chī jǐ gè jiǎozi?** How many dumplings do you want to eat?

ASKING QUESTIONS AND REPLYING TO QUESTIONS 28.6

Content question word	Meaning	What it questions	Example phrase
多少 **duōshǎo**	how many? (larger number; used with mass nouns)	quantity	你有多少钱? 你有多少錢? **Nǐ yǒu duōshǎo qián?** How much money do you have?
多 **duō**	how? (used with adjectival verbs)	intensity	你多大? **Nǐ duō dà?** How old are you? 那本书有多贵啊? 那本書有多貴啊? **Nà běn shū yǒu duō guì a?** How expensive is that book?

The following content question words and phrases are more common in formal, literary texts than in spoken Mandarin.

Content question word	Meaning	What it questions	Example phrase
何必 **hébì**	why?	reason	你何必生那么大的气? 你何必生那麼大的氣? **Nǐ hébì shēng nàme dà de qì?** Why are you so angry?
何妨 **héfáng**	why not?	reason	如果你没事，何妨多坐一会儿? 如果你沒事，何妨多坐一會兒? **Rúguǒ nǐ méi shì, héfáng duō zuò yīhuìr?** If you are not busy, why not stay for a while longer?
何时 何時 **héshí**	when?	time	飞机何时到达? 飛機何時到達? **Fēijī héshí dào dá?** What time is the plane arriving?
何故 **hégù**	why?	reason	他何故杀人? 他何故殺人? **Tā hégù shā rén?** Why did he kill someone?
为何 為何 **wèihé**	why?	reason	为何惊慌? 為何驚慌? **Wèihé jīnghuāng?** Why are (you) so frightened?
何为 何為 **héwéi**	what is (noun phrase)?	identification	何为科学方法? 何為科學方法? **Héwéi kēxué fāngfǎ?** What is the scientific method?
何尝 何嘗 **hécháng**	how could (you) not (verb phrase)?	rhetorical request for reason	我何尝不想上大学? 我何嘗不想上大學? **Wǒ hécháng bù xiǎng shàng dàxué?** How could I not be thinking about going to university?

28.6 Content questions

In Mandarin, questions and answers use the same phrase order.

In Mandarin, the content question word goes where the answer goes.

Question	Answer
你找谁？ 你找誰？ **Nǐ zhǎo *shéi*?** *Who* are you looking for?	我找王老师。 我找王老師。 **Wǒ zhǎo *Wáng lǎoshī*.** I am looking for *Professor Wang*.
这是什么？ 這是甚麼？ **Zhè shì *shénme*?** *What* is this?	这是手机。 這是手機。 **Zhè shì *shǒujī*.** This is *a cell phone*.
你今天喝什么茶？ 你今天喝甚麼茶？ **Nǐ jīntiān hē *shénme* chá?** *What* tea are you drinking today?	(我喝)龙井(茶)。 (我喝)龍井(茶)。 **(Wǒ hē) *lóngjǐng* (chá).** (I'm drinking) *Longjing* (tea).
你什么时候有空？ 你甚麼時候有空？ **Nǐ *shénme shíhòu* yǒu kōng?** *When* do you have free time?	我今天下午有空。 **Wǒ *jīntiān xiàwǔ* yǒu kōng.** I have free time *this afternoon*.
你在哪儿(哪里)学中文？ 你在哪兒(哪裏)學中文？ **Nǐ zài *nǎr (nǎlǐ)* xué Zhōngwén?** *Where* do you study Chinese?	我在大学学中文。 我在大學學中文。 **Wǒ zài *dàxué* xué Zhōngwén.** I study Chinese *in college/at university*.
你几点钟下课？ 你幾點鐘下課？ **Nǐ *jǐdiǎn zhōng* xià kè?** *What time* do you get out of class?	我四点钟下课。 我四點鐘下課。 **Wǒ *sìdiǎn zhōng* xià kè.** I get out of class *at 4 o'clock*.
你在什么地方吃午饭？ 你在甚麼地方吃午飯？ **Nǐ zài *shénme dìfang* chī wǔfàn?** *Where* do you eat lunch?	我在餐厅吃午饭。 我在餐廳吃午飯。 **Wǒ zài *cāntīng* chī wǔfàn.** I eat lunch *in the cafeteria*.

怎么/怎麼 **zěnme** 'how' asks for a process. It occurs right before the verb. The answer to a 怎么/怎麼 **zěnme** question is an explanation. It may be a short phrase or it may be a sentence or more in length. The long answer to 怎么/怎麼 **zěnme** 'how' questions involves a series of steps in which the process is described.

Question	Answer
这个字怎么写？ 這個字怎麼寫？ **Zhège zì *zěnme* xiě?** *How* do you write this character?	这个字这样写。 這個字這樣寫。 **Zhège zì *zhèyàng* xiě.** You write this character *this way*.
从这儿到公园怎么走？ 從這兒到公園怎麼走？ **Cóng zhèr dào gōngyuán *zěnme* zǒu?** *How* do you go from here to the park?	从这儿到公园往北走。 從這兒到公園往北走。 **Cóng zhèr dào gōngyuán *wǎng běi* zǒu.** From here to the park, *walk north*.

ASKING QUESTIONS AND REPLYING TO QUESTIONS 28.6

The question expression 怎么样？/ 怎麼樣？ **zěnmeyàng?** asks for a description:

那个饭馆怎么样？
那個飯館怎麼樣？
Nàge fànguǎn zěnmeyàng?
What is that restaurant like?

The expression 怎么了？/ 怎麼了？ **zěnme le**? is used to ask how someone is when the speaker believes there is something the matter:

你怎么了？
你怎麼了？
Nǐ zěnme le?
What is the matter with you?

为什么/為甚麼 **wèi shénme** 'why' questions ask for reasons, and their responses typically require a sentence or more. 为什么/為甚麼 **wèi shénme** occurs after the subject of the sentence.

Replies to 为什么/為甚麼 **wèi shénme** questions often begin with the word 因为/因為 **yīnwéi** 'because.'

Question

你为什么学中文？
你為甚麼學中文？
Nǐ *wèi shénme* xué Zhōngwén?
Why do you study Chinese?

你为什么喜欢他呢？
你為甚麼喜歡他呢？
Nǐ *wèi shénme* xǐhuan tā ne?
Why do you like him?

Answer

因为我想在中国找工作。
因為我想在中國找工作。
Yīnwéi wǒ xiǎng zài Zhōngguó zhǎo gōngzuò.
Because I want to look for a job in China.

因为他特别帅！
因為他特別帥！
Yīnwéi tā tèbié shuài!
Because he's so handsome!

In Mandarin, content question words are used in expressions that express the meanings 'any,' 'every,' 'none,' 'always,' 'never,' etc.

谁都认识他。
誰都認識他。
Shéi dōu rènshi tā.
Everyone knows him.

我什么时候都忙。
我甚麼時候都忙。
Wǒ shénme shíhòu dōu máng.
I am always busy.

他什么酒都不喝。
他甚麼酒都不喝。
Tā shénme jiǔ dōu bù hē.
He doesn't drink any alcohol.

▶ 46.4.2

29

Expressing identification, possession, and existence

29.1 Expressing identification

To identify a person, place, or thing, use the verb 是 **shì** 'to be.'

29.1.1 Identifying oneself and others

我是张明智。
我是張明智。
Wǒ shì Zhāng Míngzhì.
I am Zhang Mingzhi.

这是我太太。
這是我太太。
Zhè shì wǒ tàitai.
This is my wife.

Q:	他们是谁？ 他們是誰？ **Tāmen shì shéi?** Who are they?	A:	他们是我的朋友。 他們是我的朋友。 **Tāmen shì wǒ de péngyou.** They are my friends.
Q:	你是经理吗？ 你是經理嗎？ **Nǐ shì jīnglǐ ma?** Are you the manager?	A:	是。(我是经理。) 是。(我是經理。) **Shì. (Wǒ shì jīnglǐ.)** Yes. (I am the manager.)

▶ 22.5

29.1.2 Identifying places

Q:	这是什么地方？ 這是甚麼地方？ **Zhè shì shénme dìfang?** What is this place?	A:	这是北京饭店。 這是北京飯店。 **Zhè shì Běijīng fàndiàn.** This is the Beijing Hotel.
Q:	那是长安东路吗？ 那是長安東路嗎？ **Nà shì Cháng'ān dōng lù ma?** Is that East Chang'an Road?	A:	那不是长安东路；那是长安西路。 那不是長安東路；那是長安西路。 **Nà bù shì Cháng'ān dōng lù; nà shì Cháng'ān xī lù.** That is not East Chang'an Road; it is West Chang'an Road.

EXPRESSING IDENTIFICATION, POSSESSION, AND EXISTENCE

Q:	这是不是假日旅馆？ 這是不是假日旅館？ **Zhè shì bù shì Jiàrì Lǚguǎn?** Is this the Holiday Inn?	A:	是。 **Shì.** Yes, it is.
Q:	我们的房间是几号？ 我們的房間是幾號？ **Wǒmen de fángjiān shì jǐ hào?** What is our room number?	A:	你们的房间是479号。 你們的房間是479號。 **Nǐmen de fángjiān shì 479 hào.** Your room number is 479.

29.1.3 Identifying things

Chinese uses yes–no questions and content questions to ask about the identity of things.

▶ 28.1, 28.6

Q:	这是我们的出租车吗？ 這是我們的出租車嗎？ **Zhè shì wǒmen de chūzūchē ma?** Is this our taxi?	A:	这不是你们的。 這不是你們的。 **Zhè bù shì nǐmen de.** This is not yours.
Q:	这是什么菜？ 這是甚麼菜？ **Zhè shì shénme cài?** What is this dish?	A:	这是清蒸鱼。 這是清蒸魚。 **Zhè shì qīngzhēng yú.** It is steamed fish.

29.2 Expressing possession

This section introduces the forms used by Chinese speakers to express possession and to inquire about possession.

29.2.1 Indicating 'having something'

To say that someone or something *has* something, use the verb 有 **yǒu** 'to have.'

他有女朋友。
Tā yǒu nǚ péngyou.
He has a girlfriend.

你有弟弟吗？
你有弟弟嗎？
Nǐ yǒu dìdi ma?
Do you have a younger brother?

The negation of 有 **yǒu** is 没有/沒有 **méi yǒu**.

Q:	你有妹妹吗？ 你有妹妹嗎？ **Nǐ yǒu mèimei ma?** Do you have a younger sister?	A:	没有。 沒有 **Méi yǒu.** No.
Q:	你有没有姐姐？ 你有沒有姐姐？ **Nǐ yǒu méi yǒu jiějie?** Do you have an older sister?	A:	我没有姐姐。 我沒有姐姐。 **Wǒ méi yǒu jiějie.** I do not have an older sister.

Expressing possession 29.2

Q: 你现在有空吗?
你現在有空嗎?
Nǐ xiànzài yǒu kōng ma?
Do you have free time now?

A: 对不起。现在没有空。
對不起。現在沒有空。
Duìbuqǐ. Xiànzài méi yǒu kōng.
Sorry. I don't have free time now.

▶ 27.1.2

29.2.2 Expressing possession

To indicate one's possession, use the following structure:

possessor + 的 *de* + *possessed object*

哥哥的车　　老师的书
哥哥的車　　老師的書
gēgē de chē　　**lǎoshī de shū**
older brother's car　　teacher's book

Mandarin does not have possessive pronouns. A *pronoun* + 的 *de* is equivalent in meaning to a possessive pronoun in English.

我的钥匙　　谁的书?
我的鑰匙　　誰的書?
wǒ de yàoshi　　**shéi de shū?**
my key　　whose book?

A table of English possessive pronouns and their Mandarin equivalents is presented in Chapter 5.

▶ 5.2.4, 9.2.1.2

The *possessor* + 的 *de* may sometimes occur without the following 'possessed' noun. This is often the case when the noun is clear from the context of the sentence. In the following sentences, the noun in parentheses may be omitted.

这本书是你的(书)。
這本書是你的(書)。
Zhè běn shū shì nǐ de (shū).
This book is yours.

那个学校是他们的(学校)。
那個學校是他們的(學校)。
Nàge xuéxiào shì tāmen de (xuéxiào).
That school is theirs.

When there is a close relationship between the possessor and the possessed noun, 的 **de** may be omitted. 的 **de** is often omitted if the possessor is a pronoun.

我(的)母亲很忙。
我(的)母親很忙。
Wǒ (de) mǔqin hěn máng.
My mother is very busy.

他是我们(的)老师。
他是我們(的)老師。
Tā shì wǒmen (de) lǎoshī.
He is our teacher.

EXPRESSING IDENTIFICATION, POSSESSION, AND EXISTENCE

29.2.3 Expressing possession in formal written Chinese

属于/屬於 **shǔyú** *'belong to, be affiliated with'*

这个幼儿园是属于北京大学的。
這個幼兒園是屬於北京大學的。
Zhège yòu'éryuán shì shǔyú Běijīng Dàxué de.
This kindergarten is affiliated with Beijing University.

之 *zhī*

之 **zhī** is the formal written equivalent of 的 **de**, used in literary Chinese texts. Like 的 **de**, it occurs after the possessor and before the possessed noun.

钟鼓之声
鐘鼓之聲
zhōnggǔ zhī shēng
the sound of bells and drums

▶ 9.6

29.3 Expressing existence

There are three verbs that are commonly used to express existence.

29.3.1 有 *yǒu* 'to exist'

In addition to its use in expressing possession, the verb 有 **yǒu** is also used to express existence.

昨天晚上有很大的雾。
昨天晚上有很大的霧。
Zuótiān wǎnshang yǒu hěn dà de wù.
Last night there was a very dense fog.

附近有三个旅馆。
附近有三個旅館。
Fùjìn yǒu sān gè lǚguǎn.
There are three hotels nearby.

To ask about existence, use the question form 有没有/有沒有 **yǒu méi yǒu** or the yes–no question marker 吗/嗎 **ma**.

附近有没有旅馆？
附近有沒有旅館？
Fùjìn yǒu méi yǒu lǚguǎn?
Is there a hotel nearby?

昨天晚上有雾吗？
昨天晚上有霧嗎？
Zuótiān wǎnshang yǒu wù ma?
Was there fog last night? (Was it foggy last night?)

▶ 28.1

To give a negative reply, say 没有/沒有 **méi yǒu**.

附近没有旅馆。
附近沒有旅館。
Fùjìn méi yǒu lǚguǎn.
There is no hotel nearby.

Expressing existence

昨天晚上没有雾。
昨天晚上沒有霧。
Zuótiān wǎnshang méi yǒu wù.
There was no fog last night.

▶ 27.1.2

29.3.2 The verb 是 *shì* 'to express existence'

是 **shì** can be used to express the existence of some object at a location. 是 **shì** is often used in this way when the object fills the location.

我们房子的屋顶上都是雪。
我們房子的屋頂上都是雪。
Wǒmen fángzi de wūdǐng shàng dōu shì xuě.
The roof of our house was covered with snow.

地上都是玩具。
Dì shàng dōu shì wánjù.
Toys are all over the floor.

29.3.3 Expressing existence with change-of-state placement verbs

Change-of-state verbs that refer to placement, such as 站 **zhàn** 'to stand,' 坐 **zuò** 'to sit,' 放 **fàng** 'to put, to place,' 躺 **tǎng** 'to lie,' etc. are often used in sentences that refer to existence. In these 'existential' sentences the verbs of placement are usually followed by the verb suffix 着/著 **zhe** to emphasize the ongoing duration of the situation.

街上站着很多人。
街上站著很多人。
Jiēshang zhànzhe hěn duō rén.
There are a lot of people standing in the street.

公共汽车上坐着很多人。
公共汽車上坐著很多人。
Gōnggòng qìchē shàng zuòzhe hěn duō rén.
There are a lot of people sitting on the bus.

书桌上放着一瓶花。
書桌上放著一瓶花。
Shūzhuō shàng fàngzhe yī píng huā.
There is a vase of flowers on the desk.

▶ 17.2.2, 34.4, 39.2

30

Describing people, places, and things

30.1 Equational sentences: identifying or describing the subject with a noun phrase in the predicate

是 **shì** links the subject with a noun phrase in the predicate that identifies or describes it. Sentences with this form are *equational sentences*.

    subject 是 **shì** *noun or noun phrase*

    赵玫玲是学生。
    趙玫玲是學生。
    Zhào Méilíng *shì* **xuésheng.**
    Zhao Meiling *is* a student.

    苏州是一个城市。
    蘇州是一個城市。
    Sūzhōu *shì* **yī gè chéngshì.**
    Suzhou *is* a city.

    奔驰是一种车。
    奔馳是一種車。
    Bēnchí *shì* **yī zhǒng chē.**
    The Mercedes Benz *is* a type of car.

▶ 11.4, 29.1

30.2 Describing the subject with a predicate that is an adjectival verb

Adjectival verbs may serve as the predicate of the sentence to describe the subject. The intensifier 很 **hěn** often occurs before the adjectival verb, especially if it is a one-syllable adjectival verb. Notice that 是 **shì** is not used when the predicate is an adjectival verb.

    *subject (*很 **hěn***) adjectival verb*

    赵玫玲很聪明。
    趙玫玲很聰明。
    Zhào Méilíng hěn cōngming.
    Zhao Meiling is very smart.

    苏州很漂亮。
    蘇州很漂亮。
    Sūzhōu hěn piàoliang.
    Suzhou is very beautiful.

奔驰很贵。
奔馳很貴。
Bēnchí hěn guì.
The Mercedes Benz is very expensive.

▶ 10

30.3 Identifying or describing a noun with a modifying phrase

Phrases that describe or 'modify' the noun always occur before the noun. The particle 的 **de** typically occurs right after the modifier and before the noun that is being described. In the following examples, the *modifier* + 的 *de* is emphasized.

很聪明的女孩子
很聰明的女孩子
hěn cōngming de **nǚháizi**
a very intelligent girl

很贵的车
很貴的車
hěn guì de **chē**
a very expensive car

很有名的大学
很有名的大學
hěn yǒu míng de **dàxué**
a very famous university

很安靜的地方
hěn ānjìng de **dìfang**
a very peaceful place

▶ 9.2

30.4 Asking questions about the attributes of a person, place, or thing

30.4.1 Asking what someone or something is like

To ask what someone or something is like, say:

person/place/thing 怎么样？
怎麼樣？
zěnmeyàng?

What about this person/place/thing?
What is this person/place/thing like?

那个女孩子怎么样？
那個女孩子怎麼樣？
Nàge nǚ háizi zěnmeyàng?
What about that girl? (What is that girl like?)

那个大学怎么样？
那個大學怎麼樣？
Nàge dàxué zěnmeyàng?
What is that university like?

DESCRIBING PEOPLE, PLACES, AND THINGS

30.5

苏州怎么样?
蘇州怎麼樣?
Sūzhōu zěnmeyàng?
What is Suzhou like?

▶ 28.6

30.4.2 Asking for more information

To ask for more information about a person, place or thing, say:

什么/甚麼 **shénme** noun?
what person/place thing?

这是<u>什么</u>书?
這是<u>甚麼</u>書?
Zhè shì shénme shū?
What book is this?

or

什么样的/甚麼樣的 **shénme yàng de** noun?
what kind of noun?

这是<u>什么样的</u>地方?
這是<u>甚麼樣的</u>地方?
Zhè shì shénme yàng de dìfang?
What kind of place is this?

▶ 9.2.1.9, 28.6

30.5 Describing an item in terms of the material that it is made of

30.5.1 Describing what an item is made of

To describe an item in terms of the material that it is made of, say:

(noun) 是(用)NP做的
    shì (yòng) NP zuò de
(noun) is made of _____

那个桌子是用木头做的。
那個桌子是用木頭做的。
Nàge zhuōzi shì yòng mùtou zuò de.
That table is made of wood.

这个花瓶是(用)玻璃做的。
這個花瓶是(用)玻璃做的。
Zhège huāpíng shì (yòng) bōli zuò de.
This vase is made of glass.

我的耳环是(用)金子做的。
我的耳環是(用)金子做的。
Wǒ de ěrhuán shì (yòng) jīnzi zuò de.
My earrings are made of gold.

▶ 57.2.4

Describing people in terms of age **30.7**

30.5.2 Asking what an item is made of

To ask what an item is made of, say:

> (noun) 是用什么做的？
> 是用甚麼做的？
> **shì yòng shénme zuò de?**

What is (this object) made of?

> 这个花瓶是用什么做的？
> 這個花瓶是用甚麼做的？
> **Zhège huāpíng shì yòng shénme zuò de?**
> What is this vase made of?

> 你的耳环是用什么做的？
> 你的耳環是用甚麼做的？
> **Nǐ de ěrhuán shì yòng shénme zuò de?**
> What are your earrings made of?

30.6 Describing nouns in terms of attributes that imply comparison

In Mandarin, adjectival verbs imply comparison, even when they are not used in a comparison structure. This is especially true when the adjectival verb is not preceded by an intensifier. Here are examples. The context usually makes it clear whether a simple description or a comparison is intended.

> 那本书贵。
> 那本書貴。
> **Nà běn shū guì.**
> That book is expensive.
> or
> That book is more expensive (than some other book).

> 王老师忙。
> 王老師忙。
> **Wáng lǎoshī máng.**
> Professor Wang is busy.
> or
> Professor Wang is busier (than some other people).

▶ 10.5, 33

30.7 Describing people in terms of age

30.7.1 Describing age

To describe a person in terms of his or her age, say:

> 王明(是)二十三岁。
> 王明(是)二十三歲。
> **Wáng Míng (shì) èrshísān suì.**
> Wang Ming is 23 (years old).

If it is clear from the context, 岁/歲 **suì** 'years of age' may be omitted:

> 王明(是)二十三。
> **Wáng Míng (shì) èrshísān.**
> Wang Ming is 23.

195

DESCRIBING PEOPLE, PLACES, AND THINGS

The verb 是 **shì** is optional and is usually absent in statements in which the predicate is an age, or, in fact, any number + classifier (+ noun) phrase.

> 我的弟弟十八岁。
> 我的弟弟十八歲。
> **Wǒ de dìdi shíbā suì.**
> My younger brother is 18 (years old).

However, when negation or an adverb occurs in the sentence, 是 **shì** must also occur.

> 他不是十八岁。他只是十五岁。
> 他不是十八歲。他只是十五歲。
> **Tā bù shì shíbā suì. Tā zhǐ shì shíwǔ suì.**
> He is not 18 (years old). He is only 15 (years old).

When the adverb 已经/已經 **yǐjing** 'already' occurs, 是 **shì** may be absent.

> 他已经(是)两岁了。
> 他已經(是)兩歲了。
> **Tā yǐjing (shì) liǎng suì le.**
> He is already two (years old).

▶ 11.4

30.7.2 Asking about age

To ask the age of an adult, say:

> 你多大年纪?
> 你多大年紀?
> **Nǐ duō dà niánjì?**
> How old are you?

or

> 你多大岁数?
> 你多大歲數?
> **Nǐ duō dà suìshu?**
> How old are you?

or

> 你岁数多大?
> 你歲數多大?
> **Nǐ suìshu duō dà?**
> How old are you?

To ask the age of a young person, say:

> 你多大?
> **Nǐ duō dà?**
> How old are you?

To ask the age of a child (up to ten years of age), you can say:

> 你几岁?
> 你幾歲?
> **Nǐ jǐ suì?**
> How old are you?

Describing the weather 30.8

A formal and very polite way to inquire about the age of an older person is:

您今年高寿？
您今年高壽？
Nín jīnnián gāoshòu?
How old are you?

NOTE 几/幾 **jǐ** is a classifier that is used to ask about small numbers. Therefore, it is appropriate to use when asking the age of young children, but not when asking the age of older people.

▶ 28.6

30.8 Describing the weather

30.8.1 Statements that describe the weather

Here are common Mandarin expressions used when discussing the weather. Notice that there is no word in Mandarin that is equivalent to the 'it' used in weather descriptions in English. Mandarin weather descriptions often begin with the verb and do not have a subject.

天气/天氣	舒服	凉快
tiānqì	**shūfu**	**liángkuai**
weather	comfortable	cool
闷热/悶熱	冷	暖和
mēnrè	**lěng**	**nuǎnhuo**
muggy; hot and humid	cold	warm
热/熱	多云/多雲	温和/溫和
rè	**duō yún**	**wēnhé**
hot	cloudy	mild
下雪	下雨	刮风/刮風
xià xuě	**xià yǔ**	**guā fēng**
snowing	raining	windy

今天的天气很好。
今天的天氣很好。
Jīntiān de tiānqì hěn hǎo.
Today's weather is very good.

昨天很闷热。
昨天很悶熱。
Zuótiān hěn mēnrè.
Yesterday was very humid and hot.

今天多云。
今天多雲。
Jīntiān duō yún.
Today it is cloudy. (used in weather reports)

昨天的天气很舒服。
昨天的天氣很舒服。
Zuótiān de tiānqì hěn shūfu.
Yesterday's weather was very comfortable.

昨天很凉快/冷/热/暖和。
昨天很涼快/冷/熱/暖和。
Zuótiān hěn liángkuai/lěng/rè/nuǎnhuo.
Yesterday was cool/cold/hot/warm.

DESCRIBING PEOPLE, PLACES, AND THINGS

下雨了。
Xià yǔ le.
It's raining. (lit. 'falling the rain')

下雪了。
Xià xuě le.
It's snowing. (lit. 'falling the snow')

刮风了。
颱風了。
Guā fēng le.
It is windy. (lit. 'blowing the wind')

30.8.2 Asking about the weather

To ask about the weather or climate in general terms, use 怎么样/怎麼樣 **zěnmeyàng** 'what about it?' The following questions are followed by a typical answer.

Q: 这儿的天气怎么样?
這兒的天氣怎麼樣?
Zhèr de tiānqì zěnmeyàng?
What is the weather like here?

A: 这儿的天气很好。不冷也不热。
這兒的天氣很好。不冷也不熱。
Zhèr de tiānqì hěn hǎo. Bù lěng yě bù rè.
The weather here is very nice, neither cold nor hot.

Q: 今年这儿的天气怎么样?
今年這兒的天氣怎麼樣?
Jīnnián zhèr de tiānqì zěnmeyàng?
What was the weather like here this year?

A: 今年这儿的天气不太正常。
今年這兒的天氣不太正常。
Jīnnián zhèr de tiānqì bù tài zhèngcháng.
The weather here was not normal this year.

Q: 杭州的气候怎么样?
杭州的氣候怎麼樣?
Hángzhōu de qìhòu zěnmeyàng?
What is the climate like in Hangzhou?

A: 杭州的气候非常温和。
杭州的氣候非常溫和。
Hángzhōu de qìhòu fēicháng wēnhé.
Hangzhou's climate is very mild.

30.8.3 Asking about temperature and describing temperature

Here are expressions associated with temperature.

温度/溫度 **wēndù** temperature	度 **dù** degree	零下 **língxià** below zero
华氏/華氏 **huáshì** Fahrenheit	摄氏/攝氏 **shèshì** Celsius; centigrade	

Talking about illness and other medical conditions 30.9

Notice that when describing temperature, you can use the verb 是 **shì**. 是 **shì** is required with negation, but is otherwise usually absent. With the adverb 差不多 **chàbùduō** 'almost,' the verb may be 有 **yǒu**.

今天的温度是二十度。
今天的溫度是二十度。
Jīntiān de wēndù shì èrshí dù.
Today's temperature is 20 degrees.

Q: 今天的温度怎么样?
今天的溫度怎麼樣?
Jīntiān de wēndù zěnmeyàng?
What is today's temperature?

A: 天气预报说今天的温度差不多有三十度。
天氣預報說今天的溫度差不多有三十度。
Tiānqì yùbào shuō jīntiān de wēndù chàbùduō yǒu sānshí dù.
The weather report says today's temperature will be around 30 degrees.

Q: 你说的是华氏还是摄氏?
你說的是華氏還是攝氏?
Nǐ shuō de shì huáshì háishi shèshì?
Do you mean Fahrenheit or centigrade?

A: 在中国我们用的是摄氏。
在中國我們用的是攝氏。
Zài Zhōngguó wǒmen yòng de shì shèshì.
We use centigrade in China.

Q: 摄氏三十度是华氏多少度?
攝氏三十度是華氏多少度?
Shèshì sān shí dù shì huáshì duōshao dù?
Thirty degrees centigrade is how many degrees Fahrenheit?

A: 差不多是华氏九十度。
差不多是華氏九十度。
Chàbuduō shì huáshì jiǔshí dù.
It's about 90 degrees Fahrenheit.

今天很冷, 零下五度。
Jīntiān hěn lěng, língxià wǔ dù.
It's really cold today, five degrees below zero.

30.9 Talking about illness and other medical conditions

30.9.1 Expressing general illness or allergy

Here are the most common ways to express having an illness or an allergy.

General illness	*Cold*	*Allergy*
(我)病了。	(我)感冒了。	(我)对(青霉素)过敏。
		(我)對(青黴素)過敏。
(Wǒ) bìng le.	**(Wǒ) gǎn mào le.**	**(Wǒ) duì (qīng méi sù) guòmǐn.**
(I) have become ill.	(I) have a cold.	(I) am allergic to (penicillin).
or		
(我)有病。		
(Wǒ) yǒu bìng.		
(I) have an illness.		

199

30.9.2 Describing symptoms

In English, symptoms are described as a possession of the patient: 'I have a headache,' 'you have a broken leg,' etc. Notice how symptoms are described in Mandarin.

Fever

(我)发烧了。
(我)發燒了。
(Wǒ) fā shāo le.
(I) have fever.

(我)发高烧。
(我)發高燒。
(Wǒ) fā gāo shāo.
(I) have a high fever.

General infection

(我)发炎。
(我)發炎。
(Wǒ) fāyán.
(I) have an infection.

Stomach ache

(我)肚子疼。
(Wǒ) dùzi téng.
(I) have a stomach ache.

Cold symptoms

(我)流鼻涕。
(Wǒ) liú bítì.
(I) have a runny nose.

(我)打喷嚏。
(我)打噴嚏。
(Wǒ) dǎ pēntì.
(I) am sneezing.

Earache

(我)耳朵疼。
(Wǒ) ěrduo téng.
(I) have earache.

Diarrhea

(我)拉稀。
(Wǒ) lā xī.
(I) have diarrhea.

我泻肚了。
我瀉肚了。
Wǒ xièdù le.
I have diarrhea. (formal expression)

(我)拉肚子。
(Wǒ) lā dùzi.
(I) have diarrhea.

Sore throat

(我)咳嗽。
(Wǒ) késou.
(I) have a cough.

(我)嗓子疼。
(Wǒ) sǎngzi téng.
(I) have a sore throat.

Headache

(我)头疼。
(我)頭疼。
(Wǒ) tóu téng.
(I) have a headache.

Broken bones

他骨头断了。
他骨頭斷了。
Tā gǔtou duàn le.
He has a broken bone.
(lit. 'His bone broke.')

他腿(手)断了。
他腿(手)斷了。
Tā tuǐ (shǒu) duàn le.
He has a broken leg (arm).

30.9.3 Asking about symptoms

The following expressions are commonly used to ask about symptoms:

你什么地方不舒服?
你甚麼地方不舒服?
Nǐ shénme dìfang bù shūfu?
Where are you uncomfortable?

发不发烧?
發不發燒?
Fā bù fā shāo?
Do you have a fever?

发烧吗?
發燒嗎?
Fā shāo ma?
Do you have a fever?

(头)疼不疼?
(頭)疼不疼?
(Tóu) téng bù téng?
Do you have a headache?

(头)疼吗?
(頭)疼嗎?
(Tóu) téng ma?
Do you have a headache?

▶ 28.1, 28.6

31

Describing how actions are performed

31.1 Describing the general or past performance of an action with a manner adverbial phrase

To describe how an action is generally performed or how it was performed in the past, use the following structure:

action verb 得 *de adjectival verb*

Phrases that describe the performance of an action are often referred to as *manner complements* or *manner adverbial phrases*. The word *adverbial* means they describe the verb.

他说得快。
他說得快。
Tā shuō de kuài.
He speaks fast.

她开得慢。
她開得慢。
Tā kāi de màn.
She drives slowly.

你们都考得好。
你們都考得好。
Nǐmen dōu kǎo de hǎo.
You all did well on the exam.

NOTE The suffixes 了 **le**, 过/過 **guo**, and 着/著 **zhe** do not occur after the action verb or the adjectival verb in manner adverbial phrases.

▶ 37, 39

31.1.1 Describing the performance of an action when the verb takes an object

If the action verb takes an object, the verb is said twice, the first time followed by the object, and the second time followed by 得 *de adjectival verb*:

[action verb + object] [action verb 得 *de adjectival verb]*

他说话说得快。
他說話說得快。
Tā shuō huà shuō de kuài.
He speaks fast.

DESCRIBING HOW ACTIONS ARE PERFORMED　　　　　　　　　　　　　　　　　　**31.1**

> 他说中国话说得快。
> 他說中國話說得快。
> **Tā shuō Zhōngguó huà shuō de kuài.**
> He speaks Chinese fast.

> 她开车开得慢。
> 她開車開得慢。
> **Tā kāi chē kāi de màn.**
> She drives a car slowly.

> 你们考试都考得好。
> 你們考試都考得好。
> **Nǐmen kǎo shì dōu kǎo de hǎo.**
> You all did well on the exam.

31.1.2 Modifying the description of the action

31.1.2.1 Modifying with intensifiers

In manner adverbial phrases, the adjectival verb may be preceded by an intensifier:

> 他说话说得<u>很</u>快。
> 他說話說得<u>很</u>快。
> **Tā shuō huà shuō de *hěn* kuài.**
> He speaks *very* quickly.

> 她开车开得<u>太</u>慢。
> 她開車開得<u>太</u>慢。
> **Tā kāi chē kāi de *tài* màn.**
> She drives a car *too* slowly.

> 你们考试都考得<u>真</u>好。
> 你們考試都考得<u>真</u>好。
> **Nǐmen kǎo shì dōu kǎo de *zhēn* hǎo.**
> You all did *really* well on the exam.

▶ 10.3

31.1.2.2 Modifying with negation

In manner adverbial phrases, negation must occur before the adjectival verb, not before the action verb. Negation must be 不 **bù**.

> 他说得不快。
> 他說得不快。
> **Tā shuō de bù kuài.**
> He doesn't speak fast.

> 你们都考得不好。
> 你們都考得不好。
> **Nǐmen dōu kǎo de bù hǎo.**
> You all didn't do well on the exam.

▶ 27.1.1

31.2 Asking about the performance of an action

To ask how an action is performed, say:

(subject) action verb 得怎么样?
　　　　　　　　　得怎麼樣?
　　　　　　　　　de zěnmeyàng?
How does the subject do the action?

> 他考得怎么样?
> 他考得怎麼樣?
> **Tā kǎode zěnmeyàng?**
> How did he do on the test?

> 她开车开得怎么样?
> 她開車開得怎麼樣?
> **Tā kāi chē kāi de zěnmeyàng?**
> How does she drive?

To ask if an action is performed in a particular way, form a yes–no question with the adjectival verb using either of the following forms:

- Verb-not-verb structure

    action verb 得 **de** adjectival verb 不 **bù** adjectival verb?

    > 你(考试)考得好不好?
    > 你(考試)考得好不好?
    > **Nǐ (kǎo shì) kǎo de hǎo bù hǎo?**
    > Did you do well on the test?

    > 他说得清楚不清楚?
    > 他說得清楚不清楚?
    > **Tā shuō de qīngchu bù qīngchu?**
    > Did he speak clearly?

- 吗/嗎 **ma** structure

    > 你考得好吗?
    > 你考得好嗎?
    > **Nǐ kǎo de hǎo ma?**
    > Did you do well on the test?

    > 他说得清楚吗?
    > 他說得清楚嗎?
    > **Tā shuō de qīngchu ma?**
    > Did he speak clearly?

▶ 28.1

DESCRIBING HOW ACTIONS ARE PERFORMED

31.3 Describing the performance of an entire action with an adverbial modifier

To describe how an entire action is performed on a specific occasion, precede the verb phrase (or prepositional phrase + verb phrase if there is a prepositional phrase) with an *adverbial verb modifier* + 地 *de* as follows. Note the tone changes on the second syllable of the modifier:

adverbial verb modifier + 地 *de* + *verb phrase*

他偷偷儿地把钱拿走了。
他偷偷兒地把錢拿走了。
Tā *tōutōur de* bǎ qián názǒu le.
He *secretly* took away the money.

你们得好好儿地学。
你們得好好兒地學。
Nǐmen děi *hǎohāor de* xué.
You have to study *hard/well*.

他慢慢地把汉字学会了。
他慢慢地把漢字學會了。
Tā *mànmān de* bǎ Hàn zì xuéhuì le.
He *slowly* learned the Chinese characters.

快快地吃吧！
Kuàikuāi de chī ba!
Hurry up and eat!

孩子高高兴兴地在公园里玩。
孩子高高興興地在公園裏玩。
Háizi *gāo gāo xīng xīng de* zài gōngyuán lǐ wán.
The children are playing *happily* in the park.

他们静静地睡了一个晚上。
他們靜靜地睡了一個晚上。
Tāmen *jìngjìng de* shuì le yī gè wǎnshang.
They slept *peacefully* the whole night.

你得留心地听老师说话。
你得留心地聽老師說話。
Nǐ děi *liúxīn de* tīng lǎoshī shuō huà.
You should listen *attentively* to the teacher.

她急急忙忙地逃走了。
Tā *jíjí mángmáng de* táozǒu le.
She *hurriedly* ran away. (She ran away in a hurry.)

Phrases that frequently occur as adverbial modifiers of an entire action include the following:

慢慢地	mànmān de	slowly
快快地	kuàikuāi de	quickly
好好地	hǎohāo de	well
偷偷地	tōutōu de	secretly
靜靜地	jìngjìng de	peacefully
安靜地	ānjìng de	peacefully/quietly
急忙地	jímáng de	hurriedly/hastily
匆忙地	cōngmáng de	hurriedly/hastily
兴奋地/興奮地	xīngfèn de	excitedly
大声地/大聲地	dàshēng de	loudly

31.3 Describing the performance of an entire action with an adverbial modifier

悄悄地	**qiāoqiāo de**	quietly
严厉地/嚴厲地	**yánlì de**	sternly
残忍地/殘忍地	**cánrěn de**	cruelly
仔细地/仔細地	**zǐxì de**	meticulously
用心地	**yòngxīn de**	attentively, carefully
留心地	**liúxīn de**	attentively, cautiously
认真地/認真地	**rènzhēn de**	diligently, conscientiously
情愿地/情願地	**qíngyuàn de**	willingly
自愿地/自願地	**zìyuàn de**	willingly
使劲地/使勁地	**shǐjìn de**	using full strength/ do with all one's might
渐渐地/漸漸地	**jiànjiàn de**	gradually
安安静静地	**ānānjìngjìng de**	peacefully
仔仔细细地/仔仔細細地	**zǐzǐxìxì de**	meticulously
急急忙忙地	**jíjí mángmáng de**	hurriedly
慌慌张张地/慌慌張張地	**huānghuāng zhāngzhāng de**	in a flustered manner

NOTE These *adverbial modifiers* + 地 *de* occur in the same position in the predicate as other adverbs, that is, at the beginning of the verb phrase, before the verb and any prepositional phrase.

▶ 15.1

32

Indicating result, conclusion, potential, and extent

32.1 Indicating the result or conclusion of an action with resultative verbs

In Mandarin, action verbs refer to open-ended processes and not to their conclusions or results. For example, the verb 买/買 **mǎi** refers to 'shopping,' not 'buying.' The verb 找 **zhǎo** refers to 'looking for' something, not 'finding' it.

English sometimes uses two entirely different verbs to refer to a process and its result or conclusion. In Mandarin, processes and results are always expressed using the same verb. The process is expressed with an open-ended action verb. The result or conclusion is expressed by adding a resultative suffix to the open-ended action verb. Verbs that are formed by an action verb and a resultative suffix are often referred to as *resultative verbs*.

Resultative verb structure: *action verb + resultative ending*

NOTE Some grammars refer to the resultative suffix as a *complement of result*.

▶ 13, 18

32.1.1 Common resultative suffixes

Resultative suffixes that indicate the conclusion of an action:

Suffix	*Meaning*
完 **wán**	to finish
好 **hǎo**	to do to a successful conclusion

Resultative suffixes that indicate the result of an action:

Suffix	*Meaning*
见/見 **jiàn**	to perceive (used with verbs of perception: see, hear, smell)
到 **dào**	to attain a goal, to acquire (like 着/著 **zháo**)
着/著 **zháo**	to attain a goal, to acquire (like 到 **dào**)
错/錯 **cuò**	to do wrong, to be mistaken

Indicating the result or conclusion of an action with resultative verbs | **32.1**

Suffix	Meaning
饱/飽 **bǎo**	to be full
懂 **dǒng**	to understand
会/會 **huì**	to know
住 **zhù**	to stick
开/開 **kāi**	to open
够/夠 **gòu**	to be enough
光 **guāng**	to use up
清楚 **qīngchu**	to be clear
干净/乾淨 **gānjìng**	to be clean

32.1.2 Common resultative verbs: action verbs + resultative ending

Action verb	Meaning	Resultative verb	Meaning
说/說 **shuō**	to say	说完/說完 **shuōwán**	to finish saying
吃 **chī**	to eat	吃完 **chīwán**	to finish eating
用 **yòng**	to use	用完 **yòngwán**	to use up (to use something until finished)
说/說 **shuō**	to say	说好/說好 **shuōhǎo**	to reach a successful conclusion through discussion; to reach an agreement
听/聽 **tīng**	to listen	听见/聽見 **tīngjian**	to hear something
看 **kàn**	to look	看见 **kànjian**	to see something
闻/聞 **wén**	to smell	闻见/聞見 **wénjian**	to smell something
听/聽 **tīng**	to listen	听到/聽到 **tīngdào**	to hear something
看 **kàn**	to look	看到 **kàndào**	to see something
闻/聞 **wén**	to smell	闻到/聞到 **wéndào**	to smell something

207

INDICATING RESULT, CONCLUSION, POTENTIAL, AND EXTENT

32.1

Action verb	Meaning	Resultative verb	Meaning
买/買 **mǎi**	to shop for	买到/買到 **mǎidào**	to buy/to purchase
找 **zhǎo**	to look for	找到 **zhǎodào**	to find
买/買 **mǎi**	to shop for	买着/買著 **mǎizháo**	to buy/to purchase
找 **zhǎo**	to look for	找着/找著 **zhǎozháo**	to find
睡/睡 **shuì**	to sleep	睡着/睡著 **shuìzháo**	to fall asleep
做 **zuò**	to do	做错/做錯 **zuòcuò**	to do wrong
写/寫 **xiě**	to write	写错/寫錯 **xiěcuò**	to write incorrectly
买/買 **mǎi**	to shop for	买错/買錯 **mǎicuò**	to buy wrong (to buy the wrong thing)
用 **yòng**	to use	用错/用錯 **yòngcuò**	to use wrong (to use something the wrong way)
吃 **chī**	to eat	吃饱/吃飽 **chībǎo**	to eat until full
看 **kàn**	to read	看懂 **kàndǒng**	to read to the point of understanding something
听/聽 **tīng**	to listen	听懂/聽懂 **tīngdǒng**	to listen to the point of understanding
学/學 **xué**	to study	学会/學會 **xuéhuì**	to study to the point of knowing something; to master by studying
记/記 **jì**	to record, to remember	记住/記住 **jìzhù**	to remember
打 **dǎ**	to hit (also many idiomatic meanings)	打开/打開 **dǎkāi**	to open
吃 **chī**	to eat	吃够 **chīgòu**	to eat enough
问/問 **wèn**	to ask	问清楚 問清楚 **wènqīngchu**	to ask about something until you are clear about it
擦 **cā**	to wipe	擦干净 擦乾淨 **cāgānjìng**	to wipe something until it is clean
洗 **xǐ**	to wash	洗干净 洗乾淨 **xǐ gānjìng**	to wash something until it is clean

32.1 Indicating the result or conclusion of an action with resultative verbs

Here are example sentences with resultative verbs.

Q: 你听到了那个声音吗?
你聽到了那個聲音嗎?
Nǐ tīngdào le nàge shēngyīn ma?
Did you hear that sound?

A: 没听到。
沒聽到。
Méi tīngdào.
I didn't hear it.

Q: 你吃饱了吗?
你吃飽了嗎?
Nǐ chībǎo le ma?
Did you eat until full? (Are you full?)

A: 吃饱了。
吃飽了。
Chībǎo le.
I ate until full. (I'm full.)

我把我自己的名字写错了。
我把我自己的名字寫錯了。
Wǒ bǎ wǒ zìjǐ de míngzi xiěcuò le.
I wrote my own name wrong.

Directional suffixes may also indicate the result of movement.

我们走进来了。
我們走進來了。
Wǒmen zǒujìnlái le.
We walked *in*.

猫跳上沙发去了。
貓跳上沙發去了。
Māo tiào*shàng* shāfā qù le.
The cat jumped *onto* the sofa.

▶ 19, 48.8

32.1.3 Using the verb suffix 了 *le* with resultative verbs to indicate completion

The verb suffix 了 **le** occurs at the end of resultative verbs, after the resultative suffix, to indicate that the action is complete or the desired result has been attained.

我做完了功课。
我做完了功課。
Wǒ zuòwán le gōngkè.
I finished my homework.

我吃饱了。
我吃飽了。
Wǒ chībǎo le.
I am full. (I've eaten until full.)

了 **le** never occurs between the action verb and the resultative ending.

Say this
你找到了你的皮包吗?
你找到了你的皮包嗎?
Nǐ zhǎodào le nǐ de píbāo ma?
Have you found your wallet?

Not this
*你找了到你的皮包吗?
你找了到你的皮包嗎?
Nǐ zhǎo le dào nǐ de píbāo ma?

▶ 13.1, 18.4, 37.1

INDICATING RESULT, CONCLUSION, POTENTIAL, AND EXTENT

32.1.4 Using 没/沒 *méi* with resultative verbs to indicate lack of completion or result

The negative marker 没/沒 **méi** is used to indicate that an action has not been completed or that the desired result has not been attained. 没/沒 **méi** occurs before the entire resultative verb.

> 我没看完。
> 我沒看完。
> **Wǒ méi kànwán.**
> I haven't finished reading.
>
> 我没听懂。
> 我沒聽懂。
> **Wǒ méi tīngdǒng.**
> I didn't understand (by listening).

没/沒 **méi** never occurs between the action verb and resultative suffix.

Say this	*Not this*
我没念错。	*我念没错。
我沒唸錯。	我唸沒錯。
Wǒ méi niàncuò.	**Wǒ niàn méi cuò.**
I didn't read (it) wrong.	

▶ 13.3.2, 18.4, 37.3

32.2 Indicating the ability to reach a conclusion or result: the potential infixes 得 *de* and 不 *bu*

得 **de** and 不 **bu** may occur between an action verb and a resultative or directional suffix to indicate that it is possible or not possible to reach the result. When 得 **de** and 不 **bu** are used in this way, we refer to them as *potential infixes* and the form of the resultative or directional verb as the *potential form*.

32.2.1 The potential infix 得 *de*

To indicate that *it is possible* to perform an action and reach a conclusion or result, add the potential infix 得 **de** into the middle of the resultative verb, between the action verb and the resultative suffix:

> *action verb* + 得 *de* + *resultative suffix*
>
> 我听得懂中国电影。
> 我聽得懂中國電影。
> **Wǒ tīngdedǒng Zhōngguó diànyǐng.**
> I can understand (by listening) Chinese movies.
>
> 你吃得完那么多东西吗?
> 你吃得完那麼多東西嗎?
> **Nǐ chīdewán nàme duō dōngxi ma?**
> Can you finish eating that many things?

▶ 18.6, 19.5

32.2.2 The potential infix 不 *bu*

To indicate that *it is not possible* to reach a conclusion or result, add the potential infix 不 **bu** into the middle of the resultative or directional verb, between the action verb and the resultative suffix:

Summary of the functions of resultative verbs 32.3

action verb + 不 **bu** + *resultative suffix*

王老师的话我都听不懂。
王老師的話我都聽不懂。
Wáng lǎoshī de huà wǒ dōu tīngbudǒng.
I can't understand (by listening) what Professor Wang says.

我找不到我的皮包。
Wǒ zhǎobudào wǒ de píbāo.
I can't find my wallet.

NOTE The infixes 得 **de** and 不 **bu** are the only things that can occur between an action verb and a resultative suffix.

▶ 18.6, 19.5

32.2.2.1 Using resultative verbs to indicate that a result cannot be achieved no matter what

Resultative verbs in the negative potential form occur with the question word 怎么/怎麼 **zěnme** to indicate that a result cannot be achieved *no matter what* the subject does.

我怎么学也学不会。
我怎麼學也學不會。
Wǒ zěnme xué yě xuébuhuì.
No matter how I study I can't learn (it).

他怎么找也找不到。
他怎麼找也找不到。
Tā zěnme zhǎo yě zhǎobudào.
No matter how I look I can't find (it).

▶ 28.6

32.3 Summary of the functions of resultative verbs

The functions of resultative verbs and their occurrence with 了 **le** and negation are summarized below.

The action occurred and the result was attained	*The action occurred but the result or conclusion was not attained*
resultative verb + 了 **le**	没 **méi** + resultative verb
我吃饱了。	我没吃饱。
我吃飽了。	我沒吃飽。
Wǒ chībǎo le.	**Wǒ méi chībǎo.**
I ate until full.	I did not eat until full.
	(I ate but was not full.)
It is possible to attain the indicated result or conclusion by performing the verb	*It is impossible to attain the indicated result or conclusion by performing the verb*
action verb 得 **de** result/conclusion	action verb 不 **bu** result/conclusion
我吃得饱。	我吃不饱。
我吃得飽。	我吃不飽。
Wǒ chīdebǎo.	**Wǒ chībubǎo.**
I am able to eat until full.	I am unable to eat until full.

INDICATING RESULT, CONCLUSION, POTENTIAL, AND EXTENT

32.4 Indicating the ability to perform the verb: the potential suffixes 得了 *deliǎo* and 不了 *buliǎo*

Resultative suffixes indicate the result or conclusion of an action. To indicate that the subject is *able to* or *unable to* perform the action, add one of the following *potential suffixes* to the verb:

-得了 *deliǎo* able to perform the action
-不了 *buliǎo* unable to perform the action

▶ 18.6.2

32.4.1 The potential suffix 得了 *deliǎo*

Use this suffix to say that the subject is able to perform the action of the verb or that the subject is able to finish the action. In the latter sense, it is similar to the resultative suffix 完 **wán** 'to finish.'

他很聪明，一定做得了这件事情。
他很聰明，一定做得了這件事情。
Tā hěn cōngming, yīdìng zuòdeliǎo zhèjiàn shìqing.
He is very smart. He is certainly able to take care of this matter.

今天的功课这么多，我做不了。
今天的功課這麼多，我做不了。
Jīntiān de gōngkè zhème duō, wǒ zuòbuliǎo.
There is so much homework today. I can't do it. (can't finish it.)

你点了这么多菜，我们吃得了吗？
你點了這麼多菜，我們吃得了嗎？
Nǐ diǎn le zhème duō cài, wǒmen chīdeliǎo ma?
You've ordered so many dishes. Will we be able to eat them? (finish eating them?)

32.4.2 The potential suffix 不了 *buliǎo*

Use this suffix to say that the subject is not able to do some action.

我用不了筷子。
Wǒ yòngbuliǎo kuàizi.
I am unable to use chopsticks.

他一定走不了那么远。
他一定走不了那麼遠。
Tā yīdìng zǒubuliǎo nàme yuǎn.
He is certainly unable to walk that far.

这是他的个性，他改不了。
這是他的個性，他改不了。
Zhè shì tā de gèxìng, tā gǎibùliǎo.
This is his nature. He can't change.

▶ 18.6.2

Resultative suffixes with special meanings or properties

32.4.3 Asking about the ability to perform an action

To ask about the ability of a subject to perform an action, form a yes–no question with 吗/嗎 **ma** or with the *verb-not-verb* structure.

- 吗/嗎 *ma*

    你吃得了这么多菜吗?
    你吃得了這麼多菜嗎?
    Nǐ chīdeliǎo zhème duō cài ma?
    Are you able to eat this many dishes?

- *Verb-not-verb* structure: *verb* 得了 *deliǎo verb* 不了 *bùliǎo*

    他做得了做不了这件事情?
    他做得了做不了這件事情?
    Tā zuòdeliǎo zuòbuliǎo zhè jiàn shìqing?
    Is he able to take care of this matter or not?

    这么多菜，你吃得了吃不了?
    這麼多菜，你吃得了吃不了?
    Zhème duō cài, nǐ chīdeliǎo chībuliǎo?
    This many dishes, are you able to eat them or not?

To answer 'yes,' say *verb* 得了 *deliǎo*:

做得了。
Zuòdeliǎo.
He can do it.

吃得了。
Chīdéliǎo.
I can eat them.

To answer 'no,' say *verb* 不了 *buliǎo*:

做不了。
Zuòbuliǎo.
He can't do it.

吃不了。
Chībuliǎo.
I can't eat them.

▶ 18.6.1

32.5 Resultative suffixes with special meanings or properties

-掉 *diào*

掉 **diào** indicates completion, and often also carries negative connotations for the speaker. It may serve as a suffix on action verbs or change-of-state action verbs in which the action does not bring about a resulting state. It does not occur in the potential form.

甩掉 **shuǎidiào** 'to throw away, to discard'

他把那个孩子甩掉不管了。
他把那個孩子甩掉不管了。
Tā bǎ nàge háizi shuǎidiào bù guǎn le.
He abandoned that child.

INDICATING RESULT, CONCLUSION, POTENTIAL, AND EXTENT 32.5

扔掉 *rēngdiào* 'to throw away'

> 你怎么把我的信给扔掉了？
> 你怎麽把我的信給扔掉了？
> **Nǐ zěnme bǎ wǒ de xìn gěi rēngdiào le?**
> Why did you throw away my letter?

死掉 *sǐdiào* 'to die'

> 我忘了浇水，花儿都死掉了。
> 我忘了澆水，花兒都死掉了。
> **Wǒ wàng le jiāo shuǐ, huār dōu sǐdiào le.**
> I forgot to water (them) and all of my flowers died.

忘掉 *wàngdiào* 'to forget completely'

> 你怎么能忘掉了这么要紧的事情？
> 你怎麽能忘掉了這麽要緊的事情？
> **Nǐ zěnme néng wàngdiào le zhème yàojǐn de shìqing?**
> How could you forget such an important thing?

丢掉 *diūdiào* 'to lose'

> 我的护照丢掉了。我得去报警。
> 我的護照丢掉了。我得去報警。
> **Wǒ de hùzhào diūdiào le. Wǒ děi qù bào jǐng.**
> I lost my passport. I have to report it to the police.

-得及 *dejí*, -不及 *bují*

及 **jí** only occurs in potential form. It means to be able to do an action on time.

来得及/來得及 *láidejí* 'to be able to arrive on time'

来不及/來不及 *láibují* 'to be unable to arrive on time'

> Q: 我们现在去上课，来得及来不及？
> 我們現在去上課，來得及來不及？
> **Wǒmen xiànzài qù shàng kè, láidejí láibují?**
> If we go to class now, will we get there on time?
>
> A: 还有五分钟。快点儿走来得及。
> 還有五分鐘。快點兒走來得及。
> **Hái yǒu wǔfēn zhōng. Kuài diǎr zǒu láidejí.**
> We still have five minutes. If we go fast we can get there on time.

-得起 *deqǐ*, -不起 *buqǐ*

起 **qǐ** only occurs in potential form. Its most common meaning is to be able to afford to do the verb.

吃得起 *chīdeqǐ* 'to be able to afford to eat something'

吃不起 *chībuqǐ* 'to be unable to afford to eat something'

> Q: 天天在饭馆吃饭，吃得起吃不起？
> 天天在飯館吃飯，吃得起吃不起？
> **Tiāntiān zài fànguǎn chī fàn, chīdeqǐ chībuqǐ?**
> Can you afford to eat in a restaurant every day?
>
> A: 有的人吃得起，有的人吃不起。
> **Yǒude rén chīdeqǐ, yǒude rén chībuqǐ.**
> Some people can afford it, some can't.

32.5 Resultative suffixes with special meanings or properties

住得起 **zhùdeqǐ** 'to be able to afford to live someplace'

住不起 **zhùbuqǐ** 'to be unable to afford to live someplace'

> Q: 现在北京房子那么贵，你们住得起住不起？
> 現在北京房子那麼貴，你們住得起住不起？
> **Xiànzài Běijīng fángzi nàme guì, nǐmen zhùdeqǐ zhùbuqǐ?**
> Houses in Beijing are so expensive now, can you afford to live there?

> A: 我们住得起，可是我们的孩子住不起。
> 我們住得起，可是我們的孩子住不起。
> **Wǒmen zhùdeqǐ, kěshì wǒmen de háizi zhùbuqǐ.**
> We can afford to live there, but our children cannot afford to live there.

-得起 **deqǐ** and -不起 **buqǐ** also have idiomatic meanings when suffixed to certain verbs.

看得起 **kàndeqǐ** 'to have a good opinion of, think highly of'

看不起 **kànbuqǐ** 'to look down on, despise'

> 你不应该看不起没有钱的人。
> 你不應該看不起沒有錢的人。
> **Nǐ bù yīnggāi kànbuqǐ méi yǒu qián de rén.**
> You should not look down on people who have no money.

对得起/對得起 **duìdeqǐ** 'to show respect to someone'

对不起/對不起 **duìbuqǐ** 'to disappoint someone, cause someone to be embarrassed or lose face'

> Q: 你不好好地念书对得起对不起你的父母？
> 你不好好地唸書對得起對不起你的父母？
> **Nǐ bù hǎohāo de niàn shū duìdeqǐ duìbuqǐ nǐ de fùmǔ?**
> If you do not study hard, how can you face your parents?

> A: 我一定要好好地念书才能对得起他们。
> 我一定要好好地唸書才能對得起他們。
> **Wǒ yīdìng yào hǎohāo de niànshū cái néng duìdeqǐ tāmen.**
> I certainly want to study hard so that I can make them happy.

-上 shàng

上 **shàng** has a special meaning when used in the resultative verb 考上 **kǎoshàng** 'to pass an entrance exam' (especially a university entrance exam). The potential forms are:

考得上 **kǎodeshàng** 'to be able to pass the entrance exam'

考不上 **kǎobushàng** 'to be unable to pass the entrance exam'

> Q: 你想我今年考得上考不上北大？
> **Nǐ xiǎng wǒ jīnnián kǎodeshàng kǎobushàng Běi Dà?**
> Do you think I will be able to pass the entrance exam for Beijing University this year?

> A: 我想你一定考得上。
> **Wǒ xiǎng nǐ yīdìng kǎodeshàng.**
> I think you will certainly pass the exam.

-不定 budìng

-不定 **budìng** has a restricted use as a resultative verb ending:

说不定/說不定 **shuōbudìng** 'perhaps'

> 他现在还没来，说不定他不会来了。
> 他現在還沒來，說不定他不會來了。
> **Tā xiànzài hái méi lái, shuōbudìng tā bù huì lái le.**
> He hasn't come yet. Perhaps he won't come.

▶ 18.6, 18.7

INDICATING RESULT, CONCLUSION, POTENTIAL, AND EXTENT

32.6 Indicating the extent or result of a situation

Resultative verbs indicate the result of actions. To indicate the result or extent of a situation, use the following structure:

> verb 得 *de* verb phrase/clause

For adjectival verbs, 得 *de* introduces the extent of the situation, adding the meaning: *so adjectival verb that* verb phrase/clause.

> 他累得抬不起头来了。
> 他累得抬不起頭來了。
> **Tā *lèi de* táibuqǐtóu lái le.**
> He was *so tired that* he could not pick up his head.

> 她高兴得说不出话来了。
> 她高興得說不出話來了。
> **Tā *gāoxìng de* shuōbuchū huà lái le.**
> She was *so happy that* she was unable to speak.

> 他冷得发抖了。
> 他冷得發抖了。
> **Tā *lěng de* fādǒu le.**
> He was *so cold that* he was shivering.

When the verb is an action verb, 得 *de* introduces the result of the action, adding the meaning: *performed the action until* verb phrase/sentence.

> 妈妈哭得眼睛都红了。
> 媽媽哭得眼睛都紅了。
> **Māma *kū de* yǎnjing dōu hóng le.**
> Mom *cried until* her eyes were red.

> 他走得精疲力尽了。
> 他走得精疲力盡了。
> **Tā *zǒu de* jīngpí lìjìn le.**
> He *walked so much that* he was exhausted.

If the action verb takes an object, the sentence takes the following form:

> [action verb + object] action verb 得 *de* verb phrase/clause

> 他[走路]走得精疲力尽了。
> 他[走路]走得精疲力盡了。
> **Tā [zǒu lù] zǒu de jīngpí lìjìn le.**
> He walked so much that he was exhausted.

33

Making comparisons

Comparison structures are used to indicate that things are similar to or different from each other, or to indicate that something is more than or less than another thing in some way.

This chapter presents the structures used to make comparisons in Mandarin. It uses the following grammatical terms and abbreviations. Refer to the relevant chapters for more information about each grammatical category.

noun phrase (NP)			Chapter 9
adjectival verb (AV)	and	adjectival verb phrase (AVP)	Chapter 10
stative verb (SV)	and	stative verb phrase (SVP)	Chapter 11
modal verb (MV)			Chapter 12
action verb (V)	and	action verb phrase (VP)	Chapter 13

33.1 Similarity

33.1.1 Indicating that noun phrases are identical

To indicate that two noun phrases are similar or equal, say:

NP₁	跟/和	NP₂	一样
NP₁	跟/和	NP₂	一樣
NP₁	**gēn/hé**	NP₂	**yīyàng**
NP₁	and	NP₂	identical/same

这本书跟/和那本书一样。
這本書跟/和那本書一樣。
Zhè běn shū gēn/hé nà běn shū yīyàng.
This book and that book are the same.

今天的天气跟/和昨天的一样。
今天的天氣跟/和昨天的一樣。
Jīntiān de tiānqì gēn/hé zuótiān de yīyàng.
Today's weather is the same as yesterday's.

NOTE The words 跟 **gěn** and 和 **hé** are equivalent in meaning. In all of the structures in this chapter in which they occur, 跟 **gěn** and 和 **hé** are interchangeable. In some dialects, 同 **tóng** occurs in this structure instead of 跟 **gěn** or 和 **hé**.

▶ 16.1, 33.2.1

MAKING COMPARISONS — 33.1

33.1.2 Indicating that all noun phrases are the same

When a noun phrase refers to multiple entities (for example, 'houses,' 'dogs,' 'two books,' etc.), use this pattern to say that all of the entities are the same.

    NP   一样/一樣 **yīyàng**
    NP   identical/same

> 这两本书一样。
> 這兩本書一樣。
> **Zhè liǎng běn shū yīyàng.**
> These two books are identical.

> 这三个菜一样吗?
> 這三個菜一樣嗎?
> **Zhè sān gè cài yīyàng ma?**
> Are these three dishes the same?

▶ 33.2.2

33.1.3 Indicating that noun phrases share a property

To indicate that two noun phrases are alike in a particular property, say the following:

NP₁	跟/和	NP₂	一样	AV
NP₁	跟/和	NP₂	一樣	AV
NP₁	**gēn/hé**	NP₂	**yīyàng**	AV
NP₁	and	NP₂	identical/same	AV

> 我儿子跟/和我女儿一样高。
> 我兒子跟/和我女兒一樣高。
> **Wǒ érzi gēn/hé wǒ nǚ'ér yīyàng gāo.**
> My son and my daughter are the same height. (equally *tall*)

> 小狗和小猫一样可爱。
> 小狗和小貓一樣可愛。
> **Xiǎogǒu hé xiǎomāo yīyàng kě'ài.**
> Puppies and kittens are equally *cute*.

▶ 33.2.3

33.1.4 Indicating resemblance

To indicate that one noun phrase resembles another noun phrase, say:

NP₁	像	NP₂
NP₁	**xiàng**	NP₂
NP₁	looks like	NP₂ (NP₁ resembles NP₂)

> 他像他爸爸。
> **Tā xiàng tā bàba.**
> He resembles his dad.

> 他像法国人吗?
> 他像法國人嗎?
> **Tā xiàng Fǎguórén ma?**
> Does he look like a French person?

or

Similarity

> NP₁　跟/和　NP₂　很像
> NP₁　**gēn/hé**　NP₂　**hěn xiàng**

> 你儿子跟/和你女儿很像吗？
> 你兒子跟/和你女兒很像嗎？
> **Nǐ érzi gēn/hé nǐ nǚ'ér hěn xiàng ma?**
> Do your son and daughter look alike?

If the noun phrase refers to multiple entities, say:

> NP　（很）　像
> NP　**(hěn)**　**xiàng**
> NP are very similar/very much alike.

> 他们很像。
> 他們很像。
> **Tāmen hěn xiàng.**
> They look very much alike.

▶ 33.2.4

33.1.5 Indicating similarity in some property

To indicate that two noun phrases are similar enough to be considered equivalent, say:

> NP₁　有　NP₂　那么/那麼　AV
> NP₁　**yǒu**　NP₂　**nàme**　AV

> 他有他姐姐那么高。(AV)
> 他有他姐姐那麼高。
> **Tā yǒu tā jiějie nàme *gāo*.**
> He is as *tall* as his older sister.

> 他有他姐姐那么聪明吗？
> 他有他姐姐那麼聰明嗎？
> **Tā yǒu tā jiějie nàme *cōngming* ma?**
> Is he as *intelligent* as his older sister?

or

> NP₁　有　NP₂　这么/這麼　AV
> NP₁　有　NP₂　**zhème**　AV
> NP₁ is as AV as NP₂

> 他有你这么高。AV
> 他有你這麼高。
> **Tā yǒu nǐ zhème *gāo*.**
> He is as *tall* as you.

NOTE　这么/這麼 **zhème** 'this/so' and 那么/那麼 **nàme** 'that/so' are used frequently in comparison structures. They may occur before an adjectival verb. It is often not necessary to translate 这么/這麼 **zhème** and 那么/那麼 **nàme** into English.

▶ 33.4.1

219

MAKING COMPARISONS

33.1

33.1.6 Indicating identical performance of an action

To indicate that two noun phrases perform an action in a similar way, say:

NP₁	跟/和	NP₂	[verb 得]	一样	AV
NP₁	跟/和	NP₂	[verb 得]	一樣	AV
NP₁	**gēn/hé**	NP₂	[verb **de**]	**yīyàng**	AV

NP₁ and NP₂ perform the verb equally AV

> 我跟他吃得<u>一样多</u>。
> 我跟他吃得<u>一樣多</u>。
> **Wǒ gēn tā chī de *yīyàng duō*.**
> I eat *as much as* him.

> 弟弟跟妹妹写得<u>一样快</u>。
> 弟弟跟妹妹寫得<u>一樣快</u>。
> **Dìdi gēn mèimei xiě de *yīyàng kuài*.**
> Younger brother and younger sister write *equally fast*.

If the object of the action verb is included in the sentence, the action verb is said twice, once followed by the object, and once followed by 得一样 **de yīyàng** (AV).

NP₁	跟/和	NP₂	[action verb + object]	[action verb 得]	一样	AV
NP₁	跟/和	NP₂	[action verb + object]	[action verb 得]	一樣	AV
NP₁	**gēn/hé**	NP₂	[action verb + object]	[action verb **de**]	**yīyàng**	AV

NP₁ and NP₂ perform the action verb equally AV

> 我跟他<u>吃</u>饭<u>吃</u>得一样多。
> 我跟他<u>吃</u>飯<u>吃</u>得一樣多。
> **Wǒ gēn tā *chī* fàn *chī* de yīyàng duō.**
> I eat as much as him.

> 弟弟跟妹妹<u>写</u>字<u>写</u>得一样快。
> 弟弟跟妹妹<u>寫</u>字<u>寫</u>得一樣快。
> **Dìdi gēn mèimei *xiě* zì *xiě* de yīyàng kuài.**
> Younger brother and younger sister write characters equally fast.

Here are several variations in this pattern. They differ in the order of the phrases. In all of these variations, [action verb + object] occurs before [action verb 得 **de**], and 一样/一樣 **yīyàng** AV occurs at the end of the sentence.

Variation 1

NP₁	[action verb + object]	[action verb 得]	跟/和	NP₂	一样	AV
NP₁	[action verb + object]	[action verb 得]	跟/和	NP₂	一樣	AV
NP₁	[action verb + object]	[action verb **de**]	**gēn/hé**	NP₂	**yīyàng**	AV

NP₁ and NP₂ perform the action verb equally AV

> 我吃饭吃得跟他一样多。
> 我吃飯吃得跟他一樣多。
> **Wǒ chī fàn chī de gēn tā yīyàng duō.**
> I eat as much as him.

> 弟弟写字写得跟妹妹一样快。
> 弟弟寫字寫得跟妹妹一樣快。
> **Dìdi xiě zì xiě de gēn mèimei yīyàng kuài.**
> Younger brother and younger sister write characters equally fast.

220

Similarity | **33.1**

Variation 2

NP₁ [action verb + object] 跟/和 NP₂ [action verb 得] 一样 AV
NP₁ [action verb + object] 跟/和 NP₂ [action verb 得] 一樣 AV
NP₁ [action verb + object] **gēn/hé** NP₂ [action verb **de**] **yīyàng** AV
NP₁ and NP₂ perform the action verb equally AV

我吃饭跟他吃得一样多。
我吃飯跟他吃得一樣多。
Wǒ chī fàn gēn tā chī de yīyàng duō.
I eat as much as him.

The verb 有 **yǒu** can be used instead of 跟 **gēn** or 和 **hé**.

NP₁ 有 NP₂ [action verb + object] [action verb 得] (这么/那么) AV
NP₁ 有 NP₂ [action verb + object] [action verb 得] (這麼/那麼) AV
NP₁ **yǒu** NP₂ [action verb + object] [action verb **de**] (**zhème/nàme**) AV
NP₁ and NP₂ perform the action verb equally AV

弟弟有爸爸写字写得那么漂亮。
弟弟有爸爸寫字寫得那麼漂亮。
Dìdi yǒu bàba xiě zì xiě de nàme piàoliang.
Younger brother writes characters as beautifully as Dad.

or

NP₁ [action verb + object] [action verb 得] 有 NP₂ (这么/那么) AV
NP₁ [action verb + object] [action verb 得] 有 NP₂ (這麼/那麼) AV
NP₁ [action verb + object] [action verb **de**] **yǒu** NP₂ (**zhème/nàme**) AV
NP₁ performs the action verb as AV as NP₂

弟弟写字写得有爸爸那么漂亮。
弟弟寫字寫得有爸爸那麼漂亮。
Dìdi xiě zì xiě de yǒu bàba nàme piàoliang.
Younger brother writes characters as beautifully as Dad.

Be careful to repeat the verb if you include the object of the verb.

Say this	*Not this*
我吃饭吃得跟他一样多。 我吃飯吃得跟他一樣多。 **Wǒ chī fàn chī de gēn tā yīyàng duō.** I eat as much as he does.	*我吃饭得跟他一样多。 我吃飯得跟他一樣多。 **Wǒ chī fàn de gēn tā yīyàng duō.**
弟弟写字写得有爸爸那么漂亮。 弟弟寫字寫得有爸爸那麼漂亮。 **Dìdi xiě zì xiě de yǒu bàba nàme piàoliang.** Younger brother writes characters as nicely as Dad.	*弟弟写字得有爸爸那么漂亮。 弟弟寫字得有爸爸那麼漂亮。 **Dìdi xiě zì de yǒu bàba nàme piàoliang.**

▶ 31.1.2, 33.3.5, 33.4.3

MAKING COMPARISONS

33.2 Difference

33.2.1 Indicating that noun phrases are different

To indicate that two noun phrases are different, say:

NP₁	不	跟/和	NP₂	一样
NP₁	不	跟/和	NP₂	一樣
NP₁	bù	gēn/hé	NP₂	yīyàng

NP₁ and NP₂ are not identical/the same.

这本书不跟/和那本书一样。
這本書不跟/和那本書一樣。
Zhè běn shū bù gēn/hé nà běn shū yīyàng.
This book is not the same as that book.

今天的天气不跟/和昨天的天气一样。
今天的天氣不跟/和昨天的天氣一樣。
Jīntiān de tiānqì bù gēn/hé zuótiān de tiānqì yīyàng.
Today's weather is not the same as yesterday's.

or

NP₁	跟/和	NP₂	不	一样
NP₁	跟/和	NP₂	不	一樣
NP₁	gēn/hé	NP₂	bù	yīyàng

NP₁ and NP₂ are not identical/the same.

这个旅馆的房费跟/和那个旅馆的不一样。
這個旅館的房費跟/和那個旅館的不一樣。
Zhège lǚguǎn de fáng fèi gēn/hé nàge lǚguǎn de bù yīyàng.
The room charge in this hotel is not the same as the room charge in that hotel.

▶ 33.1.1

33.2.2 Indicating that all noun phrases are not identical

When a noun phrase refers to more than one entity (for example 'houses,' 'dogs,' 'two books,' etc.), use this pattern to say that the entities are not identical.

NP	不	一样
NP	不	一樣
NP	bù	yīyàng

NP are not identical/same

这两本书不一样。
這兩本書不一樣。
Zhè liǎng běn shū bù yīyàng.
These two books are not identical.

▶ 33.1.2

33.2.3 Indicating that noun phrases are different in some property

To indicate that two noun phrases are different in a particular property, say:

NP₁	不	跟/和	NP₂	一样	AV
NP₁	不	跟/和	NP₂	一樣	AV
NP₁	bù	gēn/hé	NP₂	yīyàng	AV

这个旅馆的房间不跟那个旅馆的房间一样干净。
這個旅館的房間不跟那個旅館的房間一樣乾淨。
Zhège lǚguǎn de fángjiān bù gēn nàge lǚguǎn de fángjiān yīyàng *gānjìng*.
The rooms in this hotel are not as *clean* as the rooms in that hotel.

我儿子不跟/和我女儿一样高。
我兒子不跟/和我女兒一樣高。
Wǒ érzi bù gēn/hé wǒ nǚ'ér yīyàng *gāo*.
My son is not the same *height* as my daughter.

or

NP₁	跟/和	NP₂	不	一样	AV
NP₁	跟/和	NP₂	不	一樣	AV
NP₁	gēn/hé	NP₂	bù	yīyàng	AV

NP₁ and NP₂ are not identical/the same in some property

这个旅馆的房间跟那个旅馆的房间不一样干净。
這個旅館的房間跟那個旅館的房間不一樣乾淨。
Zhège lǚguǎn de fángjiān gēn nàge lǚguǎn de fángjiān bù yīyàng *gānjìng*.
The rooms in this hotel are not as *clean* as the rooms in that hotel.

我儿子跟/和我女儿不一样高。
我兒子跟/和我女兒不一樣高。
Wǒ érzi gēn/hé wǒ nǚ'ér bù yíyàng *gāo*.
My son and my daughter are not the same height. (not equally *tall*)

▶ 33.1.3

33.2.4 Indicating that one noun phrase does not resemble another

To indicate that one noun phrase does not resemble another noun phrase, say:

| NP₁ | 不 | 像 | NP₂ |
| NP₁ | bù | xiàng | NP₂ |

NP₁ does not look like NP₂/NP₁ does not resemble NP₂

他(一点也)不像法国人。
他(一點也)不像法國人。
Tā (yīdiǎn yě) bù xiàng Fǎguórén.
He doesn't look like a French person (at all).

▶ 33.1.4

33.3 More than

'More than' comparisons indicate that some noun phrase has more of some property than another noun phrase. The property can be expressed as an adjectival verb, a stative verb, or a verb phrase with a modal verb.

MAKING COMPARISONS | 33.3

33.3.1 Comparing noun phrases in terms of adjectival verbs

NP₁ 比 NP₂ AV
NP₁ **bǐ** NP₂ AV
NP₁ is more AV than NP₂

中国比日本大。
中國比日本大。
Zhōngguó bǐ Rìběn dà.
China is *bigger* than Japan.

我的身体比以前好了。
我的身體比以前好了。
Wǒ de shēntǐ bǐ yǐqián hǎo le.
My health is *better* than before.

吃饭比做饭容易。
吃飯比做飯容易。
Chī fàn bǐ zuò fàn róngyì.
Eating is *easier* than cooking.

写字比认字难。
寫字比認字難。
Xiě zì bǐ rèn zì nán.
Writing characters is *harder* than recognizing characters.

NOTE: In the third and fourth example sentences in this section, the phrases that are being compared are a *verb + object*. In these sentences, the verb + object together function as a noun phrase, serving as the subject of the sentence or as the object of 比 **bǐ**.

33.3.2 Comparing noun phrases in terms of stative verbs

Stative verbs such as **ài** 'to love' and **xǐhuan** 'to like to,' 'to prefer' take noun phrase objects or verb phrase complements. The stative verb and its object or complement is a stative verb phrase (SVP). When comparing two noun phrases in terms of a stative verb phrase, say:

NP₁ 比 NP₂ SVP
NP₁ **bǐ** NP₂ SVP
NP₁ is more SVP than NP₂

他比我爱吃中国饭。
他比我愛吃中國飯。
Tā bǐ wǒ ài chī Zhōngguó fàn.
He *loves to eat Chinese food* more than I.

张先生比张太太喜欢买书。
張先生比張太太喜歡買書。
Zhāng xiānsheng bǐ Zhāng tàitai xǐhuan mǎi shū.
Mr. Zhang *likes to buy books* more than Mrs. Zhang.

▶ 11

33.3.3 Comparing noun phrases in terms of modal verb phrases

To compare noun phrases in terms of verb phrases that begin with a modal verb, say:

NP₁ 比 NP₂ MVP
NP₁ **bǐ** NP₂ MVP
NP₁ is more MVP than NP₂

我姐姐比我哥哥会唱歌。(MV)
我姐姐比我哥哥會唱歌。
Wǒ jiějie bǐ wǒ gēge huì chàng gē.
My older sister *can sing* better than my older brother.

33.3.4 Indicating quantity in 'more than' comparisons

When comparing noun phrases, it is possible to indicate *how much more* one noun phrase is than the other. The phrase that indicates the quantity occurs at the end of the sentence, after the adjectival verb or stative verb.

224

More than 33.3

3.3.4.1 Indicating a specific quantity

When the quantity is a specific number, say:

    NP₁   比   NP₂   AV [number + classifier (+ noun)]
    NP₁   **bǐ**   NP₂   AV [number + classifier (+ noun)]
    NP₁ is more AV than NP₂ by [number + classifier (+ noun)]

> 她先生比她大六岁。
> 她先生比她大六歲。
> **Tā xiānsheng bǐ tā** *dà liù suì.*
> Her husband is *six years older* than her.

> 这个旅馆比那个旅馆贵九十块钱。
> 這個旅館比那個旅館貴九十塊錢。
> **Zhège lǚguǎn bǐ nàge lǚguǎn** *guì jiǔ shí kuài qián.*
> This hotel is *ninety dollars more expensive* than that one.

> 这个旅馆比那个旅馆贵一倍。
> 這個旅館比那個旅館貴一倍。
> **Zhège lǚguǎn bǐ nàge lǚguǎn guì yī bèi.**
> This hotel is *twice as expensive* as that one.

The adjectival verbs 早 **zǎo** 'early,' 晚 **wǎn** 'late,' 多 **duō** 'more,' and 少 **shǎo** 'less' may be followed by an action verb. The *number + classifier and optional noun* sequence occurs after the *adjectival verb + action verb*.

    NP₁   比   NP₂   AV action verb [number + classifier (+ noun)]
    NP₁   **bǐ**   NP₂   AV action verb [number + classifier (+ noun)]
    NP₁ does verb more AV than NP₂ by [number + classifier (+ noun)]

> 今天他比我早来了五分钟。
> 今天他比我早來了五分鐘。
> **Jīntiān tā bǐ wǒ zǎo lái le** *wǔ fēn zhōng.*
> He came *five minutes* earlier than I did today.

> 昨天我比老板晚走了一个钟头。
> 昨天我比老闆晚走了一個鐘頭。
> **Zuótiān wǒ bǐ lǎobǎn wǎn zǒu le** *yí gè zhōngtou.*
> Yesterday I left *an hour* later than my boss did.

> 我今年比去年多挣了两百块钱。
> 我今年比去年多掙了兩百塊錢。
> **Wǒ jīnnián bǐ qùnián duō zhèng le** *liǎng bǎi kuài qián.*
> I earned *two hundred dollars* more this year than last year.

3.3.4.2 Noun phrase₁ is *much more* AV than noun phrase₂

To indicate that one noun phrase is *much more* AV than another noun phrase, say the following.

    NP₁   比   NP₂   AV   得多
    NP₁   **bǐ**   NP₂   AV   **de duō**
    NP₁ is much more AV than NP₂

> 今天比昨天冷得多。
> **Jīntiān bǐ zuótiān lěng de duō.**
> Today is *much colder* than yesterday.

> 中文比英文难得多。
> 中文比英文難得多。
> **Zhōngwén bǐ Yīngwén nán de duō.**
> Chinese is *much more difficult* than English.

MAKING COMPARISONS

or

NP₁ 比 NP₂ AV 多了
NP₁ bǐ NP₂ AV duō le
NP₁ is much more AV than NP₂

今天比昨天冷多了。
Jīntiān bǐ zuótiān *lěng duō le.*
Today is *much colder* than yesterday.

中文比英文难多了。
中文比英文難多了。
Zhōngwén bǐ Yīngwén *nán duō le.*
Chinese is *much more difficult* than English.

NOTE | Intensifiers cannot occur before the adjectival verb in the 比 **bǐ** comparison pattern.

Say this   *Not this*

今天比昨天冷得多。   *今天比昨天很冷。
Jīntiān bǐ zuótiān lěng de duō.   **Jīntiān bǐ zuótiān hěn lěng.**
Today is a lot colder than yesterday.

他比我用功得多。   *他比我非常用功。
Tā bǐ wǒ yònggōng de duō.   **Tā bǐ wǒ fēicháng yònggōng.**
He is much more hardworking than I am.

The following pattern with 真 **zhēn** conveys a very similar meaning to the above patterns.

NP₁ 真 比 NP₂ AV
NP₁ zhēn bǐ NP₂ AV
NP₁ is really more AV than NP₂

今天真比昨天冷。
Jīntiān *zhēn* **bǐ zuótiān** *lěng.*
Today is *really much colder* than yesterday.

中文真比英文难。
中文真比英文難。
Zhōngwén *zhēn* **bǐ Yīngwén** *nán.*
Chinese is *really more difficult* than English.

33.3.4.3 Noun phrase₁ is *a little more* AV than noun phrase₂

To indicate that one noun phrase is *a little more* AV than another noun phrase, say the following.

NP₁ 比 NP₂ AV 一点儿/一點兒
NP₁ bǐ NP₂ AV yīdiǎr
NP₁ is a little more AV than NP₂

我们的房子比他们的小一点儿。
我們的房子比他們的小一點兒。
Wǒmen de fángzi bǐ tāmen de *xiǎo yīdiǎr.*
Our house is *a little smaller* than theirs.

哥哥比弟弟用功一点。
哥哥比弟弟用功一點。
Gēge bǐ dìdi *yònggōng yīdiǎn.*
Older brother is *a little more hardworking* than younger brother.

More than 33.3

3.3.4.4 Noun phrase₁ is *more adjectival verb than* noun phrase₂ *by half*

To indicate that one noun phrase is *more* of some quality *by half*, put the phrase 一半 **yí bàn** 'one half' after the adjectival verb.

> Q: 这两件衣服，哪一件便宜？
> 這兩件衣服，哪一件便宜？
> **Zhè liǎng jiàn yīfú, nǎ yí jiàn piányi?**
> Of these two dresses which one is cheaper?

> A: 这件衣服比那件便宜一半。
> 這件衣服比那件便宜一半。
> **Zhè jiàn yīfú bǐ nà jiàn piányi *yí bàn*.**
> This dress is half the price of that one.

3.3.4.5 Noun phrase₁ is *more adjectival verb than* noun phrase₂ *by a specific percent*

The phrase X 分之 Y occurs after the adjectival verb.

> 今年学中文的学生比去年多四分之一。
> 今年學中文的學生比去年多四分之一。
> **Jīnnián xué Zhōngwén de xuésheng bǐ qùnián duō *sì fēn zhī yī*.**
> There are 25% more students studying Chinese this year.

▶ 6.6

33.3.5 Comparing the performance of an action

To indicate that one noun phrase does some action *more AV than* another noun phrase, say:

NP₁ 比 NP₂ [verb 得] AV
NP₁ **bǐ** NP₂ [verb **de**] AV
NP₁ performs the verb more AV than NP₂

> 他比我吃得多。
> **Tā bǐ wǒ *chī de duō*.**
> He *eats more* than me.

> 弟弟比妹妹写得快。
> 弟弟比妹妹寫得快。
> **Dìdi bǐ mèimei *xiě de kuài*.**
> Younger brother *writes faster* than younger sister.

If the object of the action verb is included in the sentence, the action verb must be said twice, once followed by the object, and once followed by 得 + AV.

NP₁ 比 NP₂ [action verb + object] [action verb 得] AV
NP₁ **bǐ** NP₂ [action verb + object] [action verb **de**] AV
NP₁ performs the action verb more AV than NP₂

> 他比我吃饭吃得多。
> 他比我吃飯吃得多。
> **Tā bǐ wǒ *chī* fàn *chī de duō*.**
> He *eats* more food than me.

> 弟弟比妹妹写字写得快。
> 弟弟比妹妹寫字寫得快。
> **Dìdi bǐ mèimei *xiě* zì *xiě de kuài*.**
> Younger brother *writes* characters faster than younger sister.

MAKING COMPARISONS

33.4

Here are several variations in this pattern. They differ in the order of the phrases. In all of them, [action verb + object] occurs before [action verb 得 de], and AV occurs at the end of the sentence.

Variation 1

    NP$_1$ [action verb + object] [action verb 得]   比   NP$_2$ AV
    NP$_1$ [action verb + object] [action verb de]   **bǐ**   NP$_2$ AV
NP$_1$ performs the action verb more AV than NP$_2$

    他吃饭吃得比我多。
    他吃飯吃得比我多。
    Tā *chī* fàn *chī* de bǐ wǒ duō.
    He *eats* more food than me

    弟弟写字写得比妹妹快。
    弟弟寫字寫得比妹妹快。
    Dìdi *xiě* zì *xiě* de bǐ mèimei kuài.
    Younger brother *writes* characters faster than younger sister.

Variation 2

    object, NP$_1$ [action verb 得]   比   NP$_2$ AV
    object, NP$_1$ [action verb **de**]   **bǐ**   NP$_2$ AV
As for the object, NP$_1$ performs the action verb more AV than NP$_2$

    中国字，弟弟写得比妹妹快。
    中國字，弟弟寫得比妹妹快。
    Zhōngguó zì, dìdi xiě de bǐ mèimei kuài.
    As for Chinese characters, younger brother writes them faster than younger sister.

Variation 3

    NP$_1$ + object [action verb 得]   比   NP$_2$ AV
    NP$_1$ + object [action verb **de**]   **bǐ**   NP$_2$ AV
NP$_1$ performs the action verb more AV than NP$_2$

    弟弟的中国字，写得比妹妹快。
    弟弟的中國字，寫得比妹妹快。
    Dìdi de Zhōngguó zì, xiě de bǐ mèimei kuài.
    Younger brother's Chinese characters, (he) writes them faster than younger sister.

Be careful to repeat the verb if you include the object of the verb.

Say this	*Not this*
他吃饭吃得比我多。	*他吃饭得比我多。
他吃飯吃得比我多。	他吃飯得比我多。
Tā chī fàn chī de bǐ wǒ duō.	**Tā chī fàn de bǐ wǒ duō.**
He eats more than I do.	
弟弟写字写得比妹妹快。	*弟弟写字得比妹妹快。
弟弟寫字寫得比妹妹快。	弟弟寫字得比妹妹快。
Dìdi xiě zì xiě de bǐ mèimei kuài.	**Dìdi xiě zì de bǐ mèimei kuài.**
Younger brother writes faster than younger sister.	

▶ 31.1.1, 33.1.6

33.4 Less than

The following patterns indicate the relationship of 'less than.'

Less than **33.4**

33.4.1 Indicating 'less than' with 没有/沒有 *méi yǒu*

NP₁　没有/沒有　NP₂　AV
NP₁　**méi yǒu**　NP₂　AV
NP₁ is not as AV as NP₂

我没有他高。
我沒有他高。
Wǒ méi yǒu tā *gāo*.
I am not as *tall* as him.

我没有他用功。
我沒有他用功。
Wǒ méi yǒu tā *yònggōng*.
I am not as *hardworking* as him.

我没有他(那么)高。
我沒有他(那麼)高。
Wǒ méi yǒu tā (nàme) *gāo*.
I am not as *tall* as him.

他没有你(这么)用功。
他沒有你(這麼)用功。
Tā méi yǒu nǐ (zhème) *yònggōng*.
He is not as *hardworking* as you.

33.4.2 Indicating 'less than' with 不如 *bùrú*

不如 **bùrú** can be used when comparing two noun phrases, or when comparing noun phrases in terms of some property. It is used in formal, literary contexts.

NP₁　不如　NP₂
NP₁　**bùrú**　NP₂
NP₁ is not as good as NP₂

论学问，谁都不如赵教授。
論學問，誰都不如趙教授。
Lùn xuéwen, shéi dōu bùrú Zhào jiàoshòu.
As for scholarship, no one is the equal to Professor Zhao.

我的嗓子不如我妹妹。
Wǒ de sǎngzi bùrú wǒ mèimei.
My voice is not as good as my younger sister's.

NP₁　不如　NP₂　AV
NP₁　**bùrú**　NP₂　AV
NP₁ is not as AV as NP₂

弟弟不如哥哥用功。
Dìdi bùrú gēge *yònggōng*.
Younger brother is not as *hardworking* as older brother.

走路不如骑自行车快。
走路不如騎自行車快。
Zǒu lù bùrú qí zìxíngchē *kuài*.
Walking is not as *fast* as riding a bike.

229

MAKING COMPARISONS

33.4.3 Indicating performance that is less than another's in some way

To indicate that one noun phrase does *not* perform some action *as AV* as another noun phrase, say:

NP₁　　没有/沒有　　NP₂　　[action verb 得]　　AV
NP₁　　**méi yǒu**　　NP₂　　[action verb **de**]　　AV
NP₁ does not perform the action verb as AV as NP₂

> 我没有他吃得多。
> 我沒有他吃的多。
> **Wǒ méi yǒu tā chī de duō.**
> I don't eat as much as him.

> 妹妹没有弟弟写得快。
> 妹妹沒有弟弟寫得快。
> **Mèimei méi yǒu dìdi xiě de kuài.**
> Younger sister doesn't write as fast as younger brother.

那么/那麼 **nàme** and 这么/這麼 **zhème** optionally occur before the AV.

> 我没有他吃得那么多。
> 我沒有他吃得那麼多。
> **Wǒ méi yǒu tā chī de nàme duō.**
> I don't eat as much as him.

> 妹妹没有弟弟写得这么快。
> 妹妹沒有弟弟寫得這麼快。
> **Mèimei méi yǒu dìdi xiě de zhème kuài.**
> Younger sister doesn't write as fast as younger brother.

If the object of the action verb is included in the sentence, the action verb is said twice, once followed by the object, and once followed by 得 + AV.

NP₁　没有/沒有　NP₂　[action verb + object] [action verb 得]　（那么/那麼）　AV
NP₁　**méi yǒu**　NP₂　[action verb + object] [action verb **de**]　**(nàme)**　AV
NP₁ does not perform the action verb as AV as NP₂

> 我没有他吃饭吃得多。
> 我沒有他吃飯吃得多。
> **Wǒ méi yǒu tā chī fàn chī de duō.**
> I don't eat as much food as he does.

> 妹妹没有弟弟写字写得(那么)快。
> 妹妹沒有弟弟寫字寫得(那麼)快。
> **Mèimei méi yǒu dìdi xiě zì xiě de (nàme) kuài.**
> Younger sister doesn't write characters as fast as younger brother.

Here are several variations in this pattern. They differ in the order of the phrases. In all of them, [action verb + object] occurs before [action verb 得 **de**], and AV occurs at the end of the sentence.

Variation 1

NP₁　[action verb + object] [action verb 得]　没有/沒有　NP₂　（那么/那麼）　AV
NP₁　[action verb + object] [action verb **de**]　**méi yǒu**　NP₂　**(nàme)**　AV
NP₁ does not perform the action verb as AV as NP₂

> 我吃饭吃得没有他多。
> 我吃飯吃得沒有他多。
> **Wǒ chī fàn chī de méi yǒu tā duō.**
> I don't eat as much food as he does.

Comparative degree 33.5

妹妹写字写得没有弟弟(那么)快。
妹妹寫字寫得沒有弟弟(那麼)快。
Mèimei xiě zì xiěde méi yǒu dìdi (nàme) kuài.
Younger sister doesn't write characters as fast as younger brother.

Variation 2

| object, NP₁ | [action verb 得] | 没有/沒有 | NP₂ | (那么/那麼) | AV |
| object, NP₁ | [action verb **de**] | **méi yǒu** | NP₂ | **(nàme)** | AV |

As for the object, NP₁ does not perform the action verb as AV as NP₂

中国字，妹妹写得没有弟弟那么快。
中國字，妹妹寫得沒有弟弟那麼快。
Zhōngguó zì, mèimei xiě de méi yǒu dìdi nàme kuài.
(As for) Chinese characters, younger sister doesn't write them as fast as younger brother.

Be careful to repeat the action verb if you include its object.

Say this

我没有他吃饭吃得多。
我沒有他吃飯吃得多。
Wǒ méi yǒu tā chī fàn chī de duō.
I do not eat as much as he does.

妹妹没有弟弟写字写得(那么)快。
妹妹沒有弟弟寫字寫得(那麼)快。
Mèimei méi yǒu dìdi xiě zì xiě de (nàme) kuài.
Younger sister doesn't write as fast as younger brother.

Not this

*我没有他吃饭得多。
我沒有他吃飯得多。
Wǒ méi yǒu tā chī fàn de duō.

*妹妹没有弟弟写字得(那么)快。
妹妹沒有弟弟寫字得(那麼)快。
Mèimei méi yǒu dìdi xiě zì de (nàme) kuài.

▶ 31.1.2, 33.1.6, 33.3.5

33.5 Comparative degree

To indicate the comparative form in Mandarin, place the intensifier 更 **gèng** or the expression 还(要)/還(要) **hái (yào)** before the stative verb or adjectival verb.

哥哥喜欢看电影。妹妹更喜欢。(SV)
哥哥喜歡看電影。妹妹更喜歡。
Gēge xǐhuan kàn diànyǐng. Mèimei *gèng xǐhuan*.
Older brother likes to watch movies. Younger sister *likes to even more*.

日本车很贵。德国车更贵。(AV)
日本車很貴。德國車更貴。
Rìběn chē hěn guì. Déguó chē *gèng guì*.
Japanese cars are very expensive. German cars are *even more expensive*.

日本车很贵。德国车还(要)贵。(AV)
日本車很貴。德國車還(要)貴。
Rìběn chē hěn guì. Déguó chē *hái (yào) guì*.
Japanese cars are very expensive. German cars are *even more expensive*.

更 **gèng** and 还要/還要 **hái yào** may be used in 比 **bǐ** comparison sentences.

德国车比日本车更贵。
德國車比日本車更貴。
Déguó chē bǐ Rìběn chē *gèng guì*.
German cars are *even more expensive* than Japanese cars.

231

MAKING COMPARISONS 33.7

> 天气预报说明天比今天还要冷。
> 天氣預報說明天比今天還要冷。
> **Tiānqì yùbào shuō míngtiān bǐ jīntiān *hái yào lěng*.**
> The weather report says tomorrow will be *even colder* than today.

▶ 10.5

33.6 Superlative degree

The intensifier 最 **zuì** indicates a superlative degree: *most stative verb/most adjectival verb*. Sentence final 了 **le** is sometimes used at the end of the sentence to emphasize that the information is new for the addressee. The superlative form is also used for exaggeration.

> 万里长城是世界上最长的城了。(AV)
> 萬裏長城是世界上最長的城了。
> **Wànlǐ Chángchéng shì shìjiè shàng *zuì cháng* de chéng le.**
> The Great Wall is the *longest* wall in the world.

> 我妹妹最喜欢吃冰激凌了。(SV)
> 我妹妹最喜歡吃冰激凌了。
> **Wǒ mèimei *zuì xǐhuan* chī bīngjilíng le.**
> My younger sister *loves* to eat ice cream *the most*.

▶ 10.6

33.7 Relative degree

The following intensifiers may occur before a stative verb or adjectival verb to indicate relative degree.

| 比较/比較 | **bǐjiào** | relatively |
| 相当/相當 | **xiāngdāng** | relatively, quite |

▶ 10, 11

> 今天比较热。(AV)
> 今天比較熱。
> **Jīntiān *bǐjiào rè*.**
> Today is *relatively hot*.

> 那个女孩子相当高。(AV)
> 那個女孩子相當高。
> **Nàge nǚ háizi *xiāngdāng gāo*.**
> That girl is *quite tall*.

> 我比较喜欢喝法国酒。(SV)
> 我比較喜歡喝法國酒。
> **Wǒ *bǐjiào xǐhuan* hē Fǎguó jiǔ.**
> I *prefer to drink* French wine.

> 四川人比较喜欢吃辣的。(SV)
> 四川人比較喜歡吃辣的。
> **Sìchuān rén *bǐjiào xǐhuan* chī là de.**
> People from Sichuan *prefer to eat* spicy food.

34

Talking about the present

Here are the expressions and structures most often used to indicate that a state exists at the present time or that an action is occurring at the present time.

34.1 Time expressions that indicate present time

现在/現在 *xiànzài* 'now'

> 你现在去哪儿?
> 你現在去哪兒?
> **Nǐ xiànzài qù nǎr?**
> Where are you going now?

目前 *mùqián* 'at present'

> 他目前在学中文。
> 他目前在學中文。
> **Tā mùqián zài xué Zhōngwén.**
> He is presently studying Chinese.

今天 *jīntiān* 'today'

> 他今天很忙。
> **Tā jīntiān hěn máng.**
> He is very busy today.

这个星期/這個星期 *zhège xīngqī* 'this week'

or

这个礼拜/這個禮拜 *zhège lǐbài* 'this week'

> 这个星期很冷。
> 這個星期很冷。
> **Zhège xīngqī hěn lěng.**
> This week it is very cold.

这个月/這個月 *zhège yuè* 'this month'

> 她这个月在纽约。
> 她這個月在紐約。
> **Tā zhège yuè zài Niǔyuē.**
> She is in New York this month.

今年 *jīnnián* 'this year'

> 今年是二零一四年。
> **Jīnnián shì èr líng yī sì nián.**
> This year is 2014. (It's 2014.)

▶ 49.2

TALKING ABOUT THE PRESENT

34.2 Using 在 *zài* and 正在 *zhèngzài* to indicate ongoing actions in present time

在 **zài** or 正在 **zhèngzài** can occur before action verbs that have duration to indicate that the action is ongoing at the present time.

> 哥哥在打球。
> **Gēgē zài dǎ qiú.**
> Elder brother is playing ball.

> 他正在洗澡，不能接电话。
> 他正在洗澡，不能接電話。
> **Tā zhèngzài xǐ zǎo, bù néng jiē diànhuà.**
> He's bathing right now (and) can't get the phone.

NOTE   在 **zài** and 正在 **zhèngzài** are only used when talking about actions. They are not used when the main verb of the sentence is an adjectival verb, a stative verb, or a modal verb. 现在/現在 **xiànzài** 'now' can be used when talking about states or actions that occur in the present time.

Say this	Not this
汽油现在贵了。(AV) 汽油現在貴了。 **Qìyóu xiànzài guì le.** Gasoline is expensive now.	*汽油正在贵了。 汽油正在貴了。 **Qìyóu zhèngzài guì le.**
他现在很高兴。(AV) 他現在很高興。 **Tā xiànzài hěn gāoxìng.** He is happy right now.	*他正在很高兴。 他正在很高興。 **Tā zhèngzài hěn gāoxìng.**
她现在喜欢那个男的。(SV) 她現在喜歡那個男的。 **Tā xiànzài xǐhuan nàge nán de.** She likes that boy now.	*她正在喜欢那个男的。 她正在喜歡那個男的。 **Tā zhèngzài xǐhuan nàge nán de.**

▶ 13.4.1, 17.2, 39.2

34.3 Using the final particle 呢 *ne* to indicate ongoing situations in present time

The final particle 呢 **ne** may be used at the end of a sentence when an action is ongoing in the present time. 呢 **ne** often co-occurs with 在 **zài** and 正在 **zhèngzài**.

> 他跳舞呢。
> **Tā tiào wǔ ne.**
> He is dancing.

> 你在想什么呢？
> 你在想甚麼呢？
> **Nǐ zài xiǎng shénme ne?**
> What are you thinking?

> 他们正在开会呢。
> 他們正在開會呢。
> **Tāmen zhèng zài kāi huì ne.**
> They are having a meeting now.

234

34.4 Using 着/著 *zhe* to emphasize ongoing duration or an ongoing state in the present time

Open-ended action verbs may be suffixed with 着/著 **zhe** to emphasize ongoing duration at the present time. 着/著 **zhe** often co-occurs with 在 **zài**, 正在 **zhèngzài**, and/or 呢 **ne**.

他在说着话呢。
他在說著話呢。
Tā zài shuōzhe huà ne.
He is speaking.

Change-of-state verbs that describe posture or placement such as 站 **zhàn** 'to stand,' 坐 **zuò** 'to sit,' 躺 **tǎng** 'to lie,' 存 **cún** 'to save/to deposit,' 放 **fàng** 'to put/to place,' 挂/掛 **guà** 'to hang,' and 停 **tíng** 'to park' may be suffixed with 着/著 **zhe** to indicate that the state is ongoing in the present time. 呢 **ne** may occur at the end of the sentence.

谁在门口站着?
誰在門口站著?
Shéi zài ménkǒu zhànzhe?
Who is standing at the door?

客人在客厅里坐着呢。
客人在客廳裏坐著呢。
Kèren zài kètīng lǐ zuòzhe ne.
The guests are sitting in the living room.

病人在床上躺着。
病人在床上躺著。
Bìngrén zài chuángshàng tǎngzhe.
The patient is lying on the bed.

我们的钱都在银行里存着呢。
我們的錢都在銀行裏存著呢。
Wǒmen de qián dōu zài yínháng lǐ cúnzhe ne.
All of our money is (saved) in the bank.

那张画在墙上挂着呢。
那張畫在牆上掛著呢。
Nà zhāng huà zài qiáng shàng guàzhe ne.
That painting is hanging on the wall.

我的书在哪儿放着呢?
我的書在哪兒放著呢?
Wǒ de shū zài nǎr fàngzhe ne?
Where is my book? (Where is my book placed?)

我的车在停车场停着呢。
我的車在停車場停著呢。
Wǒ de chē zài tíngchēchǎng tíngzhe ne.
My car is parked in the parking lot.

▶ 25.3.3, 17.2, 39.2

TALKING ABOUT THE PRESENT

34.5 Indicating present time by context

Time expressions are optional when the context makes it clear that the sentence refers to a present time situation. For example, in the following conversation, 现在/現在 **xiànzài** 'now' can be included, but it is not necessary, because the question and response clearly refer to the present time.

妈妈：你(现在)做什么功课？
媽媽：你(現在)做甚麼功課？
Māma: Nǐ (xiànzài) zuò shénme gōngkè?
Mom: What homework are you doing (now)?

孩子：我(现在)做数学。
孩子：我(現在)做數學。
Háizi: Wǒ (xiànzài) zuò shùxué.
Child: I am doing math (now).

34.6 Negation in present time situations

Present time situations are negated with 不 **bù**, with one exception: the verb 有 **yǒu** is always negated with 没 **méi**.

他今天不来上课。
他今天不來上課。
Tā jīntiān bù lái shàng kè.
He is not coming to class today.

我没有钱。
我沒有錢。
Wǒ méi yǒu qián.
I don't have money.

▶ 11.6, 27.1

Action verbs may be negated with 没/沒 **méi** or 没有/沒有 **méi yǒu**, but when so negated, they do not refer to present time. Instead, they indicate that the action did not happen in the past.

你为什么没来上课？
你為甚麼沒來上課？
Nǐ wèi shénme méi lái shàng kè?
Why didn't you come to class?

▶ 13.3, 17.1, 37.3

34.7 Talking about actions that begin in the past and continue to the present

To indicate that an action began in the past and continues to the present, end the sentence with sentence final 了 **le**. If the verb is followed by an object or a duration expression, the sentence will have two instances of 了 **le**, one following the verb, and the other at the end of the sentence. Sentences like these are sometimes described as having 'double 了 **le**.' Sentence final 了 **le** is sometimes described as indicating the 'present relevance' of the situation.

▶ 38.1.3

我看了两本书了。
我看了兩本書了。
Wǒ kàn le liǎng běn shū le.
I've read two books (so far).

他在美国住了十年了。
他在美國住了十年了。
Tā zài Měiguó zhù le shínián le.
He has lived in America for ten years (and is still there).

Describing situations that are generally true 34.8

The adverb 已经/已經 **yǐjing** 'already' often occurs in these sentences to emphasize the fact that the situation has been ongoing from some time in the past up to the present time.

> 她已经学了三年的中文了。
> 她已經學了三年的中文了。
> **Tā yǐjing xué le sān nián de Zhōngwén le.**
> She has already studied three years of Chinese.

> 我教中文已经有二十多年了。
> 我教中文已經有二十多年了。
> **Wǒ jiāo Zhōngwén yǐjing yǒu èrshí duō nián le.**
> I've already taught Chinese for over twenty years.

34.8 Describing situations that are generally true

To indicate that a situation is generally true, the verb is presented without any modifiers that indicate time phrase: no time phrases, no adverbs, no verb suffixes.

> 中国人口很多。
> 中國人口很多。
> **Zhōngguó rénkǒu hěn duō.**
> China has a very large population.

> 这儿的天气很热。
> 這兒的天氣很熱。
> **Zhèr de tiānqì hěn rè.**
> The weather is very hot here.

35

Talking about habitual actions

Habitual actions are actions that occur regularly. The following time expressions and adverbs are used to express habitual actions in Chinese.

35.1 Expressing habitual time with the word 每 *měi* 'every/each'

Time expressions that indicate habitual action include the word 每 **měi** 'every/each.' As with other expressions that indicate the time when an action occurs, these expressions occur right after the subject, at the beginning of the predicate. Commonly used time expressions include:

每个小时/每個小時	měi gè xiǎoshí	every hour
每个钟头/每個鐘頭	měi gè zhōngtóu	every hour
每天	měitiān	every day
每天晚上	měitiān wǎnshang	every evening
每个礼拜/每個禮拜	měi gè lǐbài	every week
每个星期/每個星期	měi gè xīngqī	every week
每个月/每個月	měi gè yuè	every month
每年	měi nián	every year

The adverb 都 **dōu** may also occur with these expressions, right before the verb or, if there is a prepositional phrase, right before the prepositional phrase.

我每天八点半都去上班。
我每天八點半都去上班。
Wǒ měitiān bādiǎn bàn dōu qù shàng bān.
I go to work every day at 8:30.

她每个星期都回家看父母一次。
她每個星期都回家看父母一次。
Tā měi gè xīngqī dōu huí jiā kàn fùmǔ yīcì.
She goes home once every week to see her parents.

我每个月都跟朋友去看电影。
我每個月都跟朋友去看電影。
Wǒ měi gè yuè dōu gēn péngyou qù kàn diànyǐng.
Every month I go with my friends to see a movie.

35.2 Expressing habitual time with 天天 *tiāntiān* and 年年 *niánnián*

天 **tiān** and 年 **nián** may also occur in the following phrases to indicate habitual action.

| 天天 | tiāntiān | every day |
| 年年 | niánnián | every year |

大学生天天都很忙。
大學生天天都很忙。
Dàxuéshēng tiāntiān dōu hěn máng.
University students are busy every day.

35.3 Adverbs that describe habitual action

Adverbs that describe habitual action include:

常常 *chángcháng* 'often'

> 我们常常去网吧上网。
> 我們常常去網吧上網。
> **Wǒmen chángcháng qù wǎngbā shàng wǎng.**
> We frequently go to an internet café to surf the web.

平常 *píngcháng* 'ordinarily, usually'

> 学生平常在周末跟朋友玩儿。
> 學生平常在週末跟朋友玩兒。
> **Xuésheng píngcháng zài zhōumò gēn péngyou wár.**
> Students often have fun with their friends on the weekend.

经常/經常 *jīngcháng* 'usually, often'

> 弟弟经常上课迟到。
> 弟弟經常上課遲到。
> **Dìdi jīngcháng shàng kè chídào.**
> My younger brother is often late for class.

时常/時常 *shícháng* 'regularly'

> 你得时常运动运动，锻链身体。
> 你得時常運動運動，鍛鍊身體。
> **Nǐ děi shícháng yùndòng yùndòng, duànliàn shēntǐ.**
> You should exercise regularly and strengthen your body.

总/總 *zǒng* 'always'

> 她总跟男朋友在一起，不愿意一个人出去。
> 她總跟男朋友在一起，不願意一個人出去。
> **Tā zǒng gēn nán péngyou zài yīqǐ, bù yuànyi yī gè rén chūqu.**
> She's always with her boyfriend; (she's) not willing to go out by herself.

总是/總是 *zǒngshì* 'always'

> 他真是好人，总是帮助朋友。
> 他真是好人，總是幫助朋友。
> **Tā zhēn shì hǎo rén, zǒngshì bāngzhù péngyou.**
> He really is a good person; (he) always helps his friends.

都 *dōu* 'all/always'

> 我每天都看报。
> 我每天都看報。
> **Wǒ měitiān dōu kàn bào.**
> I read the news every day.

老 *lǎo* 'always'

> 我不要老待在家。
> **Wǒ bù yào lǎo dāi zài jiā.**
> I don't want to always stay home.

向来/向來 *xiànglái* 'always in the past'

> 他向来都听父母的话。
> 他向來都聽父母的話。
> **Tā xiànglái dōu tīng fùmǔ de huà.**
> He always listened to his parents.

TALKING ABOUT HABITUAL ACTIONS 35.3

一向 *yīxiàng* 'always in the past'

> 他一向很可靠。我们一定可以信任他。
> 他一向很可靠。我們一定可以信任他。
> **Tā yīxiàng hěn kěkào. Wǒmen yīdìng kéyǐ xìnrèn tā.**
> He has always been very reliable. We can certainly trust him.

NOTE   向来/向來 **xiànglái** and 从来/從來 **cónglái** are opposites.

- 向来/向來 **xiànglái** is used to indicate that an action *habitually occurred* in the past.
- 从来/從來 **cónglái** indicates that an action *does not happen* or *has not happened*.
  从来/從來 **cónglái** always occurs with negation:

> 从来/從來 **cónglái** + 不 **bù** indicates that an action never occurs.
> 从来/從來 **cónglái** + 没 **méi** indicates that an action has never occurred in the past.

> 他从来不喝酒。
> 他從來不喝酒。
> **Tā cónglái bù hē jiǔ.**
> He never drinks alcohol.

> 我从来没给他打过电话。
> 我從來沒給他打過電話。
> **Wǒ cónglái méi gěi tā dǎguo diànhuà.**
> I have never called him on the phone before.

▶ 27.3.1

36

Talking about the future

Mandarin has no distinct future tense. Instead, future time is expressed by words and phrases that refer to the future.

36.1 Time words that refer to future time

Here are some common time words that refer to future time.

今天下午	jīntiān xiàwǔ	this afternoon
今天晚上	jīntiān wǎnshang	tonight
明天	míngtiān	tomorrow
后天/後天	hòutiān	the day after tomorrow
大后天/大後天	dà hòutiān	three days from now
下个星期/下個星期	xià gè xīngqī	next week
下个礼拜/下個禮拜	xià gè lǐbài	next week
下个月/下個月	xià gè yuè	next month
明年	míngnián	next year
将来/將來	jiānglái	in the future

The neutral position for 'time when' expressions is after the subject, at the beginning of the predicate. To emphasize the time when a situation occurs, put the 'time when' expression at the beginning of the sentence, before the subject.

我们今天晚上去看电影。
我們今天晚上去看電影。
Wǒmen *jīntiān wǎnshang* qù kàn diànyǐng.
We are going to see a movie *tonight*.

今天晚上我们去看电影。
今天晚上我們去看電影。
***jīntiān wǎnshang* wǒmen qù kàn diànyǐng.**
Tonight we are going to see a movie.

▶ 4.5, 49.2, 57.3.2

36.2 Adverbs that refer to future time

Common adverbs that refer to the future include the following. (Note that adverbs always occur before the [prepositional phrase +] verb phrase.)

就要 *jiù yào* 'soon will'

他就要结婚了。
他就要結婚了。
Tā *jiù yào* jiéhūn le.
He *is going to* get married soon.

TALKING ABOUT THE FUTURE

再 **zài** '(do) again in the future'

> 再见!
> 再見!
> **Zài jiàn!**
> See you *again*! (Goodbye)

> 我没听清楚，请你再说一次。
> 我沒聽清楚，請你再說一次。
> **Wǒ méi tīng qīngchu, qǐng nǐ zài shuō yīcì.**
> I didn't hear clearly, please say it *again*.

可能 **kěnéng** 'possible'

> 她可能不学中文了。
> 她可能不學中文了。
> **Tā kěnéng bù xué Zhōngwén le.**
> She *may* not study Chinese any more.

▶ 15

Notice that the adverb 再 **zài** is closely related to the adverb 又 **yòu**. The adverb 再 **zài** means (to do) again in the future, and the adverb 又 **yòu** means (to do) again in the past. Sentences with 又 **yòu** '(to do) again in the past' always end with 了 **le**.

> 你前天迟到了。昨天又迟到了。
> 你前天遲到了。昨天又遲到了。
> **Nǐ qiántiān chídào le. Zuótiān yòu chídào le.**
> You were late the day before yesterday. Yesterday you were late again.

▶ 37.5

36.3 Indicating future time with the modal verb 会/會 *huì*

The modal verb 会/會 **huì** can be used to indicate future time. The meaning of 'future' is associated with the meanings of 'possibility' and 'prediction' conveyed by 会/會 **huì**.

> 我想他不会来了。
> 我想他不會來了。
> **Wǒ xiǎng tā bù huì lái le.**
> I don't think he *will* come.

Sometimes, 会/會 **huì** simply indicates future.

> 天气预报说，明天一定会下雨。
> 天氣預報說，明天一定會下雨。
> **Tiānqì yùbào shuō, míngtiān yīdìng huì xià yǔ.**
> The weather report says tomorrow it *will* definitely rain.

▶ 12.1

Verbs that refer to the future

36.4 Verbs that refer to the future

Verbs involving thinking or planning refer to events that will take place in the future. The most common include the following:

要 *yào* 'to want'

> 我要出去买东西。
> 我要出去買東西。
> **Wǒ yào chūqu mǎi dōngxi.**
> I want to go out to buy some things.

想 *xiǎng* 'to think'

> 我今天想早一点回家。
> 我今天想早一點回家。
> **Wǒ jīntiān xiǎng zǎo yīdiǎn huí jiā.**
> I want to return home a little earlier today.

愿意/願意 *yuànyi* 'to be willing'

> 我愿意跟他结婚。
> 我願意跟他結婚。
> **Wǒ yuànyi gēn tā jiéhūn.**
> I am willing to marry him.

准备/準備 *zhǔnbèi* 'to prepare to, to get ready to'

> 请你准备下车。
> 請你準備下車。
> **Qǐng nǐ zhǔnbèi xià chē.**
> Please get ready to get off the bus.

打算 *dǎsuan* 'to plan to'

> 我将来打算住在日本。
> 我將來打算住在日本。
> **Wǒ jiānglái dǎsuan zhù zài Rìběn.**
> I plan to live in Japan in the future.

37

Indicating completion and talking about the past

Mandarin has no grammatical structure that is entirely equivalent to past tense in English. Instead, it has structures that signal the completion of an event or that indicate that an event occurred or did not occur at some time in the past, or that a situation existed at some time in the past. The primary strategies for indicating completion and talking about the past are presented in this chapter.

37.1 Marking an action as complete: perfective aspect 了 *le*

Mandarin uses the verb suffix 了 **le** to mark an action as bounded and complete. When an action is marked as complete with respect to now (speech time), completion also indicates that the action happened in the past.

Only action verbs can be marked as complete. If a stative verb, adjectival verb, or modal verb is followed by 了 **le**, the meaning is one of *change* rather than *completion*.

▶ 10, 11, 12, 11.3, 13.1, 17.1, 38.1

In the main clause of a sentence, perfective 了 **le** follows the verb or the verb + object phrase, depending upon the properties of the object.

When the object is an unmodified noun, perfective 了 **le** follows the object.

> 他昨天晚上唱歌了。
> **Tā zuótiān wǎnshang chàng gē le.**
> He sang last night.

When the object of the verb is a modified noun – that is, a noun preceded by a specifier, number, and classifier, and/or any other description phrase – perfective 了 **le** ordinarily follows the verb.

> 她昨天晚上唱了几首歌。
> 她昨天晚上唱了幾首歌。
> **Tā zuótiān wǎnshang chàng le jǐ shǒu gē.**
> She sang a few songs last night.

> 她今天穿了她姐姐的衣服。
> **Tā jīntiān chuān le tā jiějie de yīfu.**
> She wore her older sister's clothes today.

In some contexts, Mandarin speakers may put perfective 了 **le** after the object whether the object noun is modified or not. When in doubt about where to put 了 **le**, consult your Chinese teacher or a native speaker of Mandarin.

The adverb 已经/已經 **yǐjing** *already* often occurs before an action has been marked as complete.

Indicating that an action did not occur in the past   **37.3**

> 我已经吃晚饭了。
> 我已經吃晚飯了。
> **Wǒ yǐjing chī wǎnfàn le.**
> I already ate dinner.

> Q: 那件事，你什么时候做完？
> 那件事，你甚麼時候做完？
> **Nà jiàn shì, nǐ shénme shíhòu zuòwán?**
> When will you finish that matter?

> A: 我已经做完了。
> 我已經做完了。
> **Wǒ yǐjing zuòwán le.**
> I've already finished.

37.2 Talking about sequence with perfective 了 le

To indicate that two actions occur in sequence, follow the first action verb with 了 **le**.

> 他吃了饭就走。
> 他吃了飯就走。
> **Tā chī le fàn jiù zǒu.**
> He will eat and then leave. (After he eats, he will leave.)

As the translation of this sentence indicates, this sentence refers to a sequence that will take place in the future: 了 **le** indicates that 吃 **chī** 'eat' occurs before 走 **zǒu** 'leave.'

To indicate that a *sequence* of events is complete, follow the second verb or the object of the second verb with 了 **le**.

> 他吃了饭就走了。
> 他吃了飯就走了。
> **Tā chī le fàn jiù zǒu le.**
> After he ate, he left.

> 学生做完了功课就交给老师了。
> 學生做完了功課就交給老師了。
> **Xuésheng zuòwán le gōngkè jiù jiāo gěi lǎoshī le.**
> After the students finished their work they handed it to the teacher.

These sentences have two instances of 了 **le**. The one that follows the first verb indicates sequence. The one that follows the second verb or its object indicates that the sequence is complete, and by implication, past.

37.3 Indicating that an action did not occur in the past

To indicate that an action did not occur in the past, negate the verb with 没/沒 **méi** or 没有/沒有 **méi yǒu**. Do not use 不 **bù** as the marker of negation, and do not use 了 **le** after the verb when talking about an action that did not occur.

> 我寒假没回家。
> 我寒假沒回家。
> **Wǒ hánjià méi huí jiā.**
> I didn't go home for winter break.

> 我昨天一天都没看见他。
> 我昨天一天都沒看見他。
> **Wǒ zuótiān yī tiān dōu méi kànjian tā.**
> I didn't see him at all yesterday.

245

INDICATING COMPLETION AND TALKING ABOUT THE PAST

他没(有)买那本书。
他沒(有)買那本書。
Tā méi (yǒu) mǎi nà běn shū.
He didn't buy that book.

The adverb 还/還 **hái** may occur in sentences negated with 没(有)/沒(有) **méi (yǒu)**. 还没(有)/還沒(有) **hái méi (yǒu)** means 'not yet.'

我还没吃早饭。
我還沒吃早飯。
Wǒ hái méi chī zǎofàn.
I haven't yet eaten breakfast.

他才十三岁。当然还没结婚。
他才十三歲。當然還沒結婚。
Tā cái shísān suì. Dāngrán hái méi jiéhūn.
He's only 13. Of course he hasn't yet married.

▶ 13.3.2, 17.1.1.2, 27.1.2

37.4 Asking whether an action has occurred

To ask whether an action has occurred, use a yes–no question:

Yes–no questions with 吗/嗎 *ma*

Q: 你买飞机票了吗?
你買飛機票了嗎?
Nǐ mǎi fēijī piào le ma?
Did you buy the airplane ticket?

Verb-not-verb yes–no questions

verb 了 **le** (object) 没有/沒有 **méi yǒu**

Q: 你买了飞机票没有?   or   Q: 你买飞机票了没有?
你買了飛機票沒有?   你買飛機票了沒有?
Nǐ mǎi le fēijī piào méi yǒu?   **Nǐ mǎi fēijī piào le méi yǒu?**
Have you bought (the) airplane ticket yet?   Have you bought (the) airplane ticket yet?

Yes–no questions with 有没有/有沒有 *yǒu méi yǒu (Taiwan usage)*

有没有/有沒有 **yǒu méi yǒu** + [prepositional phrase +] verb phrase

Q: 你有没有买飞机票?
你有沒有買飛機票?
Nǐ yǒu méi yǒu mǎi fēijī piào?
Have you bought the airplane ticket?

To answer 'yes' to 吗/嗎 **ma** or verb-not-verb yes–no questions, reply with V 了:

A: 买了。
買了。
Mǎi le.
[I] bought [it].

To answer 'yes' to 有没有/有沒有 **yǒu méi yǒu** questions, say:

A: 有。
Yǒu.
Yes.

Talking about past experience: verb suffix 过/過 *guo*

37.6

To answer 'no' to any form of these yes–no questions, say:

A: 没有。
没有。
Méi yǒu.
No.

▶ 17.1, 28.1

37.5 Indicating that an action occurred again in the past: 又 *yòu* verb 了 *le*

To indicate that an action occurred *again* in the past, precede the [prepositional phrase +] verb phrase with the adverb 又 **yòu** and follow the verb with 了 **le**.

他前天来了。今天早上又来了。
他前天來了。今天早上又來了。
Tā qiántiān lái le. Jīntiān zǎoshang *yòu* lái *le*.
He came the day before yesterday. This morning he came *again*.

Notice that the adverb 又 **yòu** '(to do) again in the past' is closely related to the adverb 再 **zài** '(to do) again in the future.'

我昨天晚上又吃饺子了。明天不要再吃了。
我昨天晚上又吃餃子了。明天不要再吃了。
Wǒ zuótiān wǎnshang yòu chī jiǎozi le. Míngtiān bù yào zài chī le.
I ate dumplings again last night. I don't want to eat them again tomorrow.

▶ 36.2

NOTE 又 **yòu** ... 又 **yòu** ... means 'both ... and ...' and can be used to link stative verbs or adjectival verbs.

他们又饿又渴。
他們又餓又渴。
Tāmen yòu è yòu kě.
They are hungry and thirsty.

▶ 10.8, 39.9, 43.4

37.6 Talking about past experience: verb suffix 过/過 *guo*

To indicate that an action has been experienced at least once in the indefinite past, follow the verb with the verb suffix 过/過 **guo**.

我吃过中国饭。
我吃過中國飯。
Wǒ chīguo Zhōngguó fàn.
I've eaten Chinese food (before).

The verb suffix 过/過 **guo** is appropriate in the following circumstances:

- when talking about actions that the subject does not perform on a regular basis,
- when talking about actions that happened in the remote past,

247

INDICATING COMPLETION AND TALKING ABOUT THE PAST — 37.6

- when talking about actions that are repeatable. Actions that are not repeatable cannot be suffixed with 过/過 **guo**.

    Do not say

    *她大学毕业过。
    她大學畢業過。
    Tā dàxué bìyè guò.
    intended: She has graduated from university before.

▶ 13.2, 17.3

The suffix 过/過 **guo** and perfective 了 **le** can sometimes occur together in the same sentence. When they do, 过/過 **guo** always occurs before 了 **le**.

今天的报我已经看过了。
今天的報我已經看過了。
Jīntiān de bào wǒ yǐjing kànguo le.
I've already read today's paper.

长城我已经登过了。
長城我已經登過了。
Chángchéng wǒ yǐjing dēngguo le.
I have already climbed the Great Wall.

To indicate that an action has never been experienced before, precede the [prepositional phrase +] verb phrase with 没/沒 **méi** or 没有/沒有 **méi yǒu** and follow the verb with 过/過 **guo** as follows:

没/沒(有) **méi (yǒu)** + verb 过/過 **guo**

我没吃过中国饭。
我沒吃過中國飯。
Wǒ méi chīguo Zhōngguó fàn.
I have never eaten Chinese food before.

他没坐过飞机。
他沒坐過飛機。
Tā méi zuòguo fēijī.
He has never ridden on a plane before.

When talking about events that have never been experienced before, the adverb 从来/從來 **cónglái** 'in the past' often occurs before the verb for additional emphasis:

我从来没吃过中国饭。
我從來沒吃過中國飯。
Wǒ cónglái méi chīguo Zhōngguó fàn.
I have never eaten Chinese food before.

NOTE   从来/從來 **cónglái** is only used in negative sentences.

▶ 17.3, 27.3, 35.3

37.7 Comparing the aspect markers 过/過 guo and 了 le

The aspect markers 过/過 **guo** and 了 **le** overlap in meaning, but they are not identical. As illustrated in Section 37.6, they may sometimes be used together. However, in many contexts, only 过/過 **guo** or 了 **le** is appropriate.

Here is a table that summarizes the meanings associated with 过/過 **guo** and 了 **le**, and illustrates their differences.

	过/過 *guo*	了 *le*
The action is complete.	过/過 **guo** is acceptable 我去过中国。 我去過中國。 **Wǒ qùguo Zhōngguó.** I've been to China before.	了 **le** is acceptable 我去了中国。 我去了中國。 **Wǒ qù le Zhōngguó.** I went to China.
The action has never been performed by the subject.	过/過 **guo** is acceptable 我没去过中国。 我沒去過中國。 **Wǒ méi qùguo Zhōngguó.** I have never been to China before.	了 **le** is acceptable, but simply indicates that the action did not happen 我没去中国。 我沒去中國。 **Wǒ méi qù Zhōngguó.** I didn't go to China.
The action refers to a repeatable event.	This condition is necessary for 过/過 **guo** 我看过那个电影。 我看過那個電影。 **Wǒ kànguo nàge diànyǐng.** I have seen that movie before. If the action is not repeatable, 过/過 **guo** is not acceptable *她大学毕业过。 她大學畢業過。 **Tā dàxué bìyèguo.** She graduated from university.	了 **le** can be used for repeatable or non-repeatable events 我看了那个电影。 我看了那個電影。 **Wǒ kànle nàge diànyǐng.** I saw that movie. 她大学毕业了。 她大學畢業了。 **Tā dàxué bìyè le.** She graduated from university.
The action is not customary. It is unusual for the subject to do it.	This condition is usually implied by 过/過 **guo** 我吃过蛇肉。 我吃過蛇肉。 **Wǒ chīguo shé ròu.** I have had the experience of eating snake before.	了 **le** can be used with customary or unusual actions 我吃了蛇肉。 **Wǒ chīle shé ròu.** I ate snake. (There is no implication about how common this action is for me.)

37.8 Time words and adverbs that refer to past time

37.8.1 Time words that refer to past time

Here are some common time words that refer to past time.

昨天	zuótiān	yesterday
前天	qiántiān	the day before yesterday
大前天	dàqiántiān	three days before now
上个星期/上個星期	shàng gè xīngqī	last week
上个礼拜/上個禮拜	shàng gè lǐbài	last week
上个月/上個月	shàng gè yuè	last month

INDICATING COMPLETION AND TALKING ABOUT THE PAST   37.8

| 去年 | qùnián | last year |
| 前年 | qiánnián | the year before last |

▶ 49.2

37.8.1 Adverbs that refer to past time

Adverbs that refer to past time may be used with action verbs, stative verbs, or adjectival verbs. When the verb is a stative verb or adjectival verb, an adverb may be the only marker of past time. Here are the most common adverbs that refer to past time.

以前 *yǐqián* 'before, previously, in the past'

我以前在外国住了几年。(action verb)
我以前在外國住了幾年。
Wǒ yǐqián zài wàiguó *zhù* le jǐnián.
I previously *lived* abroad for a few years.

小英以前是大明的女朋友。(stative verb)
Xiǎoyīng yǐqián *shì* Dàmíng de nǚ péngyou.
Xiaoying used to *be* Daming's girlfriend.

我以前很喜欢他。(stative verb)
我以前很喜歡他。
Wǒ yǐqián hěn *xǐhuan* tā.
I used to *like* him a lot.

汽油以前很便宜。(adjectival verb)
Qìyóu yǐqián hěn *piányi*.
In the past, gasoline was *cheap*.

过去/過去 *guòqù* 'in the past'

他过去是英文老师。(stative verb)
他過去是英文老師。
Tā guòqù *shì* Yīngwén lǎoshī.
He used to *be* an English teacher.

从前/從前 *cóngqián* 'previously'

中国从前有很多人不识字。(stative verb)
中國從前有很多人不識字。
Zhōngguó cóngqián *yǒu* hěn duō rén bù shí zì.
In the past, China *had* a lot of people who were illiterate.

These adverbs may also be used when talking about situations that customarily occurred in the past.

我从前天天去公园散步。
我從前天天去公園散步。
Wǒ cóngqián tiāntiān qù gōngyuán sànbù.
I used to take a walk in the park every day.

我过去每年都带孩子到海边去玩。
我過去每年都帶孩子到海邊去玩。
Wǒ guòqù měi nián dōu dài háizi dào hǎibiān qù wán.
In the past, every year I used to take the children to the beach to play.

37.9 Focusing on a detail of a past event with 是...的 *shì...de*

To focus on a specific detail of an event, such as the time or place of the event, use 是...的 **shì...de**.

是 **shì** occurs right before the phrase that is being focused on.
的 **de** occurs right after the verb or at the end of the sentence.

是...的 **shì...de** is used to focus on:

- the time when an event occurred:

    他是一年以前去中国的。
    他是一年以前去中國的。
    Tā shì *yīnián yǐqián* qù Zhōngguó de.
    He went to China *a year ago*.

    你的新车是什么时候买的?
    你的新車是甚麼時候買的?
    Nǐ de xīn chē shì *shénme shíhòu* mǎi de?
    When did you buy your new car?

- the one who performed the activity:

    这本书是谁写的?
    這本書是誰寫的?
    Zhè běn shū shì *shéi* xiě de?
    Who wrote this book?

- location:

    你的大衣是在哪儿买的?
    你的大衣是在哪兒買的?
    Nǐ de dàyī shì *zài nǎr* mǎi de?
    Where did you buy your coat?

    这件衣服是在哪儿买的?
    這件衣服是在哪兒買的?
    Zhè jiàn yīfú shì *zài nǎr* mǎi de?
    Where did you buy this item of clothing?

- a prepositional phrase:

    他是跟谁结婚的?
    他是跟誰結婚的?
    Tā shì *gēn shéi* jiéhūn de?
    Who (*with whom*) did he marry?

If the verb has an object and the object is not a pronoun, 的 **de** can come either after the verb or at the end of the sentence.

昨天晚上是谁给你做的晚饭?
昨天晚上是誰給你做的晚飯?
Zuótiān wǎnshàng shì *shéi* gěi nǐ zuò de wǎnfàn?
Who cooked dinner for you last night?

or

昨天晚上是谁给你做晚饭的?
昨天晚上是誰給你做晚飯的?
Zuótiān wǎnshàng shì *shéi* gěi nǐ zuò wǎnfàn de?
Who cooked dinner for you last night?

INDICATING COMPLETION AND TALKING ABOUT THE PAST　　　　　　　　**37.9**

If the object of the verb is a pronoun, 的 **de** can only occur after the pronoun, at the end of the sentence.

Say this　　　　　　　　　　　　　*Not this*

你是在<u>哪儿</u>认识他的？　　　　　　*你是在哪儿认识的他？
你是在<u>哪兒</u>認識他的？　　　　　　你是在哪兒認識的他？
Nǐ shì zài *nǎr* rènshi tā de?　　**Nǐ shì zài nǎr rènshi de tā?**
Where did you meet him?

是 **shì** may be omitted in affirmative sentences.

这件衣服(是)在网上买的。
這件衣服(是)在網上買的。
Zhè jiàn yīfú (shì) zài wǎngshàng mǎi de.
This item of clothing was bought online.

是 **shì** may not be omitted in negated sentences.

Say this　　　　　　　　　　　　　　　　　　*Not this*

这件衣服不是在网上买的。　　　　　　　　　*这件衣服不在网上买的。
這件衣服不是在網上買的。　　　　　　　　　這件衣服不在網上買的。
Zhè jiàn yīfú bù shì zài wǎngshàng　　　　**Zhè jiàn yīfú bù zài wǎngshàng**
mǎi de.　　　　　　　　　　　　　　　　　**mǎi de.**
This item of clothing was not bought online.

▶ 11.4, 57.2.4, 57.3

38

Talking about change, new situations, and changing situations

Mandarin has a number of ways to indicate that a situation represents a change from the past or that it is in the process of change. **38.1** and **38.3** present grammatical patterns that are used to talk about change. **38.4** presents words that are used to talk about change.

38.1 Indicating that a situation represents a change

To indicate that a situation represents a change, add the particle 了 **le** to the end of the sentence that describes the situation. We refer to this use of 了 **le** as 'sentence final 了 **le**.' Here are the most common types of change associated with sentence final 了 **le**. Notice that in English this sense of change is sometimes expressed with the word 'become' (verb) or (verb) 'now' or 'gotten' (verb).

38.1.1 New information for the addressee

他们订婚了!
他們訂婚了!
Tāmen dìng hūn le!
They have become engaged!

我有两个孩子了。
我有兩個孩子了。
Wǒ yǒu liǎng gè háizi le.
I have two children now (and this is information that is new for you).

38.1.2 Change of state

When the main verb of a sentence is a stative verb, sentence final 了 **le** indicates a change of state.

东西都贵了。
東西都貴了。
Dōngxi dōu guì le.
Things have become expensive.

他有女朋友了。
Tā yǒu nǚ péngyou le.
He has a girlfriend now. (He didn't have one before.)

TALKING ABOUT CHANGE, NEW SITUATIONS, AND CHANGING SITUATIONS

38.1.3 Actions that continue into the future: double 了 *le* sentences

Sentence final 了 **le** can be used with the perfective aspect suffix 了 **le** to signal that a certain portion of an action is complete but that the action is continuing into the future. Sentences like these are sometimes described as having 'double 了 **le**,' and the function of the sentence final 了 **le** is sometimes described as indicating the 'present relevance' of the situation.

> 他已经睡了十个钟头了。
> 他已經睡了十個鐘頭了。
> **Tā yǐjing shuì le shí gè zhōngtóu le.**
> He has already slept for ten hours.

▶ 34.7

38.1.4 Situations that do not exist anymore

To indicate that a situation does not exist anymore, add sentence final 了 **le** to the end of a negated sentence:

negated sentence + sentence final 了 le

> 她不吃肉了。
> **Tā bù chī ròu le.**
> She doesn't eat meat anymore.

> 太阳出来了。不冷了。
> 太陽出來了。不冷了。
> **Tàiyáng chūlái le. Bù lěng le.**
> The sun has come out. (It) isn't cold anymore.

38.1.5 Imminent occurrences and imminent change

Sentence final 了 **le** can be used to indicate that a situation will happen soon. Often, an adverb or adverbial phrase such as 快 **kuài**, 快要 **kuài yào**, or 就要 **jiù yào** occurs before the [prepositional phrase +] verb phrase to emphasize the fact that the situation will happen soon.

> 我们快到了。
> 我們快到了。
> **Wǒmen kuài dào le.**
> We will be arriving soon.

> 我快要做完了。
> **Wǒ kuài yào zuòwán le.**
> I'm just about done.

38.2 Comparing sentences with and without sentence final 了 *le*

Notice how sentence final 了 **le** changes the meaning of the sentence. Without sentence final 了 **le**, the sentence is a description of a situation. With sentence final 了 **le**, the sentence focuses on a change.

No sentence final 了 le	*Sentence final 了 le*
我会看中文报。	我会看中文报了。
我會看中文報。	我會看中文報了。
Wǒ huì kàn Zhōngwén bào.	**Wǒ huì kàn Zhōngwén bào le.**
I can read Chinese newspapers.	I can read Chinese newspapers now.

38.3 Indicating change over time

No sentence final 了 **le**	*Sentence final* 了 **le**
汽油很贵。 汽油很貴。 **Qìyóu hěn guì.** Gasoline is very expensive.	汽油很贵了。 汽油很貴了。 **Qìyóu hěn guì le.** Gasoline has become very expensive.
我不喜欢吃肉。 我不喜歡吃肉。 **Wǒ bù xǐhuan chī ròu.** I don't like to eat meat.	我不喜欢吃肉了。 我不喜歡吃肉了。 **Wǒ bù xǐhuan chī ròu le.** I don't like to eat meat anymore.

38.3 Indicating change over time

38.3.1 More and more of some situation

越来越   yuè lái yuè   AV/SV/MV
more and more AV/SV/MV

This pattern is used to indicate that something is becoming *more and more* adjectival verb (AV), stative verb (SV), or modal verb (MV) over time.

Sentence final 了 **le** can optionally occur with this pattern to emphasize the sense of change that the pattern conveys.

'more and more' adjectival verb

东西越来越贵(了)。
東西越來越貴(了)。
Dōngxi yuè lái yuè guì (le).
Things are getting more and more expensive.

天气越来越冷(了)。
天氣越來越冷(了)。
Tiānqì yuè lái yuè lěng (le).
The weather is getting colder and colder.

'more and more' stative verb

他长大了，越来越懂事(了)。
他長大了，越來越懂事(了)。
Tā zhǎng dà le, yuè lái yuè dǒng shì (le).
He has grown up. More and more he knows how to behave.

中国的生活，我越来越习惯了。
中國的生活，我越來越習慣了。
Zhōngguó de shēnghuó, wǒ yuè lái yuè xíguàn le.
(As for) life in China, I am getting used to it.

'more and more' modal verb

你越来越会做饭(了)。
你越來越會做飯(了)。
Nǐ yuè lái yuè huì zuò fàn (le).
You are getting better and better at cooking.

他们越来越会说中文(了)。
他們越來越會說中文(了)。
Tāmen yuè lái yuè huì shuō Zhōngwén (le).
They are getting more and more proficient in speaking Chinese.

TALKING ABOUT CHANGE, NEW SITUATIONS, AND CHANGING SITUATIONS | 38.4

越來越 **yuè lái yuè** can be used to express negative situations.

> 我越来越不喜欢他了。
> 我越來越不喜歡他了。
> **Wǒ yuè lái yuè bù xǐhuan tā le.**
> I dislike him more and more.

> 他们家越来越没有钱了。
> 他們家越來越沒有錢了。
> **Tāmen jiā yuè lái yuè méi yǒu qián le.**
> Their family has less and less money.

38.3.2 Indicating change caused by changing events

To indicate that one change causes another change, say:

> 越　　　VP　　　越　　　AV/SV/MV
> **yuè**　　VP　　**yuè**　　AV/SV/MV
> the more VP the more AV/SV/MV

越 *yuè* VP 越 *yuè* adjectival verb

> 我越吃冰淇淋越胖。
> **Wǒ yuè chī bīngqilín yuè pàng.**
> The more I eat ice cream, the fatter I get.

越 *yuè* VP 越 *yuè* stative verb

> 我越吃豆腐，越喜欢吃。
> 我越吃豆腐，越喜歡吃。
> **Wǒ yuè chī dòufu, yuè xǐhuan chī.**
> The more I eat beancurd, the more I like to eat it.

越 *yuè* VP 越 *yuè* modal verb

> 我越学中文越会说中国话。
> 我越學中文越會說中國話。
> **Wǒ yuè xué Zhōngwén yuè huì shuō Zhōngguó huà.**
> The more I study Chinese, the more I am able to speak Chinese.

Note that this pattern indicates both change and result.

▶ 10.9, 12.6.4

38.4 Nouns and verbs that express change

Nouns

变化/變化 *biànhuà* 'a change'

> 最近十年来，北京变化很大。
> 最近十年來，北京變化很大。
> **Zuìjìn shínián lái, Běijīng biànhuà hěn dà.**
> In the past ten years, Beijing has had a lot of changes.
> (lit. 'In the past ten years, Beijing's changes have been big.')

> 这附近没有什么变化。
> 這附近沒有甚麼變化。
> **Zhè fùjìn méi yǒu shénme biànhuà.**
> The area around here hasn't had much change.

38.4 Nouns and verbs that express change

Verbs

变/變 **biàn** 'change' [does not take an object]

> 情况变了。
> 情況變了。
> **Qíngkuàng biàn le.**
> The circumstances have changed.

换 **huàn** 'change (something)' [takes an object]

> 这句话不容易懂，请你换一个说法。
> 這句話不容易懂，請你換一個說法。
> **Zhè jù huà bù róngyì dǒng, qǐng nǐ huàn yī gè shuōfa.**
> This sentence is difficult to understand. Please put it another way.

成 **chéng** 'change into (something), turn into (something), become (something)' [takes an object]

> 他成了一个很有名的人了。
> 他成了一個很有名的人了。
> **Tā chéng le yī gè hěn yǒu míng de rén le.**
> He has become a very famous person.

Some common expressions with 成 **chéng**:

| 成名 | **chéng míng** | 'become famous' |
| 成年 | **chéng nián** | 'grow up, become an adult; come of age' |

改变/改變 **gǎibiàn** 'change' [does not take an object]

> 他的样子改变了。
> 他的樣子改變了。
> **Tā de yàngzi gǎibiàn le.**
> His appearance has changed.

变成/變成 **biànchéng** 'turn into (something), change into (something)' [takes an object]

> 你觉得坏人能变成好人吗？
> 你覺得壞人能變成好人嗎？
> **Nǐ juéde huàirén néng biànchéng hǎorén ma?**
> Do you think that bad people can turn into good people?

成为/成為 **chéngwéi** 'become (something), turn into (something)' [takes an object]

> 他成为一个科学家了。
> 他成為一個科學家了。
> **Tā chéngwéi yī gè kēxuéjiā le.**
> He became a scientist.

改 **gǎi** 'change (something), reform (something), correct (something)' [takes an object]

> 请你帮我改我的文章。
> 請你幫我改我的文章。
> **Qǐng nǐ bāng wǒ gǎi wǒ de wénzhāng.**
> Please help me correct my essay.

改 **gǎi** is also used as the first part of the following verbs:

改写/改寫 **gáixiě** 'rewrite'

> 这本书，我已经改写三次了。你还不满意吗？
> 這本書，我已經改寫三次了。你還不滿意嗎？
> **Zhè běn shū, wǒ yǐjing gáixiě sāncì le. Nǐ hái bù mǎnyì ma?**
> I've rewritten this book three times. Are you still not satisfied?

TALKING ABOUT CHANGE, NEW SITUATIONS, AND CHANGING SITUATIONS 38.4

改正 *gǎizhèng* 'correct, rectify'

请你改正我的错误。
請你改正我的錯誤。
Qǐng nǐ gǎizhèng wǒ de cuòwù.
Please correct my mistakes.

改造 *gǎizào* 'remodel, reform' [this expression has political overtones]

你的思想意识太旧，真应该改造改造。
你的思想意識太舊，真應該改造改造。
Nǐ de sīxiǎng yìshi tài jiù, zhēn yīnggāi gǎizào gǎizào.
Your ideological awareness is out of date and needs to be reformed.

改善 *gǎishàn* 'improve'

政府应该设法改善人民的生活。
政府應該設法改善人民的生活。
Zhèngfǔ yīnggāi shèfǎ gǎishàn rénmín de shēnghuó.
(The) government should think of ways to improve people's livelihood.

改良 *gǎiliáng* 'improve'

中国帮助非洲国家改良农业。
中國幫助非洲國家改良農業。
Zhōngguó bāngzhù Fēizhōu guójiā gǎiliáng nóngyè.
China has helped African nations improve their agriculture.

改换(成)/改換(成) *gǎihuàn (chéng)* 'change (something)'; 'exchange for some equivalent item'

现在朝代已经改换了。
現在朝代已經改換了。
Xiànzài cháodài yǐjing gǎihuàn le.
The dynasty has changed (to another dynasty).

改进/改進 *gǎijìn* 'improve'

我们的税收制度，仍得改进。
我們的稅收制度，仍得改進。
Wǒmen de shuìshōu zhìdù, réng děi gǎijìn.
Our tax system still needs to be improved.

39

Talking about duration and frequency

When we talk about duration, we can specify the length of an action ('we walked *for an hour*'), or we can focus on the ongoing duration of the action without reference to its length ('while *we were walking*, it started to rain'). When we talk about frequency, we indicate how often an action occurs. This chapter will show you how to express both duration and frequency in Mandarin.

39.1 Specifying the length of an action with a duration phrase

Duration phrases can be used to indicate *how long* an action occurs. To indicate the duration of an action, follow the verb with a time phrase:

subject + verb + duration

Only open-ended actions have duration. Open-ended actions include 买/買 **mǎi** 'to shop,' 学/學 **xué** 'to study,' 看 **kàn** 'to look at,' 'to watch,' 'to read,' 吃 **chī** 'to eat,' 睡 **shuì** 'to sleep,' 唱 **chàng** 'to sing,' 洗 **xǐ** 'to wash,' etc.

▶ 13.5, 18.1, 18.2

39.1.1 Indicating duration when there is no object noun phrase

When the action verb does not have an object noun phrase, the duration phrase simply follows the verb. If the verb is suffixed with 了 **le**, the duration phrase follows 了 **le**.

我想在中国住一年。
我想在中國住一年。
Wǒ xiǎng zài Zhōngguó *zhù* yīnián.
I plan to live in China for a year.

他病了三天。
Tā *bìng* le sāntiān.
He was *sick* for three days.

39.1.2 Indicating duration when the verb takes an object

When the verb takes an object noun phrase, duration may be indicated using the following sentence patterns. In all of these patterns, the verb is followed by its object or by a duration phrase. A single verb is never followed directly by both an object and a duration phrase, with one exception. If the object is a pronoun, the pronoun may occur after the verb and before the duration phrase.

259

TALKING ABOUT DURATION AND FREQUENCY | 39.1

我等了他三个小时了。
我等了他三個小時了。
Wǒ děng le tā sān gè xiǎoshí le.
I've been waiting for him for three hours.

Pattern 1: verb + object verb + duration

The verb occurs twice in the verb phrase. First it is followed by the object, then it is followed by the duration phrase.

Say this	*Not this*
我每天晚上看书看四个小时。 我每天晚上看書看四個小時。 **Wǒ měitiān wǎnshang *kàn* shū *kàn* sì gè xiǎoshí.**	*我每天晚上看书四个小时。 我每天晚上看書四個小時。 **Wǒ měitiān wǎnshang *kàn* shū sì gè xiǎoshí.**

Every night I read (books) for four hours.

If the sentence refers to a past event, the second occurrence of the verb is followed by 了 **le**.

我睡觉睡了八个钟头。
我睡覺睡了八個鐘頭。
Wǒ shuì jiào *shuì* le bā gè zhōngtóu.
I slept for eight hours.

我等他等了三个小时。
我等他等了三個小時。
Wǒ děng tā *děng* le sān gè xiǎoshí.
I waited for him for three hours.

▶ 37.1

Pattern 2: verb + object 有 yǒu + duration

The verb and its object are stated first, followed by 有 **yǒu** and the duration phrase. 有 **yǒu** is not directly followed by 了 **le**, though 了 **le** may occur at the end of the sentence.

我等王明有三个小时了。
我等王明有三個小時了。
Wǒ *děng* Wáng Míng *yǒu* sān gè xiǎoshí le.
I have been waiting for Wang Ming for three hours.

Pattern 3: verb + duration 的 de object noun phrase

The duration phrase plus 的 **de** occurs immediately before the object noun phrase. This pattern cannot be used when the object noun phrase is a pronoun.

我学了两年的中文。
我學了兩年的中文。
Wǒ *xué* le liǎng nián de Zhōngwén.
I studied Chinese for two years.

我睡了八个钟头的觉。
我睡了八個鐘頭的覺。
Wǒ *shuì* le bā gè zhōngtóu de jiào.
I slept for eight hours.

的 **de** is sometimes omitted.

那个学生已经学了两年(的)中文了。
那個學生已經學了兩年(的)中文了。
Nàge xuésheng yǐjing xué le liǎng nián (de) Zhōngwén le.
That student has been studying Chinese for two years already.

Specifying the length of an action with a duration phrase　　**39.1**

Pattern 4: object noun phrase, verb + duration

The object noun phrase may occur at the beginning of the sentence, before the subject, as a topic. The verb is then directly followed by the duration phrase. This pattern cannot be used when the object noun phrase is a pronoun or a default object.

> 这个问题，我已经想了很久了。
> 這個問題，我已經想了很久了。
> **Zhège wèntí, wǒ yǐjing xiǎng le hěn jiǔ le.**
> This problem, I have already thought about (it) for a long time.

> 中文，我已经学了四年了。
> 中文，我已經學了四年了。
> **Zhōngwén, wǒ yǐjing xué le sìnián le.**
> Chinese, I've already studied (it) for four years.

> 中文，我至少会学两年。
> 中文，我至少會學兩年。
> **Zhōngwén, wǒ zhìshǎo huì xué liǎng nián.**
> Chinese, at the very least I will study (it) for two years.

▶ 57.1.2.1

39.1.3 Duration vs. time when

Note the difference between phrases that indicate *duration* and those that indicate *time when*.

Time phrases that indicate the *duration* of a situation always occur after the verb.

> 我学了两个小时了。
> 我學了兩個小時了。
> **Wǒ xué le liǎng gè xiǎoshí le.**
> I studied for two hours.

Time phrases that indicate the *time when* a situation takes place always occur before the verb:

> 我昨天学了中文。
> 我昨天學了中文。
> **Wǒ zuótiān xué le Zhōngwén.**
> I studied Chinese yesterday.

A sentence may include both a time when phrase and a duration phrase.

> 我昨天学了两个小时。
> 我昨天學了兩個小時。
> **Wǒ zuótiān xué le liǎng gè xiǎoshí.**
> Yesterday I studied for two hours.

39.1.4 Indicating how long it has been that something has not occurred

In Mandarin, only situations that occur can be described in terms of their duration. If a situation *does not occur*, the duration pattern cannot be used to describe it. To indicate the length of time that something has not occurred, put the time phrase before the [prepositional phrase +] verb or verb phrase.

> 我两天没睡觉。
> 我兩天沒睡覺。
> **Wǒ liǎng tiān méi shuì jiào.**
> I haven't slept for two days.

TALKING ABOUT DURATION AND FREQUENCY

他三年没有抽烟。
他三年沒有抽煙。
Tā sān nián méi yǒu chōu yān.
He hasn't smoked for three years.

39.2 Emphasizing ongoing duration

39.2.1 Emphasizing the ongoing duration of an action

To emphasize the ongoing duration of an action without specifying the length of the duration, follow the verb with the suffix 着/著 **zhe**. To indicate that an action is ongoing at the moment of speaking, 在 **zài** or 正在 **zhèngzài** may also precede the verb. 呢 **ne** may occur at the end of the sentence.

他在说着话呢。
他在說著話呢。
Tā zài shuōzhe huà ne.
He is speaking.

她正在吃着早饭呢。
她正在吃著早飯呢。
Tā zhèngzài chīzhe zǎofàn ne.
She is eating breakfast right now.

在 **zài** before the verb may also mark duration without the verb suffix 着/著 **zhe**.

他在说话呢。
他在說話呢。
Tā zài shuō huà ne.
He is speaking.

我们在吃饭呢。
我們在吃飯呢。
Wǒmen zài chī fàn ne.
We are eating right now. (We are right in the middle of eating.)

▶ 13.4, 17.2, 34.2, 34.3

The duration suffix 着/著 **zhe** is often used with verbs that refer to the placement or location of an object.

街上站着很多人。
街上站著很多人。
Jiēshàng zhànzhe hěn duō rén.
There are a lot of people standing in the street.

公共汽车上坐着很多人。
公共汽車上坐著很多人。
Gōnggòng qìchē shàng zuòzhe hěn duō rén.
There are a lot of people sitting on the bus.

▶ 34.4

This use of 着/著 **zhe** is similar to the use of the present progressive verb suffix '-ing' in English in its focus on ongoing actions. However, 着/著 **zhe** and '-ing' are not always equivalent. For example, 着/著 **zhe** can be used in Mandarin to emphasize the duration of an adjectival verb. The English equivalent does not typically use '-ing.'

Indicating the ongoing duration of a background event | **39.3**

她的脸红着呢。(AV)
她的臉紅著呢。
Tā de liǎn hóngzhe ne.
Her face is red. (Not 'Her face is being red.')

汤热着呢。(AV)
湯熱著呢。
Tāng rèzhe ne.
The soup is hot. (Not 'The soup is being hot.')

In Mandarin, 着/著 **zhe** may also be suffixed to certain verbs in commands. The English equivalent does not ordinarily involve '-ing.'

拿着！/拿著！	**Názhe!**	Hold it!/Take it!
记着！/記著！	**Jìzhe!**	Remember!
等着！/等著！	**Děngzhe!**	Wait!
坐着！/坐著！	**Zuòzhe!**	Sit!

▶ 51.1.1

39.2.2 Emphasizing the ongoing duration of a situation or state

To emphasize the ongoing duration of a situation or state, use the adverb 还/還 **hái** before the [prepositional phrase +] verb or verb phrase. In affirmative sentences and questions, this use of 还/還 **hái** can often be translated into English with the word 'still.'

他还在中国。
他還在中國。
Tā hái zài Zhōngguó.
He is still in China.

你还喜欢他吗？
你還喜歡他嗎？
Nǐ hái xǐhuan tā ma?
Do you still like him?

In negative sentences, this use of 还/還 **hái** can often be translated into English with the phrase 'not yet.'

他还没结婚。
他還沒結婚。
Tā hái méi jiéhūn.
He has not yet married. (He still hasn't married.)

我还没看那个电影。
我還沒看那個電影。
Wǒ hái méi kàn nàge diànyǐng.
I have not yet seen that movie. (I still haven't seen that movie.)

▶ 15.2.3, 40.2

39.3 Indicating the ongoing duration of a background event

When two events occur at the same time, we sometimes consider one event to be the main event and the other to be the background event. To signal that a background event is ongoing as the main event occurs, follow the verb of the background event with the verb suffix 着/著 **zhe**.

TALKING ABOUT DURATION AND FREQUENCY

> 我们喝着咖啡谈话。
> 我們喝著咖啡談話。
> **Wǒmen hēzhe kāfēi tán huà.**
> We talked while drinking coffee. ('drinking coffee' is the background event)

> 他看着电视吃早饭。
> 他看著電視吃早飯。
> **Tā kànzhe diànshì chī zǎofàn.**
> He eats breakfast while watching television. ('watching television' is the background event)

To indicate that an event is a background event without focusing on its duration, use 的时候/的時候 **de shíhou** 'when, while.'

> 我在中国的时候认识他了。
> 我在中國的時候認識他了。
> **Wǒ zài Zhōngguó de shíhou rènshi tā le.**
> While I was in China, I met him.

▶ 43.1

39.4 Indicating frequency

39.4.1 Words used to indicate frequency

The classifiers 次 **cì** 'number of times' and 遍 **biàn** 'a time' are used to indicate frequency. They are always preceded by a number or the question words 几/幾 **jǐ** or 多少 **duōshǎo** 'how many.' 次 **cì** can be used to refer to the frequency of any kind of action. 遍 **biàn** is more restricted in its use and refers only to actions that have been performed from beginning to end.

39.4.2 The grammar of the frequency expression

To indicate the frequency of an action, follow the action verb with number + 次 **cì** or 遍 **biàn** 'times' to indicate the 'number of times' that the action occurs. If the verb is suffixed with 了 **le** or 过/過 **guo**, the frequency phrase occurs after the verb suffix.

> 我已经说了三次，你怎么还不懂？
> 我已經說了三次，你怎麼還不懂？
> **Wǒ yǐjing shuō le sān cì, nǐ zěnme hái bù dǒng?**
> I've already said it three times, how can you still not understand? (遍 **biàn** can be used instead of 次 **cì** in this sentence.)

A verb may be followed by both a frequency expression and an object. The frequency expression always precedes the object.

There are several ways to indicate frequency.

Pattern 1: verb + object, verb + frequency

If the verb takes an object, the verb may be repeated, once followed by the object, and once followed by the frequency expression.

> 我去年<u>坐</u>飞机<u>坐</u>了<u>三次</u>。(遍 **biàn** cannot be used here.)
> 我去年<u>坐</u>飛機<u>坐</u>了<u>三次</u>。
> **Wǒ qùnián *zuò* fēijī *zuò* le *sān cì*.**
> Last year I *rode* airplanes *three times*.

264

Indicating frequency | **39.4**

Pattern 2: verb + frequency + object noun phrase

The frequency expression can occur between the verb and its object.

> 她坐过一次飞机。(遍 **biàn** cannot be used here.)
> 她坐過一次飛機。
> **Tā zuòguo yī cì fēijī.**
> She's ridden on a plane once.
>
> 我给他打了两次电话。(遍 **biàn** cannot be used here.)
> 我給他打了兩次電話。
> **Wǒ gěi tā dǎ le liǎng cì diànhuà.**
> I called him on the phone twice.

Pattern 3: object noun phrase, verb + frequency

If the verb takes an object, the object may be topicalized and presented first in the sentence:

> 那个电影，我看过两次。(遍 **biàn** can be used here.)
> 那個電影，我看過兩次。
> **Nàge diànyǐng, wǒ kànguo *liǎng cì*.**
> That movie, I have seen it twice.
>
> 西安，我去过一次。(遍 **biàn** can be used here)
> 西安，我去過一次。
> **Xī'ān, wǒ qùguo yīcì.**
> Xi'an, I've been there once.

▶ 57.1.2.1

265

40

Expressing additional information

Mandarin uses the following expressions to provide additional information.

40.1 也 *yě* 'also'

也 **yě** is an adverb and is always followed by a [prepositional phrase +] verb or verb phrase.

也 **yě** can be used to introduce additional information about the subject of the sentence.

> 张美丽学英文。她也学日文。
> 張美麗學英文。她也學日文。
> **Zhāng Měilì xué Yīngwén. Tā yě xué Rìwén.**
> Zhang Meili studies English. She also studies Japanese.

也 **yě** can be used to indicate that two different subjects share similar characteristics or perform the same action.

> 张美丽很高。她妹妹也很高。
> 張美麗很高。她妹妹也很高。
> **Zhāng Měilì hěn gāo. Tā mèimei yě hěn gāo.**
> Zhang Meili is very tall. Her younger sister is also very tall.

> 张美丽学英文。她妹妹也学英文。
> 張美麗學英文。她妹妹也學英文。
> **Zhāng Měilì xué Yīngwén. Tā mèimei yě xué Yīngwén.**
> Zhang Meili studies English. Her younger sister also studies English.

▶ 15.2.1

40.2 还/還 *hái* 'in addition, also'

还/還 **hái** is an adverb and is always followed by a [prepositional phrase +] verb or verb phrase. 还/還 **hái** overlaps in meaning with 也 **yě**, but they are not identical in function. 也 **yě** introduces any kind of new information. 还/還 **hái** only introduces new actions or situations.

还/還 **hái** can be used to introduce additional actions performed by the subject.

> 他要学中文，还要学日文。
> 他要學中文，還要學日文。
> **Tā yào xué Zhōngwén, hái yào xué Rìwén.**
> He wants to study Chinese, (and) he also wants to study Japanese.

> 他买了一条裤子，还买了一件衬衫。
> 他買了一條褲子，還買了一件襯衫。
> **Tā mǎi le yī tiáo kùzi, hái mǎi le yī jiàn chènshān.**
> He bought a pair of slacks, and in addition he bought a shirt.

而 *ér* 'and, but'

还/還 **hái** is also used to indicate the continuation of a situation.

> 他还在这儿。
> 他還在這兒。
> **Tā hái zài zhèr.**
> He is still here.

▶ 15.2.3, 39.2.2

40.3 还有/還有 *hái yǒu* 'in addition'

还有/還有 **hái yǒu** begins a new sentence or clause. It introduces additional information related to the topic of the conversation.

> 别忘了明天考试。还有，可以用字典。
> 別忘了明天考試。還有，可以用字典。
> **Bié wàng le míngtiān kǎo shì. Hái yǒu, kéyǐ yòng zìdiǎn.**
> Don't forget we have a test tomorrow. In addition, you can use a dictionary.

40.4 并且/並且 *bìngqiě* 'moreover'

并且/並且 **bìngqiě** begins a new sentence and provides additional information to support a preceding statement.

> 我觉得那个电影的故事没有意思。并且，太长。
> 我覺得那個電影的故事沒有意思。並且，太長。
> **Wǒ juéde nàge diànyǐng de gùshì méi yǒu yìsi. Bìngqiě, tài cháng.**
> I think that movie's story wasn't interesting. Moreover, it was too long.

40.5 再说/再說 *zài shuō* 'besides, moreover, to put it another way'

再说/再說 **zài shuō** begins a new sentence and presents information that continues and clarifies information presented in the preceding sentence.

> 我们很喜欢去中国旅行。再说在那儿也可以练习说中文。
> 我們很喜歡去中國旅行。再說在那兒也可以練習說中文。
> **Wǒmen hěn xǐhuan qù Zhōngguó lǚxíng. Zài shuō zài nàr yě kěyǐ liànxí shuō Zhōngwén.**
> We like to go to China to travel. Moreover, we can practice speaking Chinese there.

40.6 而 *ér* 'and, but'

而 **ér** joins adjectival verbs and introduces additional though contrasting information. It is literary in usage.

> 办奥运是一个艰辛而光荣的任务。
> 辦奧運是一個艱辛而光榮的任務。
> **Bàn ào yùn shì yī gè jiānxīn ér guāngróng de rènwu.**
> Organizing the Olympics is a difficult but prestigious responsibility.

EXPRESSING ADDITIONAL INFORMATION　　　　　　　　　　　　　　　**40.10**

40.7 和 *hé* and 跟 *gēn* 'and'

和 **hé** and 跟 **gēn** are conjunctions, and they are identical in meaning. They join nouns or noun phrases.

> 哥哥和弟弟都很像爸爸。
> **Gēge hé dìdi dōu hěn xiàng bàba.**
> Older brother and younger brother both resemble Dad.

For more on these and related conjunctions, see

▶ 16.1

跟 **gēn** is also a preposition.

▶ 14

40.8 不但 ... 而且 ... *bùdàn ... érqiě ...* 'not only ... but also ...'

This expression introduces related information about a subject. 不但 **bùdàn** and 而且 **érqiě** are always followed by a [prepositional phrase +] verb or verb phrase or clause.

> 那个饭馆，不但菜好吃，而且服务也很好。
> 那個飯館，不但菜好吃，而且服務也很好。
> **Nàge fànguǎn, bùdàn cài hǎo chī, érqiě fúwù yě hěn hǎo.**
> (As for) that restaurant, not only is the food good, but so is the service.
> (lit. 'That restaurant, not only is the food good, but the service is also good.')

不但 **bùdàn** can occur without 而且 **érqiě**. In the following examples, it occurs with the adverbs 还/還 **hái** and 也 **yě**.

> 哈佛大学不但录取了他，还给了他一笔很大的奖学金。
> 哈佛大學不但錄取了他，還給了他一筆很大的獎學金。
> **Hāfó dàxué bùdàn lùqǔ le tā, hái gěi le tā yī bǐ hěn dà de jiǎngxuéjīn.**
> Harvard University not only admitted him but also gave him a big scholarship.

> 那个饭馆，不但菜好吃，服务也很好。
> 那個飯館，不但菜好吃，服務也很好。
> **Nàge fànguǎn, bùdàn cài hǎo chī, fúwù yě hěn hǎo.**
> (As for) that restaurant, not only is the food good, so is the service.

40.9 又 ... 又 ... *yòu ... yòu ...* 'both ... and ...'

This expression is used to indicate two similar properties about a subject. Each instance of 又 **yòu** must be followed by an adjectival verb.

> 中国梨，又甜又脆，特别好吃。
> 中國梨，又甜又脆，特別好吃。
> **Zhōngguó lí, yòu tián yòu cuì, tèbié hǎo chī.**
> Chinese pears (are) both sweet and crisp. (They are) especially delicious.

▶ 10.8, 37.5, 43.4

40.10 除了 ... 以外 *chúle ... yǐwài* 'besides ...'

This expression can be used to introduce additional information or it can be used to introduce an exception. When it introduces additional information, the additional information is always related in meaning to the phrase that occurs between 除了 **chúle** and 以外 **yǐwài**.

另外 lìngwài 'in addition,' '(an)other' ### 40.11

The phrase that occurs between 除了 **chúle** and 以外 **yǐwài** can be a subject noun phrase, an object noun phrase, or a time phrase.

Subject noun phrase

> 除了妹妹以外，弟弟也想去中国留学。
> 除了妹妹以外，弟弟也想去中國留學。
> **Chúle mèimei yǐwài,** *dìdi* **yě xiǎng qù Zhōngguó liúxué.**
> Besides younger sister, *younger brother* also wants to go to China to study.

Object noun phrase

> 除了中国以外，弟弟也想去越南旅行。
> 除了中國以外，弟弟也想去越南旅行。
> **Chúle Zhōngguó yǐwài, dìdi yě xiǎng qù** *Yuènán* **lǚxíng.**
> Besides China, younger brother also wants to go to *Vietnam* to travel.

Time phrase

> 除了夏天以外，我们冬天也放假。
> 除了夏天以外，我們冬天也放假。
> **Chúle xiàtiān yǐwài, wǒmen** *dōngtiān* **yě fàng jià.**
> Besides the summer, we also have (a) vacation in the *winter*.

除了 **chúle** and 以外 **yǐwài** need not both occur in the same sentence. One or the other may be omitted.

> 除了中国，弟弟也想去越南旅行。
> 除了中國，弟弟也想去越南旅行。
> **Chúle Zhōngguó, dìdi yě xiǎng qù** *Yuènán* **lǚxíng.**
> Besides China, younger brother also wants to go to *Vietnam* to travel.

> 妹妹以外，弟弟也想去中国留学。
> 妹妹以外，弟弟也想去中國留學。
> **Mèimei yǐwài,** *dìdi* **yě xiǎng qù Zhōngguó liúxué.**
> Besides younger sister, *younger brother* also wants to go to China to study.

▶ 57.2.2

40.11 另外 lìngwài 'in addition,' '(an)other'

另外 **lìngwài** functions as an adverb, occurring before the verb phrase to indicate an additional action:

> 她买了裙子，另外(也)买了毛衣。
> 她買了裙子，另外(也)買了毛衣。
> **Tā mǎi le qúnzi, lìngwài (yě) mǎi le máoyī.**
> She bought a skirt, and in addition also bought a sweater.

It can also occur before a *number + classifier phrase + noun* to indicate 'another' (number of nouns).

> 那是另外一种方法。
> 那是另外一種方法。
> **Nà shì lìngwài yī zhǒng fāngfǎ.**
> That is another method.

> 我还有另外几个问题。
> 我還有另外幾個問題。
> **Wǒ hái yǒu lìngwài jǐ gè wèntí.**
> I still have several other questions.

41

Expressing contrast

41.1 Expressing contrast with paired connecting words

Mandarin uses the following paired connecting words to express contrast.

虽然...可是	or	虽然...但是	or	虽然...不过
雖然...可是		雖然...但是		雖然...不過
suīrán...kěshì		suīrán...dànshì		suīrán...bùguò
although...but		although...but		although...however

可是 kěshì and 但是 dànshì are identical in meaning and are interchangeable. 不过/不過 bùguò conveys a slightly stronger sense of contrariness to expectation.

The Chinese connecting words occur at the beginning of their clauses or right before the predicate. Both members of the pair can occur in the same sentence. Although English permits only a single contrast connector in a sentence, in order to best illustrate the usage of the Mandarin words, the English translations in this section translate each connector in the Mandarin sentences.

虽然他是中国人，可是他还喜欢吃日本菜。
雖然他是中國人，可是他還喜歡吃日本菜。
Suīrán tā shì Zhōngguó rén, kěshì tā hái xǐhuan chī Rìběn cài.
Although he is Chinese, but he still likes to eat Japanese food.

虽然他是中国人，但是他没去过北京。
雖然他是中國人，但是他沒去過北京。
Suīrán tā shì Zhōngguó rén, dànshì tā méi qùguo Běijīng.
Although he is Chinese, but he has never been to Beijing.

虽然他很有钱，可是我还不愿意嫁给他。
雖然他很有錢，可是我還不願意嫁給他。
Suīrán tā hěn yǒu qián, kěshì wǒ hái bù yuànyi jiàgěi tā.
Although he has a lot of money, but I'm still not willing to marry him.

41.1.1 The placement of connecting words

If the subjects of the two clauses are identical in reference and the second one is not omitted, 虽然/雖然 **suīrán** typically occurs before the subject.

虽然我哥哥已经三十岁了，但是他还没结婚。
雖然我哥哥已經三十歲了，但是他還沒結婚。
Suīrán wǒ gēge yǐjing sānshí suì le, dànshì tā hái méi jiéhūn.
Although my older brother is already 30 years old, but he still hasn't married.

When subjects of the two clauses in contrast sentences are identical in reference, the second one is sometimes omitted. When this is the case, the connecting word 虽然/雖然 **suīrán** typically occurs after the subject of the first clause.

Adverbs that indicate contrast

我哥哥虽然已经三十岁了可是还没结婚。
我哥哥雖然已經三十歲了可是還沒結婚。
Wǒ gēge suīrán yǐjing sānshí suì le kěshì hái méi jiéhūn.
Although my older brother is already 30 years old, but (he) still hasn't married.

41.1.2 Relative order of the clauses in contrast sentences

The position of the clauses is fixed. The 虽然/雖然 **suīrán** clause comes first. The 可是 **kěshì**, 但是 **dànshì**, or 不过/不過 **bùguò** clause comes second.

Say this	Not this
虽然他认识很多人， 可是他没有很好的朋友。 雖然他認識很多人， 可是他沒有很好的朋友。 **Suīrán tā rènshi hěn duō rén, kěshì tā méi yǒu hěn hǎo de péngyou.** Although he knows a lot of people, he doesn't have any very good friends.	*(可是)他没有很好的朋友， 虽然他认识很多人。 (可是)他沒有很好的朋友， 雖然他認識很多人。 **(Kěshì) tā méi yǒu hěn hǎo de péngyou, suīrán tā rènshi hěn duō rén.**
虽然他很小不过他胆子很大。 雖然他很小不過他膽子很大。 **Suīrán tā hěn xiǎo bùguò tā dǎnzi hěn dà.** Although he is little, he is very brave (his courage is big).	*他胆子很大虽然他很小。 他膽子很大雖然他很小。 **Tā dǎnzi hěn dà suīrán tā hěn xiǎo.**

41.1.3 Omission of the connecting words

虽然/雖然 **suīrán** can be freely omitted:

他很有钱，可是我还不愿意嫁给他。
他很有錢，可是我還不願意嫁給他。
Tā hěn yǒu qián, kěshì wǒ hái bù yuànyi jiàgěi tā.
He has a lot of money, but I'm still not willing to marry him.

可是 **kěshì**, 但是 **dànshì**, or 不过 **bùguò** can be omitted when the second clause contains the adverb 还/還 **hái** or an adverb that indicates contrast. Adverbs that indicate contrast are presented in 41.2.

虽然他很有钱，我还不愿意嫁给他。
雖然他很有錢，我還不願意嫁給他。
Suīrán tā hěn yǒu qián, wǒ hái bù yuànyi jiàgěi tā.
Although he has a lot of money, I'm still not willing to marry him.

41.2 Adverbs that indicate contrast

41.2.1 Adverbs that must occur before the [prepositional phrase +] verb or verb phrase

却 **què** 'in contrast'

却 **què** may occur with other contrast connectors.

虽然他很有钱，可是我却不愿意嫁给他。
雖然他很有錢，可是我卻不願意嫁給他。
Suīrán tā hěn yǒu qián, kěshì wǒ què bù yuànyi jiàgěi tā.
Although he is rich, I am not willing to marry him.

EXPRESSING CONTRAST

他很有钱，我却不愿意嫁给他。
他很有錢，我卻不願意嫁給他。
Tā hěn yǒuqián, wǒ què bù yuànyi jiàgěi tā.
He is rich, but I am still not willing to marry him.

倒是 *dǎoshì* 'contrary to one's expectations'

房子不大，布置得倒是很讲究。
房子不大，佈置得倒是很講究。
Fángzi bù dà, bùzhì de dǎoshì hěn jiǎngjiu.
The house isn't big, but it is fixed up really nicely.

41.2.2 Contrast adverbs that can occur at the beginning of a sentence or before a verb or verb phrase

不过/不過 *bùguò* 'however, nevertheless'

中国字很难写，不过语法比较简单。
中國字很難寫，不過語法比較簡單。
Zhōngguó zì hěn nán xiě, bùguò yǔfǎ bǐjiào jiǎndān.
Chinese characters are very difficult to write, but the grammar is relatively easy.

吃四川菜可以，不过不能太辣。
吃四川菜可以，不過不能太辣。
Chī Sìchuān cài kěyǐ, bùguò bù néng tài là.
It is okay (with me) to eat Sichuan food, but it can't be too hot.

然而 *rán'ér* 'however, nevertheless'

他虽然没考上大学，然而他并不灰心。
他雖然沒考上大學，然而他並不灰心。
Tā suīrán méi kǎoshàng dàxué, rán'ér tā bìng bù huīxīn.
Although he didn't pass the college entrance exam, he did not lose heart.

他小的时候体弱多病，然而长大后却非常强壮。
他小的時候體弱多病，然而長大後卻非常強壯。
Tā xiǎo de shíhòu tǐruò duō bìng, rán'ér zháng dà hòu què fēicháng qiáng zhuàng.
When he was young he was weak and sickly, but after he grew up he was extremely strong.

反而 *fǎn'ér* 'on the contrary, in contrast'

难的字他都记住了，容易的反而忘了。
難的字他都記住了，容易的反而忘了。
Nán de zì tā dōu jìzhù le, róngyì de fǎn'ér wàng le.
He remembers all of the difficult characters; the easy characters he forgets.

你不但不帮我忙，反而批评我。
你不但不幫我忙，反而批評我。
Nǐ búdàn bù bāng wǒ máng, fǎn'ér pīpíng wǒ.
Not only don't you help me, but on the contrary you criticize me.

反过来/反過來 *fǎnguòlái* 'conversely'

有的人认为学数学快的人学语言学也快，反过来也一样。
有的人認為學數學快的人學語言學也快，反過來也一樣。
Yǒu de rén rènwéi xué shùxué kuài de rén xué yǔyánxué yě kuài, fǎnguolái yě yīyàng.
Some people think that people who learn math quickly also learn linguistics quickly. The converse is also true. (The converse is the same.)

Qualifying a statement with an adjectival verb or stative verb

你们是好朋友，看到他做错了就应该跟他说。反过来，如果不跟他说就不是真正的朋友了。
你們是好朋友，看到他做錯了就應該跟他說。反過來，如果不跟他說就不是真正的朋友了。
Nǐmen shì hǎo péngyou, kàndào tā zuòcuò le jiù yìnggāi gēn tā shuō. Fǎnguolái, rúguǒ bù gēn tā shuō jiù bù shì zhēnzhèng de péngyou le.
You are good friends. When you see him do something wrong you should speak with him. Conversely, if you don't speak with him, you are not a real friend.

41.3 Qualifying a statement with an adjectival verb or stative verb

To qualify a statement involving an adjectival verb or stative verb, use this pattern:

AV/SV 是 **shì** AV/SV, 可是 **kěshì** . . .
　　　　　　　　　　但是 **dànshì**
　　　　　　　　　　不过/不過 **bùguò**
　　　　　　　　　　就是 **jiù shì**

'AV/SV all right, but . . .'

那个电影好是好，就是太长。(AV)
那個電影好是好，就是太長。
Nàge diànyǐng hǎo shì hǎo, jiù shì tài cháng.
That movie is *good all right*, but it is too long.

那双鞋子贵是贵，可是我还想买。(AV)
那雙鞋子貴是貴，可是我還想買。
Nà shuāng xiézi guì shì guì, kěshì wǒ hái xiǎng mǎi.
That pair of shoes is expensive *all right*, but I still want to buy them.

我喜欢是喜欢他，就是他有一点太无聊。(SV)
我喜歡是喜歡他，就是他有一點太無聊。
Wǒ xǐhuan shì xǐhuan tā, jiù shì tā yǒu yīdiǎn tài wúliáo.
I *like him all right*, he's just a little boring.

42

Expressing sequence

42.1 Expressing the relationship 'before'

42.1.1 The structure of the 以前 yǐqián 'before' sentence

以前 **yǐqián** is used to indicate the relationship 'before one event occurs, another event occurs.'

event₁ 以前 **yǐqián**, event₂
before event₁, event₂

> 我上大学以前，想去澳大利亚旅游。
> 我上大學以前，想去澳大利亞旅遊。
> **Wǒ shàng dàxué yǐqián, xiǎng qù Àodàlìyà lǚyóu.**
> Before I attend university, I want to go to Australia to travel.

> 妈妈上班以前，都吃早饭。
> 媽媽上班以前，都吃早飯。
> **Māma shàng bān yǐqián, dōu chī zǎofàn.**
> Before Mom goes to work, she always eats breakfast.

To indicate that a sequence occurred in the past, follow the verb of the second clause with perfective 了 **le**.

> 我来中国以前，在日本住了一年。
> 我來中國以前，在日本住了一年。
> **Wǒ lái Zhōngguó yǐqián, zài Rìběn zhù le yīnián.**
> Before I came to China, I lived in Japan for a year.

NOTE The more literary form of 以前 **yǐqián** is 之前 **zhīqián**.

▶ 9.6

42.1.2 Comparing 以前 yǐqián with 'before'

以前 **yǐqián** signals the same relationship of sequence as the English word 'before.' However, there are important differences between 以前 **yǐqián** and 'before.'

- 以前 **yǐqián** occurs at the end of the first clause:

    妈妈上班以前
    妈妈上班以前
    Māma shàng bān *yǐqián*

'Before' occurs at the beginning of the first clause:

before Mom goes to work

Expressing the relationship 'after' in a single sentence

- In Mandarin, the clause that ends with 以前 **yǐqián** must come first in the sentence. In English, the order of the clauses in the 'before' sentence is not fixed. Either can come first in the sentence. Compare the following sentences.

Good English	Good Mandarin
Before Mom went to work she ate breakfast.	妈妈上班以前吃了早饭。 媽媽上班以前吃了早飯。 **Māma shàng bān yǐqián** chī le zǎofàn.

Good English	Bad Mandarin
Mom ate breakfast *before* she went to work.	*妈妈吃了早饭上班以前。 媽媽吃了早飯上班以前。 **Māma chī le zǎofàn** *shàng bān yǐqián.*

42.2 Expressing the relationship 'after' in a single sentence

In Mandarin, the relationship of 'after' is expressed using some combination of the word 以后/以後 **yǐhòu** 'after,' perfective 了 **le**, and adverbs, usually 就 **jiù** or 才 **cái**.

These markers of sequence can occur together in a single sentence to express the relationship of sequence, or they can occur independently.

Native speakers of Mandarin differ in their preference for the use of these markers of sequence.

▶ 6.9, 37.2, 42.2.2

42.2.1 Indicating sequence with 以后/以後 *yǐhòu* 'after'

以后/以後 **yǐhòu** 'after' is used to express the following relationship: 'after an event occurs, another event occurs.'

event₁ 以后/以後 **yǐhòu**, event₂
after event₁, event₂

我们吃了饭以后，就去看电影。
我們吃了飯以後，就去看電影。
Wǒmen chī le fàn *yǐhòu*, jiù qù kàn diànyǐng.
After we eat, we will go to a movie.

我下了课以后，就回家。
我下了課以後，就回家。
Wǒ xià le kè *yǐhòu*, jiù huí jiā.
After I get out of class, I go home.

孩子睡了觉以后，父母就看电视。
孩子睡了覺以後，父母就看電視。
Háizi shuì le jiào *yǐhòu*, fùmǔ jiù kàn diànshì.
After the children go to sleep, the parents watch television.

To signal that a sequence occurred in the past, follow the verb of the second clause with 了 **le**, using the guidelines for the placement of perfective 了 **le** presented in Chapter 17.

▶ 17.1.1.1

EXPRESSING SEQUENCE

If the verb takes a one-syllable object, 了 **le** may also follow the object.

> 他吃了饭<u>以后</u>就看电视了。
> 他吃了飯<u>以後</u>就看電視了。
> **Tā chī le fàn** *yǐhòu* **jiù kàn diànshì le.**
> *After* he ate, he watched television.

> 他吃了晚饭<u>以后</u>就喝了一杯茶。
> 他吃了晚飯<u>以後</u>就喝了一杯茶。
> **Tā chī le wǎnfàn** *yǐhòu* **jiù hē le yī bēi chá.**
> *After* he ate dinner, he drank a cup of tea.

以后/以後 **yǐhòu** signals the same relationship of sequence as the English word 'after.' However, there are important differences between 以后/以後 **yǐhòu** and 'after.'

- 以后/以後 **yǐhòu** occurs at the end of the first clause:

    > 我下了课<u>以后</u>
    > 我下了課<u>以後</u>
    > **wǒ xià le kè** *yǐhòu*

    'After' occurs at the beginning of the clause:

    > *after* I get out of class

- In Mandarin, the clause that ends with 以后/以後 **yǐhòu** must come first in the sentence. In English, the order of the clauses in the 'after' sentence is not fixed. Either can come first in the sentence. Compare the following sentences.

Good English	Good Mandarin
After I get out of class, I go home.	我下了课以后回家。 我下了課以後回家。 **Wǒ xià le kè yǐhòu huí jiā.**

Good English	Bad Mandarin
I go home *after I get out of class*.	*我回家下了课以后。 我回家下了課以後。 **Wǒ huí jiā xià le kè yǐhòu.**

NOTE The more literary form of 以后/以後 **yǐhòu** is 之后/之後 **zhīhòu**.

▶ 9.6

42.2.2 Adverbs that occur in sequence sentences

42.2.2.1 就 *jiù*

The adverb 就 **jiù** has several functions. One function is to signal a relationship of sequence between events that occur in a series. The relationship of sequence indicated by 就 **jiù** reinforces the meaning of sequence indicated by 以后/以後 **yǐhòu**. Therefore, 就 **jiù** often occurs with 以后/以後 **yǐhòu** in sequence sentences.

> 我学了中国历史以后就想去中国。
> 我學了中國歷史以後就想去中國。
> **Wǒ xué le Zhōngguó lìshǐ yǐhòu jiù xiǎng qù Zhōngguó.**
> After I studied Chinese history, I wanted to go to China.

The meaning of 就 **jiù** is related to the meaning of 以后/以後 **yǐhòu**, but the two words are independent. 就 **jiù** may occur without 以后/以後 **yǐhòu**, and 以后/以後 **yǐhòu** may occur without 就 **jiù**.

Expressing the relationship 'after' in a single sentence | 42.2

The following two sentences, one with 就 **jiù** and the other with 以后/以後 **yǐhòu**, are equivalent in meaning. Compare them to the sentence above in which 就 **jiù** and 以后/以後 **yǐhòu** both occur.

> 我学了中国历史就想去中国。
> 我學了中國歷史就想去中國。
> **Wǒ xué le Zhōngguó lìshǐ jiù xiǎng qù Zhōngguó.**
> After I studied Chinese history I wanted to go to China.

> 我学了中国历史以后想去中国。
> 我學了中國歷史以後想去中國。
> **Wǒ xué le Zhōngguó lìshǐ yǐhòu xiǎng qù Zhōngguó.**
> After I studied Chinese history I wanted to go to China.

▶ 15.2.4

42.2.2.2 Indicating that one event happens 'only after' another event: sequence with the adverb 才 *cái*

To indicate that some event happens 'only after' another event, use the adverb 才 **cái** before the second verb of a sequence. 才 **cái** can occur with 以后/以後 **yǐhòu** and 了 **le**. 才 **cái** and 就 **jiù** cannot both occur before the same verb.

> 她在中国住了两年才会说中国话。
> 她在中國住了兩年才會說中國話。
> **Tā zài Zhōngguó zhù le liǎng nián cái huì shuō Zhōngguó huà.**
> She lived in China for two years and only then was able to speak Chinese.
> (After she lived in China for two years, only then was she able to speak Chinese.)

> 你长大了以后才懂这种事情。
> 你長大了以後才懂這種事情。
> **Nǐ zhǎng dà le yǐhòu cái dǒng zhè zhǒng shìqing.**
> After you grow up, only then will you understand this kind of situation.

▶ 15.2.6

Pay attention to the difference between the adverbs 才 **cái** and 就 **jiù** in the following sentences. Since 就 **jiù** indicates simple sequence, it is used much more frequently than 才 **cái**. For many speakers of Mandarin, a verb phrase with 才 **cái** cannot include 了 **le**.

就 *jiù*	才 *cái*
他吃了药就好了。 他吃了藥就好了。 **Tā chī le yào jiù hǎo le.** After he ate the medicine, he recovered.	他吃了药才好(了)。 他吃了藥才好(了)。 **Tā chī le yào cái hǎo (le).** Only after he ate the medicine did he recover. (He ate the medicine and only then recovered.)
就 *jiù*	才 *cái*
他开了空调就舒服了。 他開了空調就舒服了。 **Tā kāi le kōngtiáo jiù shūfu le.** After he turned on the air conditioner, he was comfortable.	他开了空调才舒服。 他開了空調才舒服。 **Tā kāi le kōngtiáo cái shūfu.** Only after he turned on the air conditioner was he comfortable. (He turned on the air conditioner and only then was comfortable.)

▶ 37.2

EXPRESSING SEQUENCE

42.2.2.3 便 *biàn*

便 **biàn**, like 就 **jiù**, is used to reinforce a relationship of sequence between two events.

> 每天一下课他便到图书馆去工作。
> 每天一下課他便到圖書館去工作。
> **Měitiān yī xià kè tā biàn dào túshūguǎn qù gōngzuò.**
> Every day, as soon as he gets out of class he goes to the library to work.

便 **biàn** is largely restricted to formal, literary contexts.

> 自从毕业以后，我们便没有来往。
> 自從畢業以後，我們便沒有來往。
> **Zìcóng bìyè yǐhòu, wǒmen biàn méi yǒu láiwǎng.**
> Since we've graduated, we haven't had any contact.

42.2.3 Indicating sequence with perfective 了 *le*

Like the adverbs 就 **jiù**, 才 **cái**, and 便 **biàn**, the verb suffix 了 **le** can be used to signal a relationship of sequence between two events. 了 **le** is optional, but when it occurs, it normally follows the first verb in a series of verb phrases. Notice that 就 **jiù** or 才 **cái** often occurs with 了 **le** and 以后/以後 **yǐhòu** in sequence sentences that indicate the relationship 'after.'

> 她买了照相机以后就照了很多照片。
> 她買了照相機以後就照了很多照片。
> **Tā mǎi le zhàoxiàngjī yǐhòu jiù zhào le hěn duō zhàopiàn.**
> After she bought a camera, she took a lot of pictures.

> 我做完了功课以后才睡觉。
> 我做完了功課以後才睡覺。
> **Wǒ zuòwán le gōngkè yǐhòu cái shuì jiào.**
> Only after I finish my homework will I go to sleep.
> (I will finish my homework and only then go to sleep.)

Follow the guidelines for the placement of perfective 了 **le** presented in Chapter 17.

▶ 17.1.1.1, 37.2

42.2.4 Indicating 'after' in a single sentence: a summary of the use of 以后/以後 *yǐhòu*, 了 *le*, and sequence adverbs

- 以后/以後 **yǐhòu**, 了 **le**, and sequence adverbs all signal a sequence of events within a single sentence.
- Sequence sentences can contain any combination of 以后/以後 **yǐhòu**, 了 **le**, and sequence adverbs.
- None of these markers of sequence is obligatory, and native speakers of Mandarin differ in their preferences in using them.
- Events that are related in terms of sequence need not have any of these sequence markers.

> 我每天下课回家。
> 我每天下課回家。
> **Wǒ měitiān xià kè huí jiā.**
> Every day, after I get out of class I return home.
> (Every day I get out of class and return home.)

Indicating that one event happens first and another event happens afterwards — **42.3**

42.3 Indicating that one event happens first and another event happens afterwards

The following pairs of adverbs are used to indicate that one event happens first and another event happens afterwards. The adverbs always occur before [prepositional phrases +] verb phrases. The order of the adverbs and their following verb phrases is fixed. They are often used when giving instructions and describing processes.

42.3.1 Indicating the relationship 'first . . . then . . .'

The following pairs of adverbs are commonly used to indicate the relationship 'first . . . then . . .'

先 **xiān** VP$_1$ 再 **zài** VP$_2$
first VP$_1$ then VP$_2$

> 你先买票，再上公共汽车。
> 你先買票，再上公共汽車。
> **Nǐ xiān mǎi piào, zài shàng gōnggòng qì chē.**
> You first buy a ticket, then get on the bus.

先 **xiān** VP$_1$ 然后/然後 **ránhòu** VP$_2$
first VP$_1$ then/afterwards VP$_2$

> 我们得先去换钱，然后去买东西。
> 我們得先去換錢，然後去買東西。
> **Wǒmen děi xiān qù huàn qián, ránhòu qù mǎi dōngxi.**
> We have to first change money and then go shopping.

先 **xiān** VP$_1$ 以后/以後 **yǐhòu** VP$_2$
first VP$_1$ then/afterwards VP$_2$

> 我们先吃饭，以后讨论那件事情。
> 我們先吃飯，以後討論那件事情。
> **Wǒmen xiān chī fàn, yǐhòu tǎolùn nà jiàn shìqing.**
> We will eat first and discuss this matter afterwards.

42.3.2 Indicating the relationship 'first . . . only then . . .'

To indicate that some event occurs 'only after' another event, say:

先 **xiān** VP$_1$ 才 **cái** VP$_2$
first VP$_1$ only then VP$_2$

> 你先买票，才上公共汽车。
> 你先買票，才上公共汽車。
> **Nǐ xiān mǎi piào, cái shàng gōnggòng qìchē.**
> You first buy a ticket and only then get on the bus.

▶ 15.2.6

EXPRESSING SEQUENCE

42.3.3 Indicating the relationship 'as soon as ... then ...'

To indicate that some event occurs 'as soon as' another event occurs, say:

一 **yī** VP₁ 就 **jiù** VP₂
as soon as VP₁ then VP₂

> 我们一到北京，就去爬长城。
> 我們一到北京，就去爬長城。
> **Wǒmen yī dào Běijīng, jiù qù pá chángchéng.**
> As soon as we get to Beijing we will go climb the Great Wall.

NOTE When 一 **yī** occurs immediately before a [prepositional phrase +] verb or verb phrase, it always means 'as soon as.' When 一 **yī** occurs immediately before a classifier, it is always the number 'one.'

42.4 Indicating 'afterwards' in a separate sentence

Mandarin has a number of *sentence adverbs*, adverbs that occur at the beginning of a sentence, to introduce an event that happens afterwards. The most common are 以后/以後 **yǐhòu**, 然后/然後 **ránhòu**, and 后来/後來 **hòulái**.

以后/以後 **yǐhòu** *'afterwards, later'*
以后/以後 **yǐhòu** is the most neutral of the sentence adverbs used to indicate 'afterwards.'

> 请先喝点茶吧！以后我们出去吃晚饭。
> 請先喝點茶吧！以後我們出去吃晚飯。
> **Qǐng xiān hē diǎn chá ba! Yǐhòu wǒmen chūqu chī wǎnfàn.**
> Drink a little tea first. Afterwards we will go out to eat dinner.

然后/然後 **ránhòu** *'afterwards/after that'*
然后/然後 **ránhòu** can only be used to indicate sequence between two events that occur in close temporal sequence to each other.

> 我们看了电影。然后我们去了咖啡店喝咖啡。
> 我們看了電影。然後我們去了咖啡店喝咖啡。
> **Wǒmen kàn le diànyǐng. Ránhòu wǒmen qù le kāfēi diàn hē kāfēi.**
> We saw a movie. Afterwards, we went to a coffee shop and drank coffee.

后来/後來 **hòulái** *'afterwards'*
后来/後來 **hòulái** can only be used to indicate sequence between two events that have already occurred.

> 我昨天早上考了中文。后来我回宿舍睡觉了。
> 我昨天早上考了中文。後來我回宿舍睡覺了。
> **Wǒ zuótiān zǎoshang kǎo le Zhōngwén. Hòulái wǒ huí sùshè shuì jiào le.**
> Yesterday morning I had a Chinese test. Afterwards I went back to the dormitory and went to sleep.

42.5 Comparing 以前 *yǐqián* 'before' with 以后/以後 *yǐhòu* 'after'

In some ways, the uses of 以前 **yǐqián** 'before' and 以后/以後 **yǐhòu** 'after' are parallel. Both must occur in the first clause of a sequence sentence, and both words occur at the end of their clause.

However, the words are different in their occurrence with perfective 了 **le**. The perfective 了 **le** may occur in the 以后/以後 **yǐhòu** clause but it may not occur in the 以前 **yǐqián** clause. Compare these sentences.

Comparing 以前 *yǐqián* 'before' **with** 以后/以後 *yǐhòu* 'after'   42.5

Say this	Not this
我去中国以前学了两年的中文。 我去中國以前學了兩年的中文。 **Wǒ qù Zhōngguó yǐqián xué le liǎng nián de Zhōngwén.** Before I went to China I studied two years of Chinese.	*我去了中国以前学了两年的中文。 我去了中國以前學了兩年的中文。 **Wǒ qù le Zhōngguó yǐqián xué le liǎng nián de Zhōngwén.**
他考试以前复习功课了。 他考試以前復習功課了。 **Tā kǎo shì yǐqián fùxí gōngkè le.** Before he took the test he reviewed the lessons.	*他考试了以前复习了功课。 他考試了以前復習了功課。 **Tā kǎo shì le yǐqián fùxí le gōngkè.**

For many Mandarin speakers, the sequence use of 就 **jiù** is also not acceptable in 以前 **yǐqián** sentences. For these speakers, if 就 **jiù** occurs in an 以前 **yǐqián** sentence, it has the sense of 'only,' and not of sequence.

我去中国以前就学了两年的中文。
我去中國以前就學了兩年的中文。
Wǒ qù Zhōngguó yǐqián *jiù* xué le liǎng nián de Zhōngwén.
Before I went to China I *only* studied two years of Chinese.

43

Expressing simultaneous situations

43.1 Indicating that one situation is the background for another situation

To indicate that one situation is the background for another situation, say:

S₁ 的时候 S₂/S₁ 的時候 S₂
S₁ **de shíhou** S₂
while/when S₁, S₂

S₁ and S₂ can be actions or states.

S₁ and S₂ are states

我小的时候，生活很苦。
我小的時候，生活很苦。
Wǒ xiǎo de shíhou, shēnghuó hěn kǔ.
When I was young, life was very hard (bitter).

S₁ and S₂ are actions

我看书的时候，常听音乐。
我看書的時候，常聽音樂。
Wǒ kàn shū de shíhou, cháng tīng yīnyuè.
When I read, I often listen to music.

的时候/的時候 **de shíhou** can be used when one situation overlaps with the start of another one.

你来的时候，我们正在上课。
你來的時候，我們正在上課。
Nǐ lái de shíhou, wǒmen zhèngzài shàng kè.
When you arrived, we were in class.

However, 的时候/的時候 **de shíhou** cannot be used when the relationship between S₁ and S₂ is that of sequence. When S₁ and S₂ are related in terms of sequence, use 以后/以後 **yǐhòu**.

▶ 42.2

The events in the following sentence are related in terms of sequence. Therefore, they should be connected by 以后/以後 **yǐhòu** 'after' and not 的时候/的時候 **de shíhou** 'when.' Notice that in English, 'when' can be used with sequential situations or with simultaneous situations.

Say this	Not this
你吃(完)了晚饭以后请给我打电话。 你吃(完)了晚飯以後請給我打電話。 **Nǐ chī(wán) le wǎnfàn yǐhòu qǐng gěi wǒ dǎ diànhuà.** After (when) you finish dinner, please call me.	*你吃完了晚饭的时候请给我打电话。 你吃完了晚飯的時候請給我打電話。 **Nǐ chīwán le wán fàn de shíhou qǐng gěi wǒ dǎ diànhuà.**

Describing a subject in terms of two qualities that exist at the same time | **43.4**

43.2 Indicating that two actions occur at the same time

43.2.1 Focusing on each action separately

(subject) 一边/邊 VP₁ 一边/邊 VP₂
(subject) **yībiān** VP₁ **yībiān** VP₂
subject does both VP₁ and VP₂ at the same time

一边/一邊 **yībiān** must occur before each verb phrase:

> 我儿子一边听音乐，一边作功课。
> 我兒子一邊聽音樂，一邊作功課。
> **Wǒ érzi yìbiān tīng yīnyuè, yìbiān zuò gōngkè.**
> My son listens to music and does homework at the same time.

43.2.2 Focusing on the shared time

(subject) 同时/同時 VP₁ VP₂
(subject) **tóngshí** VP₁ VP₂
subject simultaneously does VP₁ and VP₂

同时/同時 **tóngshí** occurs before the list of actions that occur at the same time:

> 你为什么同时听音乐作功课？
> 你為甚麼同時聽音樂作功課？
> **Nǐ wèi shénme tóngshí tīng yīnyuè zuò gōngkè?**
> Why do you listen to music and do your homework at the same time?

43.3 Indicating that two actions occur in the same time frame

To indicate that two actions occur in the same time frame, though not necessarily at the same time, say:

> 又 action VP₁ 又 action VP₂
> **yòu** VP₁ **yòu** VP₂
> (subject) does both VP₁ and VP₂

> 他特别忙，又念书，又做事。
> **Tā tèbié máng, yòu niàn shū, yòu zuò shì.**
> He is really busy. He both studies and has a job.

43.4 Describing a subject in terms of two qualities that exist at the same time

(subject) 又 AV/SV₁ 又 AV/SV₂
(subject) **yòu** AV/SV₁ **yòu** AV/SV₂
(subject) is both AV/SV₁ and AV/SV₂

> 那个男的又高又大。
> 那個男的又高又大。
> **Nàge nán de yòu gāo yòu dà.**
> That guy is both tall and big.

▶ 10.8, 40.9

EXPRESSING SIMULTANEOUS SITUATIONS

43.5 Indicating that a situation is reached at a specific point in time

到 dào + time phrase/S$_1$, S$_2$
when/by that time phrase/S$_1$, S$_2$

> 到六月，我就在这儿教了十五年书了。
> 到六月，我就在這兒教了十五年書了。
> **Dào liù yuè, wǒ jiù zài zhèr jiào le shíwǔ nián shū le.**
> In June, I will have been teaching here for fifteen years.

> 到三月，我就三十岁了。
> 到三月，我就三十歲了。
> **Dào sānyuè, wǒ jiù sānshí suì le.**
> When March comes, I will be 30.

等 děng + S$_1$, S$_2$
when/by the time that S$_1$, S$_2$

> 等你学完这本书，你就学了很多中文了。
> 等你學完這本書，你就學了很多中文了。
> **Děng nǐ xuéwán zhè běn shū, nǐ jiù xué le hěn duō Zhōngwén le.**
> By the time you finish this book, you will have studied a lot of Chinese.

> 等菜来了我们都饿死了。
> 等菜來了我們都餓死了。
> **Děng cài lái le wǒmen dōu è sǐ le.**
> By the time the food arrived, we were all starving to death.

等到 děngdào + S$_1$, S$_2$
when/by the time that S$_1$, S$_2$

> 等到你毕业，你的中国话一定会说得很好。
> 等到你畢業，你的中國話一定會說得很好。
> **Děngdào nǐ bìyè, nǐ de Zhōngguó huà yīdìng huì shuō de hěn hǎo.**
> By the time you graduate, your spoken Chinese will be very good.

> 等到爸爸回家了，孩子都睡觉了。
> 等到爸爸回家了，孩子都睡覺了。
> **Děngdào bàba huí jiā le, háizi dōu shuì jiào le.**
> By the time Dad returned home, the children were already asleep.

43.6 Presenting simultaneous situations

To present two parallel circumstances that exist at the same time and describe the same situation, say:

一方面 S$_1$ 一方面 S$_2$
yī fāngmiàn S$_1$ **yī fāngmiàn** S$_2$
on the one hand S$_1$, on the other hand S$_2$

> 她一定考得上大学。一方面她很聪明，一方面她很用功。
> 她一定考得上大學。一方面她很聰明，一方面她很用功。
> **Tā yīdìng kǎodeshàng dàxué. Yīfāngmiàn tā hěn cōngming, yīfāngmiàn tā hěn yònggōng.**
> She will certainly pass the college entrance exam. On the one hand, she is very smart; on the other hand, she is very hardworking.

> 他的体重不会减轻。一方面，他吃得太多，一方面他不愿意运动。
> 他的體重不會減輕。一方面，他吃得太多，一方面他不願意運動。
> **Tā de tǐzhòng bù huì jiǎnqīng. Yīfāngmiàn, tā chī de tài duō, yīfāngmiàn tā bù yuànyi yùndòng.**
> He can't lose weight. On the one hand, he eats too much; on the other hand, he isn't willing to exercise.

44

Expressing cause and effect or reason and result

44.1 Expressing cause and effect or reason and result in a single sentence

Mandarin uses the paired connecting words 因为/因為 **yīnwei** 'because/since'... 所以 **suǒyǐ** 'therefore'... to express cause and effect or reason and result. 因为/因為 **yīnwei** and 所以 **suǒyǐ** occur at the beginning of their clauses or right before the predicate. They can occur in the same sentence.

因为他没有很多钱，所以他不随便买东西。
因為他沒有很多錢，所以他不隨便買東西。
Yīnwei tā méi yǒu hěn duō qián, suǒyǐ tā bù suíbiàn mǎi dōngxi.
Because he doesn't have a lot of money, therefore he doesn't casually buy things.

44.1.1 Omission of subjects in 因为/因為 *yīnwei*... 所以 *suǒyǐ*... sentences

When the subjects of the 因为/因為 **yīnwei** clause and the 所以 **suǒyǐ** clause are identical, the subject is often omitted in the second (所以 **suǒyǐ**) clause. In that case, 因为/因為 **yīnwei** is usually placed after the subject of the first clause.

我最近因为忙，所以没给你打电话。
我最近因為忙，所以沒給你打電話。
Wǒ zuìjìn yīnwei máng, suǒyǐ méi gěi nǐ dǎ diànhuà.
Because I have been busy recently, I haven't called you.

When the subjects of the two clauses are identical, the subject may also be omitted from the first clause. This sentence is acceptable with or without 所以 **suǒyǐ**.

因为有事，(所以)王先生请假了。
因為有事，(所以)王先生請假了。
Yīnwei yǒu shì, (suǒyǐ) Wáng xiānsheng qǐng jià le.
Because he had business to attend to, Mr. Wang asked for time off.

44.1.2 Relative order of the 因为/因為 *yīnwei* and 所以 *suǒyǐ* clauses

The position of the 所以 **suǒyǐ** clause is fixed. It must come second in the sentence, after a clause that introduces the cause.

Say this

因为他是中国人，所以他会说中国话。
因為他是中國人，所以他會說中國話。
Yīnwei tā shì Zhōngguó rén, suǒyǐ tā huì shuō Zhōngguó huà.
Because he is Chinese, (*therefore*) he can speak Chinese.

Not this

*所以他会说中国话，因为他是中国人
 所以他會說中國話，因為他是中國人
Suǒyǐ tā huì shuō Zhōngguó huà, yīnwei tā shì Zhōngguó rén.

EXPRESSING CAUSE AND EFFECT OR REASON AND RESULT

However, the 因为/因為 **yīnwei** clause may occur either first or second in the sentence. As the sentences above illustrate, when 因为/因為 **yīnwei** occurs in the second clause, 所以 **suǒyǐ** cannot be included in the first clause.

> 他会说中国话，因为他是中国人。
> 他會說中國話，因為他是中國人。
> **Tā huì shuō Zhōngguó huà, yīnwei tā shì Zhōngguó rén.**
> He can speak Chinese *because* he is Chinese.

> 王先生请假了，因为他有事。
> 王先生請假了，因為他有事。
> **Wáng xiānsheng qǐng jià le, *yīnwei* tā yǒu shì.**
> Mr. Wang asked for time off *because* he had a matter (to attend to).

44.1.3 Omission of the connecting words

Although you can include 因为/因為 **yīnwei** and 所以 **suǒyǐ** in the same sentence, it is often possible to have only 因为/因為 **yīnwei** or only 所以 **suǒyǐ** in a cause and effect sentence.

所以 *suǒyǐ* and not 因为/因為 *yīnwei*

> 我最近很忙，所以没给你打电话。
> 我最近很忙，所以沒給你打電話。
> **Wǒ zuì jìn hěn máng, suǒyǐ méi gěi nǐ dǎ diànhuà.**
> I have been very busy recently, so I haven't called you.

因为/因為 *yīnwei* and not 所以 *suǒyǐ*

> 他因为病了，没来上课。
> 他因為病了，沒來上課。
> **Tā yīnwei bìng le, méi lái shàng kè.**
> Because he was sick, he didn't come to class.

44.2 Introducing the cause or reason

The following expressions introduce a cause or reason for some situation.

> 因为 (noun phrase) 的关系，...
> 因為 (noun phrase) 的關係，...
> **yīnwei (noun phrase) de guānxi, ...**
> because of/due to (noun phrase), ...

> 因为他朋友的关系，汽车的价格减少了。
> 因為他朋友的關係，汽車的價格減少了。
> **Yīnwei tā péngyou *de guānxi*, qìchē de jiàgé jiǎnshǎo le.**
> *Because of* his friend, the price of the car was reduced.

(noun phrase)(之)所以 situation₁, 是因为 situation₂
(noun phrase)(之)所以 situation₁, 是因為 situation₂
(noun phrase)**(zhī) suǒyǐ** situation₁, **shì yīnwei** situation₂
(nouns phrase's) reason for situation₁ is situation₂

> 有些人之所以对工作不认真，是因为缺乏责任感。
> 有些人之所以對工作不認真，是因為缺乏責任感。
> **Yǒu xiē rén *zhī suǒyǐ* duì gōngzuò bù rènzhēn, *shì yīnwei* quēfá zérèngǎn.**
> *The reason why* some people don't work conscientiously *is because* they lack a sense of responsibility.

Introducing the cause or reason   44.2

> 我之所以不去美国，是因为身体不好。
> 我之所以不去美國，是因為身體不好。
> **Wǒ zhī suǒyǐ bù qù Měiguó, shì yīnwei shēntǐ bù hǎo.**
> *The reason why* I am not going to America *is that* my health isn't good.

由于/由於 (situation)
yóu yú (situation)
owing to, due to, because of, as a result of (situation)

由于/由於 **yóu yú** may be placed before or after the subject.

> 由于我的粗心大意，这次考试的成绩不好。
> 由於我的粗心大意，這次考試的成績不好。
> *Yóuyú* wǒ de cūxīn dàyì, zhè cì kǎoshì de chéngjī bù hǎo.
> *Because of* my carelessness, my grade on this exam was not good.

> 他由于不了解情况，造成了一个大错误。
> 他由於不瞭解情況，造成了一個大錯誤。
> Tā *yóuyú* bù liáojiě qíngkuàng, zàochéng le yī gè dà cuòwù.
> *Because* he did not understand the situation, he made a big mistake.

The inclusion of 所以 **suǒyǐ** 'therefore,' or 因而 **yīn'ér** 'therefore,' etc., makes the relationship between cause and effect or reason and result clearer.

由于/由於 (situation₁), 所以 (situation₂)
yóu yú (situation₁), **suǒyǐ** (situation₂)

or

由于/由於 (situation₁), 因而 (situation₂)
yóu yú (situation₁), **yīn'ér** (situation₂)
due to/because of (situation₁), therefore (situation₂)

> 由于买不到票，所以我们上不了火车。
> 由於買不到票，所以我們上不了火車。
> *Yóuyú* mǎibudào piào, *suǒyǐ* wǒmen shàngbuliǎo huǒchē.
> *Because* we could not get tickets, we couldn't get on the train.

> 由于各自坚持自己的意见，因而无法达成协议。
> 由於各自堅持自己的意見，因而無法達成協議。
> *Yóuyú* gèzì jiānchí zìjǐ de yìjiàn, *yīn'ér* wú fǎ dáchéng xiéyì.
> *Owing to the fact* that everyone held onto his own opinion, there was no way to reach an agreement.

The result may be stated first in the sentence. The reason is then introduced with 由于/由於 **yóu yú**. 由于/由於 **yóu yú** must be preceded by 是 **shì**:

(situation₂) 是由于/由於 (situation₁)
(situation₂) **shì yóu yú** (situation₁)
situation₂ is because of situation₁

> 碰到一点儿困难就退缩，这都是由于你缺乏信心。
> 碰到一點兒困難就退縮，這都是由於你缺乏信心。
> **Pèngdào yīdiǎr kùnnan jiù tuìsuō, zhè dōu shì *yóuyú* nǐ quēfá xìnxīn.**
> (If) you retreat when you meet a little difficulty, this is *because of* your lack of confidence.

EXPRESSING CAUSE AND EFFECT OR REASON AND RESULT

为了/為了 **wéi le** can be used to identify some noun phrase as the reason for performing some action.

为了/為了 (noun phrase)
wéi le (noun phrase)
because of/for the sake of (noun phrase)

> 我这样做，完全是为了你。
> 我這樣做，完全是為了你。
> **Wǒ zhèyàng zuò, wánquán shì *wéi le* nǐ.**
> My doing this is completely *for* you. (I'm doing this all *for* you.)

44.3 Introducing the effect or result

In this pattern, 为了/為了 **wéi le** introduces a desired effect or result.

为了 situation 起见 . . . ,
為了 situation 起見 . . . ,
wéi le situation **qǐjiàn**, . . .
in order to, for the purpose of (obtaining the situation)

> 为了安全起见，绝对禁止司机酒后开车。
> 為了安全起見，絕對禁止司機酒後開車。
> ***Wéi le** ānquán **qǐjiàn**, juéduì jìnzhǐ sījī jiǔ hòu kāi chē.*
> *For the sake of* safety, drivers are absolutely forbidden to drink and drive.

44.4 Inquiring about cause or reason

To inquire about the cause or reason for something, use the following expressions:

为什么/為甚麼? **wèi shénme?** *'why?'*
为什么/為甚麼 **wèi shénme** is the most common and neutral expression used to inquire about the cause or reason for something.

> 你昨天为什么没来上课？
> 你昨天為甚麼沒來上課？
> **Nǐ zuótiān *wèi shénme* méi lái shàng kè?**
> *Why* didn't you come to class yesterday?

> 你为什么还在这儿？
> 你為甚麼還在這兒？
> **Nǐ *wèi shénme* hái zài zhèr?**
> *Why* are you still here?

怎么?/怎麼? **zěnme?** *'why? how come?'*
怎么/怎麼 **zěnme** is used to inquire about the reason for something, at the same time conveying surprise or disapproval. It may not require an answer.

> 他说今天来，怎么没来？
> 他說今天來，怎麼沒來？
> **Tā shuō jīntiān lái, *zěnme* méi lái?**
> He said he was coming today. *Why* hasn't he come?

> 你不说，我怎么知道？
> 你不說，我怎麼知道？
> **Nǐ bù shuō, wǒ *zěnme* zhīdao?**
> If you don't say (if you don't tell me), how can I know?

Inquiring about cause or reason

44.4

什么理由？/ 甚麼理由？ **shénme lǐyóu?** *'what is the reason?'*

什么理由/甚麼理由 **shénme lǐyóu** is used to inquire about the reason for something. When the speaker uses this expression, he or she expects an answer.

> 你有什么理由要跟我离婚？
> 你有甚麼理由要跟我離婚？
> **Nǐ yǒu shénme lǐyóu yào gēn wǒ lí hūn?**
> *What is the reason why you want to divorce me?*

> 什么理由你不给我们工钱？
> 甚麼理由你不給我們工錢？
> **Shénme lǐyóu nǐ bù gěi wǒmen gōngqian?**
> *What is the reason why you haven't given us our wages?*

凭什么？/ 憑甚麼？ **píng shénme?** *'on what basis?' 'by what right?'*

凭什么/憑甚麼 **píng shénme** is a colloquial expression, most often used in speaking.

> 你凭什么打人？
> 你憑甚麼打人？
> **Nǐ píng shénme dǎ ren?**
> *What right do you have to hit people?*

> 你凭什么逮捕我？
> 你憑甚麼逮捕我？
> **Nǐ píng shénme dàibǔ wǒ?**
> *On what grounds are you arresting me?*

何故 **hégù?** and 为何/為何 **wéi hé?** *'for what reason?' 'why?'*

何故 **hégù** and 为何/為何 **wéi hé** are used only in formal (usually written) language.

> 他何故杀人？
> 他何故殺人？
> **Tā hégù shā rén?**
> *Why did he kill someone?*

> 为何惊慌？
> 為何驚慌？
> **Wéi hé jīnghuāng?**
> *Why are (you) so frightened?*

▶ 28.6

45

Expressing conditions

45.1 'If . . . then' conditional sentences

Mandarin uses the following words to express 'if' in conditional sentences.

要是 **yàoshi**
如果 **rúguǒ**
假如 **jiǎrú**
假使 **jiǎshǐ**
倘若 **tǎngruò**
倘使 **tǎngshǐ**

要是 **yàoshi** and 如果 **rúguǒ** are commonly used in formal and informal speech or writing.

假如 **jiǎrú** is used in more formal speech or writing.

假使 **jiǎshǐ**, 倘若 **tǎngruò**, and 倘使 **tǎngshǐ** are most commonly used in formal, written Chinese.

The 'if' word is placed before or after the subject in the first clause of a sentence.

Mandarin does not have a word that specifically corresponds to 'then' in conditional sentences. Instead, the adverb 就 **jiù** typically occurs in the second clause, immediately before the [prepositional phrase +] verb phrase.

▶ 15.2.4

NOTE 便 **biàn** or 则/則 **zé** are sometimes used instead of 就 **jiù** before the [prepositional phrase +] verb phrase of the second clause.

Here are examples of conditional sentences.

要是 *yàoshi*

要是你不给他钱，他就不会给你做事。
要是你不給他錢，他就不會給你做事。
Yàoshi nǐ bù gěi tā qián, tā jiù bù huì gěi nǐ zuò shì.
If you don't pay him, he won't work for you.

如果 *rúguǒ*

如果你是我，你也不会同意他的看法的。
如果你是我，你也不會同意他的看法的。
Rúguǒ nǐ shì wǒ, nǐ yě bù huì tóngyì tā de kànfa de.
If you were me, you wouldn't agree with his viewpoint either.

45.1 'If...then' conditional sentences

假如 *jiǎrú*

这篇文章写得不错，假如再短一点儿那就更好了。
這篇文章寫得不錯，假如再短一點兒那就更好了。
Zhè piān wénzhāng xiě de bù cuò, jiǎrú zài duǎn yīdiǎr nà jiù gèng hǎo le.
This essay is very good; if it were a little shorter it would be even better.

假使 *jiǎshǐ*

假使人人都骑自行车或坐公共汽车，环境污染的问题就容易解决了。
假使人人都騎自行車或坐公共汽車，環境污染的問題就容易解決了。
Jiǎshǐ rénrén dōu qí zìxíngchē huò zuò gōnggòng qìchē, huánjìng wūrǎn de wèntí jiù róngyì jiějué le.
If everyone rode a bicycle or took the bus, the pollution problem would be easy to solve.

假使我是老师，我每天都给学生考试。
假使我是老師，我每天都給學生考試。
Jiǎshǐ wǒ shì lǎoshī, wǒ měitiān dōu gěi xuéshēng kǎo shì.
If I were a teacher, I would give students a test every day.

倘若/儻若 *tǎngruò*

倘若学生都一看就懂，那老师还有什么用呢？
儻若學生都一看就懂，那老師還有甚麼用呢？
Tǎngruò xuéshēng dōu yī kàn jiù dǒng, nà lǎoshī hái yǒu shénme yòng ne?
If students understood as soon as they looked at something, then what use would there be for teachers?

倘使 *tǎngshǐ*

倘使放假不能回家，请及时写信告知。
儻使放假不能回家，請及時寫信告知。
Tǎngshǐ fàng jià bù néng huí jiā, qǐng jí shí xiě xìn gào zhī.
If you have a vacation and cannot return home, please write me right away to let me know.

则/則 *zé*

大家共同努力则一定能把事情做好。
大家共同努力則一定能把事情做好。
Dàjiā gòngtóng nǔlì zé yīdìng néng bǎ shìqíng zuòhǎo.
(If) everyone works hard together, we certainly can take care of this matter.

坚持不懈则会成功。
堅持不懈則會成功。
Jiānchí bù xiè zé huì chénggōng.
(If)(we) persist, (we) can definitely succeed.

'if... then' sentences with ...的话/的話 de huà

The 'if' clause may end with 的话/的話 **de huà**. Here are examples with 要是 **yàoshi**...的话/的話 **de huà** and 如果 **rúguǒ**...的话/的話 **de huà**.

要是你愿意的话，我们可以今天去市场。
要是你願意的話，我們可以今天去市場。
Yàoshi nǐ yuànyì de huà, wǒmen kěyǐ jīntiān qù shìchǎng.
If you are interested, we can go to the market today.

要是方便的话，就请你给我买一份人民日报。
要是方便的話，就請你給我買一份人民日報。
Yàoshi fāngbiàn de huà, jiù qǐng nǐ gěi wǒ mǎi yī fèn Rénmín Rìbào.
If it is convenient, could you buy me a copy of today's *People's Daily*.

EXPRESSING CONDITIONS

> 如果不是你帮助他的话，他是不会成功的。
> 如果不是你幫助他的話，他是不會成功的。
> **Rúguǒ bù shì nǐ bāngzhù tā de huà, tā shì bù huì chénggōng de.**
> If you hadn't helped him, he wouldn't have succeeded.

45.2 'even if'

就是 **jiùshì** situation, (subject) 也/ **yě** [prepositional phrase +] verb phrase
就是 **jiùshì** situation, (subject) 还/還 **hái** [prepositional phrase +] verb phrase
Even if (situation), (subject) still ([prepositional phrase +] verb phrase)

> 就是你去我也不去。
> **Jiùshì nǐ qù wǒ yě bù qù.**
> Even if you go, I still won't go.

> 那本字典特别好。就是很贵我还要买。
> 那本字典特別好。就是很貴我還要買。
> **Nà běn zìdiǎn tèbié hǎo. Jiùshì hěn guì wǒ hái yào mǎi.**
> That dictionary is particularly good. Even if it is expensive, I still want to buy it.

> 我爱她。就是她不爱我我还爱她。
> 我愛她。就是她不愛我我還愛她。
> **Wǒ ài tā. Jiùshì tā bù ài wǒ wǒ hái ài tā.**
> I love her. Even if she doesn't love me, I still love her.

45.3 'as long as'

Use 只要 **zhǐyào** to express this meaning:

> 只要我们一起努力合作，我们一定会成功。
> 只要我們一起努力合作，我們一定會成功。
> **Zhǐyào wǒmen yīqǐ nǔlì hézuò, wǒmen yīdìng huì chénggōng.**
> As long as we work hard together, we will definitely succeed.

45.4 'only if,' 'unless'

Use 除非 **chúfēi** to express this meaning.

> 除非你是百万富翁，要不然你最好别去看那边的房子。
> 除非你是百萬富翁，要不然你最好別去看那邊的房子。
> **Chúfēi nǐ shì bǎiwàn fùwēng, yàobùrán nǐ zuì hǎo bié qù kàn nàbian de fángzi.**
> Unless you are a millionaire, you'd best not go look at the houses over there.

> 除非多修几个水库，否则无法解决饮水的问题。
> 除非多修幾個水庫，否則無法解決飲水的問題。
> **Chúfēi duō xiū jǐ gè shuǐkù, fǒuzé wúfǎ jiějué yǐnshuǐ de wèntí.**
> Unless we build more reservoirs, there is no way to solve the drinking water problem.

45.5 'otherwise'

Use the following words to express this meaning. Notice that they occur before the subject of the second clause or sentence.

'otherwise'

45.5

要不然 *yàoburán* 'otherwise'

快一点走吧，要不然上课又要迟到了。
快一點走吧，要不然上課又要遲到了。
Kuài yīdiǎn zǒu ba, yàobùrán shàng kè yòu yào chídào le.
Hurry up, otherwise we will be late for class.

我的汽车坏了，要不然我不会不来上班。
我的汽車壞了，要不然我不會不來上班。
Wǒ de qìchē huài le, yàobùrán wǒ bù huì bù lái shàng bān.
My car is broken, otherwise I wouldn't miss work.

不然 *bùrán* 'otherwise'

他让我跟他一起去买东西，不然他不帮我练习中文。
他讓我跟他一起去買東西，不然他不幫我練習中文。
Tā ràng wǒ gēn tā yīqǐ qù mǎi dōngxi, bùrán tā bù bāng wǒ liànxí Zhōngwén.
He makes me go with him to buy things (to go shopping with him). Otherwise, he won't help me study Chinese.

幸亏我的身体好，不然一定会生病。
幸虧我的身體好，不然一定會生病。
Xìngkuī wǒ de shēntǐ hǎo, bùrán yīdìng huì shēng bìng.
It is a good thing I am healthy. Otherwise I would get sick.

否则 *fǒuzé* 'otherwise'

幸亏我多带了点钱，否则我们就回不去了。
幸虧我多帶了點錢，否則我們就回不去了。
Xìngkuī wǒ duō dài le diǎn qián, fǒuzé wǒmen jiù huí bù qù le.
Luckily I brought a little extra money with me. Otherwise we wouldn't be able to get back.

要走人行横道，否则撞死了也是白撞。
要走人行橫道，否則撞死了也是白撞。
Yào zǒu rén xíng héng dào, fǒuzé zhuàngsǐ le yě shì bái zhuàng.
You should walk in the crosswalk. Otherwise, if you get killed it's your fault.
(lit. 'Otherwise, if you get killed (by being hit) it would have been avoidable.')

46

Expressing 'both,' 'all,' 'every,' 'any,' 'none,' 'not any,' and 'no matter how'

46.1 Expressing 'both' and 'all'

46.1.1 Expressing 'both' and 'all' with 都 *dōu*

Mandarin does not have separate words for 'both' and 'all.' It uses the same word, 都 **dōu**, to indicate that a situation is true for the entire plural subject or object. 都 **dōu** is an adverb and always occurs before the verb. When the sentence occurs in neutral *subject-verb-object* form, 都 **dōu** usually indicates 'both' or 'all' of the subject.

我们都喜欢他。
我們都喜歡他。
Wǒmen dōu xǐhuan tā.
We all like him.

To indicate 'both' or 'all' of the object noun phrase using 都 **dōu**, 'topicalize' the object noun phrase by placing it before the subject.

那样的音乐，我都喜欢听。
那樣的音樂，我都喜歡聽。
Nà yàng de yīnyuè, wǒ dōu xǐhuan tīng.
That kind of music, I like to listen to all of it.

中国菜我都喜欢吃。
中國菜我都喜歡吃。
Zhōngguó cài wǒ dōu xǐhuan chī.
(As for) Chinese food, I like to eat everything.

▶ 15.2.2, 57.1.2

Mandarin does not have a distinct word for 'both.' To specify that a situation is true for precisely *two* nouns, your noun phrase must include the number two:

那两本书都很有意思。
那兩本書都很有意思。
Nà liǎng běn shū dōu hěn yǒu yìsī.
Those two books are both very interesting.

Expressing 'both' and 'all' 46.1

46.1.2 Expressing 'all' with 所有的 *suǒyǒu de*

所有的 **suǒyǒu de** occurs before any noun with plural reference to indicate *all of the noun*. It generally refers to nouns that represent a relatively large number of objects.

> 所有的车都太贵。
> 所有的車都太貴。
> **Suǒyǒu de chē dōu tài guì.**
> All of the cars are too expensive.

> 那个饭馆，所有的菜都太咸。
> 那個飯館，所有的菜都太鹹。
> **Nàge fànguǎn, suǒyǒu de cài dōu tài xián.**
> (In) that restaurant, all of the dishes are too salty.

> 我校的足球队，所有的男的都很帅。
> 我校的足球隊，所有的男的都很帥。
> **Wǒ xiào de zúqiú duì, suǒyǒu de nán de dōu hěn shuài.**
> (In) our school's football team, all of the guys are really cute.

46.1.3 Expressing the concept 'all' with 全 *quán*

全 **quán** occurs before certain nouns to indicate *all of the noun* or *the entire noun*.

Commonly occurring phrases with 全 **quán** include:

全家	quán jiā	all of the family/the whole family
全班	quán bān	all of the class/the whole class
全国/全國	quán guó	the whole country
全民	quánmín	all of the people
全年	quán nián	the whole year

> 上个星期我们全家人都去法国旅行了。
> 上個星期我們全家人都去法國旅行了。
> **Shàng gè xīngqī wǒmen quán jiā rén dōu qù Fǎguó lǚxíng le.**
> Last week, our whole family went to France for vacation.

> 全班都考得很好。
> **Quán bān dōu kǎo de hěn hǎo.**
> The whole class did well on the exam.

46.1.4 Expressing 'double' or 'both' with 双/雙 *shuāng*

双/雙 **shuāng** 'pair' is a classifier:

> 一双鞋子/一雙鞋子
> **yī shuāng xiézi**
> a pair of shoes

双/雙 **shuāng** also occurs before a noun to indicate *double noun* or *both nouns*. It is often used to describe objects that come in pairs:

双面/雙面	shuāngmiàn	both sides; reversible
双方/雙方	shuāngfāng	both parties (both people)
双亲/雙親	shuāngqīn	both parents
双姓/雙姓	shuāngxìng	two-character family name
双人床/雙人牀	shuāngrén chuáng	double bed
双胞胎/雙胞胎	shuāngbāotāi	twins

295

'BOTH,' 'ALL,' 'EVERY,' 'ANY,' 'NONE,' 'NOT ANY,' AND 'NO MATTER HOW' | **46.3**

46.2 Expressing 'none'

Mandarin does not have a single word for 'none.' Instead, 'none' is expressed as:

都 **dōu** + negation
'all not' = 'none'

> 孩子都不愿意睡觉。
> 孩子都不願意睡覺。
> **Háizi dōu bù yuànyi shuì jiào.**
> The children are all not willing to sleep. = None of the children is willing to sleep.

> 我的朋友都没上过大学。
> 我的朋友都沒上過大學。
> **Wǒ de péngyou dōu méi shàngguo dàxué.**
> All of my friends have not attended college. = None of my friends has attended college.

46.3 Expressing 'every'

46.3.1 Expressing 'every' with 每 *měi*

每 **měi** + number + classifier (+ noun)
every + number + classifier (+ noun)
If the number is 'one,' it is usually omitted.

> 那些书，每(一)本都很贵。
> 那些書，每(一)本都很貴。
> **Nà xiē shū, měi (yī) běn dōu hěn guì.**
> Those books, every volume is expensive.

> 每(一)个学生都考得很好。
> 每(一)個學生都考得很好。
> **Měi (yī) gè xuésheng dōu kǎo de hěn hǎo.**
> Every student did well on the exam.

> 我每天都上课。
> 我每天都上課。
> **Wǒ měitiān dōu shàng kè.**
> I attend class every day.

> 你每两天可以借一本书。
> 你每兩天可以借一本書。
> **Nǐ měi liǎng tiān kěyǐ jiè yī běn shū.**
> Every two days you can borrow one book.

▶ 35.1

46.3.2 Expressing 'every' with double negatives

没有/沒有 **méi yǒu** + noun phrase + negation
'there is no noun phrase that is not' = 'every noun phrase'

> 没有人不喜欢她。
> 沒有人不喜歡她。
> **Méi yǒu rén bù xǐhuan tā.**
> There is no one who doesn't like her. = Everyone likes her.

Expressing 'every,' 'any,' 'not any,' and 'no matter how' with question words 46.4

那个学生没有一天不迟到。
那個學生沒有一天不遲到。
Nàge xuésheng méi yǒu yī tiān bù chídào.
That student, there is not one single day that he is not late. = That student, he is late every day.

46.3.3 Expressing 'every' with reduplication

Certain nouns and classifiers can be reduplicated (repeated) to mean 'every noun' or 'every classifier.' The most common of these include the following.

人人 *rénrén* 'everyone'

> 人人都喜欢吃好吃的东西。
> 人人都喜歡吃好吃的東西。
> **Rénrén dōu xǐhuan chī hǎo chī de dōngxi.**
> Everyone likes to eat delicious food.

个个/個個 *gègè* 'everyone'

> 他们的孩子，个个都很聪明。
> 他們的孩子，個個都很聰明。
> **Tāmen de háizi, gègè dōu hěn cōngming.**
> All their children are very bright.

年年 *niánnián* 'every year'

> 他们的生活不变。年年都一样。
> 他們的生活不變。年年都一樣。
> **Tāmen de shēnghuó bù biàn. Niánnián dōu yīyàng.**
> Their lives do not change. Every year is the same.

本本 *běnběn* 'every volume'

> 他写的书，本本都很好。
> 他寫的書，本本都很好。
> **Tā xiě de shū, běn běn dōu hěn hǎo.**
> The books that he writes, every volume (every one) is very good.

天天 *tiāntiān* 'every day'

> 我们天天吃中国饭。
> 我們天天吃中國飯。
> **Wǒmen tiāntiān chī Zhōngguó fàn.**
> We eat Chinese food every day.

46.4 Expressing 'every,' 'any,' 'not any,' and 'no matter how' with question words

46.4.1 Expressing 'every' and 'any' with question words

In Mandarin, questions words + 都 **dōu** or 也 **yě** are commonly used to convey the meaning 'every' or 'any.'

Here is a list of question words + 都 **dōu** or 也 **yě** with translations and examples. Note that in some expressions, the question word is part of a larger noun phrase.

'BOTH,' 'ALL,' 'EVERY,' 'ANY,' 'NONE,' 'NOT ANY,' AND 'NO MATTER HOW' — 46.4

谁/誰 + 都 or 也
shéi + dōu or yě
everyone

> 谁都会做这个工作。
> 誰都會做這個工作。
> **Shéi dōu huì zuò zhège gōngzuò.**
> Anyone can do this job.

> 谁都要跟张三做生意。
> 誰都要跟張三做生意。
> **Shéi dōu yào gēn Zhāng Sān zuò shēngyì.**
> Everyone wants to do business with Zhang San.

什么/甚麼 + 都 or 也
shénme + dōu or yě
everything, anything

> 他什么事情都懂。
> 他甚麼事情都懂。
> **Tā shénme shìqing dōu dǒng.**
> He understands everything.

> 弟弟什么书都喜欢看。
> 弟弟甚麼書都喜歡看。
> **Dìdi shénme shū dōu xǐhuan kàn.**
> Little Brother enjoys reading everything.

哪 + classifier + 都 or 也
nǎ + classifier + dōu or yě
everything, anything

> 这儿的天气很好。哪天都很舒服。
> 這兒的天氣很好。哪天都很舒服。
> **Zhèr de tiānqì hěn hǎo. Nǎ tiān dōu hěn shūfu.**
> The weather here is very good. Every day is very comfortable.

> 我特别喜欢看王老师的书。他写的书，哪本都很有意思。
> 我特別喜歡看王老師的書。他寫的書，哪本都很有意思。
> **Wǒ tèbié xǐhuan kàn Wáng lǎoshī de shū. Tā xiě de shū, nǎ běn dōu hěn yǒu yìsi.**
> I especially like to read Professor Wang's books. Of the books that he has written, every book is very interesting.

哪儿/哪兒 + 都 or 也
nǎr + dōu or yě
everywhere

> 他妹妹哪儿都想去。
> 他妹妹哪兒都想去。
> **Tā mèimei nǎr dōu xiǎng qù.**
> His little sister wants to go everywhere.

> Q: 你想去哪儿吃饭？ A: 哪儿都行。
> 你想去哪兒吃飯？   哪兒都行。
> **Nǐ xiǎng qù nǎr chī fàn?**   **Nǎr dōu xíng.**
> Where do you want to go to eat?   Any place is okay.

Expressing 'every,' 'any,' 'not any,' and 'no matter how' with question words   **46.4**

什么地方/甚麼地方 + 都 or 也
shénme dìfang + dōu or yě
everywhere/anywhere

> 中国人口很多。什么地方都是人。
> 中國人口很多。甚麼地方都是人。
> **Zhōngguó rénkǒu hěn duō. Shénme dìfang dōu shì rén.**
> China's population is very big. There are people everywhere.
> (. . . Every place is full of people.)

> 我听说意大利什么地方都很漂亮。
> 我聽說意大利甚麼地方都很漂亮。
> **Wǒ tīngshuō Yìdàlì shénme dìfang dōu hěn piàoliang.**
> I've heard it said that in Italy, every place is very pretty.

几点钟/幾點鐘 + 都 or 也
jǐdiǎn zhōng + dōu or yě
always/at any hour

> Q: 我们几点钟去看电影？   A: 几点钟都可以。
>   我們幾點鐘去看電影？   幾點鐘都可以。
>   **Wǒmen jǐdiǎn zhōng qù kàn diànyǐng?**   **Jǐdiǎn zhōng dōu kěyǐ.**
>   What time should we go to see a movie?   Anytime is okay.

什么时候/甚麼时候 + 都 or 也
shénme shíhòu + dōu or yě
always/any time/whenever

> 爸爸什么时候都很忙。
> 爸爸甚麼時候都很忙。
> **Bàba shénme shíhòu dōu hěn máng.**
> Dad is always busy.

> Q: 你什么时候有空？   A: 我什么时候都有空。
>   你甚麼時候有空？   我甚麼時候都有空。
>   **Nǐ shénme shíhòu yǒu kòng?**   **Wǒ shénme shíhòu dōu yǒu kòng.**
>   When do you have free time?   I always have free time.

The following expressions with 多 **duō** also express the meaning 'no matter how.'

多么/多麼 + adjectival verb
duóme + adjectival verb
no matter how adjectival verb

> 那件衣服多么贵我还想买。
> 那件衣服多麼貴我還想買。
> **Nà jiàn yīfú duóme guì wǒ hái xiǎng mǎi.**
> No matter how expensive that item of clothing is I still want to buy it.

多少
duōshǎo
however many

> 我跟你说了多少次你还不听。
> 我跟你說了多少次你還不聽。
> **Wǒ gēn nǐ shuō le duōshǎo cì nǐ hái bù tīng.**
> No matter how many times I've told you, you still don't listen.

299

'BOTH,' 'ALL,' 'EVERY,' 'ANY,' 'NONE,' 'NOT ANY,' AND 'NO MATTER HOW' | **46.4**

46.4.2 Expressing 'not any' with question words

Question words with 都 **dōu** or 也 **yě** and negation are used to express the concept 'not any.'

Here is a list of question words + 都 **dōu** or 也 **yě** + negation, with translations and examples. 也 **yě** is much more commonly used than 都 **dōu** when expressing 'not any.'

谁/誰 + 都 or 也 + negation
shéi + **dōu** or **yě** + negation
no one/not anyone

> 谁也不会做这个工作。
> 誰也不會做這個工作。
> **Shéi yě bù huì zuò zhège gōngzuò.**
> No one can do this job.

> 谁都不要跟张三做生意。
> 誰都不要跟張三做生意。
> **Shéi dōu bù yào gēn Zhāng Sān zuò shēngyì.**
> No one wants to do business with Zhang San.

什么/甚麼 + 都 or 也 + negation
shénme + **dōu** or **yě** + negation
nothing/not anything

> 他什么事情也不懂。
> 他甚麼事情也不懂。
> **Tā shénme shìqing yě bù dǒng.**
> He doesn't understand anything.

> 弟弟什么书都不喜欢看。
> 弟弟甚麼書都不喜歡看。
> **Dìdi shénme shū dōu bù xǐhuan kàn.**
> Little Brother doesn't like to read any book.

哪/哪 + classifier + 都 or 也 + negation
nǎ + classifier + **dōu** or **yě** + negation
nothing/not anything

> 他哪个菜也不喜欢吃。
> 他哪個菜也不喜歡吃。
> **Tā nǎge cài yě bù xǐhuan chī.**
> He doesn't like to eat any dish.

> 他哪个车都没买。
> 他哪個車都沒買。
> **Tā nǎge chē dōu méi mǎi.**
> He didn't buy a car.

哪儿/哪兒 + 都 or 也 + negation
nǎr + **dōu** or **yě** + negation
nowhere/not anyplace

> 他妹妹哪儿也不想去。
> 他妹妹哪兒也不想去。
> **Tā mèimei nǎr yě bù xiǎng qù.**
> His little sister doesn't want to go anywhere.

> 我哪儿都没去过。
> 我哪兒都沒去過。
> **Wǒ nǎr dōu méi qùguo.**
> I haven't been anywhere.

Expressing 'every,' 'any,' 'not any,' and 'no matter how' with question words   **46.4**

什么地方/甚麼地方 + 都 or 也 + negation
shénme dìfang + dōu or yě + negation
nowhere/not anyplace

> 我刚到这儿来。什么地方都不认识。
> 我剛到這兒來。甚麼地方都不認識。
> **Wǒ gāng dào zhèr lái. Shénme dìfang dōu bù rènshi.**
> I've just come here. (I'm new here.) I don't recognize any place.

> 怎么了？什么地方都没有人。
> 怎麼了？甚麼地方都沒有人。
> **Zěnme le? Shénme dìfang dōu méi yǒu rén.**
> What's going on? There aren't any people anywhere.

什么时候/甚麼時候 + 都 or 也 + negation
shénme shíhòu + dōu or yě + negation
never/not anytime

> Q: 你什么时候有空？   A: 我什么时候也没有空。
> 你甚麼時候有空？   我甚麼時候也沒有空。
> **Nǐ shénme shíhòu yǒu kòng?**   **Wǒ shénme shíhòu yě méi yǒu kòng.**
> When do you have free time?   I never have free time.

> Q: 你什么时候看电视？   A: 我什么时候都不看电视。
> 你甚麼時候看電視？   我甚麼時候都不看電視。
> **Nǐ shénme shíhòu kàn diànshì?**   **Wǒ shénme shíhòu dōu bù kàn diànshì.**
> When do you watch television?   I never watch television.

46.4.3 Expressing 'no matter how' with 怎么/怎麼 *zěnme*

怎么/怎麼 verb₁ 也 + verb₂
zěnme verb₁ yě + verb₂
no matter how much one does verb₁ (the anticipated goal or result is not attained)

When 怎么/怎麼 **zěnme** is used, verb₂ is often a resultative verb.

> 这个字，我怎么写，也写不对。
> 這個字，我怎麼寫，也寫不對。
> **Zhège zì, wǒ zěnme xiě, yě xiě bù duì.**
> This character, no matter how I write it, I write it incorrectly.

> 这件事，我怎么做也不好。
> 這件事，我怎麼做也不好。
> **Zhè jiàn shì, wǒ zěnme zuò yě bù hǎo.**
> This situation, no matter how I handle it, is not good.

> 你做的菜太多了！怎么吃，也吃不完。
> 你做的菜太多了！怎麼吃，也吃不完。
> **Nǐ zuò de cài tài duō le! Zěnme chī, yě chībuwán.**
> You made too much food! No matter how we eat, we can't finish it.

> 这个谜语，怎么猜也猜不着。
> 這個謎語，怎麼猜也猜不著。
> **Zhège míyǔ, zěnme cāi yě cāibuzháo.**
> This riddle, no matter how I guess, I can't figure it out.

'BOTH,' 'ALL,' 'EVERY,' 'ANY,' 'NONE,' 'NOT ANY,' AND 'NO MATTER HOW' 46.4

The expression 不论/不論 **búlùn** 'regardless/no matter how' may occur before 怎么/怎麼 **zěnme**. The meaning of the expression is the same: no matter how much one does verb$_1$ (the anticipated goal or result is not attained).

这个字，我不论怎么写，也写错。
這個字，我不論怎麼寫，也寫錯。
Zhège zì, wǒ búlùn zěnme xiě yě xiěcuò.
This character, no matter how I write it, I write it wrong.

这件事，我不论怎么做也不好。
這件事，我不論怎麼做也不好。
Zhè jiàn shì, wǒ búlùn zěnme zuò yě bù hǎo.
This situation, no matter how I handle it, is not good.

▶ 28.6, 32

47

Expressing location and distance

47.1 Location

47.1.1 Words that indicate location and compass direction

47.1.1.1 Location words

Mandarin location words consist of a base form and a location suffix. Base forms never occur alone. Some base forms occur with several different suffixes with no change in meaning. Here are the Mandarin location words and their English equivalents.

Base form	Mandarin location words			English
里/裏 lǐ	里头/裏頭 lǐtou	里面/裏面 lǐmiàn	里边/裏邊 lǐbiān	in
外 wài	外头/外頭 wàitou	外面 wàimiàn	外边/外邊 wàibiān	out
上 shàng	上头/上頭 shàngtou	上面 shàngmiàn	上边/上邊 shàngbiān	over
下 xià	下头/下頭 xiàtou	下面 xiàmiàn	下边/下邊 xiàbiān	under
前 qián	前头/前頭 qiántou	前面 qiánmiàn	前边/前邊 qiánbiān	in front of
后/後 hòu	后头/後頭 hòutou	后面/後面 hòumiàn	后边/後邊 hòubiān	behind
左 zuǒ		左面 zuǒmiàn	左边/左邊 zuǒbiān	left
右 yòu		右面 yòumiàn	右边/右邊 yòubiān	right
对/對 duì		对面/對面 duìmiàn		across from
旁 páng			旁边/旁邊 pángbiān	next to
中 zhōng	中间/中間 zhōngjiān			between

NOTES

1 In traditional characters, the character 裏 lǐ is also written as 裡.
2 The choice of suffix is determined by the region of China and the personal preference of the speaker.
3 Mandarin has a second word for 'in,' 内 nèi. 内 nèi does not occur with suffixes and is very restricted in usage. It is used in fixed expressions such as:

国内/國內 guónèi	domestic (vs. 国外/國外 guówài foreign)
内部 nèibù	internal
内人 nèiren	my wife

EXPRESSING LOCATION AND DISTANCE

47.1

47.1.1.2 Compass direction

The words for north, east, south, and west are also formed with a base form and a suffix. The suffix can be 面 **miàn** or 边/邊 **biān**.

The combination compass direction words (northeast, southwest, etc.) usually occur without a suffix. If a suffix occurs, it is 面 **miàn** or 边/邊 **biān**.

Base form	Mandarin compass direction words		English
东/東 **dōng**	东面/東面 **dōngmiàn**	东边/東邊 **dōngbiān**	east
南 **nán**	南面 **nánmiàn**	南边/南邊 **nánbiān**	south
西 **xī**	西面 **xīmiàn**	西边/西邊 **xībiān**	west
北 **běi**	北面 **běimiàn**	北边/北邊 **běibiān**	north
	东南(面)/東南(面) **dōngnán (miàn)**	东南(边)/東南(邊) **dōngnán (biān)**	southeast
	东北(面)/東北(面) **dōngběi (miàn)**	东北(边)/東北(邊) **dōngběi (biān)**	northeast
	西南(面) **xīnán (miàn)**	西南(边)/西南(邊) **xīnán (biān)**	southwest
	西北(面) **xīběi (miàn)**	西北(边)/西北(邊) **xīběi (biān)**	northwest

47.1.2 Spatial orientation with respect to a reference point

47.1.2.1 Indicating location with respect to a reference using location words

To indicate that something is 'inside,' 'outside,' 'over,' 'under,' etc. a reference point, use the following structure:

> *reference point* 的 *de* *location word*

In the following phrases, the reference point is the house. Note that 的 **de** may be omitted.

房子(的)里头/房子(的)裏頭
fángzi (de) lǐtou
inside the house

房子(的)外头/房子(的)外頭
fángzi (de) wàitou
outside the house

房子(的)上头/房子(的)上頭
fángzi (de) shàngtou
on the house/over the house

房子(的)下头/房子(的)下頭
fángzi (de) xiàtou
below the house/under the house

房子(的)前头/房子(的)前頭
fángzi (de) qiántou
in front of the house

房子(的)后头/房子(的)後頭
fángzi (de) hòutou
behind the house

Location

47.1

房子(的)左边/房子(的)左邊
fángzi (de) zuǒbiān
to the left of the house

房子(的)右边/房子(的)右邊
fángzi (de) yòubiān
to the right of the house

房子(的)对面/房子(的)對面
fángzi (de) duìmiàn
across from the house

房子(的)中间/房子(的)中間
fángzi (de) zhōngjiān
between the houses

房子的旁边/房子的旁邊
fángzi (de) pángbiān
next to the house

The location base forms 里/裹 **lǐ** 'inside,' 外 **wài** 'outside,' 上 **shàng** 'above,' and 下 **xià** 'below' can directly follow the reference point. When they occur this way, 的 **de** does not occur.

reference point + location base form

房子(的)里头/房子(的)裹頭 **fángzi (de) lǐtou** inside the house	or	房子里/房子裹 **fángzi lǐ** inside the house
房子(的)外头/房子(的)外頭 **fángzi (de) wàitou** outside the house	or	房子外 **fángzi wài** outside the house
房子(的)上头/房子(的)上頭 **fángzi (de) shàngtou** on top of the house	or	房子上 **fángzi shàng** on top of the house
房子(的)下头/房子(的)下頭 **fángzi (de) xiàtou** below the house	or	房子下 **fángzi xià** below the house

47.1.2.2 Indicating location with compass direction words

To indicate that something is 'east of,' 'west of,' 'north of,' or 'south of' a reference point, use the following structure. Keep in mind that compass direction words can be used with the 面 **miàn** or 边/邊 **biān** suffix.

reference point 的 **de** *compass direction word*

EXPRESSING LOCATION AND DISTANCE

47.1.3 Describing and asking about the location of an object

47.1.3.1 Describing the location of an object

To describe the location of an object, say:

> object 在 *zài* location

咖啡馆在后边。
咖啡館在後邊。
Kāfēiguǎn zài hòubiān.
The coffee shop is in the back.

To describe the location of an object with respect to a reference point, say:

> object 在 *zài* reference point 的 ***de*** location word

In these examples, the object is the cat, and the reference point is the house.

猫在房子(的)里头。
貓在房子(的)裏頭。
Māo zài fángzi (de) lǐtou.
The cat is inside the house.

猫在房子(的)外头。
貓在房子(的)外頭。
Māo zài fángzi (de) wàitou.
The cat is outside the house.

猫在房子(的)上头。
貓在房子(的)上頭。
Māo zài fángzi (de) shàngtou.
The cat is on the house/over the house.

猫在房子(的)下头。
貓在房子(的)下頭。
Māo zài fángzi (de) xiàtou.
The cat is below the house/under the house.

猫在房子(的)前头。
貓在房子(的)前頭。
Māo zài fángzi (de) qiántou.
The cat is in front of the house.

猫在房子(的)后头。
貓在房子(的)後頭。
Māo zài fángzi (de) hòutou.
The cat is behind the house.

猫在房子(的)左边。
貓在房子(的)左邊。
Māo zài fángzi (de) zuǒbian.
The cat is to the left of the house.

猫在房子(的)右边。
貓在房子(的)右邊。
Māo zài fángzi (de) yòubian.
The cat is to the right of the house.

Location

猫在房子(的)对面。
貓在房子(的)對面。
Māo zài fángzi (de) duìmiàn.
The cat is across from the house.

猫在房子(的)中间。
貓在房子(的)中間。
Māo zài fángzi (de) zhōngjiān.
The cat is between the houses.

猫在房子(的)旁边。
貓在房子(的)旁邊。
Māo zài fángzi (de) pángbiān.
The cat is next to the house.

Use the same pattern to indicate location in terms of compass direction:

object 在 **zài** reference point 的 **de** compass location word

房子在路(的)西北(边)。
房子在路(的)西北(邊)。
Fángzi zài lù (de) xīběi (biān).
The house is to the northwest of the road.

路在房子(的)东南(边)。
路在房子(的)東南(邊)。
Lù zài fángzi (de) dōngnán (biān).
The road is to the southeast of the house.

Asking about the location of an object

To ask about the location of an object, say:

(object) 在哪儿？/哪兒？ **zài nǎr?**
or
(object) 在哪里/哪裏 **zài nǎli?**
Where is (the object)?

猫在哪儿？（猫在哪里？）
貓在哪兒？（貓在哪裏？）
Māo zài nǎr? (Māo zài nǎli?)
Where is the cat?

▶ 28.6

To ask if an object is at a location, ask a yes–no question with 吗/嗎 **ma**.

(object) 在 **zài** (location) 吗/嗎 **ma?**
Is (the object) at (this location)?

猫在里边吗？
貓在裏邊嗎？
Māo zài lǐbiān ma?
Is the cat inside?

▶ 28.1

EXPRESSING LOCATION AND DISTANCE

To ask where an object is with respect to a reference point, say:

(object) 在 **zài** reference point 的 **de** 哪边/哪邊 **nǎbiān**?

咖啡馆在车站的哪边？
咖啡館在車站的哪邊？
Kāfēiguǎn zài chēzhàn de nǎbiān?
The coffee shop is on which side of the train station? (Which side of the train station is the coffee shop on?)

To ask if an object is at one or the other of two locations, use a 还是/還是 **háishi** question and ask:

(object) 在 **zài** reference point 的 **de** location₁ 还是/還是 **háishi** 在 **zài** reference point 的 **de** location₂?

咖啡馆在车站的里边还是在车站的外边呢？
咖啡館在車站的裡邊還是在車站的外邊呢？
Kāfēiguǎn zài chēzhàn de lǐbiān háishi zài chēzhàn de wàibiān ne?
Is the coffee shop inside the station or outside the station?

▶ 28.3

47.2 Indicating that an object exists or does not exist at a location

To indicate that an object exists at a location, use the following pattern. Note that 在 **zài** is optional at the beginning of the sentence.

(在 **zài**) location 有 **yǒu** object

At location there is object (there are objects).

(在)桌子上有书。
(在)桌子上有書。
(Zài) zhuōzi shàng yǒu shū.
On the table there is a book (there are books).

(在)房子后边有猫。
(在)房子後邊有貓。
(Zài) fángzi hòubiān yǒu māo.
Behind the house there is a cat (there are cats).

有 **yǒu** object 在 **zài** location

There is object (there are objects) at location.

有两本书在桌子上。
有兩本書在桌子上。
Yǒu liǎng běn shū zài zhuōzi shàng.
There are two books on the table.

有一只猫在房子的后边。
有一只貓在房子的後邊。
Yǒu yīzhī māo zài fángzi de hòubiān.
There is a cat behind the house.

Using location as a description

To indicate that an object does not exist at a location, use the following structure:

(在 zài) location 没有/沒有 méi yǒu object

At location there is no object.

> (在)房子里没有人。
> (在)房子裏沒有人。
> **(Zài) fángzi lǐ méi yǒu rén.**
> There are no people in the house.
> (lit. 'In the house there are no people.')

> (在)屋子里没有桌子。
> (在)屋子裏沒有桌子。
> **(Zài) wūzi lǐ méi yǒu zhuōzi.**
> There aren't any tables in the room.
> (lit. 'In the room there aren't any tables.')

or

没有/沒有 méi yǒu object 在 zài location

> 没有人在房子里。
> 沒有人在房子裏。
> **Méi yǒu rén zài fángzi lǐ.**
> There are no people in the house.

> 没有桌子在屋子里。
> 沒有桌子在屋子裏。
> **Méi yǒu zhuōzi zài wūzi lǐ.**
> There aren't any tables in the room.

▶ 11.6

47.3 Using location as a description

Location phrases may also be used to describe a noun. When used as a description, the location phrase precedes the noun, as follows:

> location phrase 的 de noun
> the noun at this location [or] the noun in this direction

To help you to understand this structure, the location phrase in each of the following examples is presented in square brackets. Notice that the words 'that,' 'who,' and 'which' that occur in the description in English are not translated into Mandarin. In Mandarin, the noun can be understood as singular or plural.

> [沙发上]的猫
> [沙發上]的貓
> **[shāfā shàng] de māo**
> the cat [(that is) on the sofa]

> [房子里]的人
> [房子裏]的人
> **[fángzi lǐ] de rén**
> the person [(who is) in the house]

> [北边]的湖
> [北邊]的湖
> **[běibiān] de hú**
> the lake [(that is) in the north]

EXPRESSING LOCATION AND DISTANCE

[左边]的人
[左邊]的人
[zuǒbiān] de rén
the person [(who is) on the left]

The location phrase may itself include a noun with a description:

[房子(的)后头]的人
[房子(的)後頭]的人
[fángzi de hòutou] de rén
the person [(who is) behind the house]

[图书馆(的)对面]的学校
[圖書館(的)對面]的學校
[túshūguǎn (de) duìmiàn] de xuéxiào
the school [(that is) across from the library]

▶ 9.2, 30.3

Compare the use of the location phrase as a description of a noun, with the use of the location phrase to indicate the location of a noun. Keep in mind that location phrases follow the noun and description phrases precede the noun.

Location: noun 的 *de* location phrase	Description: location phrase 的 *de* noun
房子的后头 房子的後頭 **fángzi de hòutou** behind the house	后头的房子 後頭的房子 **hòutou de fángzi** the house that is behind
房子的北面 **fángzi de běimiàn** to the north of the house	北面的房子 **běimiàn de fángzi** the house to the north
孩子的右边 孩子的右邊 **háizi de yòubiān** to the right of the child	右边的孩子 右邊的孩子 **yòubiān de háizi** the child on the right
前头的人 前頭的人 **qiántou de rén** the person who is in front	人的前头 人的前頭 **rén de qiántou** in front of the person
书的上头 書的上頭 **shū de shàngtou** on top of the book	上头的书 上頭的書 **shàngtou de shū** the book on top

47.4 Talking about distance

In Mandarin, distance is always expressed with the word 离/離 **lí** 'to be separated from.' All expressions of distance use the following structure. The noun phrases refer to objects or locations.

noun phrase$_1$ 离/離 **lí** noun phrase$_2$ close/far/x distance
noun phrase$_1$ is close/far/x distance from noun phrase$_2$

Talking about distance

47.4

47.4.1 Talking about 'near' and 'far'

To say that one object or place is (very) far from another object or place, say:

noun phrase₁ 离/離 **lí** noun phrase₂ (很) 远/遠 **(hěn) yuǎn**

> 我家离图书馆很远。
> 我家離圖書館很遠。
> **Wǒ jiā lí túshūguǎn hěn yuǎn.**
> My house is very far from the library.

To say that one object or place is (very) close to another object or place, say:

noun phrase₁ 离/離 **lí** noun phrase₂ (很) 近 **(hěn) jìn**

> 公园离学校(很)近。
> 公園離學校(很)近。
> **Gōngyuán lí xuéxiào (hěn) jìn.**
> The park is very close to the school.

To say that an object or place is close to your present location, say:

noun phrase₁ 离/離这儿/這兒(很)近 **lí zhèr (hěn) jìn**

or

noun phrase₁ 离/離这里/這裏(很)近 **lí zhèlǐ (hěn) jìn**

> 公园离这儿(很)近。
> 公園離這兒(很)近。
> **Gōngyuán lí zhèr (hěn) jìn.**
> The park is (very) close to here.

> 学校离这里(很)近。
> 學校離這裏(很)近。
> **Xuéxiào lí zhèlǐ (hěn) jìn.**
> The school is (very) close to here.

To say that an object or place is far from your present location, say:

noun phrase₁ 离/離这儿/這兒(很)远/遠 **lí zhèr (hěn) yuǎn**

or

noun phrase₁ 离/離这里/這裏(很)远/遠 **lí zhèlǐ (hěn) yuǎn**

> 公园离这儿(很)远。
> 公園離這兒(很)遠。
> **Gōngyuán lí zhèr (hěn) yuǎn.**
> The park is (very) far from here.

> 学校离这里(很)远。
> 學校離這裏(很)遠。
> **Xuéxiào lí zhèlǐ (hěn) yuǎn.**
> The school is (very) far from here.

EXPRESSING LOCATION AND DISTANCE

Be careful to use 离/離 **lí** 'to be separated from,' and not the prepositions 到 **dào** 'from' or 从/從 **cóng** 'from' when talking about distance.

Say this

我家离图书馆很近。
我家離圖書館很近。
Wǒ jiā lí túshūguǎn hěn jìn.
My house is close to the library.

Not this

*我家到图书馆很近。
我家到圖書館很近。
Wǒ jiā dào túshūguǎn hěn jìn.

*我家很近到图书馆。
我家很近到圖書館。
Wǒ jiā hěn jìn dào túshūguǎn.

47.4.2 Talking about specific distance

To indicate the specific distance between two objects or places, say:

noun phrase₁ 离/離 **lí** noun phrase₂ (有) (**yǒu**) distance

公园离图书馆(有)三里(路)。
公園離圖書館(有)三里(路)。
Gōngyuán lí túshūguǎn (yǒu) sān lǐ (lù).
The park is three miles from the library.

Commonly used distance words include:

里	**lǐ**	Chinese mile (.5 kilometers)
公里	**gōnglǐ**	kilometer
米	**mǐ**	meter
英里	**Yīng lǐ**	English mile
哩	**lǐ**	English mile

47.5 Asking about distance

47.5.1 Asking about 'near' and 'far'

To ask if an object or place is far from another object or place, say:

noun phrase₁ 离/離 **lí** noun phrase₂ 远吗/遠嗎 **yuǎn ma?**

or

noun phrase₁ 离/離 **lí** noun phrase₂ 远不远/遠不遠 **yuǎn bù yuǎn?**

你家离图书馆远吗?
你家離圖書館遠嗎?
Nǐ jiā lí túshūguǎn yuǎn ma?
Is your house far from the library?

or

你家离图书馆远不远?
你家離圖書館遠不遠?
Nǐ jiā lí túshūguǎn yuǎn bù yuǎn?
Is your house far from the library?

Asking about distance

47.5

To ask if an object or place is near to another object or place, say:

noun phrase₁ 离/離 **lí** noun phrase₂ 近吗/近嗎 **jìn ma?**

> 你家离图书馆近吗?
> 你家離圖書館近嗎?
> **Nǐ jiā lí túshūguǎn jìn ma?**
> Is your house close to the library?

NOTE: As in English, the question 'is it far?' is more neutral than the question 'is it close?' When the speaker asks 'is it far?' he or she typically does not necessarily expect the answer to be 'far.' However, when the question is 'is it close?' the speaker often expects the answer to be 'close.'

To ask if an object or place is far from your present location, say:

> 图书馆离这儿远吗?
> 圖書館離這兒遠嗎?
> **Túshūguǎn lí zhèr yuǎn ma?**
> Is the library far from here?

or

> 图书馆离这里远吗?
> 圖書館離這裏遠嗎?
> **Túshūguǎn lí zhèlǐ yuǎn ma?**
> Is the library far from here?

▶ 28.1

47.5.2 Asking about specific distances

To ask how far one object or place is from another object or place, say:

> 你家离图书馆多(么)远?
> 你家離圖書館多(麼)遠?
> **Nǐ jiā lí túshūguǎn duō(me) yuǎn?**
> How far is your house from the library?

or

> 你家离图书馆有多远?
> 你家離圖書館有多遠?
> **Nǐ jiā lí túshūguǎn yǒu duō yuǎn?**
> How far is your house from the library?

▶ 28.6

48

Talking about movement, directions, and means of transportation

48.1 Talking about 'going' and 'coming'

Expressions used to talk about going and coming usually involve a preposition indicating 'to,' 'from,' or 'toward,' and a verb indicating 'going' or 'coming.' The structures used to indicate going and coming are presented here. In Mandarin, the prepositional phrase always occurs before the verb.

▶ 14

Note the difference between 走 **zǒu** and 去 **qù**.

The verb 走 **zǒu** 'to go' is used with movement *toward* a direction.

The verb 去 **qù** is used with movement that *terminates* at a location.

48.1.1 Talking about 'going toward' a direction

[往/向/朝　　(direction)] 走
[**wǎng/xiàng/cháo** (direction)] **zǒu**

> 往东走。　　　　朝南走。　　　　向西走。
> 往東走。
> **Wǎng dōng zǒu.**　**Cháo nán zǒu.**　**Xiàng xī zǒu.**
> Go east.　　　　Go south.　　　　Go west.

To tell someone to go straight ahead, say:

> 一直走。
> **Yī zhí zǒu.**
> Go straight ahead.

To tell someone to go straight toward a direction, say:

> [一直]　[往/向/朝　　(direction)] 走
> [**yī zhí**] [**wǎng/xiàng/cháo** (direction)] **zǒu**

or

> [往/向/朝　　(direction)] [一直] 走
> [**wǎng/xiàng/cháo** (direction)] [**yī zhí**] **zǒu**
> go straight toward (direction)

>> 一直往北走。　　or　　往北一直走。
>> **Yīzhí wǎng běi zǒu.**　　　**Wǎng běi yīzhí zǒu.**
>> Go straight north.　　　　　Go straight north.

Talking about turning

48.1.2 Talking about 'going to' a destination

到 destination 去
dào destination **qù**
to [a destination] go = go to a destination

or

去 **qù** destination
go (to) a destination

> 我想到图书馆去。　　　　　　or　　我想去图书馆。
> 我想到圖書館去。　　　　　　　　我想去圖書館。
> **Wǒ xiǎng dào túshūguǎn qù.**　　**Wǒ xiǎng qù túshūguǎn.**
> I want to go to the library.　　　　I want to go to the library.

48.1.3 Talking about 'coming to' a destination

到 destination 来/來
dào destination **lái**
to [a place] come (come to a place)

or

来/來 **lái** destination
come to a destination

> 你什么时候到我家来？　　　　or　　你什么时候来我家？
> 你甚麼時候到我家來？　　　　　　你甚麼時候來我家？
> **Nǐ shénme shíhòu dào wǒ jiā lái?**　　**Nǐ shénme shíhòu lái wǒ jiā?**
> When are you coming to my house?　　When are you coming to my house?

48.1.4 Talking about 'coming from' a location

从/從 location 来/來
cóng location **lái**
from location come (come from a location)

> 她刚从美国来。
> 她剛從美國來。
> **Tā gāng cóng Měiguó lái.**
> She just came from America.

▶ 14.2.4

48.2 Talking about turning

Turning is a type of movement *toward* a direction. Therefore, it may be expressed with the prepositions 往 **wǎng**, 向 **xiàng**, and 朝 **cháo**.

To talk about turning, say:

> [往/向/朝]　　　(direction) 拐
> **[wǎng/xiàng/cháo]** (direction) **guǎi**
> turn toward (direction)

> [往]左拐。　　　　[向]右拐。　　　　[朝]北拐。
> **[Wǎng] zuǒ guǎi.**　**[Xiàng] yòu guǎi.**　**[Cháo] běi guǎi.**
> Turn left.　　　　Turn right.　　　　Turn north.

TALKING ABOUT MOVEMENT, DIRECTIONS, AND MEANS OF TRANSPORTATION | **48.5**

or

拐 (direction)
guǎi (direction)

拐北。
Guǎi běi.
Turn north.

▶ 14.2.4

48.3 Talking about crossing

过一条街。
過一條街。
Guò yī tiáo jiē.
Cross one street or go one block.

过两个红绿灯。
過兩個紅綠燈。
Guò liǎng gè hóng lǜ dēng.
Pass two traffic lights.

过一个路口。
過一個路口。
Guò yī gè lùkǒu.
Cross one intersection.

48.4 Talking about arriving

The verb 到 **dào** means 'to arrive.'

我们到了。
我們到了。
Wǒmen dào le.
We've arrived (at our destination).

你到了奶奶家请给我打电话。
你到了奶奶家請給我打電話。
Nǐ dào le nǎinai jiā qǐng gěi wǒ dǎ diànhuà.
After you arrive at (get to) grandma's house, please call me.

这个包裹，今天寄，什么时候到？
這個包裹，今天寄，甚麼時候到？
Zhège bāoguǒ, jīntiān jì, shénme shíhòu dào?
This package, if I mail it today, when will it arrive?

48.5 Talking about means of transportation

48.5.1 Describing means of transportation

Means of transportation include locomotion: 走 **zǒu** 'to walk,' 跑 **pǎo** 'to run,' 跳 **tiào** 'to hop/ to jump,' 游 **yóu** 'to swim,' 飞/飛 **fēi** 'to fly'; or transportation by a vehicle: 车/車 **chē** 'car,' 出租车/出租車 **chūzū chē** 'taxi cab,' 火车/火車 **huǒchē** 'train,' 地铁/地鐵 **dìtiě** 'subway,' 公共汽车/公共汽車 **gōnggòng qìchē** 'public bus,' 飞机/飛機 **fēijī** 'plane,' 摩托车/摩托車 **mótuōchē** 'motorcycle,' or 自行车/自行車 **zìxíngchē** (in Taiwan: 脚踏车/腳踏車 **jiǎotàchē**) 'bicycle.'

Talking about means of transportation | **48.5**

The expression used to describe riding on a vehicle depends upon the vehicle.

For vehicles in which you sit on a seat, the verb is 坐 **zuò** 'sit.'

坐 **zuò** sit	车/車 **chē**	ride in a car (go by car)
	出租车/出租車 **chūzū chē**	ride in a taxi cab/take a cab/(go) by cab
	火车/火車 **huǒchē**	take a train/by train
	地铁/地鐵 **dìtiě**	take the subway
	飞机/飛機 **fēijī**	take an airplane/by plane
	公共汽车/公共汽車 **gōnggòng qìchē** or 公车/公車 **gōngchē**	take a bus/(go)by bus

For things that you ride astraddle, such as bicycles, motorcycles, and horses, the verb is 骑/騎 **qí**:

骑/騎 **qí** ride	自行车/自行車 **zìxíngchē**	ride a bicycle
	摩托车/摩托車 **mótuōchē**	ride a motorcycle
	马/馬 **mǎ**	ride a horse

The expression used to get on or into a vehicle is 上 **shàng** [vehicle]:

上飞机/上飛機   **shàng fēijī**   get on the plane; board the plane

The expression used to get off or out of a vehicle is 下 **xià** [vehicle]:

下火车/下火車   **xià huǒchē**   get off the train

To indicate that you wish to get off a public vehicle, you say:

下车/下車
Xià chē!
Getting off!

48.5.2 Including the means of transportation in a directional expression

The means of transportation normally occurs before the verb, or before the prepositional phrase and the verb.

他想坐船到中国去。
他想坐船到中國去。
Tā xiǎng *zuò chuán* dào Zhōngguó qù.
He's thinking about *taking a boat* to China.
(He's thinking about going to China *by boat*.)

你可以坐地铁去天安门。
你可以坐地鐵去天安門。
Nǐ kěyǐ *zuò dìtiě* qù Tiān'ānmén.
You can take the subway to Tiananmen.

TALKING ABOUT MOVEMENT, DIRECTIONS, AND MEANS OF TRANSPORTATION

48.6 Asking about locations and asking for directions

48.6.1 Asking about locations

To ask where a place is located, say:

(place) 在哪儿？ or (place) 在哪里？
(place) 在哪兒？   (place) 在哪裏？
(place) **zài nǎr**?   (place) **zài nǎlǐ**?
Where is (the place)?   Where is (the place)?

图书馆在哪儿？   图书馆在哪里？
圖書館在哪兒？   圖書館在哪裏？
Túshūguǎn zài nǎr?   **Túshūguǎn zài nǎlǐ?**
Where is the library?   Where is the library?

48.6.2 Asking how to go from one place to another

To ask how to get from one place to another, say:

怎么走？
怎麼走？
Zěnme zǒu?
How do you go?

(从 place₁) 到 place₂ 怎么走？
(從 place₁) 到 place₂ 怎麼走？
(**cóng** place₁) **dào** place₂ **zěnme zǒu**?
How do you go (from place₁) to place₂?

(从这儿) 到图书馆怎么走？
(從這兒) 到圖書館怎麼走？
(**Cóng zhèr**) **dào túshūguǎn zěnme zǒu?**
How do you go (from here) to the library?

48.6.3 Asking about alternative directions

To ask about alternative directions, use 还是/還是 **háishi** 'or':

往北拐还是往南拐？
往北拐還是往南拐？
Wǎng běi guǎi háishi wǎng nán guǎi?
(Do you) turn north *or* turn south?

▶ 28.3

48.6.4 What to say when you do not know the way

我不太清楚。
Wǒ bù tài qīngchu.
I am not too clear (about this).

(对不起，) 我不知道怎么去。
(對不起，) 我不知道怎麼去。
(**Duìbuqǐ,**) **wǒ bù zhīdao zěnme qù.**
(Sorry,) I don't know how to go.

(对不起，) 我不认识这个地方。
(對不起，) 我不認識這個地方。
(**Duìbuqǐ,**) **wǒ bù rènshi zhèige dìfang.**
(Sorry,) I don't know this place.

Talking about directional movement

(对不起，) 我不知道。
(對不起，) 我不知道。
(Duìbuqǐ,) wǒ bù zhīdao.
(Sorry,) I don't know.

48.7 Asking for and giving directions: sample conversations

Notice that the adverb 再 **zài** can be used to connect a series of directions.

▶ 36.2

Conversation 1

A: 请问，火车站在哪儿？
请問，火車站在哪兒？
Qǐngwèn, huǒchēzhàn zài nǎr?
May I ask, where is the train station?

B: 从这儿一直往前走，过三条街，向右拐就可以看见了。
從這兒一直往前走，過三條街，向右拐就可以看見了。
Cóng zhèr yī zhí wǎng qián zǒu, guò sān tiáo jiē, xiàng yòu guǎi, jiù kěyǐ kànjiàn le.
Go straight ahead, pass three blocks, turn right and you will see it.

Conversation 2

A: 劳驾，去邮政局怎么走？
勞駕，去郵政局怎麼走？
Láojià, qù yóuzhèngjú zěnme zǒu?
May I trouble you? How does one get to the post office?

B: 从这儿往东走，过一个十字路口，往南拐，再走几分钟，在左边有一个红房子就是邮政局。
從這兒往東走，過一個十字路口，往南拐，再走幾分鐘，在左邊有一個紅房子就是郵政局。
Cóng zhèr wǎng dōng zǒu, guò yī gè shí zì lùkǒu, wǎng nán guǎi, zài zǒu jǐ fēn zhōng, zài zuǒbiān yǒu yī gè hóng fángzi jiù shì yóuzhèngjú.
Go east, pass one intersection, turn south, then walk for a few minutes. On your left there is a red building; that is the post office.

Conversation 3

A: 请您告诉我去地铁站怎么走？
請您告訴我去地鐵站怎麼走？
Qǐng nín gàosu wǒ qù dìtiě zhàn zěnme zǒu?
Please tell me how to get to the subway station.

B: 对不起，我也不知道。你问别人吧！
對不起，我也不知道。你問別人吧！
Duìbuqǐ, wǒ yě bù zhīdao. Nǐ wèn biéren ba!
Sorry, I don't know either. You'd better ask someone else.

48.8 Talking about directional movement

Action verbs that refer to movement, such as 跑 **pǎo** 'to run,' 走 **zǒu** 'to walk,' 跳 **tiào** 'to jump,' 开/開 **kāi** 'to drive,' 飞/飛 **fēi** 'to fly,' 划 **huá** 'to row,' 游 **yóu** 'to swim,' and even 穿 **chuān** 'to put on,' 吃 **chī** 'to eat,' and 喝 **hē** 'to drink' may be suffixed with directional endings that indicate the direction of the movement.

319

TALKING ABOUT MOVEMENT, DIRECTIONS, AND MEANS OF TRANSPORTATION   48.8

The directional suffix always ends in 来/來 **lái** 'to come' or 去 **qù** 'to go.' 来/來 **lái** 'to come' is used when the movement is toward the speaker or addressee. 去 **qù** 'to go' is used when the movement is away from the speaker or addressee.

> 我们走进来了。
> 我們走進來了。
> **Wǒmen zǒujìnlái le.**
> We walked in.

> 他跑出去了。
> **Tā pǎochūqù le.**
> He ran out.

These directional suffixes behave like resultative endings. 得 **de** and 不 **bu** may occur between the action verb and the direction suffix to indicate that the subject was able or unable to move in the direction indicated by the suffix.

> 你开得进去吗?
> 你開得進去嗎?
> **Nǐ kāidejìnqu ma?**
> Can you drive in?

> 车太大。我开不进去。
> 車太大。我開不進去。
> **Chē tài dà. Wǒ kāibujìnqu.**
> The car is too big. I can't drive in.

▶ 19.4, 19.5, 32.2

The object of the action verb may also be included in these directional endings. When it is included, it occurs between the direction word and 来/來 **lái** 'to come' or 去 **qù** 'to go.'

> 她走进屋子来了。
> 她走進屋子來了。
> **Tā zǒujìn wūzi lái le.**
> She walked into the room.

> 我们开进城里去了。
> 我們開進城裏去了。
> **Wǒmen kāijìn chénglǐ qù le.**
> We drove into the city.

▶ 19

49

Talking about clock time and calendar time

49.1 Clock time

49.1.1 Talking about hours

There are two Mandarin words for 'hour': 钟头/鐘頭 **zhōngtóu** and 小时/小時 **xiǎoshí**. Speakers in different regions of China prefer one or the other word, but the meanings are identical. Hours are counted with the classifier 个/個 **gè**:

one hour	一个钟头/一個鐘頭 **yī gè zhōngtóu**	or	一个小时/一個小時 **yī gè xiǎoshí**
two hours	两个钟头/兩個鐘頭 **liǎng gè zhōngtóu**	or	两个小时/兩個小時 **liǎng gè xiǎoshí**
three hours	三个钟头/三個鐘頭 **sān gè zhōngtóu**	or	三个小时/三個小時 **sān gè xiǎoshí**

To say 'half an hour,' place 半 **bàn** *before* the classifier 个/個 **gè**.

半个钟头/半個鐘頭 **bàn gè zhōngtóu** half an hour	or	半个小时/半個小時 **bàn gè xiǎoshí** half an hour

To indicate one or more hours and a half, place 半 **bàn** *after* the classifier 个/個 **gè**.

一个半钟头/一個半鐘頭 **yī gè bàn zhōngtóu** one and a half hours	or	一个半小时/一個半小時 **yī gè bàn xiǎoshí** one and a half hours
两个半钟头/兩個半鐘頭 **liǎng gè bàn zhōngtóu** two and a half hours	or	两个半小时/兩個半小時 **liǎng gè bàn xiǎoshí** two and a half hours

▶ 6.6.4

49.1.2 Talking about minutes and seconds

The word for 'minute' is 分 **fēn**. The word for 'second' is 秒 **miǎo**. 分 **fēn** and 秒 **miǎo** are classifiers and are directly preceded by a number. A phrase indicating the number of minutes or seconds may optionally end with the noun 钟/鐘 **zhōng** 'clock.'

一分(钟/鐘) **yī fēn (zhōng)** one minute	两分(钟)/兩分(鐘) **liǎng fēn (zhōng)** two minutes	or	二分(钟)/二分(鐘) **èr fēn (zhōng)** two minutes
一秒(钟/鐘) **yī miǎo (zhōng)** one second	两秒(钟)/兩秒(鐘) **liǎng miǎo (zhōng)** two seconds	or	二秒(钟)/二秒(鐘) **èr miǎo (zhōng)** two seconds

TALKING ABOUT CLOCK TIME AND CALENDAR TIME

To indicate half a minute or half a second, place 半 **bàn** before the word for minute or second.

半分
bàn fēn
half a minute

半秒
bàn miǎo
half a second

To indicate one or more minutes or seconds and a half, place 半 **bàn** immediately after the word for minute/second.

Minutes

一分半
yī fēn bàn
one and a half minutes

两分半/兩分半
liǎng fēn bàn
two and a half minutes

Seconds

一秒半
yī miǎo bàn
one and a half seconds

两秒半/兩秒半
liǎng miǎo bàn
two and a half seconds

▶ 6.6.4

49.1.3 Telling time

49.1.3.1 o'clock: time on the hour

o'clock time is expressed as follows. 钟/鐘 **zhōng** is optional and is often not used. The '(X) o'clock' phrase literally means '(X) dots of the clock.'

1 o'clock	一点钟/一點鐘 **yī diǎn zhōng**	7 o'clock	七点钟/七點鐘 **qī diǎn zhōng**
2 o'clock	两点钟/兩點鐘 **liǎng diǎn zhōng** or 二点钟/二點鐘 **èr diǎn zhōng**	8 o'clock	八点钟/八點鐘 **bā diǎn zhōng**
3 o'clock	三点钟/三點鐘 **sān diǎn zhōng**	9 o'clock	九点钟/九點鐘 **jiǔ diǎn zhōng**
4 o'clock	四点钟/四點鐘 **sì diǎn zhōng**	10 o'clock	十点钟/十點鐘 **shí diǎn zhōng**
5 o'clock	五点钟/五點鐘 **wǔ diǎn zhōng**	11 o'clock	十一点钟/十一點鐘 **shí'yī diǎn zhōng**
6 o'clock	六点钟/六點鐘 **liù diǎn zhōng**	12 o'clock	十二点钟/十二點鐘 **shí'èr diǎn zhōng**

49.1.3.2 Reciting time as digital time

The most common way to tell time is to say it the way it appears on a digital clock.

3:50   三点五十分(钟)
       三點五十分(鐘)
       sān diǎn wǔ shí fēn (zhōng)

4:27   四点二十七分(钟)
       四點二十七分(鐘)
       sì diǎn èr shí qī fēn (zhōng)

Reciting time with 零 **líng** *'zero'*
When time is recited as digial time, if the number of minutes is smaller than ten, minutes may optionally begin with 零 **líng** 'zero.' 零 **líng** 'zero' is also written as ○.

Clock time　　　　　　　　　　　　　　　　　　　　　　　　**49.1**

    2:02　　两点零二分
               兩點零二分
               liǎng diǎn líng èr fēn

To indicate half past the hour, use 半 **bàn**.

    6:30　　六点半
               六點半
               liù diǎn bàn

The phrases 一刻 **yī kè** 'one quarter' and 三刻 **sān kè** 'three quarters' can be used to express a quarter after or a quarter to and 45 minutes after the hour.

    7:15　　七点一刻（钟）
               七點一刻（鐘）
               qī diǎn yī kè (zhōng)

    7:45　　七点三刻（钟）
               七點三刻（鐘）
               qī diǎn sān kè (zhōng)

9.1.3.3　Telling time specifying 'minutes to' and 'minutes past' the hour

过/過 **guò** 'pass' introduces minutes past the hour. When reciting time with 过/過 **guò**, the order of information is as follows. 钟/鐘 **zhōng** is optional and is often omitted.

x hour	past	x minutes	
x 点/點 **diǎn**	过/過 **guò**	x 分 **fēn**	钟/鐘 **zhōng**

    3:10　　三点过十分（钟）
               三點過十分（鐘）
               sān diǎn guò shí fēn (zhōng)

    4:27　　四点过二十七分（钟）
               四點過二十七分（鐘）
               sì diǎn guò èr shí qī fēn (zhōng)

    7:15　　七点过一刻（钟）
               七點過一刻（鐘）
               qī diǎn guò yī kè (zhōng)

    7:45　　七点过三刻（钟）
               七點過三刻（鐘）
               qī diǎn guò sān kè (zhōng)

NOTE　　过/過 **guò** cannot be used with 半 **bàn** 'half.'

差 **chà** 'lack' introduces minutes before the hour. The '差 **chà** + minutes' phrase can occur either before or after the hour phrase, as follows. 钟/鐘 **zhōng** is optional and is often omitted.

Pattern 1

x 点/點 **diǎn**　　差 **chà**　　x 分 **fēn**　　（钟/鐘 **zhōng**）
(lit. 'x o'clock lacking x minutes')

    6:50　　七点差十分（钟）
               七點差十分（鐘）
               qī diǎn chà shí fēn (zhōng)

    7:45　　八点差一刻（钟）
               八點差一刻（鐘）
               bā diǎn chà yī kè (zhōng)

TALKING ABOUT CLOCK TIME AND CALENDAR TIME

Pattern 2

差 **chà**   x 分 **fēn**   x 点/點 **diǎn**   (钟/鐘 **zhōng**)
(lit. 'lacking x minutes, x o'clock')

    6:50   差十分七点(钟)
             差十分七點(鐘)
             chà shífēn qī diǎn (zhōng)

    7:45   差一刻八点(钟)
             差一刻八點(鐘)
             chà yī kè bā diǎn (zhōng)

49.1.4 Indicating a.m. and p.m.

In Mandarin, instead of the two-way distinction between a.m. and p.m., time is categorized as follows:

morning (the early hours, approximately 6–8 or 9 a.m.)	早上 **zǎoshang** or 早晨 **zǎochén**
before noon (approximately 8 or 9 a.m. until noon)	上午 **shàngwǔ**
midday (12 noon or the time around noon.)	中午 **zhōngwǔ**
afternoon (approximately 1 p.m. to 6 p.m.)	下午 **xiàwǔ**
evening (beginning approximately 6 p.m.)	晚上 **wǎnshang**
midnight – middle of the night (approximately midnight to 3 a.m.)	半夜 **bànyè**

These expressions occur at the beginning of the clock time phrase:

下午三点钟
下午三點鐘
xiàwǔ sān diǎn zhōng
3 o'clock in the afternoon (3 p.m.)

早上六点半
早上六點半
zǎoshang liù diǎn bàn
6:30 in the morning (6:30 a.m.)

上午十点
上午十點
shàngwǔ shí diǎn
10 in the morning (10 a.m.)

晚上七点三刻
晚上七點三刻
wǎnshang qī diǎn sānkè
7:45 in the evening (7:45 p.m.)

半夜两点
半夜兩點
bànyè liǎng diǎn
2 o'clock in the morning

Calendar time

49.1.5 The location of clock time phrases in the sentence

Clock time, like all phrases that indicate the time when a situation takes place, occurs at the beginning of the predicate, right after the subject.

他每天中午十二点钟吃饭。
他每天中午十二點鐘吃飯。
Tā měitiān zhōngwǔ shí'èr diǎn zhōng chī fàn.
He eats every day around 12:00 noon.

The position of the clock time phrase in the sentence is the same whether the sentence is a statement or a question.

Q:	什么时候吃晚饭？ 甚麼時候吃晚飯？ **Shénme shíhòu chī wǎnfàn?** When will we have dinner?		A:	我们六点吃晚饭。 我們六點吃晚飯。 **Wǒmen liù diǎn chī wǎnfàn.** We will eat dinner at 6:00.
Q:	我们什么时候见？ 我們甚麼時候見？ **Wǒmen shénme shíhòu jiàn?** When shall we meet?		A:	我们明天上午九点见。 我們明天上午九點見。 **Wǒmen míngtiān shàngwǔ jiǔ diǎn jiàn.** We will meet at 9:00 tomorrow morning.

▶ 4.5, 4.11

49.1.6 Asking about time

To ask for the present hour of the day, say:

现在几点钟？
現在幾點鐘？
Xiànzài jǐ diǎn zhōng?
What time (hour) is it now?

More general questions about the present time are the following:

现在(是)什么时候？ 現在(是)甚麼時候？ **Xiànzài (shì) shénme shíhòu?** What time is it now?	or	现在(是)什么时间？ 現在(是)甚麼時間？ **Xiànzài (shì) shénme shíjiān?** What time is it now?

▶ 28.6

49.2 Calendar time

China uses two different calendar systems. The Western calendar, called 阳历/陽曆 **yánglì**, is used in nearly all official and public contexts, such as school, business, publishing, civil administration, military affairs, and politics. The 阴历/陰曆 **yīnlì** (lunar calendar), sometimes called 农历/農曆 **nónglì** (agricultural calendar), is used to mark birthdays, and traditional Chinese holidays such as the Chinese New Year, the Dragon Festival, the Mid-Autumn festival, etc. Until the nineteenth century, the lunar calendar was the primary calendar. Nowadays, the Western calendar is more widely used than the lunar calendar, especially in urban China.

TALKING ABOUT CLOCK TIME AND CALENDAR TIME

49.2.1 Years

49.2.1.1 Counting years and asking about the number of years

To count years, precede the word 年 **nián** 'year' by a number. No additional classifier occurs between the number and the word for 'year.'

one year	一年	yī nián
two years	两年/兩年	liǎng nián
three years	三年	sān nián

To ask how many years, say:

几年？/ 幾年？
jǐ nián?
how many years?

or

多少年？
duōshǎo nián?
how many years?

▶ 28.6

49.2.1.2 Referring to years

this year	今年	jīnnián
next year	明年	míngnián
two years from now	后年/後年	hòunián
three years from now	大后年/大後年	dà hòunián
four years from now	四年以后/四年以後	sì nián yǐhòu
last year	去年	qùnián
the year before last	前年	qiánnián
three years ago	大前年	dà qiánnián
four years ago	四年以前	sì nián yǐqián

49.2.1.3 Reciting years

To recite a year, read the year as a series of single numbers followed by 年 **nián**:

| 2004 | 二零零四年 | èr líng líng sì nián |
| 1976 | 一九七六年 | yī jiǔ qī liù nián |

To indicate BC and AD, say:

公元 **gōngyuán** or 公历/公曆 **gōnglì** 'AD'
公元前 **gōngyuánqián** or 前 **qián** 'BC'

> 公元2002年
> **gōngyuán 2002 nián**
> 2002 AD

> 公元前146年
> **gōngyuánqián 146 nián**
> 146 BC

In Taiwan, years are counted from the founding of the Republic of China in 1911:

民国/民國47年 **Mínguó 47 nián** = 1958
民国/民國93年 **Mínguó 93 nián** = 2004

Calendar time **49.2**

49.2.1.4 Asking about years

To ask about a year, say:

哪年?
nǎ nián? or **něi nián?**
which year?

你是哪年毕业的?
你是哪年畢業的?
Nǐ shì nǎ nián bì yè de?
In what year did you graduate?

这个大学是哪年建立的?
這個大學是哪年建立的?
Zhège dàxué shì nǎ nián jiànlì de?
In what year was this university established?

49.2.2 Months

月 **yuè** is the word for 'month,' and it is also part of the name of the months. When months are counted or referred to in expressions such as 'one month,' 'this month,' or 'next month,' the classifier 个/個 **gè** occurs between the specifier and/or number and 月 **yuè** 'month.' The names of the months do not include a classifier.

49.2.2.1 Counting months and asking about the number of months

To count months, precede the word 月 **yuè** 'month' by a number and the classifier 个/個 **gè**:

one month	一个月/一個月	yī gè yuè
two months	两个月/兩個月	liǎng gè yuè
three months	三个月/三個月	sān gè yuè

To ask how many months, say:

几个月?   or   多少月?
幾個月?
jǐ gè yuè?   **duōshǎo yuè?**
how many months?   how many months?

一年有几个月?
一年有幾個月?
Yī nián yǒu jǐ gè yuè?
One year has how many months? (How many months are there in a year?)

你已经学了多少月了?
你已經學了多少月了?
Nǐ yǐjing xué le duōshǎo yuè le?
How many months have you studied already?

49.2.2.2 Referring to months with respect to 'now'

To refer to the months, use these expressions:

this month	这个月/這個月	zhège yuè
next month	下个月/下個月	xià gè yuè
last month	上个月/上個月	shàng gè yuè

TALKING ABOUT CLOCK TIME AND CALENDAR TIME

49.2.2.3 The names of the months

January	一月	yīyuè	July	七月	qīyuè
February	二月	èryuè	August	八月	bāyuè
March	三月	sānyuè	September	九月	jiǔyuè
April	四月	sìyuè	October	十月	shíyuè
May	五月	wǔyuè	November	十一月	shíyī yuè
June	六月	liùyuè	December	十二月	shí'èr yuè

To ask which month it is, say 几月? 幾月? **jǐ yuè?** 'which month?'

你是几月生的?
你是幾月生的?
Nǐ shì jǐ yuè shēng de?
In which month were you born?

49.2.3 Weeks

Mandarin has two words for 'week': 礼拜/禮拜 **lǐbài** and 星期 **xīngqī**.

礼拜/禮拜 **lǐbài** was originally associated with religious services, but no longer has religious connotations. Different regions of China have different preferences in the choice of the word for week. 星期 **xīngqī** is the word used in calendars, newspapers, and formal documents.

49.2.3.1 Counting weeks and asking about the number of weeks

To count weeks, use the classifier 个/個 **gè**:

one week	一个星期/一個星期 **yī gè xīngqī**	or	一个礼拜/一個禮拜 **yī gè lǐbài**
two weeks	两个星期/兩個星期 **liǎng gè xīngqī**	or	两个礼拜/兩個禮拜 **liǎng gè lǐbài**
three weeks	三个星期/三個星期 **sān gè xīngqī**	or	三个礼拜/三個禮拜 **sān gè lǐbài**

To ask how many weeks, say:

几个星期?/幾個星期? or 几个礼拜?/幾個禮拜?
jǐ gè xīngqī? **jǐ gè lǐbài?**
how many weeks? how many weeks?

49.2.3.2 Referring to weeks and weekends with respect to 'now'

Expressions that refer to weeks:

this week	这个星期/這個星期	zhège xīngqī
next week	下个星期/下個星期	xià gè xīngqī
last week	上个星期/上個星期	shàng gè xīngqī

Expressions that refer to weekends:

this weekend	这个周末/這個週末	zhège zhōumò
next weekend	下个周末/下個週末	xià gè zhōumò
last weekend	上个周末/上個週末	shàng gè zhōumò

49.2.4 Days

45.2.4.1 Counting days and asking about the number of days

To count days, put the number right before the word for 'day.' No additional classifier is used:

one day	一天	yī tiān
two days	两天/兩天	liǎng tiān
three days	三天	sān tiān

Calendar time

49.2

To ask about the number of days, say:

| 几天？幾天？ | **jǐ tiān?** | how many days? (small number expected) |
| 多少天？ | **duōshǎo tiān?** | how many days? |

9.2.4.2 Referring to days of the week and asking about days of the week

There are two sets of words for the days of the week. One is based on the word 礼拜/禮拜 **lǐbài** and the other is based on the word 星期 **xīngqī**. In both sets, the names of the days of the week from Monday to Saturday include a number. Pay attention to the words for Sunday.

Sunday	礼拜天/禮拜天 **lǐbài tiān** or 礼拜日/禮拜日 **lǐbài rì**	星期天 **xīngqī tiān** or 星期日 **xīngqī rì**
Monday	礼拜一/禮拜一 **lǐbài yī**	星期一 **xīngqī yī**
Tuesday	礼拜二/禮拜二 **lǐbài èr**	星期二 **xīngqī èr**
Wednesday	礼拜三/禮拜三 **lǐbài sān**	星期三 **xīngqī sān**
Thursday	礼拜四/禮拜四 **lǐbài sì**	星期四 **xīngqī sì**
Friday	礼拜五/禮拜五 **lǐbài wǔ**	星期五 **xīngqī wǔ**
Saturday	礼拜六/禮拜六 **lǐbài liù**	星期六 **xīngqī liù**

To say 'last Tuesday,' say:

上(个)星期二 or 上(个)礼拜二
上(個)星期二 or 上(個)禮拜二
shàng (gè) xīngqī èr or **shàng (gè) lǐbài èr**

To say 'next Saturday,' say:

下(个)星期六 or 下(个)礼拜六
下(個)星期六 or 下(個)禮拜六
xià (gè) xīngqī liù or **xià (gè) lǐbài liù**

To ask about days of the week, say:

| 星期几？
星期幾？
xīngqī jǐ?
what day of the week? | or | 礼拜几？
禮拜幾？
lǐbài jǐ?
what day of the week? |

今天(是)星期几？
今天(是)星期幾？
Jīntiān (shì) xīngqī jǐ?
What day of the week is it today?

明天(是)礼拜几？
明天(是)禮拜幾？
Míngtiān (shì) lǐbài jǐ?
What day of the week is it tomorrow?

▶ 34.1, 36.1, 37.8.1

TALKING ABOUT CLOCK TIME AND CALENDAR TIME

49.2.4.3 Referring to days before and after today

大前天	dà qiántiān	three days ago
前天	qiántiān	the day before yesterday
昨天	zuótiān	yesterday
今天	jīntiān	today
明天	míngtiān	tomorrow
后天/後天	hòutiān	the day after tomorrow
大后天/大後天	dà hòutiān	three days from now

49.2.4.4 Referring to the date of the month (the first, second, third of the month, etc.)

There are two words for 'date' that are used when referring to the date of the month, 号/號 **hào** and 日 **rì**. 日 **rì** is more formal than 号/號 **hào** and is used in calendars and other written documents. To indicate the date, put the number directly before 日 **rì** or 号/號 **hào**:

the 5th (of the month)	五号/五號	or	五日
	wǔ hào		wǔ rì
the 22nd (of the month)	二十二号 二十二號	or	二十二日
	èrshí'èr hào		èrshí'èr rì

To ask about the date, say:

| 几号?
幾號?
jǐ hào?
what is the date? | or | 几日?
幾日?
jǐ rì?
what is the date? |
| 今天几号?
今天幾號?
Jīntiān jǐ hào?
What is today's date? | or | 今天几月几号?
今天幾月幾號?
Jīntiān jǐ yuè jǐ hào?
What is today's date?
(What is today's month and date?) |

49.2.4.5 Reciting complete days and asking about dates

In Mandarin, complete dates are presented from the largest unit of time to the smallest unit of time as follows:

year + month + date

一九九八年，七月，三十一日
yī jiǔ jiǔ bā nián, qīyuè, sānshí yī rì
July 31, 1998

二零零零年一月一日
èr líng líng líng nián yī yuè yī rì
January 1, 2000

一九八二年十月五号
一九八二年十月五號
yī jiǔ bā èr nián shí yuè wǔ hào
October 5, 1982

Calendar time

49.2

To ask about complete dates, say:

哪年几月几日?	or	哪年几月几号?
哪年幾月幾日?		哪年幾月幾號?
nǎ nián jǐ yuè jǐ rì?		**nǎ nián jǐ yuè jǐ hào?**
which year which month which date		which year which month which date

你是哪年几月几号生的?
你是哪年幾月幾號生的?
Nǐ shì nǎ nián jǐ yuè jǐ hào shēng de?
You were born in which year, which month, which date?
(When were you born?)

他们是哪年几月几日结婚的?
他們是哪年幾月幾日結婚的?
Tāmen shì nǎ nián jǐ yuè jǐ rì jiéhūn de?
In which year, which month, and on which date were they married?
(When were they married?)

▶ 37.9

49.2.5 Talking about semesters

学期/學期 **xuéqī** means 'semester' (of a school year).

49.2.5.1 Counting semesters

To count semesters, put the classifier 个/個 **gè** after the number and before the word 学期/學期 **xuéqī** 'semester.'

one semester	一个学期/一個學期	yī gè xuéqī
two semesters	两个学期/兩個學期	liǎng gè xuéqī
three semesters	三个学期/三個學期	sān gè xuéqī

49.2.5.2 Referring to semesters

学期/學期 **xuéqī** are referred to in the same way as weeks, weekends, and months.

this semester	这个学期/這個學期	zhège xuéqī
next semester	下个学期/下個學期	xià gè xuéqī
last semester	上个学期/上個學期	shàng gè xuéqī

50

Expressing obligations and prohibitions

50.1 Expressing obligations

50.1.1 Expressing strong obligations: must

Here are the words used to express 'strong obligations' in Mandarin, with sentences illustrating their use. All of these words can be translated with the English word 'must.'

得 *děi*

> 明天你得早点儿起来。
> 明天你得早點兒起來。
> **Míngtiān nǐ *děi* zǎo diǎr qǐlái.**
> You *have to* get up earlier tomorrow morning.

必得 *bìděi*

> 你必得按时来上课。
> 你必得按時來上課。
> **Nǐ *bìděi* ànshí lái shàng kè.**
> You *must* come to class on time.

必须/必須 *bìxū*

> 去中国以前你必须申请签证。
> 去中國以前你必須申請簽証。
> **Qù Zhōngguó yǐqián nǐ *bìxū* shēnqǐng qiānzhèng.**
> Before you go to China, you *must* apply for a visa.

必得 **bìděi** and 必须/必須 **bìxū** are more formal and stronger than 得 **děi**. 必须/必須 **bìxū** is also used in legal pronouncements and in other formal spoken and written contexts.

> 经济合同用货币履行义务时,... 必须用人民币计算和支付。
> 經濟合同用貨幣履行義務時,... 必須用人民幣計算和支付。
> **Jīngjì hétóng yòng huòbì lǚxíng yìwù shí, ... *bìxū* yòng rénmínbì jìsuàn hé zhīfù.**
> When economic contracts provide for the performance of obligations through money, ... Rénminbi *must* be used for calculating and paying obligations.

▶ 12.4.1

50.1.2 Expressing 'weak' social and moral obligations: should, shall, ought to

Here are the words used in Mandarin to express the kind of 'weak obligations' associated with the English words 'should' and 'ought to,' with sentences illustrating their use. In Mandarin, these words are also used to express moral obligations such as the responsibilities of parents to children or children to parents, and social obligations involving the things that a good person should do.

Expressing obligations | **50.1**

应当/應當 yīngdāng is more formal than 应该/應該 yīnggāi and can be used in formal texts including legal documents. 该/該 gāi is used in informal speech. 应/應 yīng is used in formal texts including legal documents.

应该/應該 *yīnggāi*

> 父母应该照顾他们的孩子。
> 父母應該照顧他們的孩子。
> **Fùmǔ *yīnggāi* zhàogù tāmen de háizi.**
> Parents *should* take care of their children.

应当/應當 *yīngdāng*

> 你有错误就应当改正。
> 你有錯誤就應當改正。
> **Nǐ yǒu cuòwù jiù *yīngdāng* gǎizhèng.**
> When you make a mistake, you *should* correct it.

该/該 *gāi*

> 我该去上班了。
> 我該去上班了。
> **Wǒ *gāi* qù shàngbān le.**
> I *should* go to work.

In legal documents, 应/應 yīng often means 'shall.'

> 经济合同被确认无效后，当事人依据该合同所取得的财产，应返还给对方。
> 經濟合同被確認無效後，當事人依據該合同所取得的財產，應返還給對方。
> **Jīngjì hétóng bèi quèrèn wúxiào hòu, dāngshìrén yījù gāi hétóng suǒ qǔ dé de cáichǎn, *yīng* fǎnhuán gěi duìfāng.**
> After an economic contract has been confirmed to be invalid, the parties *shall* return to each other any property that they have acquired pursuant to the contract.

应/應 yīng may occur in legal texts to specify moral, though non-legal obligations. The following is an excerpt from Section 1, Article 3, of the Child Welfare Law of Taiwan.

> 父母、养父母或监护人对其儿童应负保育之责任。
> 父母、養父母或監護人對其兒童應負保育之責任。
> **Fùmǔ, yǎng fùmǔ huò jiānhù rén duì qí értóng *yīng* fù bǎoyù zhī zérèn.**
> Parents, foster parents, or legal guardians *should* bear the responsibility of rearing the children in the household.

▶ 12.4.2

50.1.3 Expressing negative obligations: need not, do not have to

The Mandarin words used to indicate that an action need not be done are 不必 **bù bì**, 不用 **bù yòng**, 甭 **béng**, 不须/不須 **bù xū**, and 无须/無須 **wú xū**.

不必 *bù bì*

> 他们明天不必来上课。
> 他們明天不必來上課。
> **Tāmen míngtiān bù bì lái shàng kè.**
> They don't have to come to class tomorrow.

不用 *bù yòng*

> 你不用谢我。谢她。
> 你不用謝我。謝她。
> **Nǐ bù yòng xiè wǒ. Xiè tā.**
> You don't have to thank me. Thank her.

EXPRESSING OBLIGATIONS AND PROHIBITIONS

甭 béng

甭 béng is the contraction of 不用 bù yòng. It is used in informal speech.

> 我们都是自己人。甭那么客气。
> 我們都是自己人。甭那麽客氣。
> **Wǒmen dōu shì zìjǐ rén. Béng nàme kèqi.**
> We are all friends. You don't have to be so polite.

不须/不須 bù xū

> 去中国以前不须打针。
> 去中國以前不須打針。
> **Qù Zhōngguó yǐqián bù xū dǎ zhēn.**
> Before going to China it is not necessary to get vaccinations.

无须/無須 wú xū

> 这件事无须告诉你父母。
> 這件事無須告訴你父母。
> **Zhè jiàn shì wú xū gàosu nǐ fùmǔ.**
> There is no need to tell your parents about this matter.
> (As for this matter, there is no need to tell your parents.)

50.1.4 Asking questions about obligations

To ask if there is an obligation to do something, use a yes–no question. 吗/嗎 **ma** questions can be used with all obligation words.

> 我们得看那本书吗?
> 我們得看那本書嗎?
> **Wǒmen děi kàn nà běn shū ma?**
> Do we have to read that book?

应该/應該 **yīnggāi** and 应当/應當 **yīngdāng** can also occur in *verb-not-verb* questions.

> 我应该不应该给他道歉?
> 我應該不應該給他道歉?
> **Wǒ yīnggāi bù yīnggāi gěi tā dàoqiàn?**
> Do I have to apologize to him?

> 我应当不应当给他道歉?
> 我應當不應當給他道歉?
> **Wǒ yīngdāng bù yīngdāng gěi tā dàoqiàn?**
> Should I apologize to him?

得 **děi**, 必得 **bìděi**, and 必须/必須 **bìxū** cannot occur in *verb-not-verb* questions.

▶ 28.1.2

50.2 Expressing prohibitions: must not, should not

50.2.1 Expressing strong prohibitions: must not

The words used to express strong prohibitions in Mandarin are 不许/不許 **bù xǔ** 'must not,' 不要 **bù yào** 'don't,' and 别 **bié** 'don't.'

> 医院里不许抽烟。
> 醫院裏不許抽煙。
> **Yīyuàn lǐ bù xǔ chōu yān.**
> Smoking is not permitted in the hospital.

Expressing prohibitions: must not, should not 50.2

别开玩笑。
別開玩笑。
Bié kāi wánxiào.
Don't joke. (Be serious.)

考试以前不要紧张。
考試以前不要緊張。
Kǎoshì yǐqián bù yào jǐnzhāng.
Before a test don't be nervous.

▶ 12.5

50.2.2 Expressing weak prohibitions: should not

The Mandarin words used to indicate that an action should not be done are 不应该/應該 **bù yīnggāi** and 不应当/應當 **bù yīngdāng**.

你不应该/应当打人。
你不應該/應當打人。
Nǐ bù yīnggāi/yīngdāng dǎ rén.
You shouldn't hit people.

不应该/應該 **bù yīnggāi** 'should not' and 不应当/應當 **bù yīngdāng** 'should not' sometimes carry negative expectations. Both of the following sentences can be used after the fact, when we have seen that the medicine had side effects, or that Zhang San is a bad person.

这个药不应该有副作用啊。
這個藥不應該有副作用啊。
Zhège yào bù yīnggāi yǒu fù zuòyòng a.
This drug is not supposed to have any side effects.

张三不应该是坏人啊。
張三不應該是壞人啊。
Zhāng Sān bù yīnggāi shì huài rén a.
Zhang San is not supposed to be a bad person.

50.2.3 Formal written words that specify prohibited activities

Here are some commonly used expressions in formal written texts that indicate prohibited activities. They are always followed by a verb phrase.

禁止	**jìnzhǐ** + verb phrase	prohibited from
免	**miǎn** + verb phrase	prohibited from
勿	**wù** + verb phrase	do not
严禁/嚴禁/	**yánjìn** + verb phrase	strictly prohibited from
不准	**bù zhǔn** + verb phrase	not permitted to

Here are the texts of actual signs posted in Chinese cities indicating prohibited activities. They illustrate the use of formal written words for prohibitions.

各种车辆禁止进入
各種車輛禁止進入
Gè zhǒng chēliàng jìnzhǐ jìnrù
No entry
(lit. 'All vehicles prohibited from entering')

严禁酒后开车
嚴禁酒後開車
Yánjìn jiǔ hòu kāi chē
Don't drink and drive
(lit. 'Driving after drinking is strictly prohibited')

EXPRESSING OBLIGATIONS AND PROHIBITIONS

自行车汽车摩托车禁止入内
自行車汽車摩托車禁止入內
Zìxíng chē qìchē mótuōchē jìnzhǐ rù nèi
Bicycles, cars and motorcycles prohibited from entering

禁止拍照
Jìnzhǐ pāi zhào
No photographs
(lit. 'Taking photographs is prohibited')

禁止吸烟
禁止吸煙
Jìnzhǐ xī yān
No smoking
(lit. 'Smoking is prohibited')

禁止停车
禁止停車
Jìnzhǐ tíng chē
No parking
(lit. 'Parking is prohibited')

禁止摘花

Jìnzhǐ zhāi huā
Do not pick the flowers
(lit. 'Picking flowers is prohibited')

禁止随地吐痰
禁止隨地吐痰
Jìnzhǐ suídì tǔtán
No spitting
(lit. 'Spitting is prohibited')

车辆行人严禁穿行
車輛行人嚴禁穿行
Chēliàng xíngrén yánjìn chuānxíng
No crossing
(lit. 'Vehicles and pedestrians are strictly prohibited from crossing')

不准乱扔瓜果皮核
不准亂扔瓜果皮核
Bùzhǔn luàn rēng guāguǒ píhé
It is not permitted to throw away melon and fruit peels and pits

闲人免进
閒人免進
Xiánrén miǎn jìn
No admission except on business
(lit. 'Persons with no business here are prohibited from entering')

请勿停车
請勿停車
Qǐng wù tíng chē
No parking
(lit. 'Please don't park')

不准随地吐痰
不准隨地吐痰
Bù zhǔn suídì tǔtán
No spitting
(lit. 'Spitting on the ground is not permitted')

请勿随地吐痰
請勿隨地吐痰
Qǐng wù suídì tǔtán
No spitting
(lit. 'Please don't spit')

51

Expressing commands and permission

51.1 Commands

51.1.1 Making a command

There is no specific command form in Mandarin, but there are several ways to make a command.

The simplest way is simply to state the verb:

吃！	说！/ 說！	坐！
Chī!	**Shuō!**	**Zuò!**
Eat!	Speak!	Sit!

The verb may sometimes be suffixed with 着/著 **zhe**:

吃着！/ 吃著！	拿着！/ 拿著！	坐着！/ 坐著！
Chīzhe!	**Názhe!**	**Zuòzhe!**
Eat!	Hold it!/Take it!	Sit!

▶ 17.2

Commands may also take the form of a statement followed by 吧 **ba**.

吃吧！	给我吧！ 給我吧！	坐吧！
Chī ba!	**Gěi wǒ ba!**	**Zuò ba!**
Eat!	Give (it) to me!	Sit!

Note that the particle 吧 **ba** at the end of the sentence may also convey suggestion:

我们看电影吧！
我們看電影吧！
Wǒmen kàn diànyǐng ba!
Let's see a movie!

or supposition:

你是王老师吧。
你是王老師吧。
Nǐ shì Wáng lǎoshī ba.
You must be Professor Wang.

Context will make the function of 吧 **ba** clear in any given sentence.

▶ 56.2

EXPRESSING COMMANDS AND PERMISSION

51.1.2 Negative commands: prohibitions

To command someone not to do something, use 不要 **bù yào** 'don't,' 别 **bié** 'don't,' or 不许/不許 **bù xǔ** 'not allow.'

> 不要在屋里吸烟!
> 不要在屋裡吸煙!
> **Bù yào zài wūlǐ xī yān!**
> Don't smoke in the house!

> 别出去!
> **Bié chūqu!**
> Don't go out!

> 喝酒以后不许开车。
> 喝酒以後不許開車。
> **Hē jiǔ yǐhòu bù xǔ kāi chē.**
> After you drink alcohol, you are not allowed to drive a car.

▶ 50.2.1

51.1.3 Reporting a command

To report a command, use the verb 叫 **jiào** 'to order,' 'to call,' 'to tell.'

> 他叫我走。
> **Tā jiào wǒ zǒu.**
> He ordered me to leave. (He told me to leave.)

> 谁叫你这样做的?
> 誰叫你這樣做的?
> **Shéi jiào nǐ zhèyàng zuò de?**
> Who told you to do it this way?

> Q: 妈妈叫你去买什么?
> 媽媽叫你去買甚麼?
> **Māma jiào nǐ qù mǎi shénme?**
> What did Mom tell you to buy?

> A: 妈妈叫我去买一瓶可口可乐。
> 媽媽叫我去買一瓶可口可樂。
> **Māma jiào wǒ qù mǎi yī píng kěkǒukělè.**
> Mom made me (told me to) buy a bottle of Coke.

Note that 叫 **jiào** has other meanings and functions that are not associated with commands. They include 'to call/to be called':

> 我叫郭美玲。
> **Wǒ jiào Guō Měilíng.**
> I am called Guo Meiling.

▶ 22.5

and the passive marker 'by':

> 饼干都叫孩子吃完了。
> 餅乾都叫孩子吃完了。
> **Bǐnggān dōu jiào háizi chīwán le.**
> The cookies were all eaten up by the children.

▶ 21

Permission

51.2 Permission

51.2.1 Giving permission

To give permission, use the modal verb 可以 **kěyǐ** 'can/permitted.' To deny permission, say 不可以 **bù kěyǐ** 'cannot/not permitted.'

> Q: 妈妈，今天晚上，我可以不可以跟朋友去看电影？
> 媽媽，今天晚上，我可以不可以跟朋友去看電影？
> **Māma, jīntiān wǎnshang, wǒ kěyǐ bù kěyǐ gēn péngyou qù kàn diànyǐng?**
> Mom, may I go to see a movie with my friends tonight?

> A: 你可以去看电影，可是不可以太晚回家。
> 你可以去看電影，可是不可以太晚回家。
> **Nǐ kěyǐ qù kàn diànyǐng, kěshì bù kěyǐ tài wǎn huí jiā.**
> Yes, you may go to see a movie, but you can't come home too late.

> Q: 这里可以不可以抽烟？
> 這裡可以不可以抽煙？
> **Zhèli kěyǐ bù kěyǐ chōu yān?**
> Can one smoke here?

> A: 这里不可以抽烟。
> 這裡不可以抽煙。
> **Zhèli bù kěyǐ chōu yān.**
> No, one can't smoke here.

> Q: 我们今天不能来，可以明天来吗？
> 我們今天不能來，可以明天來嗎？
> **Wǒmen jīntiān bù néng lái, kěyǐ míngtiān lái ma?**
> We can't come today. Can we come tomorrow instead?

> A: 当然可以。
> 當然可以。
> **Dāngrán kěyǐ.**
> Of course you can.

▶ 12.2.3

51.2.2 Reporting permission

To report that someone is allowed to do something, use 让/讓 **ràng** 'to let/to permit/to allow,' or 许/許 **xǔ** 'to permit/to allow.'

> 我父母让我去中国学习。
> 我父母讓我去中國學習。
> **Wǒ fùmǔ ràng wǒ qù Zhōngguó xuéxí.**
> My parents let me go to China to study.

> 政府许我出国。
> 政府許我出國。
> **Zhèngfǔ xǔ wǒ chū guó.**
> The government has allowed me to leave the country.

让/讓 **ràng** also functions as the passive marker 'by':

> 我的行李让人拿走了。
> 我的行李讓人拿走了。
> **Wǒ de xíngli ràng rén názǒu le.**
> My suitcase was taken away by someone.

▶ 21

EXPRESSING COMMANDS AND PERMISSION

To indicate that someone is not allowed to do something, say 不叫 **bù jiào**, 不让/不讓 **bù ràng**, or 不许/不許 **bù xǔ**.

老师不叫我们出去。
老師不叫我們出去。
Lǎoshī bù jiào wǒmen chūqu.
The teacher won't allow us to go out.

妈妈不让我看电视。
媽媽不讓我看電視。
Māma bù ràng wǒ kàn diànshì.
Mom won't let me watch television.

你不许喝酒以后开车。
你不許喝酒以後開車。
Nǐ bù xǔ hē jiǔ yǐhòu kāi chē.
You are not allowed to drive after drinking alcohol.

52

Expressing ability and possibility

52.1 Expressing ability

52.1.1 Expressing a learned ability

To express a learned or acquired ability or skill, something that you *know how* to do or have *learned how* to do, use the modal verb 会/會 **huì**.

Q: 你会说英文吗?
你會說英文嗎?
Nǐ huì shuō Yīngwén ma?
Do you know how to speak English?

A: 我会说一点儿英文。
我會說一點兒英文。
Wǒ huì shuō yīdiǎr Yīngwén.
I know how to speak a little English.

Q: 你会开车吗?
你會開車嗎?
Nǐ huì kāi chē ma?
Do you know how to drive?

A: 我还不会开车呢。
我還不會開車呢。
Wǒ hái bù huì kāi chē ne.
I don't know how to drive yet.

▶ 12.2.1

52.1.2 Expressing an innate ability or talent

To express a skill or talent or an innate ability, use the modal verb 会/會 **huì**. When expressing this meaning, 会/會 **huì** may be preceded by the intensifiers 很 **hěn** 'very,' 真 **zhēn** 'really,' or 最 **zuì** 'the most.'

我妹妹很会跳舞。你请她跳吧。
我妹妹很會跳舞。你請她跳吧。
Wǒ mèimei hěn huì tiào wǔ. Nǐ qǐng tā tiào ba.
My little sister dances very well. Ask her to dance with you.

王教授最会教数学了。
王教授最會教數學了。
Wáng jiàoshòu zuì huì jiāo shùxué le.
Professor Wang is the best at teaching math.

王: 来，干杯!
來，乾杯!
Wáng: Lái, gānbēi!
Wang: Bottoms up!

林: 我真不会喝酒。
我真不會喝酒。
Lín: Wǒ zhēn bù huì hē jiǔ.
Lin: I really can't drink.

▶ 10.3, 12.2.1

EXPRESSING ABILITY AND POSSIBILITY

52.1.3 Expressing physical ability

To express physical ability or the unobstructed ability to perform an action, use 能 **néng**.

我的身体不好。大夫说我不能游泳。
我的身體不好。大夫說我不能游泳。
Wǒ de shēntǐ bù hǎo. Dàifu shuō wǒ bù néng yóu yǒng.
My health is not so good. The doctor said I cannot swim.

他一天能作十几个小时的事。
他一天能作十幾個小時的事。
Tā yītiān néng zuò shí jǐ gè xiǎoshí de shì.
He can work more than ten hours a day.

When used to express ability, 能 **néng**, like 会/會 **huì**, can be modified by intensifiers such as 很 **hěn** 'very,' 真 **zhēn** 'really,' or 太 **tài** 'too.'

中国人很能吃苦。
中國人很能吃苦。
Zhōngguórén hěn néng chī kǔ.
The Chinese can endure a lot of hardship.

我的女儿真会花钱。
我的女兒真會花錢。
Wǒ de nǚ'ér zhēn huì huā qián.
My daughter can really spend money.

▶ 10.3, 12.2.2

52.2 Expressing possibility

52.2.1 Expressing the likely occurrence of an event

To express possibility or the likelihood of the occurrence of an event, as in 'will,' 'could possibly,' or 'would probably,' use the modal verb 会/會 **huì**.

Q: 明天会不会下雪?
明天會不會下雪?
Míngtiān huì bù huì xià xuě?
Is it going to snow tomorrow?

A: 天气预报说明天不会下雪。
天氣預報說明天不會下雪。
Tiānqì yùbào shuō míngtiān bù huì xià xuě.
According to the weather report, it won't snow tomorrow.

Q: 你想我们要坐的飞机会不会误点?
你想我們要坐的飛機會不會誤點?
Nǐ xiǎng wǒmen yào zuò de fēijī huì bù huì wùdiǎn?
Do you think the plane we are going to take will be late?

A: 航空公司说，我们要坐的飞机不会误点。
航空公司說，我們要坐的飛機不會誤點。
Hángkōng gōngsī shuō, wǒmen yào zuò de fēijī bù huì wùdiǎn.
The airline company says the plane we are going to take won't be late.

▶ 12.1, 36.3

Expressing possibility 52.2

52.2.2 Expressing feasibility

The modal 可以 **kěyǐ** is also sometimes used to express the feasibility of an event.

> 我们今天可以不考试吗?　　　　不可以。
> 我們今天可以不考試嗎?
> **Wǒmen jīntiān kěyǐ bù kǎo shì ma?**　**Bù kěyǐ.**
> Can we not have a test today?　　　No, not possible.

The most common function of 可以 **kěyǐ** is to express permission.

▶ 12.3, 51.2

52.2.3 Describing circumstances that may influence the occurrence of an event

To specify circumstantial factors that favor or obstruct the occurrence of an event, use 能 **néng**.

> 中国孩子都能上中学吗?
> 中國孩子都能上中學嗎?
> **Zhōngguó háizi dōu néng shàng zhōngxué ma?**
> Can all Chinese children go to high school?

> 今天我的车坏了, 所以不能去接你了。
> 今天我的車壞了, 所以不能去接你了。
> **Jīntiān wǒ de chē huài le, suǒyǐ bù néng qù jiē nǐ le.**
> I can't pick you up today because my car has broken down.

53

Expressing desires, needs, preferences, and willingness

53.1 Expressing desires

To express a desire for something to happen, say:

希望 xīwàng 'to hope'

> 我希望我们有机会再见。
> 我希望我們有機會再見。
> **Wǒ xīwàng wǒmen yǒu jīhuì zài jiàn.**
> I hope we have the chance to meet again.

要 yào 'to want'

> 她要看她母亲。
> 她要看她母親。
> **Tā yào kàn tā mǔqīn.**
> She wants to see her mother.

> 她要回家。
> **Tā yào huí jiā.**
> She wants to go home.

盼望 pànwang 'to hope for, long for' (+ VP)

> 母亲天天盼望哥哥回来。
> 母親天天盼望哥哥回來。
> **Mǔqīn tiāntiān pànwàng gēge huí lai.**
> Mother hopes every day that older brother will come back.

期望 qīwàng 'to expect'

> 我期望能早日回国。
> 我期望能早日回國。
> **Wǒ qīwàng néng zǎorì huí guó.**
> I hope I can return to my home country soon.

期望 qīwàng can also be used as a noun:

> 父母对孩子的期望很大。
> 父母對孩子的期望很大。
> **Fùmǔ duì háizi de qīwàng hěn dà.**
> Parents have great hopes and expectations for their children.
> (The expectations of parents regarding their children are very big.)

Expressing preferences   53.3

To express a desire for something, say:

要 *yào* 'to want'

> 他要一辆新车。
> 他要一輛新車。
> **Tā yào yī liàng xīn chē.**
> He wants a new car.

> 小狗饿了，要吃东西。
> 小狗餓了，要吃東西。
> **Xiǎo gǒu è le, yào chī dōngxi.**
> The puppy is hungry and wants to eat something.

53.2 Expressing needs

To indicate that you need something, say:

需要 *xūyào* 'to need'

> 他需要安慰和了解。
> **Tā xūyào ānwèi hé liáojiě.**
> He needs comfort and understanding.

> 我需要你的帮助。
> 我需要你的幫助。
> **Wǒ xūyào nǐ de bāngzhù.**
> I need your help.

得 *děi* [+ verb] 'to need [to do]'

> 这个汤得多加点盐。
> 這個湯得多加點鹽。
> **Zhège tāng děi duō jiā diǎn yán.**
> This soup needs a little more salt.
> (This soup needs (for us) to add a little more salt.)

> 我们得晚上十点到家。
> 我們得晚上十點到家。
> **Wǒmen děi wǎnshang shí diǎn dào jiā.**
> We need to be home by 10 p.m.

▶ 12.4, 50.1

53.3 Expressing preferences

To indicate a preference, say:

宁可/寧可 *nìngkě* 'to prefer'

> 我们宁可在家吃饭，不愿意去饭馆吃。
> 我們寧可在家吃飯，不願意去飯館吃。
> **Wǒmen nìngkě zài jiā chī fàn, bù yuànyi qù fànguǎn chī.**
> We'd prefer to eat at home. We do not want to go to a restaurant to eat.

> 他宁可死，也不愿意屈服。
> 他寧可死，也不願意屈服。
> **Tā nìngkě sǐ, yě bù yuànyi qūfú.**
> He'd prefer to die, and he is not ready to surrender.

345

EXPRESSING DESIRES, NEEDS, PREFERENCES, AND WILLINGNESS

偏爱/偏愛 *piān'ài* 'to favor, be partial to somebody or something'

老师不应该偏爱某一个学生。
老師不應該偏愛某一個學生。
Lǎoshī bù yīnggāi piān'ài mǒu yī gè xuésheng.
The teacher should not be partial to any student.

情愿/情願 *qíngyuàn* 'would rather'

我情愿一辈子不结婚，也不要跟他结婚。
我情願一輩子不結婚，也不要跟他結婚。
Wǒ qíngyuàn yī bèizi bù jiéhūn, yě bù yào gēn tā jiéhūn.
I'd rather be single all my life than marry him.

53.4 Expressing willingness

To indicate willingness, say:

愿意/願意 *yuànyi* 'to be willing'

我愿意嫁给他。
我願意嫁給他。
Wǒ yuànyi jiàgěi tā.
I am willing to marry him.

我不愿意嫁给别人。
我不願意嫁給別人。
Wǒ bù yuànyi jiàgěi biéren.
I don't want to marry anyone else.

我愿意跟你合作。
我願意跟你合作。
Wǒ yuànyi gēn nǐ hézuò.
I am willing to cooperate with you.

54

Expressing knowledge, advice, and opinions

54.1 Expressing knowledge

To express knowledge, use the following verbs:

知道	zhīdao	to know
认识/認識	rènshi	to recognize/to know
会/會	huì	to be able to, to know

54.1.1 Expressing knowledge with 知道 zhīdao and 认识/認識 rènshi

知道 zhīdao and 认识/認識 rènshi can both be translated into English as 'to know.' They are sometimes interchangeable, but they often have distinct uses.

- 知道 zhīdao means *to know information*.
- 认识/認識 rènshi means *to know of* or *to recognize*. It is used to talk about recognizing Chinese characters and locations, as well as people.

The following examples illustrate the differences between 知道 zhīdao and 认识/認識 rènshi.

Conversation 1

Q: 你认识他吗?
你認識他嗎?
Nǐ *rènshi* tā ma?
Do you *know* him?

A: 我知道他是谁，可是我不认识他。
我知道他是誰，可是我不認識他。
Wǒ *zhīdao* tā shì shéi, kěshì wǒ bù *rènshi* tā.
I *know* who he is, but I don't *know* him.

Do not say

*你知道他吗?
你知道他嗎?
Nǐ *zhīdao* tā ma?

Conversation 2

Q: 你知道火车站在哪儿吗?
你知道火車站在哪兒嗎?
Nǐ *zhīdao* huǒchēzhàn zài nǎr ma?
Do you *know* where the train station is?

A: 我不知道。对不起。
我不知道。對不起。
Wǒ bù *zhīdao*. Duìbuqǐ.
I don't *know*. Sorry.

Do not say

*你认识火车站在哪儿吗?
你認識火車站在哪兒嗎?
Nǐ *rènshi* huǒchēzhàn zài nǎr ma?

Do not say

*我不认识。对不起。
我不認識。對不起。
Wǒ bù *rènshi*. Duìbuqǐ.

54.2 EXPRESSING KNOWLEDGE, ADVICE, AND OPINIONS

Conversation 3

Q: 你认识中国字吗?
你認識中國字嗎?
Nǐ rènshi Zhōngguó zì ma?

Do you *know* Chinese characters?

Do not say

*你知道中国字吗?
你知道中國字嗎?
Nǐ zhīdao Zhōngguó zì ma?

A: 我认识，可是我不知道怎么写。
我認識，可是我不知道怎麼寫。
Wǒ rènshi, kěshì wǒ bù zhīdao zěnme xiě.

I recognize them, but I don't know how to write them.

Do not say

*我知道，可是我不认识怎么写。
我知道，可是我不認識怎麼寫。
Wǒ zhīdao, kěshì wǒ bù rènshi zěnme xiě.

Conversation 4

Q: 请问，到图书馆怎么走?
請問，到圖書館怎麼走?
Qǐngwèn, dào túshūguǎn zěnme zǒu?
Excuse me, how do you go to the library?

A: 对不起，我不认识路。
對不起，我不認識路。
Duìbuqǐ, wǒ bù rènshi lù.
Sorry, I don't know the way.

54.1.2 Expressing knowledge with 会/會 *huì*

One meaning conveyed by the modal verb 会/會 **huì** is that of ability associated with knowledge. In the following sentences, 会/會 **huì** means *to be able to* or *to know*.

Q: 你会说英文吗?
你會說英文嗎?
Nǐ huì shuō Yīngwén ma?
Do you speak English?

A: 我会说一点儿。
我會說一點兒。
Wǒ huì shuō yīdiǎr.
I can speak a little.

Q: 你会不会开车?
你會不會開車?
Nǐ huì bù huì kāi chē?
Do you know how to drive?

A: 我十八岁就会开车了。
我十八歲就會開車了。
Wǒ shíbā suì jiù huì kāi chē le.
I have known how to drive since I was eighteen.

Q: 美国人都会跳舞吧?
美國人都會跳舞吧?
Měiguórén dōu huì tiào wǔ ba?
All Americans know how to dance, right?

A: 不一定。我就不会。
不一定。我就不會。
Bù yīdìng. Wǒ jiù bù huì.
Not necessarily. I for one cannot dance.

▶ 12.1

54.2 Advice and opinions

54.2.1 Requesting and giving advice and opinions

To give your opinion or your advice, or to ask another for their opinion or advice, use these expressions.

Advice and opinions 54.2

想 *xiǎng* 'to think'

> Q: 你想我们是坐飞机好，还是坐火车好？
> 你想我們是坐飛機好，還是坐火車好？
> **Nǐ xiǎng wǒmen shì zuò fēijī hǎo, háishi zuò huǒchē hǎo?**
> Do you think we should fly or take the train?

> A: 我想我们坐飞机比较好。
> 我想我們坐飛機比較好。
> **Wǒ xiǎng wǒmen zuò fēijī bǐjiào hǎo.**
> I think it is better to fly.

The Mandarin equivalent of the English expression 'I don't think...' is 我想...不 **wǒ xiǎng...bù** 'I think...not...' and not 我不想 **wǒ bù xiǎng...**

> 我想他不聪明。
> 我想他不聰明。
> **Wǒ xiǎng tā bù cōngming.**
> I don't think he is smart.

> 我想他不会来。
> 我想他不會來。
> **Wǒ xiǎng tā bù huì lái.**
> I don't think he is going to come.

看 *kàn* 'to look at, consider, think'

> Q: 你看这件事应该怎么办？
> 你看這件事應該怎麼辦？
> **Nǐ kàn zhè jiàn shì yīnggāi zěnme bàn?**
> How do you think we should handle this matter?

> A: 我看我们得先看看大家的意见。
> 我看我們得先看看大家的意見。
> **Wǒ kàn wǒmen děi xiān kànkan dàjiā de yìjiàn.**
> I think we should consider everybody's opinion first.

觉得/覺得 *juéde* 'to feel, to consider, to think'

> 他们都觉得这样做比较妥当。
> 他們都覺得這樣做比較妥當。
> **Tāmen dōu juéde zhèyàng zuò bǐjiào tuǒdang.**
> They all feel that doing it this way is more appropriate.

说/說 *shuō* 'to say'

> 你说我应该选哪门课？
> 你說我應該選哪門課？
> **Nǐ shuō wǒ yīnggāi xuǎn nǎ mén kè?**
> Which courses do you say I should take?

认为/認為 *rènwéi* 'to believe, to suppose, to consider'

以为/以為 *yǐwéi* 'to believe, to suppose, to consider'

以为/以為 *yǐwéi* and 认为/認為 *rènwéi* overlap in meaning and usage.

> 我以为这次的旅行很有意思。(认为/認為 **rènwéi** can be used)
> 我以為這次的旅行很有意思。
> **Wǒ yǐwéi zhècì de lǚxíng hěn yǒu yìsi.**
> I *consider* this trip to be very interesting.

349

EXPRESSING KNOWLEDGE, ADVICE, AND OPINIONS — 54.2

> 大家都<u>以为</u>他是一个好人。(认为/認為 **rènwéi** can be used)
> 大家都<u>以為</u>他是一個好人。
> **Dàjiā dōu *yǐwéi* tā shì yī gè hǎorén.**
> Everyone *believes* he is a good person.

以为/以為 **yǐwéi** also means 'to mistakenly assume' something. This meaning is not shared by 认为/認為 **rènwéi**. It is illustrated in the following sentences:

> 我以为你是日本人,原来你是韩国人。
> 我以為你是日本人,原來你是韓國人。
> **Wǒ yǐwéi nǐ shì Rìběn rén, yuánlái nǐ shì Hánguó rén.**
> I thought you were Japanese, but you are Korean.

> 我以为今天不会下雨。没想到下了这么大的雨。
> 我以為今天不會下雨。沒想到下了這麼大的雨。
> **Wǒ yǐwéi jīntiān bù huì xià yǔ. Méi xiǎngdào xià le zhème dà de yǔ.**
> I assumed that it wouldn't rain today. I had no idea that it would rain this much.

When giving or requesting advice, you can make reference to obligations.

> 我想你<u>应该</u>多用功一些。
> 我想你<u>應該</u>多用功一些。
> **Wǒ xiǎng nǐ *yīnggāi* duō yònggōng yīxiē.**
> I think you *should* be a little more diligent.

▶ 12.4, 50.1

54.2.2 Making your request polite

To make your request for an opinion or advice polite, use these expressions.

请问/請問 ***qǐng wèn*** 'may I ask, excuse me'

> 请问,我应该送他什么礼物?
> 請問,我應該送他甚麼禮物?
> **Qǐngwèn, wǒ yīnggāi sòng tā shénme lǐwù?**
> May I ask, what kind of gift should I give him?

请教/請教 ***qǐng jiào*** 'please teach me/(I) request instruction'

> 我有一个问题跟您请教。
> 我有一個問題跟您請教。
> **Wǒ yǒu yī gè wèntí gēn nín qǐng jiào.**
> I'd like some advice from you on a question.

请指教/請指教 ***qǐng zhǐjiào*** 'please provide instruction'

> 我写了一篇文章请你多指教。
> 我寫了一篇文章請你多指教。
> **Wǒ xiě le yī piān wénzhāng qǐng nǐ duō zhǐjiào.**
> I've written an essay that I would like your comments on.

Advice and opinions   54.2

54.2.3 Telling someone their best or only option

These expressions can be used when giving strong, direct advice.

最好 *zuì hǎo* (+ verb phrase) 'the best thing to do is'

   Q: 下雨呢！怎么办啊？
        下雨呢！怎麼辦啊？
        Xià yǔ ne! Zěnme bàn a?
        It's raining. What should we do?

   A: 那，我们最好不去。
        那，我們最好不去。
        Nà, wǒmen zuì hǎo bù qù.
        Well then, we'd best not go.

只好 *zhǐ hǎo* (+ verb phrase) 'the only thing to do is'

    要是你要考得好，只好认真的学习。
    要是你要考得好，只好認真的學習。
    Yàoshi nǐ yào kǎo de hǎo, zhǐ hǎo rènzhēn de xuéxí.
    If you want to do well on the exam, the only thing you can do is study hard.

54.2.4 Telling someone to do as they please

To tell someone to do as they please, use the following expressions:

随便/隨便 *suíbiàn* + verb phrase '(do) as you please'

    别客气！随便吃！
    別客氣！隨便吃！
    Bié kèqì! Suíbiàn chī!
    Don't be polite. (Don't adhere strictly to the rituals of guest and host.) Eat whatever you want.

    (at a restaurant)
    Customer: 我们坐哪儿？/我們坐哪兒？
                Wǒmen zuò nǎr?
                Where should we sit?
    Waiter: 随便。/隨便。
                Suíbiàn.
                Wherever you want.

subject	怎么	verb	就	怎么	verb
subject	怎麼	verb	就	怎麼	verb
subject	**zěnme**	verb	**jiù**	**zěnme**	verb

do whatever the subject pleases

Conversation 1

   Q: 这件事我怎么作好？
        這件事我怎麼作好？
        Zhè jiàn shì wǒ zěnme zuò hǎo?
        How should I best do this?

   A: 这我可不知道，你想怎么做就怎么做吧。
        這我可不知道，你想怎麼做就怎麼做吧。
        Zhè wǒ kě bù zhīdào, nǐ xiǎng zěnme zuò jiù zěnme zuò ba.
        I don't know. Do it the way you think it should be done.

EXPRESSING KNOWLEDGE, ADVICE, AND OPINIONS

Conversation 2

Q: 你想这个周末我们去哪儿好?
你想這個週末我們去哪兒好?
Nǐ xiǎng zhège zhōumò wǒmen qù nǎr hǎo?
Where do you think we should go this weekend?

A: 你想去哪儿我们就去哪儿吧，我没意见。
你想去哪兒我們就去哪兒吧，我沒意見。
Nǐ xiǎng qù nǎr wǒmen jiù qù nǎr ba, wǒ méi yìjiàn.
We will go wherever you think we should go. I don't have an opinion.

Conversation 3

Q: 姐姐，你说我跟谁出去玩儿好?
姐姐，你說我跟誰出去玩兒好?
Jiějie, nǐ shuō wǒ gēn shéi chūqu wár hǎo?
Older sister, who do you think I should go out with?

A: 你想跟谁玩儿就跟谁玩儿。不必问我。
你想跟誰玩兒就跟誰玩兒。不必問我。
Nǐ xiǎng gēn shéi wár jiù gēn shéi wár. Bù bì wèn wǒ.
Go out with whomever you want. You don't have to ask me.

55

Expressing fear, worry, and anxiety

55.1 Expressing fear of something

To express fear of something, say:

subject 怕 **pà** something
subject is afraid of something

> 我怕狗。
> **Wǒ pà gǒu.**
> I am afraid of dogs.

> 我们不要怕困难。
> 我們不要怕困難。
> **Wǒmen bù yào pà kùnnán.**
> We shouldn't be afraid of difficulty.

> 我妈妈怕胖，不敢多吃。
> 我媽媽怕胖，不敢多吃。
> **Wǒ māma pà pàng, bù gǎn duō chī.**
> My mother is afraid of getting fat. She doesn't dare eat much.

> 这个人真是天不怕，地不怕。
> 這個人真是天不怕，地不怕。
> **Zhège rén zhēn shì tiān bù pà, dì bù pà.**
> This person is not afraid of anything.

▶ 63.3

To tell someone not to be afraid of something, say:

别怕！ *Bié pà!* 'Don't be afraid!'

> 别怕我的狗。
> **Bié pà wǒ de gǒu.**
> Don't be afraid of my dog.

不要怕！ *Bù yào pà!* 'Don't be afraid!'

> 不要怕他。他人很好。
> **Bù yào pà tā. Tā rén hěn hǎo.**
> Don't be afraid of him. He means well.

To indicate that someone is afraid, use these expressions:

怕死（了） *pàsǐ le* 'to be scared to death'

> 我怕死了。
> **Wǒ pàsǐ le.**
> I am scared to death.

▶ 18.7

353

EXPRESSING FEAR, WORRY, AND ANXIETY

55.2

害怕 *hàipà* 'to be afraid'

> 我很害怕。
> **Wǒ hěn hàipà.**
> I'm very afraid.

恐惧/恐懼 *kǒngjù* 'to be terrified' *(literary expression used in formal speech and writing)*

> 北京的雾霾让很多外国游客恐惧。
> 北京的霧霾讓很多外國遊客恐懼。
> **Běijīng de wùmái ràng hěn duō wàiguó yóukè kǒngjù.**
> The Beijing smog has frightened a lot of foreign tourists.

恐惧/恐懼 *kǒngjù* is also used as a noun, meaning 'fear' or 'terror.'

> 一想到战争的可能性，我心里就充满了恐惧。
> 一想到戰爭的可能性，我心裏就充滿了恐懼。
> **Yī xiǎngdào zhànzhēng de kěnéng xìng, wǒ xīnli jiù chōngmǎn le kǒngjù.**
> When I think about the possibility of war, my heart fills with fear.

▶ 42.3.3

55.2 Expressing nervousness or anxiety

To indicate that someone is nervous, say:

紧张/緊張 *jǐnzhāng* 'to be nervous'

> 考试以前我很紧张。
> 考試以前我很緊張。
> **Kǎoshì yǐqián wǒ hěn jǐnzhāng.**
> Before I take a test, I am very nervous.

To indicate that someone is worried or anxious, say:

着急/著急 *zháojí* 'to be worried or anxious'

> 他找不着飞机票了。非常着急。
> 他找不著飛機票了。非常著急。
> **Tā zhǎobuzháo fēijī piào le. Fēicháng zháojí.**
> He can't find the airplane ticket(s). (He is) extremely anxious.

To indicate worry about someone or something, say:

担心/擔心 *dānxīn* 'worry about'

> 我担心我的儿子。
> 我擔心我的兒子。
> **Wǒ dānxīn wǒ de érzi.**
> I am worried about my son.

为 something 着急
為 something 著急
wéi something **zháojí**
worried about something

> 我为后果着急。
> 我為後果著急。
> **Wǒ wéi hòuguǒ zháojí.**
> I am worried about the results.

Indicating that something scares someone   **55.4**

To tell someone not to worry or be nervous, say:

别着急。　　别紧张。
　　　　　　别緊張。
Bié zháojí.   **Bié jǐnzhāng.**
Don't worry.   Don't be nervous.

To ask someone in an informal context what they are worried about, say:

你着什么急啊？
你著什麼急啊？
Nǐ zháo shénme jí a?
What are you worried about?

55.3 Indicating that something is scary

To indicate that something is scary or frightening, say:

something 可怕 **kěpà**

今天看的这个电影真可怕
今天看的這個電影真可怕。
Jīntiān kàn de zhège diànyǐng zhēn kěpà.
The movie we saw today was very scary.

战争真可怕。
戰爭真可怕。
Zhànzhēng zhēn kěpà.
War is very frightening.

To describe something as scary, say:

恐怖的 noun
kǒngbù de noun
scary noun

我不喜欢看恐怖的电影。
我不喜歡看恐怖的電影。
Wǒ bù xǐhuan kàn kǒngbù de diànyǐng.
I don't like to watch horror movies.

▶ 9.2

55.4 Indicating that something scares someone

something 吓/嚇 **xià** someone

别吓着孩子。
別嚇著孩子。
Bié xiàzhe háizi.
Don't scare the child.

你别吓我好不好？
你別嚇我好不好？
Nǐ bié xià wǒ hǎo bù hǎo?
Don't scare me, okay?

你吓死我了。
你嚇死我了。
Nǐ xiàsǐ wǒ le.
You scared me to death.

355

56

Expressing speaker attitudes and perspectives

Mandarin uses interjections at the beginning of the sentence and syllables at the end of the sentence (*sentence final particles*) to indicate the attitude of the speaker toward the situation expressed in the sentence. Attitudes expressed by interjections and sentence final particles include surprise, disgust, agreement, pity, etc.

Interjections and sentence final particles stand outside of the grammar of the sentence. Their omission or inclusion never affects the grammatical status of the sentence. However, their appropriate use contributes to the naturalness of the sentence, making it sound more authentically Mandarin.

56.1 Interjections

Syllables serving as interjections always have tones. Here are some common interjections and their associated meanings.

哈 *hā satisfaction*

> 哈哈！还是我对吧！
> 哈哈！還是我對吧！
> **Hā hā! Hái shì wǒ duì ba!**
> Well (ha), so I was right after all!

嗐 *hài sorrow, regret*

> 嗐，你怎么能跟这种人结婚？
> 嗐，你怎麼能跟這種人結婚？
> **Hài, nǐ zěnme néng gēn zhè zhǒng rén jiéhūn?**
> Why, how can you marry this kind of person?

啊 *ā surprise*

> 啊！他死了？
> **Ā! Tā sǐ le?**
> What? He passed away?

啊 *á doubt, surprise*

> 啊，你会说英文！
> 啊，你會說英文！
> **Á, nǐ huì shuō Yīngwén!**
> Oh! You speak English!

啊 *ǎ puzzled surprise*

> 啊，你把飞机票弄丢了？
> 啊，你把飛機票弄丟了？
> **Ǎ, nǐ bǎ fēijī piào nòngdiū le?**
> What! You lost your airplane ticket?

Interjections

56.1

啊 *à agreement, approval, acknowledgement*

> 啊，你说得很对。
> 啊，你說得很對。
> **À, nǐ shuō de hěn duì.**
> Yes. What you said was right.

哎 *āi surprise, dissatisfaction*

> 哎，火车怎么还没来啊？
> 哎，火車怎麼還沒來啊？
> **Āi, huǒchē zěnme hái méi lái a?**
> Oh! Why isn't the train here yet?

哎哟/哎唷 *āiyō surprise, pain*

> 哎哟/哎唷！把我疼死了。
> **Āiyō! Bǎ wǒ téngsǐ le.**
> Ouch! It hurts so much.

哎呀 *āiyā wonder, admiration, shock*

> 哎呀！太晚了。我得走了。
> **Āiyā! Tài wǎn le. Wǒ děi zǒu le.**
> Gosh! It is already so late. I have to go now.

啊呀 *āyā pained surprise*

> 啊呀！我的钱包不见了。
> 啊呀！我的錢包不見了。
> **Āyā! Wǒ de qiánbāo bù jiàn le.**
> Oh no! My wallet is missing.

唉 *āi regret*

> 唉，真没想到他的车出事了。
> 唉，真沒想到他的車出事了。
> **Āi, zhēn méi xiǎngdào tā de chē chūshì le.**
> How awful. I never thought that his car would be in an accident.

噢 *ō sudden realization*

> 噢，我忘了给你钱了。
> 噢，我忘了給你錢了。
> **Ō, wǒ wàng le gěi nǐ qián le.**
> Oh, I forgot to pay you.

哦 *ó suspicion, not fully believing*

> 哦，你们认识？
> 哦，你們認識？
> **Ó, nǐmen rènshi?**
> Oh, you know each other?

喔 *ō surprise, sudden realization*

> 喔，原来你是警察啊！
> 喔，原來你是警察啊！
> **Ō, yuánlái nǐ shì jǐngchá a!**
> Oh, so you are a policeman!

357

EXPRESSING SPEAKER ATTITUDES AND PERSPECTIVES

56.2 Sentence final particles

Sentence final particles occur in neutral tone. Here are some common sentence final particles that are used to express speaker attitude.

嘛 **ma** *indicates that something is obviously true*

> 我早就告诉你他不是好人嘛。
> 我早就告訴你他不是好人嘛。
> **Wǒ zǎo jiù gàosu nǐ tā bù shì hǎo rén ma.**
> Didn't I tell you from the start that he wasn't a good person?

啊 **a** *obviousness, impatience*

> 你要多注意身体啊。
> 你要多注意身體啊。
> **Nǐ yào duō zhùyì shēntǐ a.**
> You should pay more attention to your health.

咯 **lo** *obviousness*

> 我们该走了。再不走就晚咯。
> 我們該走了。再不走就晚咯。
> **Wǒmen gāi zǒu le. Zài bù zǒu jiù wǎn lo.**
> We'd better go now. If we don't go, we will be late.

啦 **la** *exclamation*

> 好啦，好啦，别再说啦！
> 好啦，好啦，別再說啦！
> **Hǎo la, hǎo la, bié zài shuō la!**
> Okay, okay, don't say it again!

NOTE   啦 **la** is a combination of the sentence final particles 了 **le** and 啊 **a**. Its meaning varies depending upon the sentence.

吧 **ba** *suggestions; commands; suppositions*

> 多吃一点吧！
> 多吃一點吧！
> **Duō chī yīdiǎn ba!**
> Eat a little more!

> 给我吧！
> 給我吧！
> **Gěi wǒ ba!**
> Give it to me!

> 您是王教授吧！
> **Nín shì Wáng jiàoshòu ba!**
> You must be Professor Wang!

For discussion of the sentence final particles 吗/嗎 **ma**, 呢 **ne**, 了 **le**, and 吧 **ba**, see

▶ 28.1.1, 28.5, 34.3, 38.1, 51.1

57

Topic, focus, and emphasis

57.1 Introducing a topic

The topic is the thing that is being discussed or written about. Mandarin has a variety of ways to introduce and identify the topic. Here are the most common.

57.1.1 Expressions that introduce the topic of a sentence

Mandarin uses the following expressions to introduce the topic of a sentence.

至于/至於 *zhìyú* 'concerning, regarding, as for'

> 至于我们两个人的事情，你就不要管了。
> 至於我們兩個人的事情，你就不要管了。
> **Zhìyú wǒmen liǎng gè rén de shìqing, nǐ jiù bù yào guǎn le.**
> As for the matter between the two of us, you don't have to pay attention to it.

对于/對於 *duìyú* 'concerning, regarding, as for (topic)'

> 对于中国的情形，我也不太清楚。
> 對於中國的情形，我也不太清楚。
> **Duìyú Zhōngguó de qíngxing, wǒ yě bù tài qīngchu.**
> Regarding China's state of affairs, I am also not too clear (about it).

关于/關於 *guānyú* 'concerning, regarding, as for (topic)'

> 关于国家大事，我们都应该注意。
> 關於國家大事，我們都應該注意。
> **Guānyú guójiā dà shì, wǒmen dōu yīnggāi zhùyì.**
> As for the major events of (our) country, we all should pay attention.

对 *(topic)* 来说/對 *(topic)* 來說 *duì (topic) lái shuō* 'as for (topic) . . .'

> 对我来说，教书是一件很快乐的事。
> 對我來說，教書是一件很快樂的事。
> **Duì wǒ lái shuō, jiāo shū shì yī jiàn hěn kuàilè de shì.**
> As for me, teaching is a very enjoyable task.

论(到)/論(到) *lùn (dào)* 'speaking about (topic)'

> 论到足球，我是一窍不通。
> 論到足球，我是一竅不通。
> **Lùn dào zúqiú, wǒ shì yīqiào bù tōng.**
> Speaking about football, I am completely ignorant.

提(到) *tí (dào)* 'speaking about (topic)'

> 提到奥运，你觉得那个裁判公平不公平？
> 提到奧運，你覺得那個裁判公平不公平？
> **Tí dào Àoyùn, nǐ juéde nàge cáipàn gōngpíng bù gōngpíng?**
> Speaking about the Olympics, do you think that decision was fair?

TOPIC, FOCUS, AND EMPHASIS

谈(到)/談(到) **tán (dào)** 'speaking about (topic)'

谈到中英两国的历史，他比谁都有兴趣。
談到中英兩國的歷史，他比誰都有興趣。
Tán dào Zhōng Yīng liǎng guó de lìshǐ, tā bǐ shéi dōu yǒu xìngqu.
Speaking about the history of China and England, he is more interested than anyone.

至于/至於 **zhìyú**, 对于/對於 **duìyú**, and 关于/關於 **guānyú** are interchangeable, as are 提到 **tí dào** and 谈到/談到 **tán dào**.

57.1.2 Structures that identify the topic of a sentence

57.1.2.1 Topicalization

In Mandarin, a noun phrase may be identified as the topic of a sentence when it occurs at the beginning of the sentence. If another noun phrase in the sentence has the same reference as the topic, it is typically omitted. In the following sentences, the first noun phrase is the topic. The omitted phrase is indicated as ( ).

那个饭馆，服务不好。
那個飯館，服務不好。
Nàge fànguǎn, fúwù bù hǎo.
That restaurant, the service is not good.

美国大学，学费很贵。
美國大學，學費很貴。
Měiguó dàxué, xuéfèi hěn guì.
(In) *American universities*, tuition is very expensive.

中国长城，我听说（ ）冬天最美。
中國長城，我聽說（ ）冬天最美。
Zhōngguó Chángchéng, wǒ tīngshuō ( ) dōngtiān zuì měi.
The Great Wall of China, I hear (it) is prettiest in the winter.

汉字，我怎么写（ ）也写不好。
漢字，我怎麼寫（ ）也寫不好。
Hàn zì, wǒ zěnme xiě ( ) yě xiě bù hǎo.
Chinese characters, no matter how I write them I don't write (them) well.

English also topicalizes noun phrases in this way, but topicalization is much more common in Mandarin than in English.

57.1.2.2 Noun phrase omission

In English, when a series of noun phrases refer to the same entity, all instances after the first reference typically occur as pronouns. In Mandarin, noun phrase omission is more common than pronominalization as a way to mark identity of reference. Noun phrase omission is one way that Mandarin identifies a noun phrase as a topic. As we saw in the previous section, noun phrases are typically omitted if they refer to the topic of the discourse.

Noun phrases are omitted when they occur in the same grammatical role as the first noun phrase.

In this example, the first reference and the omitted noun phrases are subjects of the verb:

张美丽每天都很忙。(_)早上六点起床，(_)七点出门，(_)晚上九点才回家。
張美麗每天都很忙。(_)早上六點起牀，(_)七點出門，(_)晚上九點才回家。
Zhāng Měilì měitiān dōu hěn máng. (_) Zǎoshang liùdiǎn qǐ chuáng, (_) qīdiǎn chū mén, (_) wǎnshang jiǔdiǎn cái huí jiā.
Zhang Meili is very busy every day. (*She*) gets up at 6 o'clock, (*she*) leaves the house by 7 o'clock, and (*she*) doesn't get home at night until 9 o'clock.

Focus

In this example, the first reference and the omitted noun phrase are objects of the verb:

> 她买了裙子，到家以后马上穿上了(_)。
> 她買了裙子，到家以後馬上穿上了(_)。
> **Tā mǎi le qúnzi, dào jiā yǐhòu mǎshàng chuānshàng le (_).**
> She bought a skirt; when she got home she immediately put *it* on.

When a noun phrase with identical reference occurs in a different grammatical role from the first instance, it occurs as a pronoun and is not omitted. In this example, the first reference is the object of 喜欢/喜歡 **xǐhuan** 'to like.' In the second reference, it is the subject of the sentence.

> 我们都喜欢那个孩子。她又可爱又乖。
> 我們都喜歡那個孩子。她又可愛又乖。
> **Wǒmen dōu xǐhuan *nàge háizi*. *Tā* yòu kě'ài yòu guāi.**
> We all like that child. She is both cute and well behaved.

57.2 Focus

Mandarin uses the following expressions to *focus* or highlight a phrase. This section presents the structure and purpose of the most common focusing constructions in Mandarin.

57.2.1 把 *bǎ*

把 **bǎ** is used to indicate what a subject does to some object, while focusing on the object. 把 **bǎ** sentences can always be used to answer the question: 'What did the subject do to the object?' 把 **bǎ** sentences are sometimes called the 'disposal construction.' The structure of 把 **bǎ** sentences is as follows.

subject 把 **bǎ** object [prepositional phrase +] verb phrase

> 弟弟把饺子吃完了。
> 弟弟把餃子吃完了。
> **Dìdi bǎ jiǎozi chīwán le.**
> Younger brother ate up the dumplings.
> (Younger brother took the dumplings and ate them up.)

> 他把桌子擦干净了。
> 他把桌子擦乾淨了。
> **Tā bǎ zhuōzi cā gānjìng le.**
> He wiped the table clean.
> (He took the table and wiped it clean.)

The object of 把 **bǎ** must refer to something specific and definite.

The action must have a conclusion or completion. Therefore, 把 **bǎ** is often used with change-of-state verbs and verbs with resultative or directional endings.

> 我把他的地址忘了。(*change-of-state verb*)
> **Wǒ bǎ tā de dìzhǐ *wàng* le.**
> I *forgot* his address.
> (I took his address and forgot it.)

> 他把窗户打破了。(*verb with resultative ending*)
> **Tā bǎ chuānghu *dǎpò* le.**
> He *broke* the window.
> (He took the window and broke it.)

TOPIC, FOCUS, AND EMPHASIS 57.2

她把论文写完了。(*verb with resultative ending*)
她把論文寫完了。
Tā bǎ lùnwén *xiěwán* le.
She *finished writing* her thesis.
(She took her thesis and finished writing it.)

他把每个字都写错了。(*verb with resultative ending*)
他把每個字都寫錯了。
Tā bǎ měi gè zì dōu *xiěcuò* le.
He *wrote* every character *wrong*.
(He took every character and *wrote* it *wrong*.)

▶ 18, 19, 20, 32.1

Mandarin often uses 把 **bǎ** when English would use a passive sentence.

▶ 21

For a more detailed discussion of 把 **bǎ**, see

▶ 20

57.2.2 Indicating exception or addition with 除了 *chúle* ... 以外 *yǐwài*

除了 *chúle* noun phrase 以外 *yǐwài*
except for (noun phrase); in addition to (noun phrase)

This expression introduces an exception to a situation or an additional example of a situation. The structure itself is the same whether it focuses on an exception or an example. The context of the sentence makes it clear whether the sentence is providing an exception or an additional example.

- The noun phrase that follows 除了 *chúle* may be the subject, a 'time when' expression, or the object of the verb.
- The full expression includes both 除了 *chúle* and 以外 *yǐwài*. However, either phrase may be omitted.
- 也 *yě* or 都 *dōu* typically occurs in the predicate.

除了 *chúle* ... 以外 *yǐwài* marking exception: 'except for noun phrase'

除了 *chúle* + *subject*

除了爷爷以外，我们全家都去中国旅游。
除了爺爺以外，我們全家都去中國旅遊。
***Chúle yéye* yǐwài, wǒmen quánjiā dōu qù Zhōngguó lǚyóu.**
Except for grandfather, our whole family is going to China to travel.

除了 *chúle* + *time when*

除了星期天以外，他每天都复习中文。
除了星期天以外，他每天都復習中文。
***Chúle xīngqītiān* yǐwài, tā měitiān dōu fùxí Zhōngwén.**
Except for Sunday, he reviews Chinese every day.

除了 *chúle* + *object*

除了苦瓜以外，我弟弟什么都吃。
除了苦瓜以外，我弟弟甚麼都吃。
***Chúle kǔguā* yǐwài, wǒ dìdi shénme dōu chī.**
Except for bitter melon, my younger brother eats everything.

Focus

57.2

除了 **chúle** . . . 以外 **yǐwài** marking an additional example: 'in addition to noun phrase'

In this use of 除了 **chúle** . . . 以外 **yǐwài**, the adverb 也 **yě** usually occurs in the predicate.

除了 *chúle* + *subject*

> 除了爷爷以外，奶奶也去中国旅游。
> 除了爺爺以外，奶奶也去中國旅遊。
> **Chúle yéye yǐwài, nǎinai yě qù Zhōngguó lǚyóu.**
> Besides grandfather, grandmother will also go to China to travel.

除了 *chúle* + *time when*

> 除了晚上以外，他白天也上网。
> 除了晚上以外，他白天也上網。
> **Chúle wǎnshang yǐwài, tā báitiān yě shàng wǎng.**
> In addition to the evening, he also surfs the web during the day.

除了 *chúle* + *object*

> 除了苦瓜以外，我弟弟也吃辣椒。
> **Chúle kǔguā yǐwài, wǒ dìdi yě chī làjiāo.**
> Besides bitter melon, my younger brother also eats hot peppers.

57.2.3 Indicating inclusion with 连/連 *lián*

连/連 **lián** noun phrase 也/都 **yě/dōu** [+ prepositional phrase +] verb phrase
even noun phrase does verb phrase [+ prepositional phrase]

连/連 **lián** is used to indicate that a noun phrase is included in the situation described by the verb phrase. The noun phrase that follows 连/連 **lián** may be the subject, a 'time when' expression, or the object of the verb. 也 **yě** or 都 **dōu** typically occurs in the predicate.

连/連 *lián* + *subject noun phrase*

> 人人都喜欢吃中国饭。连外国人也喜欢。
> 人人都喜歡吃中國飯。連外國人也喜歡。
> **Rén rén dōu xǐhuan chī Zhōngguó fàn. Lián wàiguórén yě xǐhuan.**
> Everyone likes to eat Chinese food. *Even foreigners* like to (eat Chinese food).

> 我们全家都去中国旅游。连爷爷也去。
> 我們全家都去中國旅遊。連爺爺也去。
> **Wǒmen quánjiā dōu qù Zhōngguó lǚyóu. Lián yéye yě qù.**
> Our whole family is going to China to travel. *Even grandpa* will go.

连/連 *lián* + *'time when' expression*

> 他每天都复习中文。连周末也复习。
> 他每天都復習中文。連週末也復習。
> **Tā měitiān dōu fùxí Zhōngwén. Lián zhōumò yě fùxí.**
> He reviews Chinese every day. He *even* reviews *on the weekend*.

> 他每天都很忙。连礼拜天都很忙。
> 他每天都很忙。連禮拜天都很忙。
> **Tā měitiān dōu hěn máng. Lián lǐbàitiān dōu hěn máng.**
> He is busy every day. He is *even* busy *on Sundays*.

连/連 *lián* + *object noun phrase*

> 我弟弟什么都吃。连苦瓜也吃。
> 我弟弟甚麼都吃。連苦瓜也吃。
> **Wǒ dìdi shénme dōu chī. Lián kǔguā yě chī.**
> My younger brother eats anything. He *even* eats *bitter melon*.

TOPIC, FOCUS, AND EMPHASIS

谁都喜欢这个电影。连爸爸也喜欢。
誰都喜歡這個電影。連爸爸也喜歡。
Shéi dōu xǐhuan zhège diànyǐng. Lián bàba yě xǐhuan.
Everyone likes that movie. Even Dad likes it.

57.2.4 Focusing with 是 *shì* or 是 ... 的 *shì* ... *de*

是 **shì**, or 是 ... 的 **shì** ... **de** together, focus on some detail of an event: the time, the place, the actor, etc.

The phrase that is focused occurs immediately after 是 **shì**.

If the sentence refers to a situation in past time, 的 **de** occurs at the very end of the sentence, or immediately after the verb. In the following examples, the phrase that is focused is emphasized.

▶ 11.4, 30.5

Focus on the subject

是他给我们介绍的。
是他給我們介紹的。
Shì *tā* gěi wǒmen jièshào de.
It was *he* who introduced us.

Focus on the place

我是在中国学中文的。
我是在中國學中文的。
Wǒ shì *zài Zhōngguó* xué Zhōngwén de.
It was *in China* where I studied Chinese.

你们是在哪儿认识的?
你們是在哪兒認識的?
Nǐmen shì *zài nǎr* rènshi de?
Where did you meet?

Focus on the 'time when'

他是去年买的那本书。
他是去年買的那本書。
Tā shì *qùnián* mǎi de nà běn shū.
It was *last year* when he bought that book.

Focus on the prepositional phrase

我是跟朋友看电影的。
我是跟朋友看電影的。
Wǒ shì *gēn péngyou* kàn diànyǐng de.
It was *with friends* that I saw the movie.

是 **shì** may be omitted, unless it is negated.

这双鞋(是)在王府井买的。
這雙鞋(是)在王府井買的。
Zhè shuāng xié (shì) *zài Wángfǔjǐng* mǎi de.
These shoes were bought *in Wangfujing*.

这双鞋不是在王府井买的。
這雙鞋不是在王府井買的。
Zhè shuāng xié bù shì *zài Wángfǔjǐng* mǎi de.
These shoes were not bought *in Wangfujing*.

Emphasis

If the object of the verb is a pronoun, 的 **de** can only occur after the pronoun, at the end of the sentence.

Say this	Not this
你是在哪儿认识他的？	*你是在哪儿认识的他？
你是在哪兒認識他的？	你是在哪兒認識的他？
Nǐ shì *zài nǎr* rènshi tā de?	**Nǐ shì *zài nǎr* rènshi de tā.**
Where did you meet him?	

When the sentence refers to a non-past event, 是 **shì** alone can be used to focus a phrase.

我是明年毕业，不是今年毕业。
我是明年畢業，不是今年畢業。
Wǒ shì *míngnián* bìyè, bù shì *jīnnián* bìyè.
It is *next year* when I graduate, not *this year*.

是 **shì** and 的 **de** are often used to indicate contrastive focus. They contrast some situation with another situation. 是 **shì** or 不是 **bù shì** occurs before each of the phrases that is being contrasted.

这件衣服，我不是在西班牙买的。我是在法国买的。
這件衣服，我不是在西班牙買的。我是在法國買的。
Zhè jiàn yīfu, wǒ bù shì *zài Xībānyá* mǎi de. Wǒ shì *zài Fǎguó* mǎi de.
This article of clothing, I didn't buy it *in Spain*. I bought it *in France*.

这个字不是我写的。是王老师写的。
這個字不是我寫的。是王老師寫的。
Zhège zì bù shì *wǒ* xiě de. Shì *Wáng lǎoshī* xiě de.
This character, it wasn't *I* who wrote it. It was *Professor Wang* who wrote it.

▶ 11.4, 37.9

57.3 Emphasis

57.3.1 Using 是 *shì* for emphasis

Mandarin uses the word 是 **shì** to emphasize words or phrases in the sentence, especially when the sentence is used to confirm some previously mentioned situation. 是 **shì** may be added before a 'time when' phrase, a location phrase, or a [prepositional phrase +] verb phrase to emphasize the following phrase.

In English, words that are emphasized usually receive heavy stress and falling pitch. Because Mandarin is a tone language, pitch contour cannot be used for emphasis. However, 是 **shì** often receives heavy stress when it is used for emphasis, and the emphasis used in the following examples is intended to convey heavy stress.

Neutral	With emphasis
那本书很贵。	那本书是很贵。
那本書很貴。	那本書是很貴。
Nà běn shū hěn guì.	**Nà běn shū *shì* hěn guì.**
That book is expensive.	That book *is* expensive. (just like you said)
我明天走。	我是明天走。
Wǒ míngtiān zǒu	**Wǒ *shì* míngtiān zǒu.**
I'm leaving tomorrow.	I *am* going tomorrow.
他很会唱歌。	他是很会唱歌。
他很會唱歌。	他是很會唱歌。
Tā hěn huì chàng gē.	**Tā *shì* hěn huì chàng gē.**
He can sing well.	He really *can* sing.

TOPIC, FOCUS, AND EMPHASIS

Neutral
我们在小王家吃饭。
我們在小王家吃飯。
Wǒmen zài Xiǎo Wáng jiā chī fàn.
We are eating at Little Wang's house.

With emphasis
我们是在小王家吃饭。
我們是在小王家吃飯。
Wǒmen *shì* zài Xiǎo Wáng jiā chī fàn.
We *are* eating at Little Wang's house.

▶ 10, 11.4

57.3.2 Emphasizing the time when a situation occurs

To emphasize the time when a situation occurs, you can also put the 'time when' expression before the subject. This phrase order is typically used to contrast one time phrase with another time phrase.

昨天他很忙。今天他不忙。
Zuótiān tā hěn máng. Jīntiān tā bù máng.
Yesterday he was very busy. Today he is not busy.

58

Guest and host

The present-day roles of guest and host are based on centuries of tradition. In their simplest form, the roles are as follows: the host must take care of the guest, and the guest must accept the hospitality of the host without being a burden to the host. In practice, this means that the host must offer food and drink to the guest, must make the guest comfortable, and must escort the guest when he/she departs, and the guest must reject the hospitality of the host several times before eventually accepting it. Here are some general rules of behavior for guest and host.

- When visiting a Chinese host, the guest should bring a small gift. Items such as tea, fruit, flowers, and candy are usually appropriate. The host does not ordinarily open a gift in the presence of the guest.
- When a host invites a guest to participate in an activity for which there is a fee (dinner in a restaurant, coffee or ice cream in a café, attendance at a movie or show, transportation by taxi or train, etc.), it is understood that the host pays the bill.
- In most social situations, one of the participants typically assumes the role of host, paying the bill, ordering food or drink, paying for transportation, etc. It is expected that today's guest will be tomorrow's host, and the obligations (financial and otherwise) associated with the host will be reciprocated on later occasions by other members of the group. This creates a network of mutual obligations among participants and solidifies their identity as a group. It is rare for people to split the bill in China, or for individuals to pay for themselves when participating in some entertainment as part of a group. It is common for individuals to have a good-natured fight over a bill to establish the host for the occasion. The custom of 'splitting the check' is new and practiced only by young people, mostly in mainland China. It is called AA 制 **AA zhì**, the 'algebraic average.'

Many common interactions between guest and host are conducted using ritual expressions and behavior. The most common of these are presented here. Expressions used in welcoming a guest and in saying goodbye are also used toward customers in restaurants.

58.1 Welcoming the guest

To welcome a guest, say:

欢迎!
歡迎!
Huānyíng!
Welcome!

58.2 Offering food and drink

When the host offers the guest something to eat or drink, he or she either serves something or gives the guest a choice of beverages or food. For example:

> 请喝茶。
> 請喝茶。
> **Qǐng hē chá.**
> Have some tea.

or

> 你喝可乐喝茶？
> 你喝可樂喝茶？
> **Nǐ hē kělè hē chá?**
> Do you drink cola or tea?

It is not polite to ask the guest *whether* he or she wants something to eat or drink (Would you like something to drink?), or if he or she is thirsty (Are you thirsty?). These kind of questions allow a response of 'no,' and imply that the host does not wish to provide food. A good Chinese host does not give the guest the opportunity to refuse hospitality.

58.3 Inviting the guest to get comfortable

To invite a guest to get comfortable, say:

> 请坐。
> 請坐。
> **Qǐng zuò.**
> Have a seat.

> 休息一会儿。
> 休息一會兒。
> **Xiūxi yīhuìr.**
> Rest for awhile.

58.4 Saying goodbye and seeing the guest off

When it is time for guests to leave, the host has a ritual obligation to encourage them to stay. Guests have a ritual obligation to insist upon leaving. Expressions used in this ritual are presented below.

When guests leave, the host is expected to 送 **sòng** the guests, that is, to see them off. When you see guests off, you are expected to walk them a portion of the way home. Modern day interpretation requires accompanying guests at least to the doorway if not to their car or bus or train, and staying with them until they depart. Even if the host does not accompany the guest beyond the doorway, he or she does not close the door when guests walk out of the house. Instead, the host stands in view of the guests, waving, until they are out of sight.

58.4.1 Expressions that the host can say to the guest at the end of a visit

> 再来玩。
> 再來玩。
> **Zài lái wán.**
> Come again. (informal)

Additional expressions involving guest and host

> 有空再来。
> 有空再來。
> **Yǒu kòng zài lái.**
> Come again when you have time.

> 慢走。
> **Màn zǒu.**
> Don't hurry off.

> 走好。
> **Zǒu hǎo.**
> Take care.

▶ 24.2.2

58.4.2 Expressions that guests can say to the host at the end of a visit

> 请留步。
> 請留步。
> **Qǐng liú bù.**
> Don't bother to see me out.

> 别送。
> **Bié sòng.**
> There's no need to see me off.

58.5 Additional expressions involving guest and host

The opposite of *seeing a guest off* is *picking a guest up*. The verb used is 接 **jiē**.

> 我今天晚上到机场去接白经理。
> 我今天晚上到機場去接白經理。
> **Wǒ jīntiān wǎnshang dào jīchǎng qù jiē Bái jīnglǐ.**
> Tonight I am going to the airport to pick up Manager Bai.

The verb that is used for a formal visit to someone is 拜访/拜訪 **bàifǎng**.

> 我们明天拜访王教授。
> 我們明天拜訪王教授。
> **Wǒmen míngtiān bàifǎng Wáng jiàoshòu.**
> Tomorrow we will visit Professor Wang.

59
Giving and responding to compliments

59.1 Cultural conventions regarding praise

Traditionally, Chinese people do not say 谢谢/謝謝 **xièxiè** 'thank you' in response to a personal compliment of any kind. In Chinese culture, accepting a personal compliment can be interpreted as showing conceit. Thus, it is customary in China for people to reject rather than to accept compliments. To a Westerner, 谢谢/謝謝 **xièxiè** is merely thanks for the compliment. However, in Chinese culture, it is often interpreted as a boastful agreement with someone's assessment of the quality of your abilities or possessions.

59.2 Expressions used in deflecting praise

You are expected to reject compliments and deflect praise of your accomplishments, abilities, and possessions, and to deflect praise of the accomplishments and abilities of those close to you. The following expressions are commonly used to deflect praise:

Deflecting praise in neutral or informal situations

哪里，哪里。
哪裏，哪裏。
Nǎlǐ, nǎlǐ.
I have done nothing to deserve
your compliments.
(lit. 'where? where?')

哪儿的话？
哪兒的話？
Nǎr de huà?
What kind of talk is that?
What are you talking about?

没什么。
沒甚麼。
Méi shénme.
It is nothing.

不好，不好。
Bù hǎo, bù hǎo.
Not good, not good.

真的吗？
真的嗎？
Zhēnde ma?
Really?

More formal expressions used to deflect praise

过奖了。
過獎了。
Guò jiǎng le.
You are excessive in your praise.

不敢当。
不敢當。
Bùgǎndāng.
I cannot accept your praise.

59.3 Compliments and appropriate responses

The type of compliment determines the type of response. Here are some examples of compliments and appropriate responses.

Compliment	Appropriate response
你的孩子很聪明。 你的孩子很聰明。 **Nǐ de háizi hěn cōngming.** Your child is very intelligent.	不聪明。不聪明。 不聰明。不聰明。 **Bù cōngming. Bù cōngming.** (She/he) is not intelligent.
你的中国字写得真好。 你的中國字寫得真好。 **Nǐ de Zhōngguó zì xiě de zhēn hǎo.** You write Chinese characters really well.	我写得不好。 我寫得不好。 **Wǒ xiě de bù hǎo.** I do not write well.
您的讲演太精彩了。 您的講演太精彩了。 **Nín de jiǎngyǎn tài jīngcǎi le.** You gave an outstanding speech.	过奖了。 過獎了。 **Guò jiǎng le.** You are excessive in your praise.
你的医术真高明。 你的醫術真高明。 **Nǐ de yīshù zhēn gāomíng.** Your medical skill is brilliant.	不敢当。 不敢當。 **Bùgǎndāng.** I cannot accept your praise.
今天的菜太丰富了。 今天的菜太豐富了。 **Jīntiān de cài tài fēngfù le.** Today's meal is so bountiful.	没什么菜。便饭。 沒甚麼菜。便飯。 **Méi shénme cài. Biàn fàn.** There isn't anything special. It is just ordinary food.
你太太做的菜真好吃。 你太太做的菜真好吃。 **Nǐ tàitai zuò de cài zhēn hǎo chī.** The dishes that your wife made are really good.	哪里，哪里。便饭。 哪裏，哪裏。便飯。 **Nǎlǐ, nǎlǐ. Biàn fàn.** There is nothing worth praising. It is ordinary food.
你这件毛衣很漂亮。 你這件毛衣很漂亮。 **Nǐ zhè jiàn máoyī hěn piàoliang.** Your sweater is very pretty.	真的吗？很便宜。(很旧。) 真的嗎？很便宜。(很舊。) **Zhēnde ma? Hěn piányi. (Hěn jiù.)** Really? It was very cheap. (It's old.) or 是吗？ 是嗎？ **Shì ma?** Really?

60

Expressing satisfaction and dissatisfaction

60.1 Expressing satisfaction

60.1.1 Expressions used to indicate satisfaction

The following expressions are used to express satisfaction. They are arranged here according to approximate intensity ranging from least to most enthusiastic.

马马虎虎
馬馬虎虎
mámǎ hūhū
so-so

还不错	还行	还可以
還不錯	還行	還可以
hái bù cuò	**hái xíng**	**hái kěyǐ**
it's okay	it's okay	it's okay

可以
kěyǐ
fine

不错	相当好
不錯	相當好
bù cuò	**xiāngdāng hǎo**
not bad	pretty good

很好	挺好
hěn hǎo	**tǐng hǎo**
very good	very good

满意
mǎnyì
satisfied, pleased

很满意	很喜欢
	很喜歡
hěn mǎnyì	**hěn xǐhuan**
very satisfied	like it very much

非常好	好极了
	好極了
fēicháng hǎo	**hǎojíle**
excellent	excellent

▶ 10.3, 11.2

372

Expressing dissatisfaction

60.1.2 Situations in which satisfaction is expressed

Question	Response indicating satisfaction

这个菜的味道怎么样?
這個菜的味道怎麼樣?
Zhège cài de wèidao zěnmeyàng?
How is the flavor of this dish?

马马虎虎。
馬馬虎虎。
Mámǎ hūhū.
So-so.

这本书有意思吗?
這本書有意思嗎?
Zhè běn shū yǒu yìsī ma?
Is this book interesting?

还不错。
還不錯。
Hái bù cuò.
It's okay.

你们住的旅馆好吗?
你們住的旅館好嗎?
Nǐmen zhù de lǚguǎn hǎo ma?
How is the hotel that you are staying in?

不错。
不錯。
Bù cuò.
Not bad.

旅行社的服务怎么样?
旅行社的服務怎麼樣?
Lǚxíngshè de fúwù zěnmeyàng?
How is that travel agency's service?

还行。
還行。
Hái xíng.
It's okay.

这个车可以吗?
這個車可以嗎?
Zhège chē kěyǐ ma?
Is this car okay?

可以。
Kěyǐ.
It's okay.

那个电影怎么样?
那個電影怎麼樣?
Nàge diànyǐng zěnmeyàng?
How is that movie?

相当好。
相當好。
Xiāngdāng hǎo.
Rather good.

这本书好不好?
這本書好不好?
Zhè běn shū hǎo bù hǎo?
How is this book?

很好。
Hěn hǎo.
Very good.

这个博物馆怎么样?
這個博物館怎麼樣?
Zhège bówùguǎn zěnmeyàng?
How is this art museum?

好极了。
好極了。
Hǎojíle.
Extremely good.

您对我们的服务满意吗?
您對我們的服務滿意嗎?
Nín duì wǒmen de fúwù mǎnyì ma?
Are you satisfied with our service?

很满意。
Hěn mǎnyì.
Very satisfied.

60.2 Expressing dissatisfaction

60.2.1 Expressions used to indicate dissatisfaction

These expressions are arranged from mild to strong dissatisfaction.

不太好
bù tài hǎo
not too good

不好
bù hǎo
not good

不行
bù xíng
not okay

EXPRESSING SATISFACTION AND DISSATISFACTION

60.2

不合格
bù hé gé
not up to standard

很差
hěn chà
very inferior

太差了
tài chà le
too inferior

非常不好
fēicháng bù hǎo
extremely bad

非常坏	坏极了
非常壞	壞極了
fēicháng huài	**huàijíle**
extremely bad	extremely bad
完全不行	完全不好
wánquán bù xíng	**wánquán bù hǎo**
completely unacceptable	completely bad

糟透了
zāotòu le
it's a mess

60.2.2 Situations in which dissatisfaction is expressed

Question	Response indicating dissatisfaction
这个医院怎么样？ 這個醫院怎麼樣？ **Zhège yīyuàn zěnmeyàng?** How is this hospital?	不太好。 **Bù tài hǎo.** Not too good.
餐厅的菜怎么样？ 餐廳的菜怎麼樣？ **Cāntīng de cài zěnmeyàng?** How is the food in the cafeteria?	很差。 **Hěn chà.** Really inferior.
他们的服务还好吧？ 他們的服務還好吧？ **Tāmen de fúwù hái hǎo ba?** Is their service okay?	太差了。 **Tài chà le.** It's really inferior.
这儿的空气怎么样？ 這兒的空氣怎麼樣？ **Zhèr de kōngqì zěnmeyàng?** How is the air here?	非常不好。 **Fēicháng bù hǎo.** It is extremely bad.
那儿的天气怎么样？ 那兒的天氣怎麼樣？ **Nàr de tiānqì zěnmeyàng?** How is the weather here?	坏极了。 壞極了。 **Huàijíle.** Extremely bad.
那儿的交通怎么样？ 那兒的交通怎麼樣？ **Nàr de jiāotōng zěnmeyàng?** How is the transportation there?	糟透了。 **Zāotòu le.** It's a mess./It's terrible.

61

Expressing gratitude and responding to expressions of gratitude

61.1 Expressing gratitude

In Chinese culture, you thank others for actions that benefit you or show you respect. Such actions include doing something for you, taking the time to visit or write you, or helping you in some way. In Chinese culture, you do not thank others for compliments or invitations.

▶ 58

61.1.1 Direct expressions of thanks

Gratitude is expressed in Chinese with the following expressions:

谢谢/謝謝 *xièxiè* 'thank you'

> 谢谢你帮我忙。
> 謝謝你幫我忙。
> *Xièxiè nǐ bāng wǒ máng.*
> *Thank you* for helping me.

感谢/感謝 *gǎnxiè* 'gratefully thank; appreciate'

> 非常感谢您的建议。
> 非常感謝您的建議。
> *Fēicháng gǎnxiè nín de jiànyì.*
> I greatly *appreciate* your suggestions.

表示感谢/表示感謝 *biǎoshì gǎnxiè* 'to express thanks'

> 这点小礼物表示我们的感谢。请笑纳。
> 這點小禮物表示我們的感謝。請笑納。
> *Zhè diǎn xiǎo lǐwù biǎoshì wǒmen de gǎnxiè. Qǐng xiàonà.*
> This little gift expresses our *thanks*. Please accept our humble gift.

道谢/道謝 *dàoxiè* 'to thank, to express thanks'

> 我代表我们公司向您道谢。
> 我代表我們公司向您道謝。
> *Wǒ dàibiǎo wǒmen gōngsī xiàng nín dàoxiè.*
> I represent our company in *expressing our thanks* to you.

375

EXPRESSING GRATITUDE AND RESPONDING TO EXPRESSIONS OF GRATITUDE

61.1.2 Indirect expressions of gratitude

To express gratitude without saying 'thank you,' use the following expressions:

太麻烦你了。
太麻煩你了。
Tài máfan nǐ le.
This caused you too much trouble. (I've troubled you too much.)

太辛苦了。
Tài xīnkǔ le.
or
辛苦你了。
Xīnkǔ nǐ le.
This was really a lot of work for you.

真不好意思。
Zhēn bù hǎo yìsi.
I'm really embarrassed (to have caused you trouble).

61.2 Replying to expressions of gratitude

In Chinese, it is considered presumptuous or rude to accept compliments, praise, and expressions of gratitude. Chinese does not have an expression equivalent to 'you're welcome' in English. Common appropriate responses to expressions of gratitude include the following:

不谢。 不謝。 **Bù xiè.** Don't thank me.	没事。 沒事。 **Méi shì.** It wasn't anything. (It was nothing.)	没什么。 沒甚麼。 **Méi shénme.** It wasn't anything. (It was nothing.)
不客气。 不客氣。 **Bù kèqi.** Don't be polite.	不必客气。 不必客氣。 **Bù bì kèqi.** Don't be polite.	你太客气了。 你太客氣了。 **Nǐ tài kèqi le.** You are too polite.
哪里。 哪裏。 **Nǎlǐ.** It was nothing.	哪儿的话? 哪兒的話? **Nǎr de huà** What kind of talk is that?	

▶ 59.2

62

Invitations, requests, and refusals

In Chinese culture, people are connected through a web of obligations and mutual social debt often referred to as 关系/關係 **guānxi** 'relationships' or 'connections.'

This social debt is created by invitations, favors, and requests, big and small, that have been offered and accepted by others. They include buying small items for someone such as coffee, soft drinks, or ice cream, helping someone complete a task, inviting someone to dinner, or facilitating an introduction. By accepting an invitation or favor, or by making or agreeing to a request, you enter into a relationship that obliges you to reciprocate at some time in the future.

The Chinese expression that captures this social obligation is 来往/來往 **lái wǎng**, as in the expression:

> 有来有往。
> 有來有往。
> **Yǒu lái yǒu wǎng.**
> To have give and take.

A friendship is based on giving and taking, and one expects a regular exchange of giving and receiving favors and assistance with a Chinese friend. When taking is not balanced with giving, the behavior is described by the Chinese expression:

> 有来无往，非礼也。
> 有來無往，非禮也。
> **Yǒu lái wú wǎng, fēi lǐ yě.**
> Taking without giving is ill-mannered and uncivil.

In many Western cultures, the relationship between favors and social obligations is not so strong. One may accept favors without creating any obligation toward the giver. English has an expression that captures this: 'no strings attached.' The expression means that a gift or favor comes with no obligations to the recipient. In Chinese, where relationships are built on *give and take*, favors often come with the expectation of reciprocation. A Chinese friend may be more generous with you than a Western friend, but will expect more from you in return.

This chapter provides the basic strategies for negotiating invitations and requests in Chinese and for forming socially acceptable refusals.

62.1 Invitations

62.1.1 Offering invitations

In English, invitations are often expressed in terms of a choice about whether or not to participate:

> Would you like to have coffee with me?

INVITATIONS, REQUESTS, AND REFUSALS 62.1

In Chinese, giving the listener a choice about whether or not to participate is considered rude. It implies that the speaker does not want the listener to accept the invitation. Therefore, invitations are often worded as suggestions.

我们去喝咖啡吧！
我們去喝咖啡吧！
Wǒmen qù hē kāfēi ba!
Let's go drink some coffee!

An invitation may also imply that the speaker will assume the role of 'host' and pay for any expenses involved in the activity. If the speaker specifically *invites* the addressee with the word 请/請 **qǐng** 'please' (lit. 'invite'), he or she expects to pay for the activity.

我请你喝咖啡，好吗？
我請你喝咖啡，好嗎？
Wǒ qǐng nǐ hē kāfēi, hǎo ma?
Please have coffee with me.
(lit. 'I invite you to drink coffee, okay?')

▶ 58

62.1.2 Accepting and refusing invitations

Words and phrases used to accept invitations include:

好。	行。	可以。
Hǎo.	**Xíng.**	**Kěyǐ.**
Okay.	Okay.	I can.

Invitations between friends are accepted or rejected without ceremony. However, in more formal circumstances, it is often not considered polite to accept an invitation at its first offer. Typically, people refuse an invitation once or twice before accepting, even if they intend to accept all along. In the same way, the one who gives an invitation does not give up after an initial refusal, but offers a second or a third time before being certain that the refusal is genuine. This cycle of refusal and re-invitation is a social ritual in which you are expected to participate.

Expressions that are commonly used for the *ritual refusal* of an invitation to eat or drink include:

不要客气。	你太客气了。	我不(吃)/(喝)。
不要客氣。	你太客氣了。	
Bù yào kèqi.	**Nǐ tài kèqi le.**	**Wǒ bù (chī)/(hē).**
Don't be polite.	You are too polite.	I am not (eating)/(drinking).

If you are a guest, you cannot ultimately refuse an offer of a snack or a non-alcoholic drink. After the ritual refusal, you must accept it, though you need not eat or drink it. If you accept an invitation for a meal, however, you must eat.

It is acceptable to provide a direct refusal to an invitation to drink an alcoholic beverage or to smoke. If you do not or cannot drink, say:

我不喝酒。	or	我不会喝酒。
我不喝酒。		我不會喝酒。
Wǒ bù hē jiǔ.		**Wǒ bù huì hē jiǔ.**
I do not drink alcohol.		I am not able to drink alcohol.

If you do not smoke, you can refuse a cigarette by saying:

我不抽烟。
我不抽煙。
Wǒ bù chōu yān.
I do not smoke.

Invitations

62.1

In general, appropriate refusals for most other kinds of invitations are indirect and involve face-saving strategies. See section 62.3 for polite ways to refuse invitations.

▶ 58

62.1.3 Formal written invitations

Written invitations are issued for weddings and formal dinners and events. Formal Chinese events have a fixed ending time as well as a fixed beginning time. Guests come on time and the event ends at the predetermined time. Formal events typically begin with a short formal speech announcing the commencement and end with a short formal speech announcing the conclusion.

The cover of the invitation often includes one of the following expressions that identify it as an invitation.

邀请(书/信)	or	请帖
邀請(書/信)		請帖
yāoqǐng (shū/xìn)		**qǐngtiě**
invitation		invitation (lit. 'written submission')

The body of the invitation includes the following expressions.

- Expressions that say 'formally invite':

敬约/敬約	敬邀	诚邀/誠邀
jìng yuē	**jìng yāo**	**chéng yāo**
respectfully arrange an appointment/ respectfully invite	respectfully invite	respectfully invite

恭请/恭請	光临/光臨	恭请光临
		恭請光臨
gōng qǐng	**guānglín**	**gōng qǐng guānglín**
formally request	(your) presence	formally request your presence

  呈送
  chéngsòng
  formally send a
  report or petition
  (to a higher authority)

- Expressions that identify the recipient(s) of the invitation:

  (family name) 台启 **táiqǐ**
  respectfully submitted to (family name)

  or (less formal)

  致 **zhì** (the names of the invited guests)

- Expressions that identify the type of event:

  举行/舉行 **jǔxíng** (the type of event)
  hold (a ceremony)

  or (less formal)

  参加 (the type of event)
  cānjiā
  to attend an event

379

INVITATIONS, REQUESTS, AND REFUSALS　　　　　　　　62.2

- Expressions that indicate the location of the event:

  在 zài (location of event)

  or

  地点/地點 (location of event)
  dìdiǎn
  place

- Expressions that indicate the date and time of the event:

  谨订于(2012年7月14日)
  謹訂於(2012年7月14日)
  jǐndìng yǔ (2012 nián qī yuè shísì rì)
  respectfully reserve the date of (July 14, 2012)

  晚上六点举行
  晚上六點舉行
  wǎnshang liù diǎn jǔxíng
  begin at (6 p.m.)

  or (less formal)

  时间/時間 (the time)
  shíjiān
  time

晚上九点散会	or	晚上九点散会闭幕
晚上九點散會		晚上九點散會閉幕
Wǎnshang jiǔ diǎn sàn huì		**Wǎnshang jiǔ diǎn sàn huì bì mù**
the event concludes at 9 p.m.		the curtain falls at 9 p.m.
		(the event concludes at 9 p.m.)

▶ 49

62.2 Requests

62.2.1 Making requests of close relatives and close friends

Close relatives and close friends have an obligation to help you. Therefore, requests to close relatives and close friends are often indistinguishable from commands.

给我那本字典。
給我那本字典。
Gěi wǒ nà běn zìdiǎn.
Give me that dictionary.

我借用一下你的笔。
我借用一下你的筆。
Wǒ jiè yòng yī xià nǐ de bǐ.
Let me borrow your pen for a minute.

给我笔用一下。
給我筆用一下。
Gěi wǒ bǐ yòng yī xià.
Lend me a pen for a minute.

To make a request more polite, you may preface it with 请/請 **qǐng** 'please.'

请给我笔用一下。
請給我筆用一下。
Qǐng gěi wǒ bǐ yòng yī xià.
Please lend me a pen for a minute.

Refusals

62.2.2 Requesting information or assistance from teachers

Teachers have an obligation to help you with learning so requests to teachers for information can be direct. However, they should always be polite. You can preface a request with 请教/請教 **qǐng jiào** 'please teach me,' or 请问/請問 **qǐng wèn** 'may I ask.'

老师，请教...（这个字怎么用？）
老師，請教...（這個字怎麼用？）
Lǎoshī, qǐng jiào ... (zhège zì zěnme yòng?)
Professor, may I ask (lit. 'please teach me') ... (how do you use this word?)

王教授，请问，您的意思是...
王教授，請問，您的意思是...
Wáng jiàoshòu, qǐng wèn, nín de yìsi shì ...
Professor Wang, may I ask, do you mean ...

62.2.3 Face-saving strategies used in requests

When making a request to someone outside of your close personal circle, you should leave him or her room for a graceful refusal. That is, you should allow him or her the opportunity to 留面子 **liú miànzi** 'save face' if he or she has to refuse you. Here are some face-saving ways to phrase requests.

- Ask if he or she has time.

    | 你忙吗？ | 你有空吗？ | 你有工夫吗？ |
    | 你忙嗎？ | 你有空嗎？ | 你有工夫嗎？ |
    | **Nǐ máng ma?** | **Nǐ yǒu kōng ma?** | **Nǐ yǒu gōngfu ma?** |
    | Are you busy? | Do you have free time? | Do you have free time? |

- Ask if he or she has the ability to help.

    你能不能帮我一点忙？
    你能不能幫我一點忙？
    Nǐ néng bu néng bāng wǒ yīdiǎn máng?
    Can you help me?

- Be humble
  The use of 求 **qiú** 'to beg' makes this request more humble.

    我有一点事要求你。
    我有一點事要求你。
    Wǒ yǒu yīdiǎn shì yào qiú nǐ.
    May I ask you a favor? (lit. 'I have a little matter that I seek your help with.')

▶ 12.1, 52.1.3

62.3 Refusals

It is not always possible to grant a request, but it is important to phrase a refusal in such a way that it saves face for all parties involved. Here are common ways to do so.

- Promising to try
  A promise to try leaves open the possibility that your request may be granted at some point. Here are some responses that promise to try.

    | 我试试看。 | 我试一试。 | 我尽力做。 |
    | 我試試看。 | 我試一試。 | 我盡力做。 |
    | **Wǒ shì shì kàn.** | **Wǒ shì yī shì.** | **Wǒ jìnlì zuò.** |
    | I'll see what I can do. | I'll try. | I'll try my best. |

INVITATIONS, REQUESTS, AND REFUSALS 62.3

This promise to try is more formal:

> 尽力而为。
> 盡力而為。
> **Jìnlì'érwéi.**
> I will do everything possible. (formal)

- Pleading a lack of understanding

  This kind of response is a common way to avoid answering a request for information.

  > 我不太清楚。
  > **Wǒ bù tài qīngchu.**
  > I'm not too clear about that.

- Postponing the decision

  These responses are used to postpone a decision to another time.

  > 我们考虑考虑。
  > 我們考慮考慮。
  > **Wǒmen kǎolù kǎolù.**
  > We'll think about it.

  > 以后再说吧。
  > 以後再說吧。
  > **Yǐhòu zài shuō ba.**
  > Let's talk about it again another time.

  > 现在有一点不方便。
  > 現在有一點不方便。
  > **Xiànzài yǒu yīdiǎn bù fāngbiàn.**
  > It's a little inconvenient right now.

- Pleading an inability to perform the task

  > 我做不了。
  > **Wǒ zuòbuliǎo.**
  > I am unable to do it.

  > 我恐怕帮不了你的忙。
  > 我恐怕幫不了你的忙。
  > **Wǒ kǒngpà bāngbùliǎo nǐ de máng.**
  > I am afraid I am unable to help you.

  > 我没做过那样的事。
  > 我沒做過那樣的事。
  > **Wǒ méi zuòguo nèi yàng de shì.**
  > I've never done this kind of thing before.

  > 无能为力。
  > 無能為力。
  > **Wúnéng wéilì.**
  > I am powerless to help. (formal)

- Pleading a time conflict

  > 我现在有别的事。
  > 我現在有別的事。
  > **Wǒ xiànzài yǒu biéde shì.**
  > I've got something else I have to do right now.

  > 恐怕我太忙。
  > **Kǒngpà wǒ tài máng.**
  > I'm afraid I'm too busy.

382

Abandoning a request

> 我没有时间。
> 我沒有時間。
> **Wǒ méi yǒu shíjiān.**
> I don't have time.

> 对不起，我（那天）有事。
> 對不起，我（那天）有事。
> **Duìbuqǐ, wǒ (nà tiān) yǒu shì.**
> Sorry, I have something to do (that day).

To indicate that your explanation is genuine, and that you really do not have the knowledge, ability, time, or connections required to comply with a request, add 真的 **zhēnde** to your refusal.

> 我真的不会。
> 我真的不會。
> **Wǒ zhēnde bù huì.**
> I really can't do it.

> 我真的不懂。
> **Wǒ zhēnde bù dǒng.**
> I really don't understand.

You can soften a refusal with an apology by saying:

> 不好意思。
> **Bù hǎo yìsi.**
> I'm embarrassed about this.

or

> 对不起。
> 對不起。
> **Duìbuqǐ.**
> Excuse me.

不好意思 **bùhǎoyìsi** indicates the speaker's discomfort at not being able to comply with a request.

62.4 Abandoning a request

To abandon a request and indicate that you will not ask anymore, say:

算了(吧)。	不要紧。	没关系。
	不要緊。	沒關係。
Suànle (ba).	**Bù yàojǐn.**	**Méi guānxi.**
Forget it.	It is not important.	It is not important.

63

Expressing apologies, regrets, sympathy, and bad news

63.1 Apologies and regrets

Cultures differ in the kinds of things that people are expected to apologize for. This chapter presents the types of situations for which an apology is expected and provides expressions of apology that can be used in these situations.

Note that in Chinese culture, you are not expected to apologize for or otherwise acknowledge bodily functions such as coughs, sneezes, belches, flatulence, etc. In response to someone's sneeze, you can use the following expression:

> 百岁。/ 百歲。
> **Bǎi suì.**
> (May you live to be) 100 years old.

If someone sneezes a second time, you can say:

> 千岁。/ 千歲。
> **Qiān suì.**
> (May you live to be) 1000 years old.

63.1.1 Apologizing for showing disrespect: 对不起/對不起 *duìbuqǐ*

对不起/對不起 **duìbuqǐ** is the appropriate apology for actions that show disrespect toward another, including:

- Physical actions: bumping into someone, stepping on someone's foot, spilling something on someone, etc.
- Inappropriate behavior: interrupting someone, ending a conversation, etc.
- Imperfect performance: work done poorly, language spoken poorly, comprehension difficulty, etc.

> 对不起。我中文说得不好。
> 對不起。我中文說得不好。
> **Duìbuqǐ. Wǒ Zhōngwen shuō de bù hǎo.**
> Excuse me. I speak Chinese poorly.

> 对不起。我不懂。
> 對不起。我不懂。
> **Duìbuqǐ. Wǒ bù dǒng.**
> I'm sorry. I don't understand.

> 对不起。我耽误了你。
> 對不起。我耽誤了你。
> **Duìbuqǐ. Wǒ dānwu le nǐ.**
> Excuse me. I've caused you to be delayed.

Apologies and regrets

Reply to 对不起/對不起 **duìbuqǐ** by saying:

没事。	没关系。	不要紧。
沒事。	沒關係。	不要緊。
Méi shì.	**Méi guānxi.**	**Bù yàojǐn.**
It's nothing.	It's not important.	It's not important.

63.1.2 Apologizing for refusals: 不好意思 *bù hǎo yìsi*

不好意思 **bù hǎo yìsi** acknowledges embarrassment on the part of the speaker. It is commonly used when the speaker refuses an invitation or turns down a request for assistance.

王： 今天下午跟我去喝咖啡吧。
Wáng: **Jīntiān xiàwǔ gēn wǒ qù hē kāfēi ba.**
Wang: Have coffee with me this afternoon.

林： 不好意思。我今天下午有事。
Lín: **Bù hǎo yìsi. Wǒ jīntiān xiàwǔ yǒu shì.**
Lin: How embarrassing. This afternoon I've got something to do.

There is no formulaic response to 不好意思 **bù hǎo yìsi**.

▶ 62.3

63.1.3 Apologizing for mistakes or wrongs: 抱歉 *bàoqiàn* and 道歉 *dàoqiàn*

抱歉 **bàoqiàn** and 道歉 **dàoqiàn** acknowledge a wrong to another and acknowledge personal responsibility for the wrong. Formal and written contexts often call for 抱歉 **bàoqiàn** or 道歉 **dàoqiàn**. Many speakers of Mandarin use these two words interchangeably. Here are expressions in which these words are used.

抱歉。	抱歉。我来晚了。
	抱歉。我來晚了。
Bàoqiàn.	**Bàoqiàn. Wǒ lái wǎn le.**
I apologize.	I'm sorry. I've arrived late.

真抱歉。	我向你道歉。
Zhēn bàoqiàn.	**Wǒ xiàng nǐ dàoqiàn.**
I really apologize.	I apologize to you.

NOTE The use of the more formal preposition 向 **xiàng** 'toward' in the prepositional phrase 向你 **xiàng nǐ** 'toward you' makes this structure more formal.

▶ 14

The appropriate response to 抱歉 **bàoqiàn** or 道歉 **dàoqiàn** is the same as the response to 对不起/對不起 **duìbuqǐ**:

没事。	没关系。	不要紧。
沒事。	沒關係。	不要緊。
Méi shì.	**Méi guānxi.**	**Bù yàojǐn.**
It's nothing.	It's not important.	It's not important.

385

EXPRESSING APOLOGIES, REGRETS, SYMPATHY, AND BAD NEWS

63.1.4 Asking for forgiveness: 请原谅我/請原諒我 *qǐng yuánliàng wǒ* 'please forgive me'

请原谅我/請原諒我 **qǐng yuánliàng wǒ** is used in an apology acknowledging personal responsibility for an action that negatively affects others.

The response to this kind of apology is the same as for 对不起/對不起 **duìbuqǐ**, 抱歉 **bàoqiàn**, and 道歉 **dàoqiàn**.

63.2 Expressing sympathy

To acknowledge a bad situation that another is experiencing, say:

> 真可惜。
> **Zhēn kěxī.**
> What a pity. What a shame.

To express sympathy when another is ill, say:

> 多保重身体。
> 多保重身體。
> **Duō bǎozhòng shēntǐ.**
> Take care of your health.

> 希望你早日康复。
> 希望你早日康復。
> **Xīwàng nǐ zǎo rì kāngfù.**
> I hope your health is soon restored.

63.3 Conveying bad news

To introduce bad news or a negative situation use 怕 **pà** 'to fear' and 恐怕 **kǒngpà** 'to be afraid that.' Notice that 怕 **pà** requires a subject and 恐怕 **kǒngpà** does not take a subject.

(subject) 怕 *pà situation*

> 这件事，我怕他做不好。
> 這件事，我怕他做不好。
> **Zhè jiàn shì, wǒ pà tā zuòbuhǎo.**
> I am afraid that he won't be able to do this job well.

> 我怕你这次考得不好。
> 我怕你這次考得不好。
> **Wǒ pà nǐ zhècì kǎo de bù hǎo.**
> I am afraid that this time you didn't do well on the exam.

> 我怕我帮不了你的忙。
> 我怕我幫不了你的忙。
> **Wǒ pà wǒ bāngbuliǎo nǐ de máng.**
> I am afraid that I can't help you.

恐怕 *kǒngpà situation*

> 恐怕明天会下雨。
> 恐怕明天會下雨。
> **Kǒngpà míngtiān huì xià yǔ.**
> I'm afraid it will rain tomorrow.

Conveying bad news

63.3

恐怕他们今天不会来了。
恐怕他們今天不會來了。
Kǒngpà tāmen jīntiān bù huì lái le.
I am afraid that they may not come today.

恐怕你这次考得不好。
恐怕你這次考得不好。
Kǒngpà nǐ zhè cì kǎo de bù hǎo.
I'm afraid that this time you did not do well on the exam.

恐怕我帮不了你的忙。
恐怕我幫不了你的忙。
Kǒngpà wǒ bāngbuliǎo nǐ de máng.
I am afraid that I cannot help you.

▶ 55.1

64

Expressing congratulations and good wishes

64.1 General expressions of congratulations and good wishes

The following expressions may be used to extend congratulations on any occasion. Each is followed by an illustration of its use.

恭喜! *gōngxǐ!* 'congratulations'

> 恭喜! 恭喜!
> **Gōngxǐ! Gōngxǐ!**
> Congratulations!
> (As an expression of congratulations, the word is often said twice.)

> 恭喜发财!
> 恭喜發財!
> **Gōngxǐ fācái!**
> Wishing you a prosperous New Year! (standard New Year greeting)

祝贺/祝賀 *zhù hè* 'congratulations'

> 祝贺开张大吉。
> 祝賀開張大吉。
> **Zhù hè kāizhāng dàjí.**
> Wishing you extraordinary good luck on your great business opening.

庆祝/慶祝 *qìngzhù* 'celebrate'

> 庆祝结婚纪念。
> 慶祝結婚紀念。
> **Qìngzhù jiéhūn jìniàn.**
> Congratulations on your wedding anniversary.

> 庆祝新婚。
> 慶祝新婚。
> **Qìngzhù xīn hūn.**
> Congratulations on your wedding. (on your new marriage)

> 庆祝开业。
> 慶祝開業。
> **Qìngzhù kāi yè.**
> Congratulations on your new business.

> 庆祝毕业典礼。
> 慶祝畢業典禮。
> **Qìngzhù bìyè diǎnlǐ.**
> Congratulations on your graduation.

64.2 Fixed phrases of congratulations and good wishes for special events

Occasion	Phrase of congratulations and good wishes
New Year	恭喜发财！ 恭喜發財！ (traditional greeting) **Gōngxǐ fā cái!** Congratulations and get rich!
	新春大喜！ **Xīn chūn dà xǐ!** Wishing you great happiness at the New Year!
	新年快乐！ 新年快樂！ **Xīnnián kuàilè!** Happy New Year! (Western influenced greeting)
Christmas	圣诞快乐！ 聖誕快樂！ **Shèngdàn kuàilè!** Merry Christmas!
Wedding	恭喜！ **Gōngxǐ!** Congratulations!
	天作之合！ **Tiān zuò zhī hé!** A match made in heaven!
	百年好合！ **Bǎi nián hǎo hé!** A happy union lasting 100 years!
	白头偕老！ 白頭偕老！ **Báitóu xiélǎo!** Growing old together in happiness!
Birthday	恭喜！ **Gōngxǐ!** Congratulations!
	祝你生日快乐！ 祝你生日快樂！ **Zhù nǐ shēngrì kuàilè!** Wishing you a happy birthday! (Western influenced greeting)
Birth of child (a new birth is celebrated when the child is a month old)	长命百岁！ 長命百歲！ **Chángmìng bǎi suì!** May you live to be 100 years old!
Birthday of someone 60 years old or older	祝你寿比南山，福如东海。 祝你壽比南山，福如東海。 **Zhù nǐ shòu bǐ nán shān, fú rú dōng hǎi.** I wish you a long life (live as long as the south mountain) and great fortune (as great as the east sea).

EXPRESSING CONGRATULATIONS AND GOOD WISHES

Occasion	Phrase of congratulations and good wishes
Graduation	祝贺你前途无量。 祝賀你前途無量。 **Zhù hè nǐ qiántú wúliàng.** Wishing you boundless prospects. 祝你前途光明。 **Zhù nǐ qiántú guāngmíng.** Wishing you a bright future. 祝你鹏程万里。 祝你鵬程萬里。 **Zhù nǐ péngchéng wànlǐ.** Wishing you a promising future.
Good wishes for a business	开市大吉！ 開市大吉！ **Kāi shì dà jí!** 开张大吉！ 開張大吉！ **Kāi zhāng dà jí!** 开业大吉！ 開業大吉！ **Kāi yè dàjí!** Wishing you great luck in your new business! 祝贺生意兴隆！ 祝賀生意興隆！ **Zhù hè shēngyi xīnglóng!** Wishing you booming business! 祝贺财源茂盛！ 祝賀財源茂盛！ **Zhù hè cáiyuán màoshèng!** Wishing you abundant wealth!

▶ 24.3

64.3 Replying to expressions of congratulations and good wishes

When someone congratulates you, you can reply by saying:

谢谢。	or	多谢。	or	谢谢你的好意。
謝謝。		多謝。		謝謝你的好意。
Xièxiè.		**Duō xiè.**		**Xièxie nǐ de hǎoyì.**
Thanks.		Thanks.		Thank you for your good wishes.

To give a more formal reply, say:

多谢你的吉言。
多謝你的吉言。
Duō xiè nǐ de jíyán.
Thank you for your good wishes.

Index

a.m. and p.m. 49.1.4
abandoning a request 62.4
abbreviation 2.2.1.3
ability 12.2, 52.1
   expressing an innate ability or talent 52.1.2
   expressing a learned ability 52.1.1
   expressing physical ability 52.1.3
   with 会/會 **huì** 12.2, 52.1
   with 可以 **kěyǐ** 12.2.3
   with 能 **néng** 12.2.2
   with potential infixes 得 **de** and 不 **bu** 32.2
   with potential suffixes 得了 **deliǎo** and 不了 **buliǎo** 18.6.2, 32.4
absolutely (not) 并/並 **bìng** 27.3.1
across from 对面/對面 **duìmiàn** 47.1
actions and action verbs 13
   action verbs as noun modifiers 9.2.1.5
   change-of-state action verbs 13.6
   describing how actions are performed 31
   and directional movement 48.8
   indicating that actions occur in sequence 17.1.1, 37.2
   indicating that an action did not occur in the past 13.3.2, 17.1.1.2, 27.1.2, 37.3
   indicating that an action does not occur or will not occur 13.3.1, 27.1.1
   indicating the duration of an action 4.9, 13.5.1, 13.6.1, 17.2, 34.4, 39.1, 39.2, 39.3
   indicating the frequency of an action 39.4
   indicating the result or conclusion of an action using resultative verbs 18, 17.4, 32
   with manner adverbials 31.1, 31.2
   with modifiers that precede the verb phrase 27.3
   obligatory objects of action verbs 13.5.2
   open-ended action verbs 13.5
   talking about actions that begin in the past and continue to the present 34.7
   talking about habitual actions 35
   with 过/過 **guo** to indicate that an action has been experienced in the past 13.2, 17.3, 37.6, 37.7
   with 了 **le** to indicate the completion of an action 11.3, 17.1, 37.1, 37.2
   with 又 **yòu** to indicate that an action occurred again in the past 37.5
   with 在 **zài** and 正在 **zhèngzài** to indicate ongoing actions in present time 17.2.1, 34.2
   with 再 **zài** to indicate that an action will occur in the future 36.2
additional information, ways to express 也 **yě** 15.2.1, 还/還 **hái** 15.2.3, 40
additive or *and* relationship with conjunctions 16.1
addresses and addressing envelopes 22.7
addressing others and terms of address 22.4, 22.5
adjectives (*see* adjectival verbs)
adjectival verbs 10
   and comparison 10.5, 30.6
   in comparison structures 10.7, 33
   and expressions of change 10.9, 38.3
   linking adjectival verbs – with 而 **ér** 40.6, with 又 **yòu** 10.8, 40.9
   modification of adjectival verbs by intensifiers 10.3
   negation of adjectival verbs 10.1, 27.1.1
   as noun modifiers 9.2.1.3
   as predicates 10, 30.2
adverbs 15
   adverbial phrase as modifier of action 31.1, 31.3
   adverbs and modal verbs 12.6.5, 20.5
   adverbs that describe habitual action 35.3
   adverbs that indicate contrast 41.2
   adverbs that indicate past time 37.8
   adverbs that indicate sequence 42
   adverbs that occur with negation 27.3.1
   adverbs that refer to future time 36.2
   adverbs with logical function 15.2
      cái 才 15.2.6, 42.2.2.2, 32.3.2
      dōu 都 15.2.2, 35.1, 35.3, 46.1.1, 46.2, 46.4
      hái 还/還 15.2.3, 40.2, 40.3

INDEX

adverbs (cont'd)
  jiù 就 'as soon as' 一 **yī** ... 就 **jiù** 42.3.3, in conditional sentences 45.1, in sequence structures 17.1.2, 37.2, 42.2.2, indicating uniqueness 15.2.4, 'precisely, only' 15.2.4, with 怎么/怎麼 **zěnme** to tell someone to do as they please 54.2.4
  yě 也 'also' 15.2.1, 40.1, with question words 46.4, with 连/連 **lián** 'even' 57.2.3
  zhǐ 只 'only' 15.2.5, 30.7.1
position of adverbs in the sentence 4.7
relative order of adverbs and negation 27.2
(*see also* adverbs with logical function)
advice 54.2
afraid of 55.1
afraid that 63.3
after
  cái 才 'only after' 42.2.2.2
  comparing 以前 **yǐqián** 'before' with 以后/以後 **yǐhòu** 'after' 42.5
  completed sequence, sequence in the past 37.2
  hòulái 后来/後來 42.4
  minutes past (after) the hour 49.1.3.3
  referring to days before and after today 49.2.4.3
  ránhòu 然后/然後 42.4
  xiān ... zài 先 ... 再 'first ... then' 42.3.1
  yǐhòu 以后/以後 'after' in a single sentence 42.2, 42.4, 42.5
  zhīhòu 之后/之後 'after' 9.6
afterward
  expressions with 先 **xiān** 42.3
  hòulái 后来/後來 25.11.3, 42.4
  ránhòu 然后/然後 25.11.3, 42.4
  yǐhòu 以后/以後 42.4
age 30.7
agreement, asking for agreement 28.2, 56.1
all
  dōu 都 'all, both' 15.2.2, 35.1, 35.3, 46.1.1, 46.2, 46.4
  quán 全 'all' 46.1.3
although 41.1, 41.2
and
  'and' relationship between noun phrases 16.1
  'and' relationship between verb phrases 15.2
  expressing additional information 40
any
  anyone 谁/誰 **shéi** + 都 **dōu** or 也 **yě** 42.4.1
  anything 什么/甚麼 **shénme** + 都 **dōu** or 也 **yě** 46.4.1
  anywhere 哪儿/哪兒 **nǎr** + 都 **dōu** or 也 **yě** (哪里/哪裏 **nǎli** + 都 **dōu** or 也 **yě**, 什么地方/甚麼地方 **shénme dìfang** + 都 **dōu** or 也 **yě**) 46.4.1

expressing 'any' and 'every' with question words 46.4.1
  rènhé 任何 'any' 27.3.2
apology 63.1
approximations 6.5
arriving 14.2.4, 14.3, 48.5
as long as 只要 **zhǐyào** 45.3
as soon as 一 **yī** VP$_1$ 就 **jiù** VP$_2$ 6.9, 42.3.3
asking for assistance 25.1.4, in identifying characters 25.6
(*see also* requests)
asking for repetition 25.5
aspect 4.12, 13, 17
  perfective 了 **le** 17.1, 37.1, 37.2
  durative 着/著 **zhe** 17.2, 34.4, 39.1, 39.2, 39.3
  experiential 过/過 **guo** 13.2, 17.3, 37.6, 37.7
aspect vs. tense 17.1.3
associative compound characters 会意/會意 **huì yì** 3.3.3
at the same time 同时/同時 **tóngshí** 43.2.2
attracting attention 25.1
auxiliary verbs (*see* modal verbs)

bǎ 把 20, 57.2.1
ba 吧
  in commands 51.1
  in suggestions 62.1
  in suppositions 56.2
background events 39.3, 43.1
bad news
  and the passive 21.3
  conveying bad news 63.3
bàn 半 'half' 6.6.4
  in comparison structures 33.3.4.4
  in discounted prices 6.6.6
  in time expressions 49.1.2, 49.1.3.2
because
  responding to questions about cause 28.6
  yīnwei ... suǒyǐ 因为/因為 ... 所以 'because/since ... therefore' 44
  yīnwei NP **de guānxi** 因为/因為NP的关系/關係 'because of NP' 44.2
  yóu yú 由于/由於 'because of, owing to' 44.2
before
  change of state 11.3
  before the hour (time expressions) 49.1.3.3, 49.1.4, 49.2.1.2, 49.2.4.3
  yǐqián 以前 'before' 42.1
  zhīqián 之前 'before' 9.6
behind 后头/後頭 **hòutou** (后面/後面 **hòumiàn**, 后边/後邊 **hòubiān**) 47.1
běi 北 (北面 **běimiàn**, 北边/北邊 **běibiān**) 'north' 47.1.1.2
bèi 倍 '(two)fold' 6.6.5
bèi 被 passive marker 14.2.7, 21

INDEX

below, under 下头/下頭 **xiàtou** (下面 **xiàmiàn**) 47.1
béng 甭 'need not, do not have to' 50.1.3
best thing to do is 最好 **zuì hǎo** 55.2.3
best wishes (see good wishes)
between 中间/中間 **zhōngjiān** (and other location words) 47.1.1.1
bǐ 比 comparison 'more than' 33.3
bìděi 必得 'must' 12.4.1, 50.1.1
bǐfang shuō 比方说/比方說 'for example' 25.11.5
bié 别 'don't' 12.5, 50.2.1, 51.1.2
bǐjiào 比较/比較 'relatively' 10.3, 33.7
bìng 并/並 'absolutely (not)' 27.3.1
bìngqiě 并且/並且 'moreover' 40.4
bìxū 必须/必須 'must' 12.4.1, 50.1.1
both
   'both . . . and . . .' with 又 **yòu** 10.8, 40.9, 43.4
   expressing 'both' with 都 **dōu** 15.2.2, 46.1.1
   expressing 'both' with 一边/一邊 **yìbiān** 43.2.1
   expressing 'double' or 'both' with 双/雙 **shuāng** 46.1.4
bù 不 'no, not' 27.1.1
   in resultative verb structures 18.4, 18.6, 27.4, 32.2
   negating actions 13.1.1
   negating adjectival verbs 10.1
   negating modal verbs 12.6.1
   negating stative verbs 11.1
   negation in manner adverbial phrases 31.1.2.2
   negation in present time situations 34.6
   position of negation in the sentence 4.8
bù bì 不必 'need not' 12.4.3, 50.1.3
bùdàn . . . érqiě 不但 . . . 而且 . . . 'not only, but also' 40.8
bùguò 不过/不過 'but, however' 41.1, 41.2.2, 41.3
bù hǎo yìsi 不好意思 'be embarassed'
   in apologies and regrets 62.3, 63.1.2
   in expressing gratitude 61.1.2
bùlùn 不论/不論 'regardless, no matter how' 46.4.3
bùrán 不然 'otherwise' 45.5
bùrú 'not equal to' 33.4.2
business cards 22.6
but
   ér 而 40.6
   kěshì 可是, **dànshì** 但是, and **bùguò** 不过/不過 41.1, 41.2, 41.3
bù xǔ 不许/不許 'not permitted' 12.5, 50.2.1, 51.1.2
bù xū 不须/不須 'need not, do not have to' 50.1.3
bù yào 不要 'don't' 50.2.1, 51.1.2
   'don't be polite' 62.1.2
bù yòng 不用 'don't have to, need not' 50.1.3

bǔyǔ 补语/補語 complements (verbal complements)
   of degree 10.3
   of direction 19, 48.8
   of manner 31.3
   of potential 18.6, 19.5, 32.2
   of result 18, 32.1
   see also Glossary of Grammatical Terms

cái 才 'only, only then' 15.2.6
   expressing sequence 42.2.2.2, 42.3.2
calendar time 49.2
can
   expressing feasibility with 可以 **kěyǐ** 52.2.2
   expressing knowledge or possibility with 会/會 **huì** 12.2.1, 52.2.1, 54.1.2
   expressing permission with 可以 **kěyǐ** 12.2.3, 12.3, 51.2.1
   expressing physical ability with 能 **néng** 12.2.2, 52.1.3
cause and effect 44
change
   change and change-of-state with sentence-final 了 **le** 10.10, 11.3, 13.6, 38.1
   change over time: 越来越 **yuè lái yuè** 10.9.1, 12.6.4, 38.3.1
   new situations and changing situations 38
   nouns and verbs that express change 38.4
   tone changes 2.3, 2.4
   yuè 越 verb **yuè** 越 verb 10.9.2, 38.3.2
change-of-state verbs 11.3, 13.6, 20.3.1, 57.2.1
chúfēi 除非 'unless' 45.4
chúle . . . yǐwài 除了 . . . 以外 'except for, in addition to' 40.10, 57.2.2
cì 次 'times' (frequency) 39.4
classification of characters 3.3
classifiers (measure words) 8
   indicating frequency 39.4.1
   occurring without a noun 8.4
   and common nouns 5.1, 8.2
   with 半 **bàn** 6.6.4, 49.1.1
   with 这/這 **zhè** and 那 **nà** 7.2
clock time 49.1
commands 39.2.1, 51.1, 56.2
common nouns 5.1
communication strategies 25
completion and completed action 17.1, 37
   with 了 **le** 11.3, 13.1, 17.1, 37.1
   with resultative verb endings 18.4, 32.1.3, 32.1.3
comparatives and making comparisons 33
   adjectival verbs and comparative meaning 10.5
   adjectival verbs and comparison structures 10.7
   comparative degree 更 **gèng** 'even more' 10.5, 33.5

393

INDEX

comparatives and making comparisons (cont'd)
    descriptions that imply comparisons 30.6
    expressing comparative degree 33.5
    expressing difference 33.2
    expressing 'less than' 没/沒有 **méi yǒu** 33.4
    expressing 'more than' 比 **bǐ** 33.3
    expressing relative degree 33.7
    expressing similarity 33.1
    superlative degree 最 **zuì** 'most' 10.3, 10.6, 33.6, 52.1.2
compass directions 47.1.1.2
complementizer (*see* **de** 的)
complements (verb complements)
    of degree 10.3
    of direction 19, 48.8
    of manner 31.3
    of potential 18.6, 19.5, 32.2
    of result 18, 32.1
    see also Glossary of Grammatical Terms
compliments 59
    and expressions of gratitude 61.1, 61.2
concerning, regarding, as for (the topic)
    至于/至於 **zhìyú**, 对于/對于 **duìyú**,
    关于/關於 **guānyú**, 对 (topic)
    来说/對 (topic) 來說 **duì** (topic)
    lái shuō 57.1.1
conclusions
    indicating the conclusion of an action with 把 **bǎ** 20, 57.2.1
    indicating the conclusion of an action with resultative verbs 18.1, 18.32, 32.1, 32.2
conditional (if . . . then expressions) 45.1
cóng 从/從 'from' 14.2.4
    in directional expressions 48.1.4, 48.6.2
cónglái 从来/從來 'never' 13.3.1, 27.3.1, 37.6
congratulations, expressing 64
conjunctions 16
connecting words (paired connecting words) 41.1, 44.1, 45
content questions 28.6
contrary to one's expectations **dǎoshì** 倒是 41.2.1
contrast 41
    adverbs that indicate contrast 41.2
    expressing contrast with 而 **ér** 'and, but' 40.6
    expressing contrast with paired connnecting words 41.1
conversely 反过来/反過來 **fǎnguòlái** 41.2.2
counting months 49.2.2.1
coverbs (*see* Prepositions and Prepositions that function as verbs) 14
cross (streets, intersections) 过/過 **guò** 48.3

dànshì 但是 'but' 41.1
dào 到
    as a preposition 14.2.4, 48.1.2, 48.1.3
    as a resultative ending 18.3.1, 32.1.1
    as a verb 14.3, 48.4
    in expressions that introduce the topic 57.1.1
    in questions about directions 48.6.2
    indicating the time when a situation takes place 43.5
dǎoshì 倒是 'contrary to one's expectations' 41.2.1
dates
    in formal written invitations 62.1.3
    in letters 24.3.3
    reciting dates 49.2.4.5
    referring to the date of the month 49.2.4.4
days of the week 49.2.4.2
de 的
    and noun modification 9.2, 30.3
    omission of 的 **de** 9.3
    and possession 29.2.2
    是 **shì** . . . 的 **de** 57.2.4
de 得
    in comparison structures 33
    introducing the extent of a situation 32.6
    in manner adverbial phrases 31.1, 31.2
    potential infix 18.6, 19.5, 32.2
de 地 introducing pre-verbal modifiers of the verb 27.3
deliǎo 得了 potential suffix 18.6.2, 32.4
de shíhou 的时候 'when' 39.3, 43.1
decimals 6.6.3
default objects and obligatory objects 13.5.2
deflecting praise 59.2
děi 得 'must' 12.4.1, 12.6.5, 50.1.1, 53.2
degree complements, Glossary of Grammatical Terms, 10.3
demonstratives 7
děng 等, **děngdào** 等到 'when, by the time that' 43.5
desires 53.1
dì 第 ordinal number prefix 6.4, 25.11.3
dialing phone numbers 26.2
dimes 毛 **máo**, 角 **jiǎo** 8.5
difference 33.2
directional expressions 48
directional verbs 19, 48.8
directional movement 48
directions, giving 48.7
disjunction 'or' 还是/還是 **háishi** 16.2.1, 或者 **huòzhě** 16.2.2
disposal construction (*see* **bǎ** 把) 21, 57.2.1
dissatisfaction 56.1, 60.2
distance 47.4, 47.5
do not have to (*see* need not)

INDEX

do as you please 随便/隨便 **suíbiàn**, 怎么/怎麼 V 就怎么/怎麼 V **zěnme** V **jiù zěnme** V 54.2.4

dōng 东/東 (东面/東面 **dōngmiàn**, 东边/東邊 **dōngbiān**) 'east' 47.1.1.2

don't 别 **bié** 12.5, 50.2.1, 51.1.2, 不要 **bù yào** 50.2.1, 51.1.2

dōu 都 15.2.2
    and habitual action 35.3
    and habitual time 35.1
    expressing 'both' and 'all' 46.1.1
    expressing 'none' 46.2
    expressing 'every', 'any', 'not any' and 'no matter how' 46.4

double, pair, both 双/雙 **shuāng** 6.7, 46.1.4

double negatives 46.3.2

duì 对/對
    as a preposition and verb 14.3
    'correct' 28.2
    'toward' 14.3

duìbuqǐ 对不起/對不起
    asking for directions 48.6.4
    apologies 63.1
    apologizing for an intrusion 25.1.2
    apologizing for a refusal 62.3
    apologizing for interrupting a speaker 25.9

duìmiàn 对面/對面 'across from' 47.1

duìyú 对于/對於 concerning, regarding, as for (the topic) 57.1.1

duō 多 'more'
    asking about age 30.7.2
    asking about distance 47.5.2
    in comparison structures 33.3.4.2, 33.3.4.5, 33.3.5

duōshǎo 多少 'how much, how many' 28.6
    asking about money 8.5
    asking about time 49.2.1.1, 49.2.2.1, 49.2.4.1

duration and durative aspect
    and progression, with 在 **zài** and 正在 **zhèngzài** 17.2.1, 34.2, 39.2.1
    with 还/還 **hái** 39.2.2
    with 呢 **ne** 34.3
    with 着/著 **zhe** 13.5.1, 13.6.1, 17.2, 34.4, 39.1, 39.2, 39.3

east 东/東 **dōng** (东面/東面 **dōngmiàn**, 东边/東邊 **dōngbiān**) 47.1.1.2

effect (see cause and effect) 44

either–or questions 还是/還是 **háishi** 16.2.1, 28.3

email 26.1.3

embarrassment 不好意思 **bù hǎo yìsi** 'be embarassed'
    in apologies and regrets 62.3, 63.1.2
    in expressing gratitude 61.1.2

emphasis, of the direct object 13.5.2, structures used for emphasis 57.3

emphasizing details of a past event 37.9, 57.2.4

envelopes 22.7

equational sentences 11.4, 11.5, 30.1

equational verbs 是 **shì** 11.4, 30.1, 姓 **xìng** 11.5

ér 而 'and, but' 40.6

éryǐ 而已 'and that's all' 15.2.7

estimates and approximations 6.5

even (inclusion) 连/連 **lián** 57.2.3

even, go so far as to 甚至于/甚至於 **shènzhì yú** 25.11.4

even if 就是 **jiùshì** 45.2

even more 更 **gèng** (comparative degree) 10.5, 33.5

every 每 **měi** 35.1, 46.3, 46.4.1

every (day, year) 35.2, 46.3.3

except for, in addition to: 除了 **chúle** . . . 以外 **yǐwài** 40.10, 57.2.2

existence with 有 **yǒu** 11.6, 29.3, 38.1, with 有 **yǒu** and 在 **zài** 47.2

experiential aspect with 过/過 **guo** 13.2, 17.3, 37.6, 37.7

extent or result of a situation verb 得 **de** S/VP 32.6

face-saving strategies 留面子 **liú miànzi** 62.2.3

false borrowing characters 假借 **jiǎjiè** 3.3.5

family names 姓 **xìng** 11.5, 22.1

fǎn'ér 反而 'on the contrary, in contrast' 41.2.2

fǎnguòlái 反过来/反過來 'conversely' 41.2.2

far 远/遠 **yuǎn**, 47.4.1

fax 26.1.1

fear 怕 **pà** 55.1, 恐怕 **kǒngpà** 'afraid that' 63.3

feasibility 52.2.2

fēi 非 literary marker of negation 27.5

fēn 分 'cents' 8.5, 'minutes' 49.1
    in fractions and percentages 6.6.1, 9.6

fields of study 23.3

fillers in conversations 25.10

final particles (see sentence final particles)

finals (in the Mandarin syllable) 1.1.2

first 首先 **shǒuxiān**, 第一 **dì yī**, 先 **xiān** 25.11.2

first . . . then 先 **xiān** . . . 再 42.3.1

focus 11.4, 37.9, 57.2

follow-up questions 28.5

for, on behalf of, as a replacement for 替 **tì** 14.2.6

for, on behalf of, for the benefit of 为/為 **wéi** 14.2.8

for example 比方说/比方說 **bǐfang shuō** 25.11.5

for what reason? why? 为何/為何 **wéihé** 44.4

foreign words and loan words 5

formal characters for numbers 6.3

fǒuzé 否则 'otherwise' 45.5

fractions 6.6.1, 9.6

INDEX

frequency 次 **cì** 'times' 39.4
from 从/從 **cóng** (movement from a location) 14.2.4, 48.1, 由 **yóu** (source of movement) 14.2.8
future 36, 38.1.3

gè huà 个化/個化 'ge-ization' 8.2.3
gěi 给/給 'to, for'
   as a preposition 14.2.5
   as a verb and preposition compared 14.3
   in passive structures 21
   in telephone expressions 26.1.1
gēn 跟 'and, with' (*see also* 和 **hé**)
   as a conjunction 16.1.2, 40.7
   as a preposition 14.2.3
   in comparison structures 33.1, 33.2.1
gèng 更 'even more' (comparative degree) 10.5, 33.5
generally true situations 34.8
given names 22.1.2, 22.5
giving examples 25.11.5
go toward a location or in a direction 走 **zǒu** 48.1.1, go to a location 去 **qù** 48.1.2
gōngxǐ! 恭喜! 'congratulations!' 64.1, 64.2
good wishes 24.3.2, 24.3.3, 64.2, 64.3
goodbyes 24.2, 24.3
grammatical categories Glossary of Grammatical Terms
grammatical category shift Glossary of Grammatical Terms, 13.5, 14.3
gratitude, expressing 61.1
greetings 24.1, 24.3
guānxi 关系/關係 'connections' 62
guānyú 关于/關於 'concerning, regarding, as for (the topic)' 25.11.4, 57.1.1
guest and host 58
guò 过/過
   and clock time 49.1.3.3
   and movement expressions 48.3
   cross (streets, intersections) 48.3
   experiential aspect 13.2, 17.3, 37.6, 37.7

habitual action 35
habitual time 35.1, 35.2
hái 还/還
   in addition, also 15.2.3, 40.2
   emphasizing ongoing duration 39.2.2
   not yet 37.3
hái kěyǐ 还可以/還可以 'could be worse' 60.1.1
hái yào 还要/還要 'even more' 33.5
hái yǒu 还有/還有 'in addition' 15.2.3, 25.11.2, 40.3
bàn 半 'half' 6.6.4
   in comparison structures 33.3.4.4
   in discounted prices 6.6.6
   in time expressions 49.1.2, 49.1.3.2

hé 和 'and, with' (*see also* 跟 **gēn**)
   as a conjunction 16.1.2, 40.7
   in comparison structures 33.1, 33.2.2
hébì 何必 'why?' 28.6
hécháng 何尝/何嘗 'how could?' 28.6
héfáng 何妨 'why not?' 28.6
hégù 何故 'for what reason? why?' 28.6, 44.4
here (specifier) 这儿/這兒 **zhèr**, 这里/這裏 **zhèlǐ** 2.2.1.2, 7.3; in distance expressions 47.4.1
héshí 何时/何時 'when?' 28.6
héwéi 何为/何為 'what is?' 28.6
host and guest 58
hòulái 后来/後來 'afterward' 21.11.3, 38.4
hòutou 后头/後頭 (后面/後面 **hòumiàn**, 后边/後邊 **hòubiān**) 'behind' 47.1
hour 钟头/鐘頭 **zhōngtóu**, 小时/小時 **xiǎoshí** 49.1
how? 怎么? /怎麼? **zěnme?** (question word) 28.6
how do you V? 怎么? /怎麼 **zěnme?** 25.6
how could? 何尝/何嘗 **hécháng** 28.6
however, but 不过/不過 **bùguò** 41.1, 41.2.2, 41.3
however, nevertheless 然而 **rán'ér** 41.2.2
huì 会/會
   ability or knowledge 12.2, 52.1.1, 52.1.2, 54.1.2
   future time 36.3
   likelihood 52.2.1
   possibility 12.1
huì yì 会意/會意 associative compound characters 3.3.3
huòzhě 或者 'or' 16.2.2

identification
   identifying Chinese characters 25.7
   identifying people, places, and things 29.1
   with 就 **jiù**, uniqueness 15.2.4
   with 是 **shì** 29.1
ideographs 指事 **zhǐ shì** 3.3.2
if . . . then 44.1
illness 30.9
imminent occurrence and imminent change 38.1.5
impatience 56.2
imperative (*see* commands)
in 在 **zài** (preposition) 14.2
in, inside 里头/裏頭 **lǐtou** (里面/裏面 **lǐmiàn**, 里边/裏邊 **lǐbiān**) 47.1
in addition (to)
   chúle 除了 . . . **yǐwài** 以外 40.10, 57.2.2
   hái 还/還 40.2
   hái yǒu 还有/還有 40.3
   lìngwài 另外 40.11
   yě 也 40.1
in contrast 41.2

INDEX

in front of, before 前头/前頭 **qiántou** (前面 **qiánmiàn**, 前边/前邊 **qiánbiān**) 47.1
in other words 总而言之/總而言之 **zǒng ér yán zhī** 25.11.6, 再说/再說 **zài shuō** 40.5
incapability
    in resultative and directional structures 18.6, 19.5, 32.2, 32.4
    in refusals 62.3
inclusion 57.2.3
indicating understanding or lack of understanding 25.4, 62.3
innate ability 12.2.1, 52.1.2
inquiring about cause or reason 28.6, 44.4
instructions (*see* sequence *and* directions)
intensifiers 10.3, 11.2, 12.6.3
    and comparison structures 33.3.4.2
    expressing relative degree 33.7
interjections 56.1
internet 6.10, 26.3
interrupting a speaker 25.9
into 进/進 **jìn** 14.2.4, 48.8
intransitive verbs Glossary of Grammatical Terms
invitations: declining 62.3; spoken, written 62

jiǎjiè 假借 'false borrowings of characters' 3.3.5
jìn 进/進 'into' 14.2.4, 48.8
jiù shì 就是 uniqueness 15.2.4, qualifying a statement 41.3, even if 45.2
jiù 就
    in conditional structures 44.1
    indicating 'as soon as' 42.3.3
    indicating uniqueness 15.2.4
    in sequence structures 42.2.2.1
    with 怎么/怎麼 **zěnme** to tell someone to do as they please 54.2.4
jiào 叫
    greeting and addressing others 22.5, 24.1.3
    and passive structure 14.2.7, 21.4
    reporting commands 51.1.3
    reporting permission 51.2.2
jiǎo 角 'dimes' 8.5
jǐ 几/幾 'how many' 8.5, 28.6, 30.7.2, 39.4.1
jǐdiǎn zhōng 几点钟/幾點鐘 28.6, 46.4.1, 49.1.6
jìn 近 'near' 47.4, 47.5

kěshì 可是 'but' 41.1, 41.3
kěyǐ 可以 'can' 12.3, 12.6.4, 51.2, 52.2.2
kinship terms 22.2, 22.4.2, 24.3.1
knowledge
    with the modal verb 会/會 **huì** 12.2.1
    zhīdao 知道 'know,' 认识/認識 **rènshi** 'know, recognize' 54.1
kǒngpà 恐怕 'afraid that' 62.3
kuài 块/塊 'dollar' 8.5

last (week/month/year) 上 **shàng** 49.2
learned ability 12.2.1, 52.1.1
le 了
    change of state and new situations 11.3, 37.1, 38
    completion 17.1, 18, 32.1.3
    double 了 **le** 34.7, 37.2, 38.1.3
    sentence final 10.10, 33.6, 34.7, 38.1, 38.1.3, 38.1.5
    sequence 17.1.2, 42.2
    verb suffix 11.3, 17.1, 32.1.3, 32.3, 38.1.3
left side 左边/左邊 **zuǒbiān** (左面 **zuǒmiàn**) 47.1
legal use of 应/應 **yīng** 'shall' 50.1.2
less than
    less than an amount 6.5
    less than in comparisons 10.7, 33.4
    with 才 **cái** 15.2.6
letters
    addressing 22.7
    greetings and goodbyes in 24.3
lí 离/離 expressing distance: 'separated from' 47.4
lián 连/連 'even' 57.2.3
lǐbài 礼拜/禮拜 'week' 49.2.3, 'this week' 34.1, 'every week' 35.1, 'next week' 36.1
lìngwài 另外 'in addition' 40.11
lǐtou 里头/裏頭 (里面/裏面 **lǐmiàn**, 里边/裏邊 **lǐbiān**) 'in' 47.1
liú miànzi 留面子 'face-saving strategies' 62.2.3
loan words 2.5
location as description 47.3
location
    asking about the location of an object 47.1.3.2
    describing the location of an object 43.1.3.2
    expressing location with 这儿/這兒 **zhèr** 'here' and 那儿/那兒 **nàr** 'there' 7.3
    indicating that an object exists or does not exist at a location 11.6, 11.7, 47.2
    phrase order in the location phrase (spatial orientation) 47.1.2.1
    position of location phrase in the sentence 4.4, 4.6
    using location as a description 47.3
    words that indicate location and compass direction 47.1.1
zài 在
    as a preposition 'at, in, on' 14.2.1
    as a verb 11.7
lucky and unlucky numbers 6.7

ma 吗/嗎 yes–no questions 28.1.1
made of (用) NP 做的 (**yòng**) NP **zuò de** 30.5
manner adverbial (manner complement) 31.1, 31.2

INDEX

máo 毛 'dime' 8.2.2, 8.5
may (see possibility, permission)
means of transportation 48.5
measure words (see classifiers)
méi guānxi 没关系/沒關係 'it's not important' 62.4, 63.1.1
méi yǒu 没有
   and comparison structures 10.7, 29.4.1
   and existence 25.3.1, 43.2
   and non-occurrence of actions 33.3, 33.4, 33.6
   and possession 25.2.1
   negation of 有 **yǒu** 11.6.4, 24.1.4.2
minute 分 **fēn** 49.1
modal verbs 12
modifying a noun
   modification with 的 **de** 9.2, 30.3
   modification with 之 **zhī** 9.6
   modifying a noun with a location phrase 47.3
   modifying a noun with specifiers or numbers 9.1
   order of modifiers within the noun phrase 4.10
money 钱/錢 **qián** 8.5
months 月 **yuè** 49.2.2
moral obligations (see should)
more and more 越来越 **yuè lái yuè** AV 10.9.1, 12.6.4, 38.3.1
more than 比 **bǐ** 6.5, 10.7, 33.3
moreover 并且/並且 **bìngqiě** 40.4, 再说/再說 **zài shuō** 'moreover, to put it another way' 40.5
motion, verbs of 19.2, 48
movement and directions 48
must
   bìděi 必得 12.4.1, 50.1.1
   bìxū 必须/必須 12.4.1, 50.1.1
   děi 得 12.4.1, 12.6.5, 50.1.1, 53.2
must not 不许/不許 **bù xǔ** 12.5, 50.2
měi 每 'every' 35.1, 46.3, 46.4.1

nǎ, něi 哪 'which?' 2.2.1.2, 5.1, 7.4, 9.1, 28.6
nà nèi 那 'that' 5.1, 7.2, 9.1
nǎlǐ 哪里/哪裏 'where?' 2.2.1.2, 5.1, 7.4, 28.6
nàlǐ 那里/那裏 'there' 2.2.1.2, 7.3, in distance expressions 47.4.1
name cards 22.6
names 22.1
   loan words and naming foreign objects 2.5
   proper nouns 5.3
   terms of address 22.5
nán 南 (南面 **nánmiàn**, 南边/南邊 **nánbiān**) 'south' 47.1.1.2
nǎr 哪儿/哪兒 'where?' 2.2.1.2, 5.1, 7.4, 28.6
nàr 那儿/那兒 'there' 2.2.1.2, 7.3, in distance expressions 47.4.1

ne 呢
   as a sentence final particle 56.2
   in follow-up questions 28.5
   in 还是/還是 **háishi** 'or' questions 28.3
   indicating ongoing situation in present time 34.3
near 近 **jìn** 47.4, 47.5
need not 不必 **bù bì**, 不用 **bù yòng**, 甭 **béng**, 不须/不須 **bù xū**, and 无须/無須 **wú xū** 12.4.3, 50.1.3
needs, expressing 53.2
negation 27
   不 **bù** in resultative and directional verbs 18.6, 19.5, 27.4, 32.2
   literary markers of negation 無 **wú** and 非 **fēi** 27.5
   negating actions 13.3
   negation of adjectival verbs 10.1
   negation in manner adverbial phrases 31.1.2.2
   negation of modal verbs 12.6.1
   negation in present time situations 34.6
   negation of stative verbs 11.1
   negation of 有 **yǒu** 11.6.4, 28.1.4.2
   overview of the functions of 不 **bù** 27.1.1
   overview of the functions of 没/沒 **méi** and 没有/沒有 **méi yǒu** 27.1.2
   passive and negation 21.2
   position of negation in the sentence 4.8, 27.2
   words that occur with negation 27.3
neutral tone 1.1
   and sentence final particles 56.2
   and the classifier 个/個 **gè** 8.2.3
   and the suffix 子 **zǐ** 2.2.1.1
   change to neutral tone 2.4
never 从来/從來 **cónglái** 27.3.1
new information (see new situations)
new situations 38.1
new year greetings 64.1, 64.2
next to 旁边/旁邊 **pángbiān** 47.1
next (week/month/year) 49.2
nián 年 'years' 49.2.1
niánnián 年年 'every year' 35.2, 46.3.3
nìngkě 宁可/寧可 'prefer' 53.3
no matter how 怎么 V 也/怎麼 V 也 **zěnme** V **yě** 32.2.2.1, 46.4.3
no one 谁/誰 **shéi** 都 **dōu** or 也 **yě** + neg 46.4.2
none 46.2
north 北 **běi** (北面, **běimiàn**, 北边/北邊 **běibiān**) 47.1.1.2
not any 46.4.2
not anymore neg + sentence final 了 **le** 38.1.4
not have to (see need not)
not only, but also 不但 ... 而且 ... **bùdàn** ... **érqiě** 40.8
not equal to 不如 **bùrú** 33.4.2

INDEX

not permitted 不许/不許 **bù xǔ** 12.5, 50.2.1, 51.1.2
nothing
   it was nothing (replying to praise, gratitude, apologies) 59.2, 59.3, 61.2, 63.1.1
   shénme 什么/甚麼 + **dōu** 都 or **yě** 也 + neg 46.4.2
noun and noun phrase modification 4.10, 9
   (*see also* modiyfing a noun, numbers, specifiers)
noun phrase omission 8.3, 9.5, 57.1.2.2
nouns 5, Glossary of Grammatical Terms
nowhere 哪儿/哪兒 **nǎr** + 都 **dōu** or 也 **yě** + neg, 什么地方/甚麼地方 **shénme dìfang** + 都 **dōu** or 也 **yě** + neg 46.4.2
numbers 6
   reciting dates 49.2.4.5
   reciting time 49.1.3.2, 49.1.3.3
   reciting years 49.2.1.3
   tone change in numbers 2.3.2
   writing and reciting phone and fax numbers 6.1.1, 26.5

o'clock 49.1
object, direct and indirect 4.2, Glossary of Grammatical Terms
obligations 12.4, 50.1
   social obligations 58, 62
obligatory objects and action verbs 13.5.2
occupations and professional titles 22.3.2, 23.3
on, at, in 在 **zài** 14.2.1
on the contrary, in contrast 反而 **fǎn'ér** 41.2.2
on what basis? 凭什么/憑甚麼 **píng shénme** 28.6, 44.4
only if, unless 除非 **chúfēi** 45.4
open-ended actions verbs 13.5, 18, 32.1
opinions, expressing 54.2
or 还是/還是 **háishi** 16.2.1 或者 **huòzhě** 16.2.2
ordinal numbers 6.4
otherwise 要不然 **yàoburán**, 不然 **bùrán**, 否则 **fǒuzé** 45.5
ought to (*see* should)
out, outside 外头/外頭 **wàitou** (外面 **wàimiàn**) 47.1
over, on 上头/上頭 **shàngtou** (上面 **shàngmiàn**, 上边/上邊 **shàngbiān**) 47.1
ownership (*see* possession)

pà 怕 'fear' 55.1
paired connecting words 41.1, 44.1, 45
pángbiān 旁边/旁邊 'next to' 47.1
passive 14.2.7, 21, 51.1.3
past experience with V-过/過 **guo** 13.2, 17.3, 37.6, 37.7

past time 37
   adverbs that indicate past time 37.8
   focusing on a past event with 是 **shì** . . . 的 **de** 37.9, 57.2.4
   guo 过/過 and past experience 37.6
   indicating sequence in the past 37.2
   indicating that a state existed in the past 11.3
   indicating that an action occurred again in the past with 又 **yòu** 37.5
   le 了 and past time 37.1
   non-occurrence of an action in the past 37.3
percentages 6.6.2, 6.6.6, 9.6
perfective aspect with 了 **le** 17.1, 37.1, 37.2
permission
   expressing permission with 可以 **kěyǐ** 12.3, 51.2
   reporting permission with 让/讓 **ràng** or 许/許 **xǔ** 51.2.2
phonetic component in characters 3.2.2
phonetic compound characters 形声/形聲 **xíngshēng** 3.3.4
phrase order 4
   emphasizing the 'time when' phrase 4.5, 57.3.2
   phrase order in questions 4.11, 28.1, 28.6
   topicalization 57.1.2.1
physical ability
   with 能 **néng** 12.2.2, 52.1.3
   with 可以 **kěyǐ** 12.2.3
piān'ài 偏爱/偏愛 'favor' 53.3
pictograph characters 象形 **xiàngxíng** 3.3.1
píng shénme 凭什么/憑甚麼 'on what basis?' 28.6, 44.4
Pinyin romanization 1
placement verbs 29.3.3, 34.4, 39.2
please 请/請 **qǐng**
   polite requests 54.2.2
   polite invitations 62.1, 62.2
   asking for forgiveness 63.1.4
possession
   with 的 **de** 5.2.4, 9.2, 29.2.2, 30.3
   with 有 **yǒu** 11.6, 29.2.1
possibility
   expressing possibility with 会/會 **huì** 12.1, 52.2.1
   expressing possibility with the potential infixes 得 **de** and 不 **bù** 18.6, 19.5, 32.2
potential form of resultative verbs with 得 **de** and 不 **bù** 18.6, 32.2, of directional verbs 19.5
potential suffix 得 **deliǎo** 'able to V' and 不了 **buliǎo** 'unable to V' 18.6.2, 32.4
praise 59
predicate Glossary of Grammatical Terms
preferences 宁可/寧可 **nìngkě** 'prefer,' 偏爱/偏愛 **piān'ài** 'favor,' 情愿/情願 **qíngyuàn** 'would rather', 53.3

INDEX

prepositions and prepositional phrases 4.3, 14, Glossary of Grammatical Terms
prepositions in formal speech and writing 14.2.8
prepositions that function as verbs Glossary of Grammatical Terms, 14.3
present situations and present time 34
   greetings that refer to present activity 24.1.4
   ne 呢 and ongoing actions in present time 17.2, 34.3
   negation in present time situations 34.6
   time expressions that indicate present time 34.1
   zài 在 and 正在 zhèngzài and ongoing actions in present time 17.2, 34.2
   zhe 着/著 and ongoing duration in present time 34.4
   zhèngzài 正在 and 现在/現在 xiànzài compared 34.2
present relevance 38.1.3
prices 8.5
professions used as titles and terms of address 22.3.2
progressive markers 在 zài and 正在 zhèngzài 17.2, 34.2
prohibitions 12.5, 50.2
pronouns 5.2
   as noun modifiers 9.2.1.2
   and noun phrase omission 9.5, 57.1.2.2
pronominalization in discourse (*see* noun phrase omission)
proper nouns 5.3

qián 钱/錢 'money' 8.5
qiántou 前头/前頭 (前面 qiánmiàn, 前边/前邊 qiánbiān) 'in front of, before' 47.1
qǐng 请/請 'please'
   polite requests 54.2.2
   polite invitations 62.1, 62.2
   asking for forgiveness 63.1.4
qíngyuàn 情愿/情願 'would rather' 27.3, 53.3
qù 去 'go to a location' 48.1.2
quán 全 'all' 46.1.3
quarter to (差 chà) and quarter past (过/過 guò) the hour 49.1.3.3
què 却 contrast adverb 41.2.1
questions 28, and phrase order in questions 4.11
quite 相当/相當 xiāngdāng 10.3, 33.7, 60.1.1

radical 3.2.1
rán'ér 然而 'however, nevertheless' 41.2.2
rang 让/讓 as the passive marker 'by' 14.2.7, 21. 'let permit, allow' 51.2.2
ránhòu 然后/然後 'afterward' 25.11.3, 42.4
reduplication
   in adverbial modifiers 31.3
   and habitual action 35.2

reason and result 44
reflexive pronoun 自己 zìjǐ 'self' 5.2.1
refusals 62.1.2, 62.3, 63.1.2
regarding (some topic) 关于/關於 guānyú, 至于/至於 zhìyú, 对于/對於 duìyú 25.11.4, 57.1.1
regardless, no matter how 不论/不論 bùlùn 46.4.3
regrets 63.1
relative degree and intensifiers 10.3, 33.7
relatives (*see* kinship terms)
relative clause (*see* noun *and* noun phrase modification)
relatively 比较/比較 bǐjiào 10.3, 33.7, 相当/相當 xiāngdāng 10.3, 33.7, 60.1.1
rènhé 任何 'any' 27.3.2
rènshi 认识/認識 'know, recognize' 54.1
repeatable events and the aspect suffix 过/過 guo 17.3, 37.6, 37.7
repeating the verb
   in comparison structures 33.1.6, 33.3.5, 33.4.3
   in frequency expressions 39.4.2
   when expressing duration 39.1.2
requesting repetition or clarification 25.5
requests 62.2
   making a request polite 54.2.2
   requesting and giving advice and opinions 54.2.1
result or extent of a situation (extent modifier) 32.6
resultative verbs 18, 32, 46.4.3
resultative suffixes with special meanings or properties 18.7, 32.5
rhetorical questions 28.4
right side 右边/右邊 yòubiān (右面 yòumiàn) 47.1
ritual refusal 62.1.2
rúguǒ 如果 'if' 45.1

same 一样/一樣 yīyàng, in structures indicating similarity and difference 33.1, 33.2
satisfaction, expressions of 56.1, 60.1
saving face (strategies for) 留面子 liú miànzi 62.2.3
say again 再说/再說 zài shuō 25.5
semantic derivation characters 转注/轉注 zhuǎnzhù 3.3.6
semesters 学期/學期 xuéqī 49.2.5
sentence final particles 56.2
sentence final 了 le 38.1
   and actions that continue to the present 34.7
   and adjectival verbs 10.10
   and change 38.1
   and imminent action 38.1.5
   and present relevance 38.1.3
   and superlative degree 33.6

INDEX

sequence
   and perfective 了 **le** 17.1.2, 37.2, 42.2.3
   after in a single sentence 以后/以後 **yǐhòu** 42.2
   adverbs that occur in sequence sentences: 就 **jiù** 42.2.2.1, 才 **cái** 42.2.2.2, 便 **biàn** 42.2.2
      before 以前 **yǐqián** 42.1
   establishing a sequence 25.11.3
   first . . . then 先 **xiān** . . . 再 **zài** (然后/然後 **ránhòu**, 以后/以後 **yǐhòu**) 42.3.1
   first . . . only then 先 **xiān** . . . 才 **cái** 42.3.2
   sentence adverbs that indicate 'afterward': 以后/以後 **yǐhòu**, 然后/然後 **ránhòu**, 后来/後來 **hòulái** 42.4
   sequence in the past 37.2
   comparing 以前 **yǐqián** 'before' with 以后/以後 **yǐhòu** 'after' 42.5
serial verbs (*see* sequence, simultaneous situations)
shàngtou 上头/上頭 (上面 **shàngmiàn**, 上边/上邊 **shàngbiān** 'over, on' 47.1
shéi 谁/誰 'who?' 28.6
shéi dōu 谁/誰都 'everyone, no one' 42.4.1, 42.4.2
shénme 什么/甚麼 'what' 28.6
shénme dōu 什么/甚麼都 'everything, anything' 46.4.1, 46.4.2
shénme dìfang 什么地方/甚麼地方 'where?' 28.6
shénme dìfang dōu 什么地方/甚麼地方都 'anywhere, wherever' 46.4.1, 46.4.2
shénme lǐyóu 什么理由/甚麼理由 'what is the reason?' 44.4
shénme shíhòu 什么时候/甚麼時候 'when' 28.6, with clock time 49.1.5
shénme shíhòu dōu 什么时候/甚麼時候都 'whenever, any time' 46.4.1, 46.4.2
shènzhì yú 甚至于/甚至於 'even, go so far as to' 25.11.4
shì . . . de 是 . . . 的 emphasizing details 37.9, 57.2.4, 57.3
shìfǒu 是否 yes–no question form 28.1.3, 28.1.4
shì 是 'be' 11.4
   asking for agreement with 是不是 **shì bù shì** 28.2
   describing age 30.7
   expressing existence 29.3.2
   focusing on a detail of an event 37.9, 57.2.4
   for emphasis 57.3.1
   signaling understanding 25.8
should 应该/應該 **yīnggāi**, 该/該 **gāi**, 应/應当 **yīngdāng**, 应/應 **yīng** 12.4.2, 50.1.2
should not 不应该/應該 **bù yīnggāi** 50.2.2
shǒuxiān 首先 'first, in the first place' 25.11.2

shuāng 双/雙 'double, pair, both' 6.7, 46.1.4
similarity 33.1
simplified characters 3.1
simultaneous situations 43
social obligations (*see* should)
south 南 **nán** (南面 **nánmiàn**, 南边/南邊 **nánbiān**) 47.1.1.2
spatial orientation 47.1.2
specifiers 这/這 **zhè**, **zhèi** 'this/these' and 那 **nà**, **nèi** 'that/those' 2.2.1.2, 7.2, 7.4, 8.1, 9.1
stative verbs 11
   change-of-state verbs and stative verbs 13.6.2
   comparing noun phrases in terms of stative qualities 33.3.2
   as noun modifiers 9.2.1.4
   and yes–no questions 28.1.2
still, in addition 还/還 **hái** 15.2.3, 39.2.2, 40.2
stress with 是 **shì** for emphasis 57.3.1 (*see also* emphasis)
stroke order 3.4
strong obligations (*see* must)
strong prohibitions (*see* must not)
subject Glossary of Grammatical Terms
suggestions
   with 吧 **ba** 51.1.1, 56.2, 62.1.1
   with 好不好 **hǎo bù hǎo** 62.1.1
suíbiàn 随便/隨便 'as you please' 54.2.4
suīrán 虽然/雖然 'although' 41.1
suǒyǐ 所以 'therefore, so' 44.1
suǒyǒu de 所有的 'all' 46.1.2
superlative 最 **zuì** 10.3, 10.6, 33.6, 52.1.2
suppositions 56.2
surnames (*see* family names)
surprise, and passives 17.3, with 怎么/怎麼 **zěnme** 'why' 44.4
suspicion, indicating 56.1
syllable 1.1, 2
sympathy, expressing 63.2
symptoms of illness, describing and asking about 30.9.2, 30.9.3

tag questions 28.2
telecommunications 26
telephone etiquette 26.4
telephone numbers 6.1.1, 26.5
telling time 49.1–49.4
temperature 30.8.3
terms of address 22
text message 26.1.1
that/those 那 **nà**, **nèi** 5.1, 7.2, 9.1
that (demonstrative) 那 **nà** 2.2.1.2, 7.3
the more verb$_1$ the more verb$_2$ 越 **yuè** verb$_1$ 越 **yuè** verb$_2$ 10.9.2, 12.6.4, 38.3.2
there 那儿/那兒 **nàr**, 那里/那裏 **nàli** 2.2.1.2, 7.3, in distance expressions 47.4.1

401

INDEX

there is, there exists 有 **yǒu** 11.6, 29.3, 47.2
therefore 所以 **suǒyǐ** 44.1
this/these 这/這 **zhè, zhèi** 5.1, 7.2, 9.1
tì 替 'for, on behalf of' 14.2.6
tiāntiān 天天 'every day' 35.2, 46.3.3
time when
   'duration' and 'time when' compared 39.1.3
   emphasizing 'time when' a situation occurs 57.3.2
   and focusing constructions 57.2
   position of 'time when' phrases in the sentence 4.5, 49.1.5
   relative order of 'time when' and 'location' 4.6
titles 22.3
to
   prepositions that indicate action toward a reference point 对/對 **duì** 'to, toward,' 向 **xiàng** 'toward' 14.2.2
   prepositions that indicate movement to or toward a reference point 到 **dào** 'to,' 往 **wǎng**, 'toward' 14.2.4
   prepositions that indicate transfer of an object to someone or something 给/給 **gěi** 'to, for' 14.2.5
tone changes 1.1.3, 2.3, 2.4, 31.3
tone sandhi (see tone changes)
tones 1.1.3, 1.2.1, 2.3, 2.4
tóng 同 'and, with' 16.1.3, 16.1.4, 33.1.1
tóngshí 同时/同時 'at the same time' 43.2.2
topic and topicalization
   formal development of the topic 25.11
   introducing a topic 57.1
   position of topic in the sentence 4.1
traditional characters 3.1
transitive verbs Glossary of Grammatical terms

under 下头/下頭 **xiàtou** (下面 **xiàmiàn**) 47.1.1.1
unless 除非 **chúfēi** 45.4

verb complements (complements)
   of degree 10.3
   of direction 19, 48.8
   of manner 31.3
   of potential 18.6, 19.5, 32.2
   of result 18, 32.1
   see also Glossary of Grammatical Terms
verb phrase
   negation of action verbs 13.3
   negation of stative verbs 11.1
   negation of modal verbs 12.6.1
   negation of adjectival verbs 10.1
   relative order of verbs, objects, and prepositional phrases 4.2, 4.3, 4.4, Glossary of Grammatical Terms
verb repetition (see repeating the verb)

verbs (see action verbs, adjectival verbs, stative verbs, modal verbs)
verbs that function as prepositions 14.3
verb suffix 了 **le** (see perfective aspect with 了 **le**)
verb suffix 过/過 **guo** (see experiential aspect with 过/過 **guo**)

wàitou 外头/外頭 (外面 **wàimiàn**) 'out, outside' 47.1
wǎng, wáng 往 'toward' 14.2.4, 48.1.1, 48.2
we 咱们/咱們 **zánmen** (inclusive) 5.2, 5.2.2, 我们/我們 (exclusive or neutral) 5.2
weak obligations (see should)
weak prohibitions (see should not)
weather 30.8
weeks 礼拜/禮拜 **lǐbài**, 星期 **xīngqī** 49.2.3, 'this week' 34.1, 'every week' 35.1, 'next week' 36.1
worry, expressing 55
word order (see phrase order)
wéi 为/為 'for/on behalf of' 14.2.8
wéihé 为何/為何 'for what reason, why?' 44.4
wéi le 为了/為了 'because of, for the sake of' 44.2
wèi shénme 为什么/為甚麼 'why?' 28.6, 44.4
welcoming a guest (see guest and host)
west 西 **xī** (西面 **xīmiàn**, 西边/西邊 **xībiān**) 47.1.1.2
what? (question word) 什么/甚麼 **shénme** 28.6
what is? 何为/何為 **héwéi** 28.6
when? (question word) 什么时候/甚麼時候 **shénme shíhòu**, 何时/何時 **héshí** 28.6
when (simulltaneous situations) 的时候 **de shíhou** 39.3, 43.1
when, by the time that 等 **děng**, 等到 **děngdào** 43.5
whenever 什么时候/甚麼時候 **shénme shíhòu** + 都 **dōu** or 也 **yě** 46.4.1
where 哪儿/哪兒 **nǎr**, 哪里/哪裏 **nǎlǐ**, 什么地方/甚麼地方 **shénme dìfang** 28.6
wherever (anywhere) 哪儿/哪兒 **nǎr** + 都 **dōu** or 也 **yě** (哪里/哪裏 **nǎli** + 都 **dōu** or 也 **yě**, 什么地方/甚麼地方 **shénme dìfang** + 都 **dōu** or 也 **yě**) 46.4.1
which? 哪 **nǎ, něi** 2.2.1.2, 5.1, 7.4, 9.1, 28.6
who 谁/誰 **shéi**? 28.6
why? 为什么/為甚麼 **wèi shénme**, 何必 **hébì**, 何故 **hégù**, 28.6
why not? 何妨 **héfáng** 28.6
willingness
   adverbs that express willingness to perform an action 31.3
   verbs that express willingness 36.4, 53.4
word 2
wú 无 literary marker of negation 27.5
wú xū 无须/無須 'need not, do not have to' 50.1.3

INDEX

xī 西 (西面 xīmiàn, 西边/西邊 xībiān) 'west' 47.1.1.2
xiàtou 下头/下頭 (下面 xiàmiàn) 'below, under' 47.1
xiān 先 . . . cái 才 'first . . . only then' 42.3.2
xiān 先 . . . zài 再 'first . . . then' 42.3.1
xiàng 向 'to, toward' (preposition)
    action toward a reference point 14.2.2
    in expressions of apology 63.1.3
    in expressions of gratitude 61.1.1
    movement toward a reference point 48.1.1
    transfer of an object 14.2.5
xiàng 像 'resemble' 11, 33.1.4, 33.2.4
xiāngdāng 相当/相當 'quite, relatively, rather' 10.3, 33.7, 60.1.1
xiàngxíng 象形 pictographs 3.3.1
xiǎoshí 小时/小時 'hour' 49.1
xìng 姓 'family name' 11.5, 22.1
xìngmíng 姓名 'name, family name and given name' 22.1
xīngqī 星期 'week' 49.2.3, 'this week' 34.1, 'every week' 35.1, 'next week' 36.1
xíngshēng 形声/形聲 phonetic compound characters 3.3.4
xuéqī 学期/學期 semesters 49.2.5

yàoburán 要不然 'otherwise' 45.5
yàoshi 要是 'if' 45.1
yě 也 'also'
    expressing additional information 15.2.1, 40.1
    in expressions indicating 'every' and 'any' 46.4
    in expressions indicating exception and inclusion 57.2.2, 57.2.3
years 年 nián 49.2.1
yes–no questions 28.1, 29.1.3
    with action verbs 13.4
    with adjectival verbs 10.2
    with directional verbs 19.6
    with modal verbs 12.6.2, 12.6.5
    with resultative verbs 18.5, 32.4.3
yī 一 VP_1 就 jiù VP_2 'as soon as' 6.9, 42.3.3
yībiān . . . yībiān . . . 一边/一邊 . . . 一边/一邊 doing two actions at the same time 43.2.1
yī 一 . . . 就 jiù VP_2 'as soon as . . . then' 6.9, 42.3.2
yī fāngmiàn . . . yī fāngmiàn 一方面 . . . 一方面 'on the one hand, on the other hand' 43.6
yǐhòu 以后/以後 'after' 42.1.2.4, 42.4, 42.5
yǐjing 已经/已經 'already'
    in expressions of age 30.7.1
    in expressions indicating actions that continue to the present 34.7
    properties of adverbs 15.1
    with duration expressions 39.1.2
    with perfective aspect 17, 37.1

yīngdāng 应当/應當 'should' 12.4.2, 50.1.2
yīnggāi 应该/應該 'should' 12.4.2, 50.1.2
yīnwei 因为/因為 'because' 44, responding to questions about cause 28.6
yīnwei NP de guānxi 因为/因為 NP 的关系/關係 'because of NP' 44.2
yǐqián 以前 'before' 42.1
    comparing 以前 yǐqián 'before' and 以后/以後 yǐhòu 'after' 42.5
yīyàng 一样/一樣 'same,' in structures indicating similarity and difference 33.1, 33.2
yóu 由 'from' (source of movement) 14.2.8
yǒu 有 'have, exist'
    in comparisons 33.1.6
    expressing duration with 有 yǒu 39.1.2
    expressing existence with 有 yǒu 11.6.2, 29.3.1, 47.2
    expressing possession with 有 yǒu 11.6.1, 29.2.1
    expressing temperature with 有 yǒu 30.8.3
    negation of 11.6.4, 28.1.4.2, 34.6, 37.4
yòu 又 . . . yòu 又 'both . . . and' 10.8, 40.9, 43.4
右边/右邊 yòubiān (右面 yòumiàn) 'right side' 47.1
yóu yú 由于/由於 'because of, owing to' 44.2
yú 于/於 'at, in, on' 14.2.8, 62.1.3
yǔ 与/與 'and' (formal context) 16.1.4
yuán 元/圓 'dollar' 8.5
yuǎn 远/遠 'far,' 47.4.1
yuànyi 愿意/願意 'willing' 53.4
yuè 月 months 49.2.2
yuè 越 $verb_1$ yuè 越 $verb_2$ 'the more $verb_1$ the more $verb_2$' 10.9.2, 12.6.4, 38.3.2
yuè lái yuè 越来越 'more and more' 10.9.1, 12.6.4, 38.3.1

zài 在
    indicating actions in the present 30.2
    indicating location 'at, in, on' 7.3, 11.7, 14.2.1, 43.1.3, 43.2, 58.1.3
zài 再 'again'
    adverb referring to future time 36.2
    expressing sequence 42.3.1, 48.7
    in expressions conveying additional information 40.5
    in expressions of goodbye 24.2.1, 24.2.2, 24.3.2, 58.4.1
    requesting repetition 25.5
zài shuō 再说/再說 'say again' 25.5, 'moreover' 40.5
zánmen 咱们/咱們 'we' (inclusive) 5.2, 5.2.2
zěnme 怎么/怎麼 'how' 28.6
    'how do I address you?' 22.5
    'how do you go' 48.6.2
    'how do you say' 25.6
    'no matter how' 32.2.2.1, 46.4.3

INDEX

zěnme V jiù zěnme V 怎么/怎麼 V 就怎么/怎麼 V 'do as you please' 54.2.4

zěnme le 怎么了/怎麼了 'what is the matter?' 28.6

zěnmeyàng 怎么样/怎麼樣 'how about it? 28.6, 30.4.1, 31.2, 60.1.2

zháojí 着急/著急 'anxious, nervous' 55.2

zhe 着/著
  in commands 51.1.1
  with change-of-state placement verbs 29.3.3
  duration, durative aspect 13.5.1, 17.2, 34.4, 39.1, 39.2, 39.3

zhè, zhèi 这/這 'this, these' 5.1, 7.1, 7.2, 9.1

zhèlǐ 这里/這裏 'here' 2.2.1.2, 7.3, in distance expressions 47.4.1

zhèngzài 正在 'be in the process of doing' (progressive markers) 17.2, 17.2.1, 34.2, 34.3

zhèr 这儿/這兒 'here' 2.2.1.2, 7.3, in distance expressions 47.4.1

zhī 之 9.6
  in estimates and approximations 6.5
  in fractions 6.6.1
  in expressions introducing the cause or reason 44.2
  in percentages 6.6.2
  marker of noun modification and possession 9.6, 29.2.3

zhǐ 只 'only' 15.2.5, 30.7.1

zhīdao 知道 'know' 48.6.4, 54.1.1

zhǐ hǎo 只好 'the only thing to do is' 54.2.3

zhǐ shì 指事 ideographs 3.3.2

zhǐyào 只要 'as long as' 45.3

zhìyú 至于/至於 'as for (the topic)' 25.11.4, 57.1.1

zhōngjiān 中间/中間 'between' 47.1

zhōngtóu 钟头/鐘頭 'hour' 49.1

zhuǎnzhù 转注/轉注 semantic derivation characters 3.3.6

zìcóng 自从/自從 'from, ever since' 14.2.8

zìjǐ 自己 'self' (reflexive pronoun) 5.2.1

zǒng ér yán zhī 总而言之/總而言之 'in other words, to put it another way' 25.11.6

zǒu 走 'go in a direction or toward a location' 48.1.1, 'walk' 48.5.1, 48.8

zuì 最 superlative 10.3, 10.6, 33.6, 52.1.2

zuì hǎo 最好 'the best thing to do is' 55.2.3

zuì hòu 最后/最後 'finally' 25.11.6

zuǒbiān 左边/左邊 (左面 **zuǒmiàn**) 'left side' 47.1

404